CURIOUS MYTHS
OF THE
MIDDLE AGES

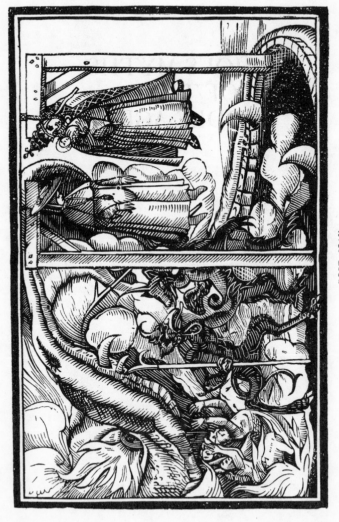

POPE JOAN.

From Joh. Wolfii Lect. Memorab. Lavingæ (1600).

CURIOUS MYTHS
OF THE
MIDDLE AGES

by Sabine Baring-Gould

Introduction by Leslie Shepard

UNIVERSITY BOOKS   *New Hyde Park, New York*

Introduction

This unusual book is a fascinating study of those wonderful and romantic stories that inspired the popular imagination of ordinary people in Medieval times and for centuries afterwards. They have a special relevance to the study of comparative religion and folklore.

Here are miracles, tall stories, travellers' tales and haunting legends of The Wandering Jew, Pope Joan, Antichrist, mermaids, tailed men, the Seven Sleepers, St. George, the Holy Grail, the Fortunate Isles (those magic lands beyond the sea) and many other marvels. Some of these myths were from an ancient pagan past, adapted to a new setting. Of particular interest is the story of the Cross, a study of pre-Christian origins of a sign which was a sacred symbol of life and regeneration long before Christ.* The tenacity of myths is well shown by the essay on

*This was later the subject of a full-length work by British antiquary John Ashton, Baring-Gould supplying a preface for the book.

William Tell, in which it transpires that earlier forms of this story were known in England, Iceland, Finland, Denmark, Persia and elsewhere. Such myths became part of a great body of European folklore, kept alive by traditional retelling and, in the last two or three centuries, by the little penny chapbooks sold by pedlars.

The author of this present book was a pioneer British folklorist. He was also one of the most remarkable men of recent times.

SABINE BARING-GOULD was born at Exeter January 28, 1834, and died January 2, 1924. His life bridged the nineteenth and twentieth centuries with all their far-reaching social changes. In 1848, when only a boy, his parents were with him on a Continental tour during the height of the French Revolution of that year.

His amazingly varied talents in many different fields seem incredible in a modern age of specialization. Parson, squire, traveller, archaeologist, popular novelist, historian, folksong collector—these are some of the versatile activities packed into his ninety years. As an author alone he was responsible for about 140 books — more than one for every year of his life! He wrote the famous hymn "Onward Christian Soldiers" and the beautiful evensong "Now the Day is Over."

When only a boy, he made three resolutions—to reform the spiritual and moral life of Lew Trenchard parish, to restore the parish church, and to improve the cottages, farms and the manor house on the estate. All three things had been accomplished against heroic odds when he died, although with genuine humility he claimed only the last two.

Baring-Gould entered Clare Hall, Cambridge University, October 1853, graduated as M.A. and became attracted to the English Catholicism of the Oxford Movement. After a brief but significant period as a master in the choir school of St. Barnabas, Pimlico, London, he became a schoolmaster at the Woodard School, Shoreham, Sussex, then at Hurstpierpoint. In 1864 he took Holy Orders in the Church of England and was ordained by Bishop Bickersteth at Ripon in Yorkshire. He became curate of Horbury, a tough industrial Yorkshire town of some 700 people. He was popular with the coal-miners and mill workers, and in great demand as a story-teller by the children.

Baring-Gould received no high ecclesiastical honors, and indeed his only academic recognition was the honorary Fellowship bestowed by Clare College, Cambridge in 1918, six years before his death. Apart from this his real memorial was local, in the hearts of his parishioners. He was the last of the great individualist country parsons of the Church of England. His grandson, the Rev. B. H. C. Dickinson, still lives at Lew Trenchard.

Baring-Gould's books on religion, folklore and mythology are of special interest and show the remarkable range of his thought and researches as well as his immense industry. His *Origin and Development of Religious Belief* (2 vols. 1869-70) is a strange but extraordinarily broadminded work. In 1874 he published *The Lost and Hostile Gos-*

pels, an important essay on the Toledoth Jeschu and the Petrine and Pauline Gospels. Between 1872 and 1889 he worked on his seventeen volume *The Lives of the Saints.*

The present book is not a dry academic treatise but a lively collection of essays by a scholar and humanitarian who was also a born story-teller. His wide reading and skilful analysis are never obtrusive. Of course one could add to most of these subjects in the light of presentday knowledge, but the spadework is Baring-Gould's, and it is important to study these essays in their original form. Baring-Gould had a great gift for presenting complex research in simple language with occasional dry humor, essentially in the homely tradition of the myths themselves. It is because of this that he is able to capture some of the hopes and fears of former generations, the romantic ideals and hidden meanings which excited the sense of wonder, without which religion lapses into formal doctrine. For many centuries myth and legend have been a magical current of symbolism that underlies and illuminates everyday piety. If doctrine is the mind of religion, myth and legend are the heart of it, timeless archetypes of the human soul.

These essays, first published in two series 1866-8 were very popular and went into many editions over fifty years. It is good to see them back in print.

London, England   Leslie Shepard
January 1967

Contents

The Wandering Jew

WHO that has looked on Gustave Doré's marvellous illustrations to this wild legend, can forget the impression they made upon his imagination?

I do not refer to the first illustration as striking, where the Jewish shoemaker is refusing to suffer the cross-laden Saviour to rest a moment on his door-step, and is receiving with scornful lip the judgment to wander restless till the Second Coming of that same Redeemer. But I refer rather to the second, which represents the Jew, after the lapse of ages, bowed beneath the burden of the curse, worn with unrelieved toil, wearied with ceaseless travelling, trudging onward at the last lights of evening, when a rayless night of unabating rain is creeping

on, along a sloppy path between dripping bushes;
and suddenly he comes over against a way-side
crucifix, on which the white glare of departing day·
light falls, to throw it into ghastly relief against the
pitch-black rain clouds.   For a moment we see the
working of the miserable shoemaker's mind.   We
feel that he is recalling the tragedy of the first
Good Friday, and his head hangs heavier on his
breast, as he recalls the part he had taken in that
awful catastrophe.

Or, is that other illustration more remarkable,
where the wanderer is amongst the Alps, at the
brink of a hideous chasm; and seeing in the con-
torted pine-branches the ever-haunting scene of
the Via dolorosa, he is lured to cast himself into
that black gulf in quest of rest,—when an angel
flashes out of the gloom with the sword of flame
turning every way, keeping him back from what
would be to him a Paradise indeed, the repose of
Death?

Or that last scene, when the trumpet sounds
and earth is shivering to its foundations, the fire
is bubbling forth through the rents in its surface,
and the dead are coming together flesh to flesh,
and bone to bone, and muscle to muscle—then
the weary man sits down and casts off his shoes!

Strange sights are around him, he sees them not; strange sounds assail his ears, he hears but one— the trumpet-note which gives the signal for him to stay his wanderings and rest his weary feet.

It is possible to linger over those noble woodcuts, and learn from them something new each time that we study them; they are picture-poems full of latent depths of thought. And now let us to the history of this most thrilling of all Mediæval myths.

The words of the Gospel contain the germs out of which the story has developed. "Verily I say unto you, There be some standing here, which shall not taste of death till they see the Son of Man coming in His kingdom [1]," are our Lord's words, which I can hardly think apply to the destruction of Jerusalem, as commentators explain it to escape the difficulty. That some should live to see Jerusalem destroyed was not very surprising, and hardly needed the emphatic Verily which Christ only used when speaking something of peculiarly solemn or mysterious import.

Besides, S. Luke's account manifestly refers the coming in the kingdom to the Judgment, for the

---

[1] Matt. xvi. 28. Mark ix. 1.

saying stands as follows : "Whosoever shall be ashamed of Me, and of My words, of him shall the Son of Man be ashamed, when He shall come in His own glory, and in His Father's, and of the holy angels. But I tell you of a truth, there be some standing here, which shall not taste of death till they see the kingdom of God [2]."

There can, I think, be no doubt in the mind of an unprejudiced person, that the words of our Lord do imply that some one or more of those then living should not die till He came again. I do not mean to insist on the literal signification, but I plead that it is compatible with our Lord's power to have fulfilled His words to the letter. That the circumstance is unrecorded in the Gospels is no evidence that it did not take place, for we are expressly told, "Many other signs truly did Jesus in the presence of His disciples, which are not written in this book [3];" and again, "There are also many other things which Jesus did, the which, if they should be written every one, I suppose that even the world itself could not contain the books that should be written [4]."

We may remember also that mysterious wit-

---

[2] Luke ix. 26, 27.   [3] John xx. 30.   [4] John xxi. 25.

nesses are to appear in the last eventful days of the world's history, and bear testimony to the Gospel truth before the antichristian world. One of these has been often conjectured to be S. John the Evangelist, of whom Christ said to Peter, "If I will that he tarry till I come, what is that to thee?" and the other has been variously conjectured to be Elias, or Enoch, or our Jew.

The historical evidence on which the tale rests is, however, too slender, for us to admit for it more than the barest claim to be more than myth. The names and the circumstances connected with the Jew and his doom vary in every account, and the only point upon which all coincide is that such an individual exists in an undying condition, wandering over the face of the earth, seeking rest and finding none.

The earliest extant mention of the Wandering Jew, is to be found in the book of the chronicles of the Abbey of S. Albans, which was copied and continued by Matthew Paris. He records that in the year 1228, "a certain Archbishop of Armenia Major came on a pilgrimage to England to see the relics of the saints, and visit the sacred places in the kingdom, as he had done in others; he also produced letters of recommendation from

his Holiness the Pope, to the religious men and
prelates of the churches, in which they were en-
joined to receive and entertain him with due reverence and honour.   On his arrival, he went to S.
Albans, where he was received with all respect by
the abbot and monks; at this place, being fatigued
with his journey, he remained some days to rest
himself and his followers, and a conversation was
commenced between him and the inhabitants of
the convent, by means of their interpreters, during
which he made many inquiries concerning the
religion and religious observances of this country,
and related many strange things concerning Eastern
countries.   In the course of conversation he. was
asked whether he had ever seen or heard any
thing of Joseph, a man of whom there was much
talk in the world, who, when our Lord suffered,
was present and spoke to Him, and who is still
alive, in evidence of the Christian faith ; in reply
to which, a knight in his retinue, who was his
interpreter, replied, speaking in French, ‘My lord
well knows that man, and a little before he took
his way to the western countries, the said Joseph
ate at the table of my lord the Archbishop in
Armenia, and he had often seen and held converse
with him.’   He was then asked about what had

passed between Christ and the same Joseph, to which he replied, 'At the time of the suffering of Jesus Christ, He was seized by the Jews, and led into the hall of judgment before Pilate, the governor, that He might be judged by him on the accusation of the Jews; and Pilate, finding no cause for adjudging Him to death, said to them, 'Take Him and judge Him according to your law;' the shouts of the Jews, however, increasing, he, at their request, released unto them Barabbas, and delivered Jesus to them to be crucified. When, therefore, the Jews were dragging Jesus forth, and had reached the door, Cartaphilus, a porter of the hall, in Pilate's service, as Jesus was going out of the door, impiously struck Him on the back with his hand, and said in mockery, 'Go quicker, Jesus, go quicker; why do you loiter?' and Jesus, looking back on him with a severe countenance, said to him, 'I am going, and you will wait till I return.' And according as our Lord said, this Cartaphilus is still awaiting His return. At the time of our Lord's suffering he was thirty years old, and when he attains the age of a hundred years, he always returns to the same age as he was when our Lord suffered. After Christ's death, when the Catholic faith gained ground, this Cartaphilus was baptized

by Ananias (who also baptized the Apostle Paul),
and was called Joseph. He often dwells in both
divisions of Armenia, and other Eastern countries, passing his time amidst the bishops and
other prelates of the Church ; he is a man of holy
conversation, and religious ; a man of few words,
and circumspect in his behaviour; for he does
not speak at all unless when questioned by the
bishops and religious men ; and then he tells of the
events of old times, and of the events which occurred
at the suffering and resurrection of our Lord, and
of the witnesses of the resurrection, namely, those
who rose with Christ, and went into the holy city,
and appeared unto men. He also tells of the creed
of the Apostles, and of their separation and
preaching. And all this he relates without smiling
or levity of conversation, as one who is well practised in sorrow and the fear of God, always looking
forward with fear to the coming of Jesus Christ,
lest at the Last Judgment he should find Him in
anger whom, when on His way to death, he had
provoked to just vengeance. Numbers came to
him from different parts of the world, enjoying his
society and conversation ; and to them, if they are
men of authority, he explains all doubts on the
matters on which he is questioned. He refuses all

gifts that are offered to him, being content with slight food and clothing. He places his hope of salvation on the fact that he sinned through ignorance, for the Lord when suffering prayed for His enemies in these words, 'Father, forgive them, for they know not what they do.' "

Much about the same date Philip Mouskes, afterwards Bishop of Tournay, wrote his rhymed chronicle (1242), which contains a similar account of the Jew, derived from the same Armenian prelate :—

> " Adonques vint un arceveskes
> De çà mer, plains de bonnes tèques
> Par samblant, et fut d'Armenie,"

and this man having visited the shrine of " St. Tumas de Kantorbire," and then having paid his devotions at " Monsigour St. Jake," he went on to Cologne to see the heads of the three kings. The version told in the Netherlands much resembled that related at S. Albans, only that the Jew, seeing the people dragging Christ to His death, exclaims :

> " Atendés moi ! g'i vois,
> S'iert mis le faus profète en crois."

Then

> " Le vrais Dieux se regarda,
> Et li a dit qu'e n'i tarda,
> Icist ne t'atenderont pas,
> Mais saces, tu m'atenderas."

We hear no more of the Wandering Jew till the sixteenth century, when we hear first of him in a casual manner, as assisting a weaver, Kokot, at the royal palace in Bohemia (1505), to find a treasure which had been secreted by the great-grandfather of Kokot, sixty years before, at which time the Jew was present. He then had the appearance of being a man of seventy years[5].

Curiously enough, we next hear of him in the East, where he is confounded with the prophet Elijah. Early in the century he appeared to Fadhilah, under peculiar circumstances.

After the Arabs had captured the city of Elvan, Fadhilah, at the head of three hundred horsemen, pitched his tents, late in the evening, between two mountains. Fadhilah having begun his evening prayer with a loud voice, heard the words "Allah akbar" (God is great) repeated distinctly, and each word of his prayer was followed in a similar manner. Fadhilah not believing this to be the result of an echo, was much astonished, and cried out, "O thou! whether thou art of the angel ranks, or whether thou art of some other order of spirits, it is well, the power of God be with thee; but if thou

---

[5] Gubitz, Gesellsch. 1845, No. 18.

art a man, then let mine eyes light upon thee, that I may rejoice in thy presence and society." Scarcely had he spoken these words, before an aged man with bald head stood before him, holding a staff in his hand, and much resembling a dervish in appearance. After having courteously saluted him, Fadhilah asked the old man who he was. Thereupon the stranger answered, "Bassi Hadhret Issa, I am here by command of the Lord Jesus, who has left me in this world, that I may live therein until He comes a second time to earth. I wait for this Lord who is the Fountain of Happiness, and in obedience to His command I dwell behind yon mountain." When Fadhilah heard these words, he asked when the Lord Jesus would appear, and the old man replied that His appearing would be at the end of the world, at the Last Judgment. But this only increased Fadhilah's curiosity, so that he inquired the signs of the approach of the end of all things, whereupon Zerib Bar Elia gave him an account of general, social, and moral dissolution, which would be the climax of this world's history [6].

In 1547 he was seen in Europe, if we are to believe the following narration :—

[6] Herbelot, Bibl. Orient. iii. p. 607.

"Paul von Eitzen, doctor of the Holy Scriptures, and Bishop of Schleswig[7], related as true for some years past, that when he was young, having studied at Wittemberg, he returned home to his parents in Hamburg in the winter of the year 1547, and that on the following Sunday, in church, he observed a tall man with his hair hanging over his shoulders, standing barefoot during the sermon, over against the pulpit, listening with deepest attention to the discourse, and, whenever the name of Jesus was mentioned, bowing himself profoundly and humbly, with sighs and beating of the breast. He had no other clothing in the bitter cold of the winter, except a pair of hose which were in tatters about his feet, and a coat with a girdle which reached to his feet; and his general appearance was that of a man of fifty years. And many people, some of high degree and title, have seen this same man in England, France, Italy, Hungary, Persia, Spain, Poland, Moscow, Lapland, Sweden, Denmark, Scotland, and other places.

"Every one wondered over the man. Now after

[7] Paul v. Eitzen was born Jan. 25th, 1522, at Hamburg; in 1562 he was appointed chief preacher for Schleswig, and died Feb. 25th, 1598. (Greve, Memor. P. ab. Eitzen. Hamb. 1744.)

the sermon, the said Doctor inquired diligently where the stranger was to be found, and when he had sought him out, he inquired of him privately whence he came, and how long that winter he had been in the place. Thereupon he replied modestly, that he was a Jew by birth, a native of Jerusalem, by name Ahasverus, by trade a shoemaker; he had been present at the crucifixion of Christ, and had lived ever since, travelling through various lands and cities, the which he substantiated by accounts he gave; he related also the circumstances of Christ's transference from Pilate to Herod, and the final crucifixion, together with other details not recorded in the Evangelists and historians; he gave accounts of the changes of government in many countries, especially of the East, through several centuries, and moreover he detailed the labours and deaths of the holy Apostles of Christ most circumstantially.

"Now when Doctor Paul v. Eitzen heard this with profound astonishment, on account of its incredible novelty, he inquired further, in order that he might obtain more accurate information. Then the man answered, that he had lived in Jerusalem at the time of the crucifixion of Christ, whom he had regarded as a deceiver of the people and a heretic; he had seen Him with his own eyes, and had done his best, along with others, to bring this deceiver, as he regarded Him, to justice, and to have Him put out of the way. When the sentence had been pronounced by Pilate, Christ was about to be dragged past his house; then he ran home, and called together his household to have a look at Christ, and see what sort of a person He was.

"This having been done, he had his little child on his arm, and was standing in his doorway to have a sight of the Lord Jesus Christ.

"As, then, Christ was led by, bowed under the weight of the heavy cross, He tried to rest a little, and stood still a moment; but the shoemaker, in zeal and rage, and for the sake of obtaining credit among the other Jews, drove the Lord Christ forward, and told Him to hasten on His way. Jesus obeying, looked at him, and said, 'I shall stand and rest, but thou shalt go till the last day.' At these words the man set down the child; and unable to remain where he was, he followed Christ, and saw how cruelly He was crucified, how He suffered, how He died. As soon as this had taken place, it came upon him suddenly that he could no more return to Jerusalem, nor see again his wife and child, but must go forth into foreign lands, one after another, like a mournful pilgrim. Now, when, years after, he returned to Jerusalem, he found it ruined and utterly razed, so that not one stone was left standing on another; and he could not recognize former localities.

"He believes that it is God's purpose in thus driving him about in miserable life, and preserving him undying, to present him before the Jews at the end, as a living token, so that the godless and unbelieving may remember the death of Christ, and be turned to repentance. For his part he would well rejoice were God in heaven to release him from this vale of tears. After this conversation, Doctor Paul v. Eitzen, along with the rector of the school of Hamburg, who was well read in history, and a traveller, questioned him about events which had taken place in the East since the death of Christ, and he was able to give them much information on many ancient matters; so that it was impossible not to be convinced of the truth of his story, and to see that what seems impossible with men is, after all, possible with God.

"Since the Jew has had his life extended, he has become silent and reserved, and only answers direct questions. When invited to become any one's guest, he eats little, and drinks in great moderation;

then hurries on, never remaining long in one place.
When at Hamburg, Dantzig, and elsewhere money
has been offered him, he never took more than
two skillings (4¼*d*.), and at once distributed it to
the poor, as token that he needed no money, for
God would provide for him, as he rued the sins
he had committed in ignorance.

" During the period of his stay in Hamburg and
Dantzig he was never seen to laugh.   In whatever
land he travelled he spoke its language, and when
he spoke Saxon, it was like a native Saxon.   Many
people came from different places to Hamburg and
Dantzig in order to see and hear this man, and
were convinced that the providence of God was
exercised in this individual in a very remarkable
manner.   He gladly listened to God's word, or
heard it spoken of always with great gravity and
compunction, and he ever reverenced with sighs the
pronunciation of the name of God, or of Jesus
Christ, and could not endure to hear curses, but
whenever he heard any one swear by God's death
or pains, he waxed indignant, and exclaimed, with
vehemence and with sighs,—' Wretched man and
miserable creature, thus to misuse the name of
thy Lord and God, and His bitter sufferings and
passion.   Hadst thou seen, as I have, how heavy

and bitter were the pangs and wounds of thy Lord, endured for thee and for me, thou wouldest rather undergo great pain thyself than thus take His sacred name in vain!'

"Such is the account given to me by Doctor Paul von Eitzen, with many circumstantial proofs, and corroborated by certain of my own old acquaintances who saw this same individual with their own eyes in Hamburg.

"In the year 1575, the Secretary Christopher Krause, and Master Jacob von Holstein, legates to the Court of Spain, and afterwards sent into the Netherlands to pay the soldiers serving his Majesty in that country, related on their return home to Schleswig, and confirmed with solemn oaths, that they had come across the same mysterious individual at Madrid in Spain, in appearance, manner of life, habits, clothing, just the same as he had appeared in Hamburg. They said that they had spoken with him, and that many people of all classes had conversed with him, and found him to speak good Spanish. In the year 1599, in December, a reliable person wrote from Brunswick to Strasburg that the same mentioned strange person had been seen alive at Vienna in Austria, and that he had started for Poland and Dantzig; and that he

purposed going on to Moscow. This Ahasverus
was at Lubeck in 1601, also about the same date in
Revel in Livonia, and in Cracow in Poland. In
Moscow he was seen of many and spoken to by
many.

"What thoughtful God-fearing persons are to
think of the said person, is at their option. God's
works are wondrous and past finding out, and are
manifested day by day, only to be revealed in full
at the last great day of account.

"Dated, Revel, August 1st, 1613.

"D. W.

"D.

"Chrysostomus Duduloeus,

"Westphalus."

The statement that the Wandering Jew appeared
in Lubeck in 1601, does not tally with the more
precise chronicle of Henricus Bangert, which gives :
—"Die 14 Januarii Anno MDCIII., adnotatum reli-
quit Lubecæ fuisse Judæum illum immortalem, qui
se Christi crucifixioni interfuisse affirmavit [8]."

In 1604, he seems to have appeared in Paris.
Rudolph Botoreus says under this date: "I fear

[8] Henr. Bangert, Comment. de Ortu, Vita, et Excessu
Coleri.

lest I be accused of giving ear to old wives' fables, if I insert in these pages what is reported all over Europe of the Jew, coeval with the Saviour Christ; however, nothing is more common, and our popular histories have not scrupled to assert it. Following the lead of those who wrote our annals, I may say that he who appeared not in one century only, in Spain, Italy, and Germany, was also in this year seen and recognized as the same individual who had appeared in Hamburg, anno MDLXVI. The common people, bold in spreading reports, relate many things of him; and this I allude to, lest any thing should be left unsaid[9]."

J. C. Bulenger puts the date of the Hamburg visit earlier. "It was reported at this time that a Jew of the time of Christ was wandering without food and drink, having for a thousand and odd years been a vagabond and outcast, condemned by God to rove, because he, of that generation of vipers, was the first to cry out for the crucifixion of Christ and the release of Barabbas; and also because soon after, when Christ, panting under the burden of the rood, sought to rest before his workshop (he was a cobbler), the fellow ordered Him off with

[9] R. Botoreus, Comm. Histor. lii. p. 305.

acerbity. Thereupon Christ replied : ' Because thou grudgest Me such a moment of rest, I shall enter into My rest, but thou shalt wander restless.' At once frantic and agitated he fled through the whole earth, and on the same account to this day he journeys through the world. It was this person who was seen in Hamburg in MDLXIV. Credat Judæus Apella! *I* did not see him or hear any thing authentic concerning him at that time when I was in Paris[1]."

A curious little book[2] written against the quackery of Paracelsus, by Leonard Doldius, a Nürnberg physician, and translated into Latin and augmented by Andreas Libavius, doctor and physician of Rotenburg, alludes to the same story, and gives the Jew a new name nowhere else met with. After having referred to a report that Paracelsus was not dead, but was seated alive, asleep or napping, in his sepulchre at Strasburg, preserved from death by some of his specifics, Libavius declares that he would sooner believe in the old man the Jew, Ahasverus, wandering over the world, called by some Buttadæus, and otherwise, again, by others.

[1] J. C. Bulenger, Historia sui Temporis, p. 357.
[2] Praxis Alchymiæ. Francfurti, MDCIV. 8vo.

He is said to have appeared in Naumburg, but the date is not given ; he was noticed in church, listening to the sermon. After the service he was questioned, and he related his story. On this occasion he received presents from the burghers[3]. In 1633 he was again in Hamburg[4]. In the year 1640, two citizens, living in the Gerberstrasse, in Brussels, were walking in the Sonian wood, when they encountered an aged man, whose clothes were in tatters and of an antiquated appearance. They invited him to go with them to a house of refreshment, and he went with them, but would not seat himself, remaining on foot to drink. When he came before the doors with the two burghers, he told them a great deal, but they were mostly stories of events which had happened many hundred years before. Hence the burghers gathered that their companion was Isaac Laquedem, the Jew who had refused to permit our Blessed Lord to rest for a moment at his doorstep, and they left him full of terror. In 1642, he is reported to have visited Leipzig. According to Peck's "History of Stamford," Upon Whitsunday, in the year of our Lord 1658, "about six of the clock, just after evensong,"

[3] Mitternacht, Diss. in Johann. xxi. 19.
[4] Mitternacht, ut supra.

one Samuel Wallis, of Stamford, who had been long wasted with a lingering consumption, was sitting by the fire, reading in that delectable book called "Abraham's Suit for Sodom." He heard a knock at the door; and, as his nurse was absent, he crawled to open it himself. What he saw there, Samuel shall say in his own style :—" I beheld a proper, tall, grave old man. Thus he said : 'Friend, I pray thee, give an old pilgrim a cup of small beere !' And I said, 'Sir, I pray you, come in and welcome.' And he said, 'I am no Sir, therefore call me not Sir; but come in I must, for I cannot pass by thy doore.'

"After finishing the beer : 'Friend,' he said, 'thou art not well.' I said, 'No, truly Sir, I have not been well this many yeares.' He said, 'What is thy disease?' I said, 'A deep consumption, Sir; our doctors say, past cure : for, truly, I am a very poor man, and not able to follow doctors' councell.' 'Then,' said he, 'I will tell thee what thou shalt do; and, by the help and power of Almighty God above, thou shalt be well. To-morrow, when thou risest up, go into thy garden, and get there two leaves of red sage, and one of bloodworte, and put them into a cup of thy small beere. Drink as often as need require, and when the cup is empty fill it again, and put in **fresh** leaves every fourth day, and thou shalt see, through our Lord's great goodness and mercy, before twelve days shall be past, thy disease shall be cured and thy body altered.'"

After this simple prescription, Wallis pressed him to eat : "But he said, ' No, friend, I will not eat ; the Lord Jesus is sufficient for me. Very seldom doe I drinke any beere neither, but that which comes from the rocke. So, friend, the Lord God be with thee.'"

So saying, he departed, and was never more heard of ; but the patient got well within the given time, and for many a long day there was war hot and fierce among the divines of Stamford, as to whether the stranger was an angel or a devil. His dress has been minutely described by honest Sam. His coat was purple, and buttoned down to the waist ; "his britches of the same couler, all new to see to ;" his stockings were very white, but whether linen or jersey, deponent knoweth not ; his beard and head were white, and he had a white stick in his hand. The day was rainy from morning to night, "but he had not one spot of dirt upon his cloathes."

Aubrey gives an almost exactly similar relation,

the scene of which he places in the Staffordshire
Moorlands. He there appears in a "purple shag
gown," and prescribes balm-leaves[5].

On the 22nd July, 1721, he appeared at the gates
of the city of Munich[6]. About the end of the
seventeenth century, or the beginning of the
eighteenth, an impostor calling himself the
Wandering Jew, attracted attention in England ;
and was listened to by the ignorant, and despised
by the educated. He however managed to thrust
himself into the notice of the nobility, who, half in
jest, half in curiosity, questioned him, and paid him
as they might a juggler. He declared that he had
been an officer of the Sanhedrim, and that he had
struck Christ as He left the judgment-hall of Pilate.
He remembered all the Apostles, and described
their personal appearance, their clothes, and their
peculiarities. He spoke many languages, claimed
the power of healing the sick, and asserted that he
had travelled nearly all over the world. Those who
heard him were perplexed by his familiarity with
foreign tongues and places. Oxford and Cambridge
sent professors to question him, and to discover the

---

[5] Notes and Queries, vol. xii. No. 322.
[6] Hormayr, Taschenbuch, 1834, p. 216.

imposition, if any. An English nobleman conversed with him in Arabic. The mysterious stranger told his questioner in that language that historical works were not to be relied upon. And on being asked his opinion of Mahomet, he replied that he had been acquainted with the father of the prophet, and that he dwelt at Ormuz. As for Mahomet, he believed him to have been a man of intelligence ; once when he heard the prophet deny that Christ was crucified, he answered abruptly by telling him he was a witness to the truth of that event. He related also that he was in Rome when Nero set it on fire ; he had known Saladin, Tamerlane, Bajazeth, Eterlane, and could give minute details of the history of the Crusades [7].

Whether this Wandering Jew was found out in London or not, we cannot tell, but he shortly after appeared in Denmark, thence travelled into Sweden, and vanished.

Some impostors assuming to be the mysterious Jew, or lunatics actually believing themselves to be him, appeared in England in 1818, 1824, 1830 [8].

[7] Calmet, Dictionn. de la Bible, t. ii. p. 472.
[8] Athenæum, Nov. 3, 1866, p. 561.

Such are the principal notices of the Wandering Jew which have appeared. It will be seen at once how wanting they are in all substantial evidence which could make us regard the story in any other light than myth.

But no myth is wholly without foundation, and there must be some substantial verity upon which this vast superstructure of legend has been raised. What that is I am unable to discover.

It has been suggested by some that the Jew Ahasverus is an impersonification of that race which wanders, Cain-like, over the earth with the brand of a brother's blood upon it, and one which is not to pass away till all be fulfilled, not to be reconciled to its angered God, till the times of the Gentiles are accomplished. And yet, probable as this supposition may seem at first sight, it is not to be harmonized with some of the leading features of the story. The shoemaker becomes a penitent, and earnest Christian, whilst the Jewish nation has still the veil upon its heart; the wretched wanderer eschews money, and the avarice of the Israelite is proverbial.

According to local legend, he is identified with the Gipsies, or rather that strange people are supposed to be living under a curse somewhat similar to that inflicted on Ahasverus, because they refused shelter to the Virgin and Child on their flight into Egypt[9]. Another tradition connects the Jew with the wild huntsman, and there is a forest at Bretten in Swabia, which he is said to haunt. Popular superstition attributes to him there a purse containing a groschen, which, as often as it is expended, returns to the spender[1].

In the Harz one form of the Wild Huntsman myth is to this effect,—that he was a Jew who had refused to suffer our Blessed Lord to drink out of a river, or out of a horse-trough, but had contemptuously pointed out to Him the hoof-print of a horse, in which a little water had collected, and had bid Him quench His thirst thence[2].

As the Wild Huntsman is the impersonification of the storm, it is curious to find in parts of France that the sudden roar of a gale at night is attributed by the vulgar to the passing of the Everlasting Jew.

A Swiss story is, that he was seen one day standing upon the Matterberg, which is below the Matterhorn, contemplating the scene with mingled

[9] Aventinus, Bayr. Chronik, viii.
[1] Meier, Schwäbischen Sagen, i. 116.
[2] Kuhn u. Schwarz, Nordd. Sagen, p. 499.

sorrow and wonder.   Once before he stood on that
spot, and then it was the site of a flourishing city,
now it is covered with gentian and wild pinks.
Once again will he revisit the hill, and that will be
on the eve of Judgment.

Perhaps, of all the myths which originated in the
Middle Ages, none is more striking than that we
have been considering ; indeed there is something
so calculated to arrest the attention and to excite
the imagination in the outline of the story, that it
is remarkable that we should find an interval of
three centuries elapse between its first introduction
into Europe by Matthew Paris and Philip Mouskes,
and its general acceptance in the sixteenth century.
As a myth, its roots lie in that great mystery of
human life which is an enigma never solved, and
ever originating speculation.

What was life ? was it of necessity limited to
fourscore years, or could it be extended indefinitely?
were questions curious minds never wearied of
asking.   And so the mythology of the past teemed
with legends of favoured or accursed mortals, who
had reached beyond the term of days set to most
men.   Some had discovered the water of life, the
fountain of perpetual youth, and were ever renew-
ing their strength.   Others had dared the power of

God, and were therefore sentenced to feel the weight of His displeasure, without tasting the repose of death.

John the Divine slept at Ephesus, untouched by corruption, with the ground heaving over his breast as he breathed, waiting the summons to come forth and witness against Antichrist. The seven sleepers reposed in a cave, and centuries glided by like a watch in the night. The monk of Hildesheim, doubting how with God a thousand years could be as yesterday, listened to the melody of a bird in the green wood during three minutes, and found that in three minutes three hundred years had flown. Joseph of Arimathæa, in the blessed city of Sarras, draws perpetual life from the Saint Graal; Merlin sleeps and sighs in an old tree, spellbound of Vivien. Charlemagne and Barbarossa wait, crowned and armed, in the heart of the mountain, till the time comes for the release of Fatherland from despotism. And, on the other hand, the curse of a deathless life has passed on the Wild Huntsman, because he desired to chase the red-deer for evermore; on the Captain of the Phantom Ship, because he vowed he would double the Cape whether God willed it or not; on the Man in the Moon, because he gathered sticks during the

Sabbath rest; on the dancers of Kolbeck, because they desired to spend eternity in their mad gambols.

I began this article intending to conclude it with a bibliographical account of the tracts, letters, essays, and books, written upon the Wandering Jew; but I relinquish my intention at the sight of the multitude of works which have issued from the press upon the subject; and this I do with less compunction as the bibliographer may at little trouble and expense satisfy himself, by perusing the lists given by Grässe in his essay on the myth, and those to be found in "Notice historique et bibliographique sur les Juifs-errants: par G. B." (Gustave Brunet), Paris, Téchener, 1845; also in the article by M. Mangin, in "Causeries et Méditations historiques et littéraires," Paris, Duprat, 1843; and, lastly, in the essay by Jacob le Bibliophile (M. Lacroix) in his "Curiosités de l'Histoire des Croyances populaires," Paris, Delahays, 1859.

Of the romances of Eugène Sue and Dr. Croly, founded upon the legend, the less said the better. The original legend is so noble in its severe simplicity, that none but a master mind could develope it with any chance of success. Nor have the poetical attempts upon the story fared better.

It was reserved for the pencil of Gustave Doré to treat it with the originality it merited, and in a series of woodcuts to produce at once a poem, a romance, and a chef-d'œuvre of art.

Prester John

Arms of the See of Chichester

A BOUT the middle of the twelfth century, a
rumour circulated through Europe that there
reigned in Asia a powerful Christian Emperor, Presbyter Johannes.   In a bloody fight he had broken
the power of the Mussulmans, and was ready to come
to the assistance of the Crusaders.   Great was the
exultation in Europe, for of late the news from
the East had been gloomy and depressing, the
power of the infidel had increased, overwhelming
masses of men had been brought into the field
against the chivalry of Christendom, and it was felt
that the cross must yield before the odious crescent.

The news of the success of the Priest-King opened a door of hope to the desponding Christian world. Pope Alexander III. determined at once to effect a union with this mysterious personage, and on the 27th of September, 1177, wrote him a letter, which he entrusted to his physician, Philip, to deliver in person.

Philip started on his embassy, but never returned. The conquests of Tschengis-Khan again attracted the eyes of Christian Europe to the East. The Mongol hordes were rushing in upon the West with devastating ferocity ; Russia, Poland, Hungary, and the Eastern provinces of Germany, had succumbed, or suffered grievously ; and the fears of other nations were roused lest they too should taste the misery of a Mongolian invasion. It was Gog and Magog come to slaughter, and the times of Antichrist were dawning. But the battle of Liegnitz stayed them in their onward career, and Europe was saved.

Pope Innocent IV. determined to convert these wild hordes of barbarians, and subject them to the cross of Christ ; he therefore sent among them a number of Dominican and Franciscan missioners, and embassies of peace passed between the Pope, the King of France, and the Mogul Khan.

The result of these communications with the East was that the travellers learned how false were the prevalent notions of a mighty Christian empire existing in central Asia. Vulgar superstition or conviction is not, however, to be upset by evidence, and the locality of the monarchy was merely transferred by the people to Africa, and they fixed upon Abyssinia, with a show of truth, as the seat of the famous Priest-King. However, still some doubted. John de Plano-Carpini and Marco Polo, though they acknowledged the existence of a Christian monarch in Abyssinia, yet stoutly maintained as well that the Prester John of popular belief reigned in splendour somewhere in the dim Orient.

But before proceeding with the history of this strange fable, it will be well to extract the different accounts given of the Priest-King and his realm by early writers; and we shall then be better able to judge of the influence the myth obtained in Europe.

Otto of Freisingen is the first author to mention the monarchy of Prester John, with whom we are acquainted. Otto wrote a chronicle up to the date 1156, and he relates that in 1145 the Catholic Bishop of Cabala visited Europe to lay certain complaints before the Pope. He mentioned the fall of Edessa, and also "he stated that a few years ago a certain King and Priest called John, who lives on the further side of Persia and Armenia in the remote East, and who, with all his people, were Christians, though belonging to the Nestorian Church, had overcome the royal brothers Samiardi, kings of the Medes and Persians, and had captured Ecbatana, their capital and residence. The said kings had met with their Persian, Median, and Assyrian troops, and had fought for three consecutive days, each side having determined to die rather than take to flight. Prester John, for so they are wont to call him, at length routed the Persians, and after a bloody battle, remained victorious. After which victory the said John was hastening to the assistance of the Church at Jerusalem, but his host, on reaching the Tigris, was hindered from passing through a deficiency in boats, and he directed his march North, since he had heard that the river was there covered with ice. In that place he had waited many years, expecting severe cold, but the winters having proved unpropitious, and the severity of the climate having carried off many soldiers, he had been forced to retreat to his own land. This king belongs to the family of the Magi, mentioned in the Gospel, and he rules over the very people formerly governed by the Magi; moreover, his fame and his wealth is so great, that he uses an emerald sceptre only.

"Excited by the example of his ancestors, who came to worship Christ in His cradle, he had proposed to go to Jerusalem, but had been impeded by the above-mentioned causes [1]."

At the same time the story crops up in other quarters, so that we cannot look upon Otto as the inventor of the myth. The celebrated Maimonides alludes to it in a passage quoted by Joshua Lorki, a Jewish physician to Benedict XIII. Maimonides lived from 1135 to 1204. The passage is as follows: —"It is evident both from the letters of Rambam (Maimonides), whose memory be blessed, and from the narration of merchants who have visited the ends of the earth, that at this time the root of our faith is to be found in the lands of Babel and Teman, where long ago Jerusalem was an exile; not reckoning those who live in the land of Paras [2] and Madai [3], of the exiles of Schomrom, the number of which people is as the sand: of these some are still under the yoke of Paras, who is called the Great-Chief Sultan by the Arabs; others live in a

---

[1] Otto, Ep. Frising., lib. vii. c. 33.
[2] Persia.   [3] Media.

place under the yoke of a strange people . . . . . .
governed by a Christian chief, Preste-Cuan by
name. With him they have made a compact, and
he with them; and this is a matter concerning
which there can be no manner of doubt."

Benjamin of Tudela, another Jew, travelled in
the East between the years 1159—1173, the last
being the date of his death. He wrote an account
of his travels, and gives in it some information
with regard to a mythical Jew king, who reigned
in the utmost splendour over a realm inhabited by
Jews alone, situate somewhere in the midst of a
desert of vast extent. About this period there
appeared a document which produced intense
excitement throughout Europe—a letter, yes! a
letter from the mysterious personage himself to
Manuel Comnenus, Emperor of Constantinople
(1143—1180). The exact date of this extraordinary epistle cannot be fixed with any certainty,
but it certainly appeared before 1241, the date of
the conclusion of the chronicle of Albericus Trium
Fontium. This Albericus relates that in the year
1165 "Presbyter Joannes, the Indian king, sent
his wonderful letter to various Christian princes,
and especially to Manuel of Constantinople, and
Frederic the Roman Emperor." Similar letters were

sent to Alexander III., to Louis VII. of France, and to the King of Portugal, which are alluded to in chronicles and romances, and which were indeed turned into rhyme and sung all over Europe by minstrels and trouvères. The letter is as follows:—

"John, Priest by the Almighty power of God and the Might of our Lord Jesus Christ, King of Kings, and Lord of Lords, to his friend Emanuel, Prince of Constantinople, greeting, wishing him health, prosperity, and the continuance of Divine favour.

"Our Majesty has been informed that you hold our Excellency in love, and that the report of our greatness has reached you. Moreover we have heard through our treasurer that you have been pleased to send to us some objects of art and interest, that our Exaltedness might be gratified thereby.

"Being human, I receive it in good part, and we have ordered our treasurer to send you some of our articles in return.

"Now we desire to be made certain that you hold the right faith, and in all things cleave to Jesus Christ, our Lord, for we have heard that your court regard you as a god, though we know that you are mortal, and subject to human infirmities.

. . . . . Should you desire to learn the greatness and excellency of our Exaltedness and of the land subject to our sceptre, then hear and believe :—I, Presbyter Johannes, the Lord of Lords, surpass all under heaven in virtue, in riches, and in power ; seventy-two kings pay us tribute. . . . In the three Indies our Magnificence rules, and our land extends beyond India, where rests the body of the holy Apostle Thomas ; it reaches towards the sunrise over the wastes, and it trends towards deserted Babylon near the tower of Babel. Seventy-two provinces, of which only a few are Christian, serve us. Each has its own king, but all are tributary to us.

" Our land is the home of elephants, dromedaries, camels, crocodiles, meta-collinarum, cametennus, tensevetes, wild asses, white and red lions, white bears, white merles, crickets, griffins, tigers, lamias, hyænas, wild horses, wild oxen and wild men, men with horns, one-eyed, men with eyes before and behind, centaurs, fauns, satyrs, pygmies, forty-ell high giants, Cyclopses, and similar women ; it is the home, too, of the phœnix, and of nearly all living animals. We have some people subject to us who feed on the flesh of men and of prematurely born animals, and who never fear death. When any of these people die, their friends and relations eat him ravenously, for they regard it as a main duty to munch human flesh. Their names are Gog and Magog, Anie, Agit, Azenach, Fommeperi, Befari, Conei-Samante, Agrimandri, Vintefolei, Casbei, Alanei. These and similar nations were shut in behind lofty mountains by Alexander the Great, towards the North. We lead them at our pleasure against our foes, and neither man nor beast is left undevoured, if our Majesty gives the requisite permission. And when all our foes are eaten, then we return with our hosts home again. These accursed fifteen nations will burst forth from the four quarters of the earth at the end of the world, in the times of Antichrist, and overrun all the abodes of the Saints as well as the great city Rome, which, by the way, we are prepared to give to our son who will be born, along with all Italy, Germany, the two Gauls, Britain and Scotland. We shall also give him Spain and all the land as far as the icy sea. The nations to which I have alluded, according to the words of the prophet, shall not stand in the judgment, on account of their offensive practices, but will be consumed to ashes by a fire which will fall on them from heaven.

"Our land streams with honey, and is overflowing with milk. In one region grows no poisonous herb, nor does a querulous frog ever quack in it, no scorpion exists, nor does the serpent glide amongst the grass, nor can any poisonous animals exist in it, or injure any one.

"Among the heathen, flows through a certain province the river Indus; encircling Paradise, it spreads its arms in manifold windings through the entire province. Here are found the emeralds, sapphires, carbuncles, topazes, chrysolites, onyxes, beryls, sardius, and other costly stones. Here grows the plant Assidos, which, when worn by any one, protects him from the evil spirit, forcing it to state its business and name; consequently the foul spirits keep out of the way there. In a certain land subject to us, all kinds of pepper is gathered, and is exchanged for corn and bread, leather and cloth. . . . At the foot of Mount Olympus bubbles up a spring which changes its flavour hour by hour, night and day, and the spring is scarcely three days' journey from Paradise, out of which Adam was driven. If any one has tasted thrice of the fountain, from that day he will feel no fatigue, but will as long as he lives be as a man of thirty years. Here are found the small stones called Nudiosi, which, if borne about the body, prevent the sight from waxing feeble, and restore it where it is lost.

The more the stone is looked at, the keener
becomes the sight.   In our territory is a certain
waterless sea, consisting of tumbling billows of sand
never at rest.   None have crossed this sea ; it lacks
water altogether, yet fish are cast up upon the
beach of various kinds, very tasty, and the like are
nowhere else to be seen.   Three days' journey from
this sea are mountains from which rolls down a
stony, waterless river, which opens into the sandy
sea.   As soon as the stream reaches the sea, its
stones vanish in it and are never seen again.   As
long as the river is in motion, it cannot be crossed ;
only four days a week is it possible to traverse it.
Between the sandy sea and the said mountains, in
a certain plain is a fountain of singular virtue,
which purges Christians and would-be Christians
from all transgressions.   The water stands four
inches high in a hollow stone shaped like a mussel-
shell.   Two saintly old men watch by it, and ask
the comers whether they are Christians, or are
about to become Christians, then whether they
desire healing with all their hearts.   If they have
answered well, they are bidden to lay aside their
clothes, and to step into the mussel.   If what they
said be true, then the water begins to rise and gush
over their heads ; thrice does the water thus lift

itself, and every one who has entered the mussel leaves it cured of every complaint.

"Near the wilderness trickles between barren mountains a subterranean rill, which can only by chance be reached, for only occasionally the earth gapes, and he who would descend must do it with precipitation, ere the earth closes again. All that is gathered under the ground there is gem and precious stone. The brook pours into another river, and the inhabitants of the neighbourhood obtain thence abundance of precious stones. Yet they never venture to sell them without having first offered them to us for our private use : should we decline them, they are at liberty to dispose of them to strangers. Boys there are trained to remain three or four days under water, diving after the stones.

"Beyond the stone river are the ten tribes of the Jews, which, though subject to their own kings, are, for all that, our slaves and tributary to our Majesty. In one of our lands, hight Zone, are worms called in our tongue Salamanders. These worms can only live in fire, and they build cocoons like silk-worms, which are unwound by the ladies of our palace, and spun into cloth and dresses, which are worn by our Exaltedness. These dresses in order to be cleaned and washed are cast into flames. . . . When we go to war, we have fourteen golden and bejewelled crosses borne before us instead of banners ; each of these crosses is followed by 10,000 horsemen, and 100,000 foot soldiers fully armed, without reckoning those in charge of the luggage and provision.

"When we ride abroad plainly, we have a wooden, unadorned cross, without gold or gem about it, borne before us, in order that we may meditate on the sufferings of Our Lord Jesus Christ ; also a golden bowl filled with earth, to remind us of that whence we sprung, and that to which we must return ; but besides these there is borne a silver bowl full of gold, as a token to all that we are the Lord of Lords.

"All riches, such as are upon the world, our Magnificence possesses in superabundance. With us no one lies, for he who speaks a lie is thenceforth regarded as dead ; he is no more thought of, or honoured by us. No vice is tolerated by us. Every year we undertake a pilgrimage, with retinue of war, to the body of the holy prophet Daniel, which is near the desolated site of Babylon. In our realm fishes are caught, the blood of which dyes purple. The Amazons and the Brahmins are sub-

ject to us. The palace in which our Supereminency
resides, is built after the pattern of the castle built
by the Apostle Thomas for the Indian king Gundo-
forus. Ceilings, joists, and architrave are of
Sethym wood, the roof of ebony, which can never
catch fire. Over the gable of the palace are, at the
extremities, two golden apples, in each of which are
two carbuncles, so that the gold may shine by day,
and the carbuncles by night. The greater gates of
the palace are of sardius, with the horn of the
horned snake inwrought, so that no one can bring
poison within.

"The other portals are of ebony. The windows
are of crystal ; the tables are partly of gold, partly
of amethyst, and the columns supporting the tables
are partly of ivory, partly of amethyst. The court
in which we watch the jousting is floored with onyx
in order to increase the courage of the combatants.
In the palace, at night, nothing is burned for light
but wicks supplied with balsam. . . . Before our
palace stands a mirror, the ascent to which consists
of five and twenty steps of porphyry, and serpen-
tine." After a description of the gems adorning this
mirror, which is guarded night and day by three
thousand armed men, he explains its use: "We

look therein and behold all that is taking place in every province and region subject to our sceptre.

"Seven kings wait upon us monthly, in turn, with sixty-two dukes, two hundred and fifty-six counts and marquises : and twelve archbishops sit at table with us on our right, and twenty bishops on the left, besides the patriarch of S. Thomas, the Sarmatian Protopope, and the Archpope of Susa. . . . Our lord high steward is a primate and king, our cup-bearer is an archbishop and king, our chamberlain a bishop and king, our marshal a king and abbot."

I may be spared further extracts from this extraordinary letter, which proceeds to describe the church in which Prester John worships, by enumerating the precious stones of which it is constructed, and their special virtues.

Whether this letter was in circulation before Pope Alexander wrote his, it is not easy to decide. Alexander does not allude to it, but speaks of the reports which have reached him of the piety and the magnificence of the Priest-King. At the same time, there runs a tone of bitterness through the letter, as though the Pope had been galled at the pretensions of this mysterious personage, and perhaps winced under the prospect of the man-eaters overrunning Italy, as suggested by John the Priest. The papal epistle is an assertion of the claims of the See of Rome to universal dominion, and it assures the Eastern Prince-Pope that his Christian professions are worthless, unless he submits to the successor of Peter. "Not every one that saith unto me, Lord, Lord," &c., quotes the Pope, and then explains that the will of God is that every monarch and prelate should eat humble pie to the Sovereign Pontiff.

Sir John Maundevil gives the origin of the priestly title of the Eastern despot, in his curious book of travels.

"So it befelle, that this emperour cam, with a Cristene knyght with him, into a chirche in Egypt: and it was Saterday in Wyttson woke. And the bishop made orders. And he beheld and listened the servyse fulle tentyfly: and he asked the Cristene knyght, what men of degree thei scholden ben, that the prelate had before him. And the knyght answerede and seyde, that thei scholde ben prestes. And then the emperour seyde, that he wolde no longer ben clept kyng ne emperour, but preest: and that he wolde have the name of the first preest, that wente out of the chirche; and his name was

John. And so evere more sittiens, he is clept Prestre John."

It is probable that the foundation of the whole Prester-John myth lay in the report which reached Europe of the wonderful successes of Nestorianism in the East, and there seems reason to believe that the famous letter given above was a Nestorian fabrication. It certainly looks un-European; the gorgeous imagery is thoroughly Eastern, and the disparaging tone in which Rome is spoken of could hardly have been the expression of Western feelings. The letter has the object in view of exalting the East in religion and arts to an undue eminence at the expense of the West, and it manifests some ignorance of European geography, when it speaks of the land extending from Spain to the Polar Sea. Moreover, the sites of the patriarchates, and the dignity conferred on that of S. Thomas are indications of a Nestorian bias.

A brief glance at the history of this heretical Church may be of value here, as showing that there really was a foundation for the wild legends concerning a Christian empire in the East, so prevalent in Europe. Nestorius, a priest of Antioch and a disciple of S. Chrysostom, was elevated by the emperor to the patriarchate of Constantinople, and in the year 428 began to propagate his heresy, denying the hypostatic union. The Council of Ephesus denounced him, and, in spite of the emperor and court, Nestorius was anathematized and driven into exile. His sect spread through the East, and became a flourishing Church. It reached to China, where the emperor was all but converted ; its missionaries traversed the frozen tundras of Siberia, preaching their maimed Gospel to the wild hordes which haunted those dreary wastes ; it faced Buddhism and wrestled with it for the religious supremacy in Thibet ; it established churches in Persia and in Bokhara ; it penetrated India ; it formed colonies in Ceylon, in Siam, and in Sumatra ; so that the Catholicos or Pope of Bagdad exercised sway more extensive than that ever obtained by the successor of S. Peter. The number of Christians belonging to that communion probably exceeded that of the members of the true Catholic Church in East and West. But the Nestorian Church was not founded on the Rock, it rested on Nestorius, and when the rain descended, and the winds blew, and the floods came, and beat upon that house, it fell, leaving scarce a fragment behind.

Rubruquis the Franciscan, who in 1253 was sent

on a mission into Tartary, was the first to let in
a little light on the fable. He writes, "The Catai
dwelt beyond certain mountains across which I
wandered, and in a plain in the midst of the mountains lived once an important Nestorian shepherd,
who ruled over the Nestorian people, called Nayman. When Coir-Khan died, the Nestorian people
raised this man to be king, and called him King
Johannes, and related of him ten times as much as
the truth. The Nestorians thereabouts have this
way with them, that about nothing they make a
great fuss, and thus they have got it noised abroad
that Sartach, Mangu-Khan, and Ken-Khan were
Christians, simply because they treated Christians
well, and showed them more honour than other
people. Yet, in fact, they were not Christians at
all. And in like manner the story got about that
there was a great King John. However, I traversed
his pastures, and no one knew any thing about him,
except a few Nestorians. In his pastures lives
Ken-Khan, at whose court was Brother Andrew,
whom I met on my way back. This Johannes had
a brother, a famous shepherd, named Unc, who
lived three weeks' journey beyond the mountains
of Caracatais."

This Unk-Khan was a real individual; he lost

his life in the year 1203. Kuschhik, prince of the Nayman, and follower of Kor-Khan, fell in 1218.

Marco Polo, the Venetian traveller (1254—1324), identifies Unk-Khan with Prester John; he says, "I will now tell you of the deeds of the Tartars, how they gained the mastery, and spread over the whole earth. The Tartars dwelt between Georgia and Bargu, where there is a vast plain and level country, on which are neither cities nor forts, but capital pasturage and water. They had no chief of their own, but paid to Prester Johannes tribute. Of the greatness of this Prester Johannes, who was properly called Un-Khan, the whole world spake; the Tartars gave him one of every ten head of cattle. When Prester John noticed that they were increasing, he feared them, and planned how he could injure them. He determined therefore to scatter them, and he sent barons to do this. But the Tartars guessed what Prester John purposed . . . . and they went away into the wide wastes of the North, where they might be beyond his reach." He then goes on to relate how Tschengis-(Jenghiz-)Khan became the head of the Tartars, and how he fought against Prester John, and, after a desperate fight, overcame and slew him.

The Syriac Chronicle of the Jacobite Primate, Gregory Bar-Hebræus (born 1226, died 1286), also identifies Unk-Khan with Prester John. "In the year of the Greeks 1514, of the Arabs 599 (A.D. 1202), when Unk-Khan, who is the Christian King John, ruled over a stock of the barbarian Hunns, called Kergis, Tschengys-Khan served him with great zeal. When John observed the superiority and serviceableness of the other, he envied him, and plotted to seize and murder him. But two sons of Unk-Khan, having heard this, told it to Tschengys, whereupon he and his comrades fled by night and secreted themselves. Next morning Unk-Khan took possession of the Tartar tents, but found them empty. Then the party of Tschengys fell upon him, and they met by the spring called Balschunah, and the side of Tschengys won the day; and the followers of Unk-Khan were compelled to yield. They met again several times, till Unk-Khan was utterly discomfited and was slain himself, and his wives, sons, and daughters carried into captivity. Yet we must consider that John, king of the Kergis, was not cast down for nought, nay rather, because he had turned his heart from the fear of Christ his Lord, who had exalted him, and had taken a

wife of the Zinish nation, called Quarakhata.
Because he forsook the religion of his ancestors
and followed strange gods, therefore God took the
government from him, and gave it to one better
than he, and whose heart was right before God."

Some of the early travellers, such as John de
Plano-Carpini and Marco Polo, in disabusing the
popular mind of the belief in Prester John as a
mighty Asiatic Christian monarch, unintentionally
turned the popular faith in that individual into
a new direction. They spoke of the black people
of Abascia in Ethiopia, which, by the way, they
called Middle India, as a great people subject to
a Christian monarch.

Marco Polo says that the true monarch of
Abyssinia is Christ; but that it is governed by
six kings, three of whom are Christians and three
Saracens, and that they are in league with the
Soudan of Aden.

Bishop Jordanus, in his description of the world,
accordingly sets down Abyssinia as the kingdom
of Prester John; and such was the popular impression, which was confirmed by the appearance
at intervals of ambassadors at European courts
from the King of Abyssinia. The discovery of
the Cape of Good Hope was due partly to a desire

manifested in Portugal to open communications
with this monarch[4], and King John II. sent two
men learned in Oriental languages through Egypt
to the court of Abyssinia. The might and dominion of this prince, who had replaced the Tartar
chief in the popular creed as Prester John, was
of course greatly exaggerated, and was supposed
to extend across Arabia and Asia to the wall of
China. The spread of geographical knowledge
has contracted the area of his dominions, and a
critical acquaintance with history has exploded
the myth which invested Unk-Khan the nomad
chief with all the attributes of a demigod, uniting
in one the utmost pretensions of a Pope and the
proudest claims of a monarch.

[4] Ludolfi, Hist. Æthiopica, lib. ii. cap. 1, 2. Petrus, Petri
filius Lusitaniæ princeps, M. Pauli Veneti librum (qui de
Indorum rebus multa : speciatim vero de Presbytero Johanne
aliqua magnifice scripsit) Venetiis secum in patriam detu-
lerat, qui (Chronologicis Lusitanorum testantibus) præcipuam
Johanni Regi ansam dedit Indicæ navigationis, quam Henricus Johannis I. filius, patruus ejus, tentaverat, prose-
quendæ, &c.

The Divining Rod

FROM the remotest period a rod has been regarded as the symbol of power and authority, and Holy Scripture employs it in the popular sense. Thus David speaks of "Thy rod and Thy staff comforting me;" and Moses works his miracles before Pharaoh with the rod as emblem of Divine commission. It was his rod which became a serpent, which turned the water of Egypt into blood, which opened the waves of the Red Sea and restored them to their former level, which "smote the rock of stone so that the water gushed out abundantly." The rod of Aaron acted an oracular part in the contest with the princes; laid up before the ark, it budded and brought forth almonds. In this instance we have it no longer as a symbol of authority, but as a means of divining the will of God. And as such it became liable to abuse; thus Hosea

rebukes the chosen people for practising similar
divinations. "My people ask counsel at their
stocks, and their staff declareth unto them[1]."

Long before this, Jacob had made a different use
of rods, employing them as a charm to make
his father-in-law's sheep bear pied and spotted
lambs.

We find rabdomancy a popular form of divination among the Greeks, and also among the
Romans. Cicero in his "De Officiis" alludes to
it. "If all that is needful for our nourishment and
support arrives to us by means of some divine rod,
as people say, then each of us, free from all care
and trouble, may give himself up to the exclusive
pursuit of study and science[2]."

Probably it is to this rod that Ennius alludes in
the passage quoted in the first book of his "De
Divinatione," wherein he laughs at those who
for a drachma will teach the art of discovering
treasures.

According to Vetranius Maurus, Varro left a
satire on the "Virgula divina," which has not been
preserved. Tacitus tells us that the Germans
practised some sort of divination by means of rods.

---

[1] Hos. iv. 12.   [2] De Officiis. lib. i. cap. 44.

"For the purpose their method is simple. They cut a rod off some fruit-tree into bits, and after having distinguished them by various marks, they cast them into a white cloth. . . . Then the priest thrice draws each piece, and explains the oracle according to the marks[3]." Ammianus Marcellinus says that the Alains employed an osier rod[4].

The fourteenth law of the Frisons ordered that the discovery of murders should be made by means of divining rods used in Church. These rods should be laid before the altar, and on the sacred relics, after which God was to be supplicated to indicate the culprit. This was called the Lot of rods, or Tan-teen, the Rod of Rods.

But the middle ages was the date of the full development of the superstition, and the divining rod was believed to have efficacy in discovering hidden treasures, veins of precious metal, springs of water, thefts, and murders. The first notice of its general use among late writers is in the "Testamentum Novum," lib. i. cap. 25, of Basil Valentine, a Benedictine monk of the fifteenth century. Basil speaks of the general faith in and adoption of this valuable instrument for the discovery of metals,

---

[3] Tacitus, German., cap. x.   [4] Ammian. Marcel. xxxi. 2.

which is carried by workmen in mines, either in
their belts or in their caps.   He says that there are
seven names by which this rod is known, and to its
excellencies under each title he devotes a chapter
of his book.   The names are:—Divine Rod, Shining
Rod, Leaping Rod, Transcendent Rod, Trembling
Rod, Dipping Rod, Superior Rod.   In his admirable
treatise on metals, Agricola speaks of the rod in
terms of disparagement ; he considers its use as a
relic of ancient magical forms, and he says that it
is only irreligious workmen who employ it in their
search after metals.   Goclenius, however, in his
treatise on the virtue of plants, stoutly does battle
for the properties of the hazel rod.   Whereupon
Roberti, a Flemish Jesuit, falls upon him tooth and
nail, disputes his facts, overwhelms him with abuse,
and gibbets him for popular ridicule.   Andreas
Libavius, a writer I have already quoted in my
article on the Wandering Jew, undertook a series
of experiments upon the hazel divining rod, and
concluded that there was truth in the popular
belief.   The Jesuit Kircher also "experimentalized
several times on wooden rods which were declared
to be sympathetic with regard to certain metals, by
placing them on delicate pivots in equilibrium, but
they never turned on the approach of metal."   (De

Arte Magnetica.) However, a similar course of experiments over water led him to attribute to the rod the power of indicating subterranean springs and watercourses; "I would not affirm it," he says, "unless I had established the fact by my own experience."

Dechales, another Jesuit, author of a treatise on natural springs, and of a huge tome entitled "Mundus Mathematicus," declared in the latter work, that no means of discovering sources is equal to the divining rod; and he quotes a friend of his who, with a hazel rod in his hand, could discover springs with the utmost precision and facility, and could trace on the surface of the ground the course of a subterranean conduit. Another writer, Saint-Romain, in his "Science dégagée des Chimères de l'École," exclaims; "Is it not astonishing to see a rod which is held firmly in the hands, bow itself and turn visibly in the direction of water or metal, with more or less promptitude, according as the metal or the water are near or remote from the surface!"

In 1659 the Jesuit Gaspard Schott writes that the rod is used in every town of Germany, and that he had frequent opportunity of seeing it used in the discovery of hidden treasures. "I searched with the greatest care," he adds, "into the question whether the hazel rod had any sympathy with gold and silver, and whether any natural property set it in motion. In like manner I tried whether a ring of metal, held suspended by a thread in the midst of a tumbler, and which strikes the hours, is moved by any similar force. I ascertained that these effects could only have arisen from the deception of those holding the rod or the pendulum, or, may be, from some diabolic impulsion, or, more likely still, because imagination sets the hand in motion."

The Sieur le Royer, a lawyer of Rouen, in 1674, published his "Traité du Bâton universel," in which he gives an account of a trial made with the rod in the presence of Father Jean François, who had ridiculed the operation in his treatise on the science of waters, published at Rennes in 1655, and which succeeded in convincing the blasphemer of the divine Rod. Le Royer denies to it the power of picking out criminals, which had been popularly attributed to it, and as had been unhesitatingly claimed for it by Debrio in his "Disquisitio Magica."

And now I am brought to the extraordinary story of Jacques Aymar, which attracted the attention of Europe to the marvellous properties of the divining rod. I shall give the history of this man in full, as such an account is rendered necessary by the mutilated versions I have seen current in English magazine articles, which follow the lead of Mrs. Crowe, who narrates the earlier portion of this impostor's career, but says nothing of his *exposé* and downfall.

On the 5th July, 1692, at about ten o'clock in the evening, a wine-seller of Lyons and his wife were assassinated in their cellar, and their money carried off. On the morrow, the officers of justice arrived, and examined the premises. Beside the corpses, lay a large bottle wrapped in straw, and a bloody hedging bill, which undoubtedly had been the instrument used to accomplish the murder. Not a trace of those who had committed the horrible deed was to be found, and the magistrates were quite at fault as to the direction in which they should turn for a clue to the murderer or murderers.

At this juncture a neighbour reminded the magistrates of an incident which had taken place four years previous. It was this. In 1688 a theft of clothes had been made in Grenoble. In the parish of Crôle lived a man named Jacques Aymar, supposed to be endowed with the faculty of using the divining rod. This man was sent for. On reaching the spot where the theft had been committed, his rod moved in his hand. He followed the track indicated by the rod, and it continued to rotate between his fingers as long as he followed a certain direction, but ceased to turn if he diverged from it in the smallest degree. Guided by his rod, Aymar went from street to street, till he was brought to a standstill before the prison gates. These could not be opened without leave of the magistrate, who hastened to witness the experiment. The gates were unlocked, and Aymar, under the same guidance, directed his steps towards four prisoners lately incarcerated. He ordered the four to be stood in a line, and then he placed his foot on that of the first. The rod remained immovable. He passed to the second, and the rod turned at once. Before the third prisoner there were no signs, the fourth trembled, and begged to be heard. He owned himself the thief, along with the second, who also acknowledged the theft, and mentioned the name of the receiver of the stolen goods. This was a farmer in the neighbourhood of Grenoble. The magistrate and officers visited him and demanded the articles he had obtained. The farmer denied all knowledge of the theft and all participation in the booty. Aymar, however, by means of his rod, discovered the secreted property, and restored it to the persons from whom it had been stolen.

On another occasion Aymar had been in quest of a spring of water, when he felt his rod turn sharply in his hand. On digging at the spot, expecting to discover an abundant source, the body of a murdered woman was found in a barrel, with a rope twisted round her neck. The poor creature was recognized as a woman of the neigbourhood who had vanished four months before. Aymar went to the house which the victim had inhabited, and presented his rod to each member of the household. It turned upon the husband of the deceased, who at once took to flight.

The magistrates of Lyons, at their wits' end how to discover the perpetrators of the double murder in the wine-shop, urged the Procureur du Roi to make experiment of the powers of Jacques Aymar. The fellow was sent for, and he boldly asserted his capacity for detecting criminals, if he were first brought to the spot of the murder, so as to be put *en rapport* with the murderers.

He was at once conducted to the scene of the outrage, with the rod in his hand. This remained stationary as he traversed the cellar, till he reached the spot where the body of the wine-seller had lain ; then the stick became violently agitated, and the man's pulse rose as though he were in an access of fever. The same motions and symptoms manifested themselves when he reached the place where the second victim had lain.

Having thus received his *impression*, Aymar left the cellar, and, guided by his rod, or rather by an internal instinct, he ascended into the shop, and then stepping into the street, he followed from one to another, like a hound upon the scent, the track of the murderers. It conducted him into the court of the archiepiscopal palace, across it, and down to the gate of the Rhone. It was now evening, and the city gates being all closed, the quest of blood was relinquished for the night.

Next morning Aymar returned to the scent. Accompanied by three officers, he left the gate and descended the right bank of the Rhone. The rod gave indications of there having been three involved in the murder, and he pursued the traces till two of them led to a gardener's cottage. Into this he entered, and there he asserted with warmth, against the asseverations of the proprietor to the contrary, that the fugitives had entered his room,

had seated themselves at his table, and had drunk
wine out of one of the bottles which he indicated.
Aymar tested each of the household with his rod,
to see if they had been in contact with the murderers. The rod moved over the two children
only, aged respectively ten and nine years. These
little things on being questioned, answered with
reluctance, that during their father's absence on
Sunday morning, against his express commands,
they had left the door open, and that two men,
whom they described, had come in suddenly upon
them, and had seated themselves and made free
with the wine in the bottle pointed out by the man
with the rod. This first verification of the talents
of Jacques Aymar convinced some of the sceptical,
but the Procurator Général forbad the prosecution
of the experiment till the man had been further
tested.

As already stated, a hedging bill had been discovered on the scene of the murder, smeared with
blood, and unquestionably the weapon with which
the crime had been committed. Three bills from
the same maker, and of precisely the same description, were obtained, and the four were taken into a
garden, and secretly buried at intervals. Aymar
was then brought, staff in hand, into the garden,

and conducted over the spots where lay the bills. The rod began to vibrate as his feet stood upon the place where was concealed the bill which had been used by the assassins, but was motionless elsewhere. Still unsatisfied, the four bills were exhumed and concealed anew. The comptroller of the province himself bandaged the sorcerer's eyes and led him by the hand from place to place. The divining rod showed no signs of movement till it approached the blood-stained weapon, when it began to oscillate.

The magistrates were now so far satisfied as to agree that Jacques Aymar should be authorized to follow the trail of the murderers, and have a company of archers to follow him.

Guided by his rod, Aymar now recommenced his pursuit. He continued tracing down the right bank of the Rhone till he came to half a league from the bridge of Lyons. Here the footprints of three men were observed in the sand, as though engaged in entering a boat. A rowing boat was obtained, and Aymar with his escort descended the river; he found some difficulty in following the trail upon water, still he was able with a little care to detect it. It brought him under an arch of the bridge of Vienne, which boats rarely passed beneath. This proved that the fugitives were without a guide. The way in which this curious journey was made was singular. At intervals Aymar was put ashore to test the banks with his rod, and ascertain whether the murderers had landed. He discovered the places where they had slept, and indicated the chairs or benches on which they had sat. In this manner, by slow degrees he arrived at the military camp of Sablon, between Vienne and Saint-Valier. There Aymar felt violent agitation, his cheeks flushed, and his pulse beat with rapidity. He penetrated the crowds of soldiers, but did not venture to use his rod, lest the men should take it ill, and fall upon him. He could not do more without special authority, and was constrained to return to Lyons. The magistrates then provided him with the requisite powers, and he went back to the camp. Now he declared that the murderers were not there. He recommenced his pursuit, and descended the Rhone again as far as Beaucaire.

On entering the town he ascertained by means of his rod that those whom he was pursuing had parted company. He traversed several streets, then crowded on account of the annual fair, and was brought to a standstill before the prison doors. One of the murderers was within, he declared, he would track the others afterwards. Having obtained permission to enter, he was brought into the presence of fourteen or fifteen prisoners. Amongst these was a hunchback who had only an hour previously been incarcerated on account of a theft he had committed at the fair. Aymar applied his rod to each of the prisoners in succession: it turned upon the hunchback. The sorcerer ascertained that the other two had left the town by a little path leading into the Nismes road. Instead of following this track, he returned to Lyons with the hunchback and the guard. At Lyons a triumph awaited him. The hunchback had hitherto protested his innocence, and declared that he had never set foot in Lyons. But as he was brought to that town by the way along which Aymar had ascertained that he had left it, the fellow was recognized at the different houses where he had lodged the night, or stopped for food. At the little town of Bagnols, he was confronted with the host and hostess of a tavern where he and his comrades had slept, and they swore to his identity, and accurately described his companions: their description tallied with that given by the children of the gardener. The wretched man was so confounded by this recognition, that he avowed having stayed there a few days before, along with two Provencals. These men, he said, were the criminals; he had been their servant, and had only kept guard in the upper room whilst they committed the murders in the cellar.

On his arrival in Lyons he was committed to prison, and his trial was decided on. At his first interrogation he told his tale precisely as he had related it before, with these additions,—the murderers spoke patois, and had purchased two bills. At ten o'clock in the evening all three had entered the wine-shop. The Provençals had a large bottle wrapped in straw, and they persuaded the publican and his wife to descend with them into the cellar to fill it, whilst he, the hunchback, acted as watch in the shop. The two men murdered the wine-seller and his wife with their bills, and then mounted to the shop, where they opened the coffer and stole from it 130 crowns, eight Louis d'ors, and a silver belt. The crime accomplished, they took refuge in the court of a large house,—this was the archbishop's palace, indicated by Aymar,—and passed the night in it. Next day, early, they left Lyons, and only stopped for a moment at a gardener's cottage. Some way down the river, they found a boat moored to the bank. This they loosed from its mooring and entered. They came ashore at the spot pointed out by the man with the stick. They stayed some days in the camp at Sablon, and then went on to Beaucaire.

Aymar was now sent in quest of the other murderers. He resumed their trail at the gate of Beaucaire, and that of one of them, after considerable *détours*, led him to the prison doors of Beaucaire, and he asked to be allowed to search among the prisoners for his man. This time he was mistaken. The second fugitive was not within ; but the gaoler affirmed that a man whom he described,—and his description tallied with the known appearance of one of the Provençals,—had called at the gate shortly after the removal of the hunch-back, to inquire after him, and on learning of his removal to Lyons, had hurried off precipitately. Aymar now followed his track from the prison, and this brought him to that of the third criminal. He pursued the double scent for some days. But it became evident that the two culprits had been alarmed at what had transpired in Beaucaire, and were flying from France. Aymar traced them to the frontier, and then returned to Lyons.

On the 30th of August, 1692, the poor hunchback was, according to sentence, broken on the wheel, in the Place des Terreaux. On his way to execution he had to pass the wine-shop. There the recorder publicly read his sentence, which had been delivered by thirty judges. The criminal knelt and asked pardon of the poor wretches in whose murder he was involved, after which he continued his course to the place fixed for his execution.

It may be well here to give an account of the authorities for this extraordinary story. There are three circumstantial accounts, and numerous letters written by the magistrate who sat during the trial, and by an eye-witness of the whole transaction, men honourable and disinterested, upon whose veracity not a shadow of doubt was supposed to rest by their contemporaries.

M. Chauvin, Doctor of Medicine, published a *Lettre à Mme. la Marquise de Senozan, sur les moyens dont on s'est servi pour découvrir les complices d'un assassinat commis à Lyon, le 5 Juillet,* 1692, Lyons, 1692. The *procès-verbal* of the Procureur du Roi, M. de Vanini, is also extant, and published in the *Physique occulte* of the Abbé de Vallemont.

Pierre Garnier, Doctor of Medicine of the

University of Montpelier, wrote a *Dissertation physique en forme de lettre, à M. de Sève, seigneur de Fléchères*, on Jacques Aymar, printed the same year at Lyons, and republished in the *Histoire critique des pratiques superstitieuses, du Père Lebrun*.

Doctor Chauvin was witness of nearly all the circumstances related, as was also the Abbé Lagarde, who has written a careful account of the whole transaction as far as to the execution of the hunchback.

Another eye-witness writes to the Abbé Bignon a letter printed by Lebrun in his *Histoire critique* cited above. "The following circumstance happened to me yesterday evening," he says; " M. le Procureur du Roi here, who, by the way, is one of the wisest and cleverest men in the country, sent for me at six o'clock, and had me conducted to the scene of the murder. We found there M. Grimaut, director of the customs, whom I knew to be a very upright man, and a young attorney named Besson, with whom I am not acquainted, but who M. le Procureur du Roi told me had the power of using the rod as well as M. Grimaut. We descended into the cellar where the murder had been committed, and where there were still traces of blood. Each time that M. Grimaut and the attorney passed the spot where the murder had been perpetrated, the rods they held in their hands began to turn, but ceased when they stepped beyond the spot. We tried experiments for more than an hour, as also with the bill, which M. le Procureur had brought along with him, and they were satisfactory. I observed several curious facts in the attorney. The rod in his hands was more violently moved than in those of M. Grimaut, and when I placed one of my fingers in each of his hands, whilst the rod turned, I felt the most extraordinary throbbings of the arteries in his palms. His pulse was at fever-heat. He sweated profusely, and at intervals he was compelled to go into the court to obtain fresh air."

The Sieur Pauthot, Dean of the College of Medicine at Lyons, gave his observations to the public as well Some of them are as follows: "We began at the cellar in which the murder had been committed ; into this the man with the rod (Aymar) shrank from entering, because he felt violent agitations which overcame him when he used the stick over the place where the corpses of those who had been assassinated had lain. On entering the cellar, the rod was put in my hands,

and arranged by the master as most suitable for
operation; I passed and repassed over the spot
where the bodies had been found, but it remained
immovable, and I felt no agitation. A lady of rank
and merit, who was with us, took the rod after me :
she felt it begin to move, and was internally
agitated. Then the owner of the rod resumed it,
and, passing over the same places, the stick rotated
with such violence that it seemed easier to break
than to stop it. The peasant then quitted our
company to faint away, as was his wont after
similar experiments. I followed him. He turned
very pale and broke into a profuse perspiration,
whilst for a quarter of an hour his pulse was
violently troubled ; indeed the faintness was so
considerable, that they were obliged to dash water
in his face and give him water to drink in order to
bring him round."   He then describes experiments
made over the bloody bill and others similar, which
succeeded in the hands of Aymar and the lady,
but failed when he attempted them himself. Pierre
Garnier, physician of the medical college of Montpelier, appointed to that of Lyons, has also
written an account of what he saw, as mentioned
above.   He gives a curious proof of Aymar's
powers.

" M. le Lieutenant-Général having been robbed by one of his lackeys, seven or eight months ago, and having lost by him twenty-five crowns which had been taken out of one of the cabinets behind his library, sent for Aymar, and asked him to discover the circumstances. Aymar went several times round the chamber, rod in hand, placing one foot on the chairs, on the various articles of furniture, and on two bureaux which are in the apartment, each of which contains several drawers. He fixed on the very bureau and the identical drawer out of which the money had been stolen. M. le Lieutenant-Général bade him follow the track of the robber. He did so. With his rod he went out on a new terrace, upon which the cabinet opens, thence back into the cabinet and up to the fire, then into the library, and from thence he went direct upstairs to the lackeys' sleeping apartment, when the rod guided him to one of the beds, and turned over one side of the bed, remaining motionless over the other. The lackeys then present cried out that the thief had slept on the side indicated by the rod, the bed having been shared with another footman, who occupied the further side." Garnier gives a lengthy account of various experiments he made along with the Lieutenant-Général, the uncle of the same, the Abbé de S. Remain, and M. de Puget, to detect whether there was imposture in the man. But all their attempts failed to discover a trace of deception. He gives a report of verbal examination of Aymar which is interesting. The man always replied with candour.

The report of the extraordinary discovery of murder made by the divining rod at Lyons attracted the attention of Paris, and Aymar was ordered up to the capital. There, however, his powers left him. The Prince de Condé submitted him to various tests, and he broke down under every one. Five holes were dug in the garden. In one was secreted gold, in another silver, in a third silver and gold, in the fourth copper, and in the fifth stones. The rod made no signs in presence of the metals, and at last actually began to move over the buried pebbles. He was sent to Chantilly to discover the perpetrators of a theft of trout made in the ponds of the park. He went round the water, rod in hand, and it turned at spots where he said the fish had been drawn out. Then, following the track of the thief, it led him to the cottage of one of the keepers, but did not move over any of the individuals then in the house. The keeper himself was absent, but arrived late at night, and on hearing what was said, he roused Aymar from his bed, insisting on having his innocence vindicated. The divining rod, however, pronounced him guilty, and the poor fellow took to his heels, much upon the principle recommended by Montesquieu a while after. Said he, "If you are accused of having stolen the towers of Notre-Dame, bolt at once."

A peasant, taken at haphazard from the street, was brought to the sorcerer as one suspected. The rod turned slightly, and Aymar declared that the man did not steal the fish, but ate of them. A boy was then introduced, who was said to be the keeper's son. The rod rotated violently at once. This was the finishing stroke, and Aymar was sent away by the Prince in disgrace. It now transpired that the theft of fish had taken place seven years before, and the lad was no relation of the keeper, but a country boy who had only been in Chantilly eight or ten months. M. Goyonnot, Recorder of the King's Council, broke a window in his house, and sent for the diviner, to whom he related a story of his having been robbed of valuables during the night. Aymar indicated the broken window as the means whereby the thief had entered the house, and pointed out the window by which he had left it with the booty. As no such robbery had been committed, Aymar was turned out of the house as an impostor. A few similar cases brought him into such disrepute that he was obliged to leave Paris, and return to Grenoble.

Some years after, he was made use of by the Maréchal Montrevel, in his cruel pursuit of the Camisards.

Was Aymar an impostor from first to last, or did his powers fail him in Paris? and was it only then that he had recourse to fraud?

Much may be said in favour of either supposition. His *exposé* at Paris tells heavily against him, but need not be regarded as conclusive evidence of imposture throughout his career. If he really did possess the powers he claimed, it is not to be supposed that these existed in full vigour under all conditions; and Paris is a place most unsuitable for testing them, built on artificial soil, and full of disturbing influences of every description. It has been remarked with others who used the rod, that their powers languished under excitement, and that the faculties had to be in repose, the attention to be concentrated on the subject of inquiry, or the action—nervous, magnetic, or electrical, or what you will—was impeded.

Now Paris, visited for the first time by a poor peasant, its saloons open to him, dazzling him with their splendour, and the novelty of finding himself in the midst of princes, dukes, marquises, and their families, not only may have agitated the countryman to such an extent as to deprive him of his peculiar faculty, but may have led him into simulating what he felt had departed from him, at the moment when he was under the eyes of the grandees of the Court. We have analogous cases in Bleton and Angelique Cottin. The former was a hydroscope, who fell into convulsions whenever he passed over running water. This peculiarity was noticed in him when a child of seven years old. When brought to Paris, he failed signally to detect the presence of water conveyed underground by pipes and conduits, but he pretended to feel the influence of water where there certainly was none. Angelique Cottin was a poor girl, highly charged with electricity. Any one touching her received a violent shock; one medical gentleman, having seated her on his knee, was knocked clean out of his chair by the electric fluid, which thus exhibited its sense of propriety. But the electric condition of Angelique became feebler as she approached Paris, and failed her altogether in the capital.

I believe that the imagination is the principal motive force in those who use the divining rod ; but whether it is so solely, I am unable to decide. The powers of nature are so mysterious and inscrutable that we must be cautious in limiting them, under abnormal conditions, to the ordinary laws of experience.

The manner in which the rod was used by certain persons renders self-deception possible. The rod is generally of hazel, and is forked like a Y ; the forefingers are placed against the diverging arms of the rod, and the elbows are brought back against the side ; thus the implement is held in front of the operator, delicately balanced before the pit of the stomach at a distance of about eight inches. Now, if the pressure of the balls of the digits be in the least relaxed, the stalk of the rod will naturally fall. It has been assumed by some, that a restoration of the pressure will bring the stem up again, pointing towards the operator, and a little further pressure will elevate it into a perpendicular position. A relaxation of force will again lower it, and thus the rotation observed in the rod be maintained. I confess myself unable to accomplish this. The lowering of the leg of the rod is easy enough, but no efforts of mine to produce a revolution on its axis have as yet succeeded. The muscles which would contract the fingers upon the arms of the stick, pass over the shoulder; and it is worthy of remark that one of the medical men who witnessed the experiments made on Bleton the hydroscope, expressly alludes to a slight rising of the shoulders during the rotation of the divining rod.

But the manner of using the rod was by no means identical in all cases. If, in all cases, it had simply been balanced between the fingers, some probability might be given to the suggestion above made, that the rotation was always effected by the involuntary action of the muscles.

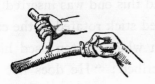

The usual manner of holding the rod, however, precluded such a possibility. The most ordinary use consisted in taking a forked stick in such a manner that the palms were turned upwards, and the fingers closed upon the branching arms of the rod. Some required the normal position of the rod to be horizontal, others elevated the point, others again depressed it.

If the implement were straight, it was held in a similar manner, but the hands were brought somewhat together, so as to produce a slight arc in the rod. Some who practised rabdomancy sustained this species of rod between their thumbs and forefingers, or else the thumb and forefingers were closed, and the rod rested on their points, or again it reposed on the flat of the hand, or on the back, the hand being held vertically and the rod held in equilibrium.

A third species of divining rod consisted in a straight staff cut in two : one extremity of the one half was hollowed out, the other half was sharpened at the end, and this end was inserted in the hollow, and the pointed stick rotated in the cavity.

The way in which Bleton used his rod is thus minutely described : " He does not grasp it, nor warm it in his hands, and he does not regard with preference a hazel branch lately cut and full of sap. He places horizontally between his forefingers a rod of any kind given to him, or picked up in the road, of any sort of wood except elder, fresh or dry, not always forked, but sometimes merely bent. If it is straight, it rises slightly at the extremities by little jerks, but does not turn. If bent, it revolves on its axis with more or less rapidity, in more or

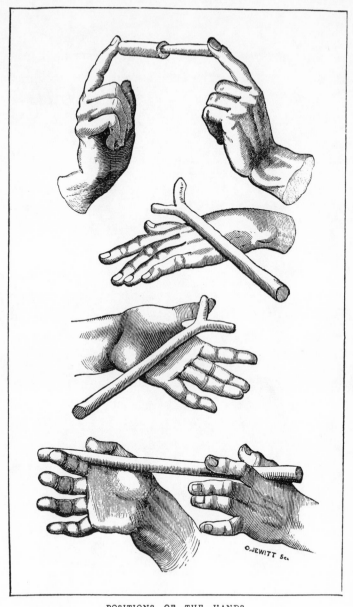

POSITIONS OF THE HANDS.

From "Lettres qui découvrent l'Illusion des Philosophes sur la Baguette."
Paris, 1693.

less time, according to the quantity and current of the water. I counted from thirty to thirty-five revolutions in a minute, and afterwards as many as eighty. A curious phenomenon is, that Bleton is able to make the rod turn between another person's fingers, even without seeing it or touching it, by approaching his body towards it when his feet stand over a subterranean watercourse. It is true, however, that the motion is much less strong and less continuous in other fingers than his own. If Bleton stood on his head, and placed the rod between his feet, though he felt strongly the peculiar sensations produced in him by flowing water, yet the rod remained stationary. If he were insulated on glass, silk, or wax, the sensations were less vivid, and the rotation of the stick ceased."

But this experiment failed in Paris under circumstances which either proved that Bleton's imagination produced the movement, or that his integrity was questionable. It is quite possible that in many instances the action of the muscles is purely involuntary, and is attributable to the imagination, so that the operator deceives himself as well as others.

This is probably the explanation of the story of Mdlle. Olivet, a young lady of tender conscience, who was a skilful performer with the divining rod, but shrank from putting her powers in operation, lest she should be indulging in unlawful acts. She consulted the Père Lebrun, author of a work already referred to in this paper, and he advised her to ask God to withdraw the power from her, if the exercise of it was harmful to her spiritual condition. She entered into retreat for two days, and prayed with fervour. Then she made her communion, asking God what had been recommended to her, at the moment when she received the Host. In the afternoon of the same day she made experiment with her rod, and found that it would no longer operate. The girl had strong faith in it before—a faith coupled with fear, and as long as that faith was strong in her, the rod moved : now she believed that the faculty was taken from her ; and the power ceased with the loss of her faith.

If the divining rod is put in motion by any other force except the involuntary action of the muscles, we must confine its powers to the property of indicating the presence of flowing water. There are numerous instances of hydroscopes thus detecting the existence of a spring or of a subterranean watercourse ; the most remarkably-endowed individuals of this description are Jean-Jacques Pa-

rangue, born near Marseilles in 1760, who expe-
rienced a horror when near water which no one
else perceived. He was endowed with the faculty
of seeing water through the ground, says l'Abbé
Sauri, who gives his history. Jenny Leslie, a
Scotch girl, about the same date claimed similar
powers. In 1790 Pennet, a native of Dauphiné,
attracted attention in Italy, but when carefully
tested by scientific men in Padua, his attempts to
discover buried metals failed ; at Florence he was
detected in an endeavour to find out, by night,
what had been secreted to test his powers on the
morrow. Vincent Amoretti was an Italian, who
underwent peculiar sensations when brought in
proximity to water, coal, and salt ; he was skilful
in the use of the rod, but made no public exhibition of his powers.

The rod is still employed, I have heard it asserted, by Cornish miners, but I have never been
able to ascertain that such is really the case. The
mining captains whom I have questioned, invariably repudiated all knowledge of its use.

In Wiltshire, however, it is still employed for
the purpose of detecting water. In the 22nd
volume of the *Quarterly Review* (p. 273, note) will
be found a very strongly-attested case, commu-

nicated to the writer of an article on "Popular Mythology," by a friend in Norfolk. A certain Lady N—— is there stated to have convinced Dr. Hutton of her possession of this mysterious gift, and to have by means of it indicated to him the existence of a spring of water in one of his fields adjoining the Woolwich College, which, in consequence of this discovery, he was enabled to sell to the College at a higher price. This power of hers Lady N—— repeatedly exhibited before credible witnesses, and the Quarterly Reviewer of that day (1820) held the fact incontrovertible. De Quincey, in two passages[5], affirms that he has frequently seen the process applied with success, and declares that, whatever science or scepticism may say, most of the tea-kettles in the Vale of Wrington, North Somersetshire, are filled by rabdomancy. In an ill-watered province this would make its professors an important class, though, as De Quincey allows, the affinity of their local appellation "jowsers," with the slang verb "to chouse," would argue some suspicion of the soundness of their pretensions. In the last number of the "Monthly Packet" (March, 1867), a curious story is told how the guests at an

---

[5] De Quincey's Collected Works, i. p. 84; iii. p. 222.

old Kentish house beset a fellow-guest, said to possess this power, with questions how they were to hold the two forks of the hazel wand. He proceeded to show them with the double stalk of a couple of twin cherries, the party being at dessert, when, lo! to the astonishment of himself and his questioners, the united portion curled quite over his hand. The master of the house alone knew that under his dining-room floor existed a strong spring of water[6].

The following extract from a letter I have just received will show that it is still in vogue on the Continent :—

"I believe the use of the divining rod for discovering springs of water has by no means been confined to Mediæval times, for I was personally acquainted with a lady, now deceased, who has successfully practised with it in this way. She was a very clever and accomplished woman ; Scotch by birth and education ; by no means credulous ; possibly a little imaginative, for she wrote not unsuccessfully ; and of a remarkably open and straightforward disposition. Captain C——, her husband, had a large estate in Holstein, near

---

[6] Quarterly Review, No. 244, p. 441.

Lubeck, supporting a considerable population, and whether for the wants of the people or for the improvement of the land, it now and then happened that an additional well was needed.

"On one of these occasions a man was sent for who made a regular profession of finding water by the divining rod ; there happened to be a large party staying at the house, and the whole company turned out to see the fun. The rod gave indications in the usual way, and water was ultimately found at the spot. Mrs. C——, utterly sceptical, took the rod into her own hands to make experiment, believing that she would prove the man an impostor, and she said afterwards she was never more frightened in her life than when it began to move, on her walking over the spring. Several other gentlemen and ladies tried it, but it was quite inactive in their hands. 'Well,' said the host to his wife, 'we shall have no occasion to send for the man again, as you are such an adept.'

"Some months after this, water was wanted in another part of the estate, and it occurred to Mrs. C—— that she would use the rod again. After some trials, it again gave decided indications, and a well was begun and carried down a very considerable depth. At last she began to shrink from incurring more expense, but the labourers had implicit faith, and begged to be allowed to persevere. Very soon the water burst up with such force that the men escaped with difficulty; and this proved afterwards the most unfailing spring for miles round.

"You will take the above for what it is worth; the facts I have given are undoubtedly true, whatever conclusions may be drawn from them. I do not propose that you should print my narrative, but I think in these cases personal testimony, even indirect, is more useful in forming one's opinion than a hundred old volumes. I did not hear it from Mrs. C——'s own lips, but I was sufficiently acquainted with her to form a very tolerable estimate of her character, and my wife, who has known her intimately from her own childhood, was in her younger days often staying with her for months together."

I remember having been much perplexed by reading a series of experiments made with a pendulous ring over metals, by a Mr. Mayo; he ascertained that it oscillated in various directions under peculiar circumstances, when suspended by a thread over the ball of the thumb. I instituted a series of experiments, and was surprised to find the ring

vibrate in an unaccountable manner in opposite
directions over different metals.   On consideration,
I closed my eyes whilst the ring was oscillating
over gold, and on opening them I found that it
had become stationary.   I got a friend to change
the metals whilst I was blindfolded—the ring no
longer vibrated.   I was thus enabled to judge of
the involuntary action of muscles, quite sufficient
to have deceived an eminent medical man like
Mr. Mayo, and to have perplexed me till I succeeded in solving the mystery[7].

[7] A similar series of experiments was undertaken, as I
learned afterwards, by M. Chevreuil in Paris, with similar
results.

The Seven Sleepers of Ephesus

ONE of the most picturesque myths of ancient days, is that which forms the subject of this article. It is thus told by Jacques de Voragine in his "Legenda Aurea :"—

"The seven sleepers were natives of Ephesus. The Emperor Decius, who persecuted the Christians, having come to Ephesus, ordered the erection of temples in the city, that all might come and sacrifice before him, and he commanded that the Christians should be sought out and given their choice, either to worship the idols, or to die. So great was the consternation in the city, that the friend denounced his friend, the father his son, and the son his father.

"Now there were in Ephesus seven Christians, Maximian, Malchus, Marcian, Dionysius, John, Serapion, and Constantine by name. These refused to sacrifice to the idols, and remained in their houses praying and fasting. They were accused before Decius, and they confessed themselves to be Christians. However, the emperor gave them a little time to consider what line they would adopt. They took advantage of this reprieve to dispense their goods among the poor, and then they retired, all seven, to Mount Celion, where they determined to conceal themselves.

"One of their number, Malchus, in the disguise of a physician, went to the town to obtain victuals. Decius, who had been absent from Ephesus for a little while, returned, and gave orders for the seven to be sought. Malchus, having escaped from the town, fled, full of fear, to his comrades, and told them of the emperor's fury. They were much alarmed; and Malchus handed them the loaves he had bought, bidding them eat, that, fortified by the food, they might have courage in the time of trial. They ate, and then, as they sat weeping and speaking to one another, by the will of God they fell asleep.

"The Pagans sought every where, but could not find them, and Decius was greatly irritated at their escape. He had their parents brought before him, and threatened them with death if they did not reveal the place of concealment; but they could only answer that the seven young men had distributed their goods to the poor, and that they were quite ignorant as to their whereabouts.

"Decius, thinking it possible that they might be hiding in a cavern, blocked up the mouth with stones, that they might perish of hunger.

"Three hundred and sixty years passed, and in the thirtieth year of the reign of Theodosius, there broke forth a heresy denying the resurrection of the dead. . . . .

"Now, it happened that an Ephesian was building a stable on the side of Mount Celion, and finding a pile of stones handy, he took them for his edifice, and thus opened the mouth of the cave. Then the seven sleepers awoke, and it was to them as if they had slept but a single night. They began to ask Malchus what decision Decius had given concerning them.

"'He is going to hunt us down, so as to force us to sacrifice to the idols,' was his reply. 'God knows,' replied Maximian, 'we shall never do that.' Then exhorting his companions, he urged Malchus to go back to the town to buy some more bread, and at the same time to obtain fresh information. Malchus took five coins and left the

cavern. On seeing the stones, he was filled with
astonishment; however, he went on towards the
city; but what was his bewilderment, on approaching the gate, to see over it a cross! He went to
another gate, and there he beheld the same sacred
sign; and so he observed it over each gate of the
city. He believed that he was suffering from the
effects of a dream. Then he entered Ephesus,
rubbing his eyes, and he walked to a baker's shop.
He heard people using our Lord's name, and he
was the more perplexed. 'Yesterday, no one dared
pronounce the name of Jesus, and now it is on
every one's lips. Wonderful! I can hardly believe
myself to be in Ephesus.' He asked a passer-by
the name of the city, and on being told it was
Ephesus, he was thunderstruck. Now he entered
a baker's shop, and laid down his money. The
baker, examining the coin, inquired whether he had
found a treasure, and began to whisper to some
others in the shop. The youth, thinking that he
was discovered, and that they were about to conduct him to the emperor, implored them to let
him alone, offering to leave loaves and money if he
might only be suffered to escape. But the shop-
men, seizing him, said: 'Whoever you are, you
have found a treasure; show us where it is, that we

may share it with you, and then we will hide you.'
Malchus was too frightened to answer. So they
put a rope round his neck, and drew him
through the streets into the market-place. The
news soon spread that the young man had discovered a great treasure, and there was presently a
vast crowd about him. He stoutly protested his
innocence. No one recognized him, and his eyes
ranging over the faces which surrounded him, could
not see one which he had known, or which was in
the slightest degree familiar to him.

"S. Martin, the bishop, and Antipater, the governor, having heard of the excitement, ordered the
young man to be brought before them, along with
the bakers.

"The bishop and the governor asked him where
he had found the treasure, and he replied that he
had found none, but that the few coins were from
his own purse. He was next asked whence he
came. He replied that he was a native of Ephesus,
'if this be Ephesus.'

"'Send for your relations—your parents, if they
live here,' ordered the governor.

"'They live here certainly,' replied the youth;
and he mentioned their names. No such names
were known in the town. Then the governor

exclaimed : 'How dare you say that this money belonged to your parents when it dates back three hundred and seventy-seven years[1], and is as old as the beginning of the reign of Decius, and it is utterly unlike our modern coinage ?   Do you think to impose on the old men and sages of Ephesus ? Believe me, I shall make you suffer the severities of the law unless you show where you made the discovery.'

"' I implore you,' cried Malchus, ' in the name of God, answer me a few questions, and then I will answer yours !   Where is the Emperor Decius gone to ?'

" The bishop answered, ' My son, there is no emperor of that name; he who was thus called died long ago.'

" Malchus replied, 'All I hear perplexes me more and more.   Follow me, and I will show you my comrades who fled with me into a cave of Mount Celion, only yesterday, to escape the cruelty of Decius.   I will lead you to them.'

" The bishop turned to the governor.   ' The hand of God is here,' he said.   Then they followed, and a great crowd after them.   And Malchus entered first into the cavern to his companions, and the

[1] This calculation is sadly inaccurate.

bishop after him. . . . And there they saw the martyrs seated in the cave, with their faces fresh and blooming as roses; so all fell down and glorified God. The bishop and the governor sent notice to Theodosius, and he hurried to Ephesus. All the inhabitants met him and conducted him to the cavern. As soon as the saints beheld the emperor, their faces shone like the sun, and the emperor gave thanks unto God, and embraced them, and said, 'I see you, as though I saw the Saviour restoring Lazarus.' Maximian replied, 'Believe us! for the faith's sake, God has resuscitated us before the great resurrection day, in order that you may believe firmly in the resurrection of the dead. For as the child is in its mother's womb living and not suffering, so have we lived without suffering, fast asleep.' And having thus spoken, they bowed their heads, and their souls returned to their Maker. The emperor, rising, bent over them and embraced them weeping. He gave orders for golden reliquaries to be made, but that night they appeared to him in a dream, and said that hitherto they had slept in the earth, and that in the earth they desired to sleep on till God should raise them again."

Such is the beautiful story. It seems to have travelled to us from the East. Jacobus Sarugiensis a Mesopotamian bishop, in the fifth or sixth century, is said to have been the first to commit it to writing. Gregory of Tours (De Glor. Mart. i. 9) was perhaps the first to introduce it to Europe. Dionysius of Antioch (ninth century) told the story in Syrian, and Photius of Constantinople reproduced it, with the remark that Mahomet had adopted it into the Koran. Metaphrastus alludes to it as well; in the tenth century Eutychius inserted it in his annals of Arabia; it is found in the Coptic and the Maronite books, and several early historians, as Paulus Diaconus, Nicephorus, &c., have inserted it in their works.

William of Malmesbury tells us a strange story concerning these sleepers. He says, that King Edward the Confessor sat, during the Easter festival, wearing his royal crown at dinner, in his palace of Westminster, surrounded by his bishops and nobles. During the banquet the king, instead of indulging in meat and drink, mused upon divine things, and sat long immersed in thought. Suddenly, to the astonishment of all present, he burst out laughing. After dinner, when he retired to his bedchamber to divest himself of his robes, three of his nobles, Earl Harold, who was afterwards king, and an abbot and a bishop, followed him, and asked the reason of his rare mirth. " I saw," said the pious monarch, "things most wonderful to behold, and therefore did I not laugh without a reason." They entreated him to explain; and after musing for a while, he informed them that the Seven Sleepers of Ephesus, who had been slumbering two hundred years in a cavern of Mount Celion, lying always on their right sides, had of a sudden, turned themselves over on their left sides; that by heavenly favour he had seen them thus turn themselves, and at the sight he had been constrained to laugh. And as Harold and the abbot and bishop marvelled at his words, the king related to them the story of the Seven Sleepers, with the shape and proportion of their several bodies, which wonderful things no man had as yet committed to writing; nay, he spake of the Ephesian sleepers, as though he had always dwelt with them. Earl Harold, on hearing this, got ready a knight, a clerk and a monk, who were forthwith sent to the emperor at Constantinople, with letters and presents from King Edward. By the emperor these messengers were forwarded to Ephesus with letters to the Bishop, commanding him to admit the three Englishmen into the cavern of the sleepers. And, lo! it fell out even as the king had seen in vision. For the Ephesians declared that they knew from their forefathers that the Seven had ever lain on their right sides ; but on the entry of the Englishmen into the cave, they were all found lying on their left sides. And this was a warning of the miseries which were to befall Christendom through the inroads of the Saracens, Turks and Tartars   For whenever sorrow threatens, the Sleepers turn on their sides.

A poem on the Seven Sleepers was composed by a trouvère named Chardri, and is mentioned by M. Fr. Michel in his "Rapports au Ministre de l'Instruction Public ;" a German poem on the same subject, of the thirteenth century, in 935 verses, has been published by M. Karajan ; and the Spanish poet, Augustin Morreto, composed a drama on it, entitled "Los Siete Durmientes," which is inserted in the 19th volume of the rare work, "Comedias Nuevas Escogidas de los Mejores Ingenios ;" last, and not least, it has formed the subject of a poem by the late Dr. Neale.

Mahomet has somewhat improved on the story. He has made the Sleepers prophecy his coming, and he has given them a dog named Kratim, or Kratimer, which sleeps with them, and which is endowed with the gift of prophecy.

As a special favour this dog is to be one of the ten animals to be admitted into his paradise, the others being Jonah's whale, Solomon's ant, Ishmael's ram, Abraham's calf, the Queen of Sheba's ass, the prophet Salech's camel, Moses' ox, Belkis' cuckoo, and Mahomet's ass.

It was perhaps too much for the Seven Sleepers to ask, that their bodies should be left to rest in earth. In ages when saintly relics were valued above gold and precious stones, their request was sure to be shelved ; and so we find that their remains were conveyed to Marseilles in a large stone sarcophagus, which is still exhibited in S. Victor's Church. In the Musæum Victorium at Rome is a curious and ancient representation of them in a cement of sulphur and plaster. Their names are engraved beside them, together with certain attributes. Near Constantine and John are two clubs, near Maximian a knotty club, near Malchus and Martinian two axes, near Serapion a burning torch, and near Danesius or Dionysius a great nail, such as those spoken of by Horace (Lib. 1, Od. 3) and S. Paulinus (Nat. 9, or Carm. 24) as having been used for torture.

In this group of figures, the seven are represented as young, without beards, and indeed in ancient martyrologies they are frequently called boys.

It has been inferred from this curious plaster representation, that the seven may have suffered under Decius, A.D. 250, and have been buried in the afore-mentioned cave ; whilst the discovery and translation of their relics under Theodosius, in 479, may have given rise to the fable.   And this I think probable enough.   The story of long sleepers and the number seven connected with it is ancient enough, and dates from heathen mythology.

Like many another ancient myth, it was laid hold of by Christian hands and baptized.

Pliny relates the story of Epimenides the epic poet, who, when tending his sheep one hot day, wearied and oppressed with slumber, retreated into a cave, where he fell asleep.   After fifty-seven years he awoke, and found every thing changed. His brother, whom he had left a stripling, was now a hoary man.

Epimenides was reckoned one of the seven sages by those who exclude Periander.   He flourished in the time of Solon.   After his death, at the age of two hundred and eighty-nine, he was revered as a God, and honoured especially by the Athenians.

This story is a version of the older legend of the perpetual sleep of the shepherd Endymion, who was thus preserved in unfading youth and beauty by Jupiter.

According to an Arabic legend, S. George thrice rose from his grave, and was thrice slain.

In Scandinavian mythology we have Siegfrid or Sigurd thus resting, and awaiting his call to come forth and fight. Charlemagne sleeps in the Odenberg in Hess, or in the Untersberg near Salzburg, seated on his throne, with his crown on his head and his sword at his side, waiting till the times of Antichrist are fulfilled, when he will wake and burst forth to avenge the blood of the saints. Ogier the Dane, or Olger Dansk, will in like manner shake off his slumber and come forth from the dream-land of Avallon to avenge the right—oh that he had shown himself in the Schleswig-Holstein war!

Well do I remember, as a child, contemplating with wondering awe the great Kyffhäuserberg in Thuringia, for therein, I was told, slept Frederic Barbarossa and his six knights. A shepherd once penetrated into the heart of the mountain by a cave, and discovered therein a hall where sat the Emperor at a stone table, and his red beard had grown through the slab. At the tread of the shepherd, Frederic awoke from his slumber, and asked, "Do the ravens still fly over the mountains?"

"Sire! they do."

"Then we must sleep another hundred years."

But when his beard has wound itself thrice round the table, then will the Emperor awake with his knights, and rush forth to release Germany from its bondage, and exalt it to the first place among the kingdoms of Europe.

In Switzerland slumber three Tells at Rütli near the Vierwaldstätter-see, waiting for the hour of their country's direst need. A shepherd crept into the cave where they rest. The third Tell rose and asked the time. "Noon," replied the shepherd lad. "The time is not yet come," said Tell, and lay down again.

In Scotland, beneath the Eildon hills, sleeps Thomas of Erceldoune ; the murdered French who fell in the Sicilian Vespers at Palermo, are also slumbering till the time is come when they may wake to avenge themselves. When Constantinople fell into the hands of the Turks, a priest was celebrating the sacred mysteries at the great silver altar of S. Sophia. The celebrant cried to God to protect the sacred host from profanation. Then the wall opened, and he entered, bearing the Blessed Sacrament. It closed on him, and there he is sleeping with his head bowed before the Body of Our Lord, waiting till the Turk is cast out of Constantinople, and S. Sophia is released from its profanation. God speed the time!

In Bohemia sleep three miners deep in the heart of the Kuttenberg. In North America, Ripp Van Winkle passed twenty years slumbering in the Katskill mountains. In Spain, Boabdil el Chico, the last Arab king of Granada, is said to lie spellbound in the mountains close to the Alhambra. In Arabia, the prophet Elijah waits till he is called forth in the days of Antichrist. In Ireland, Brian Boroimhe slumbers, waiting till a Fenian insurrection promising action and not talk summons him to his country's aid. In Wales, the legend of Arthur still dreaming through a long sleep in Avillon, has not died out. In Servia, Knez Lazar, who fell in battle against the Turks in the fight of Kossowa, in 1389, is expected to re-appear one day. A similar hope of the return of James IV. lasted for more than a hundred years after Flodden was fought. In Portugal it is believed that Sebastian, the chivalrous young monarch who did his best to ruin his country by his rash invasion of Morocco, is sleeping somewhere, but he will wake again to be his country's deliverer in the hour of need. Olaf Tryggvason is waiting a similar occasion in Norway. Even Napoleon Bonaparte is believed among some of the French peasantry to be sleeping on in a like manner.

S. Hippolytus relates that S. John the Divine is slumbering at Ephesus, and Sir John Mandeville relates the circumstances as follows : " From Pathmos men gone unto Ephesim, a fair citee and nyghe to the see. And there dyede Seynte Johne, and was buryed behynde the highe Awtiere, in a toumbe. And there is a faire chirche. For Christene mene weren wont to holden that place alweyes. And in the tombe of Seynt John is noughte but manna, that is clept Aungeles mete. For his body was translated into Paradys. And Turkes holden now alle that place and the citee and the Chirche. And all Asie the lesse is yclept Turkye. And ye shalle undrestond, that Seynt Johne bid make his grave there in his Lyf, and leyd himself there-inne all quyk. And therefore somme men seyn, that he dyed noughte, but that he resteth there till the Day of Doom. And forsoothe there is a gret marveule : For men may see there the erthe of the tombe apertly many tymes steren and moven, as there weren quykke thinges undre." The connexion of this legend of S. John with Ephesus may have had something to do with turning the seven martyrs of that city into seven sleepers.

The annals of Iceland relate that in 1403, a Finn of the name of Fethmingr, living in Halogaland, in the North of Norway, happening to enter a cave, fell asleep, and woke not for three whole years, lying with his bow and arrows at his side, untouched by bird or beast.

There certainly are authentic accounts of persons having slept for an extraordinary length of time, but I shall not mention any, as I believe the legend we are considering, not to have been an exaggeration of facts, but a Christianized myth of paganism. The fact of the number seven being so prominent in many of the tales, seems to lead to this conclusion. Barbarossa changes his position every seven years. Charlemagne starts in his chair at similar intervals. Olger Dansk stamps his iron mace on the floor once every seven years. Olaf Redbeard in Sweden uncloses his eyes at precisely the same distances of time.

I believe that the mythological core of this

picturesque legend is the repose of the earth through the seven winter months. In the North Frederic and Charlemagne certainly replace Odin.

The German and Scandinavian still heathen legends represent the heroes as about to issue forth for the defence of Fatherland in the hour of direst need. The converted and Christianized tale brings the martyr youths forth in the hour when a heresy is afflicting the Church, that they may destroy the heresy by their witness to the truth of the Resurrection.

If there is something majestic in the heathen myth, there is singular grace and beauty in the Christian tale, teaching as it does such a glorious doctrine; but it is surpassed in delicacy by the modern form which the same myth has assumed—a form which is a real transformation, leaving the doctrine taught the same. It has been made into a romance by Hoffman, and is versified by Trinius. I may perhaps be allowed to translate with some freedom the poem of the latter:—

> In an ancient shaft of Falum,
>   Year by year a body lay,
> God-preserved, as though a treasure,
>   Kept unto the waking day.

Not the turmoil, nor the passions,
    Of the busy world o'erhead,
Sounds of war, or peace rejoicings,
    Could disturb the placid dead.

Once a youthful miner, whistling,
    Hew'd the chamber, now his tomb,
Crash! the rocky fragments tumbled,
    Closed him in abysmal gloom.

Sixty years pass'd by, ere miners
    Toiling, hundred fathoms deep,
Broke upon the shaft where rested
    That poor miner in his sleep.

As the gold-grains lie untarnish'd
    In the dingy soil and sand,
Till they gleam and flicker, stainless,
    In the digger's sifting hand;

As the gem in virgin brilliance
    Rests, till usher'd into day;—
So uninjured, uncorrupted,
    Fresh and fair the body lay.

And the miners bore it upward,
    Laid it in the yellow sun,
Up, from out the neighb'ring houses,
    Fast the curious peasants run.

"Who is he?" with eyes they question.
    "Who is he?" they ask aloud:
Hush! a wizen'd hag comes hobbling,
    Panting through the wond'ring crowd.

Oh! the cry—half joy, half sorrow—
  As she flings her at his side,
" John! the sweetheart of my girlhood,
  Here am I, am I, thy bride.

" Time on thee has left no traces,
  Death from wear has shielded thee ;
I am aged, worn, and wasted,
  Oh! what life has done to me!"

Then, his smooth unfurrow'd forehead
  Kiss'd that ancient wither'd crone ;
And the Death which had divided,
  Now united them in one.

William Tell

I SUPPOSE that most people regard the story of Tell and the apple as an historical event; and with corresponding interest, when they undertake the regular Swiss round, visit the marketplace of Altorf, where is pointed out the site of the lime-tree to which Tell's child was bound, and contemplate the plaster statue which is asserted to mark the spot where Tell stood to take aim. Once, moreover, there stood another monument erected near Lucerne in commemoration of this event, a wooden obelisk, painted to look like granite, surmounted by a rosy-cheeked apple transfixed by a golden arrow. This gingerbread memorial of bad taste has perished, struck by lightning. We shall in the following pages demolish the very story which that erection was intended to commemorate.

It is one of the painful duties of the antiquarian to dispel many a popular belief, and to probe the groundlessness of many a historical statement. The antiquarian is sometimes disposed to ask with Pilate, "What is truth?" when he finds historical facts crumbling beneath his touch into mythological fables ; and he soon learns to doubt and question the most emphatic declarations of, and claims to, reliability.

Sir Walter Raleigh, in his prison, was composing the second volume of his history of the world. Leaning on the sill of his window, he meditated on the duties of the historian to mankind, when suddenly his attention was attracted by a disturbance in the court-yard before his cell.   He saw one man strike another whom he supposed by his dress to be an officer; the latter at once drew his sword and ran the former through the body.   The wounded man felled his adversary with a stick, and then sank upon the pavement.   At this juncture the guard came up and carried off the officer insensible, and then the corpse of the man who had been run through.

Next day Raleigh was visited by an intimate friend, to whom he related the circumstances of the quarrel and its issue.   To his astonishment, his friend unhesitatingly declared that the prisoner had mistaken the whole series of incidents which had passed before his eyes.

The supposed officer was not an officer at all, but the servant of a foreign ambassador ; it was he who had dealt the first blow ; he had not drawn his sword, but the other had snatched it from his side, and had run *him* through the body before any one could interfere ; whereupon a stranger from among the crowd knocked the murderer down with his stick, and some of the foreigners belonging to the ambassador's retinue carried off the corpse. The friend of Raleigh added that government had ordered the arrest and immediate trial of the murderer, as the man assassinated was one of the principal servants of the Spanish ambassador.

" Excuse me," said Raleigh, "but I cannot have been deceived as you suppose, for I was eye-witness to the events which took place under my own window, and the man fell there on that spot where you see a paving-stone standing up above the rest."

" My dear Raleigh," replied his friend, " I was sitting on that stone when the fray took place, and I received this slight scratch on my cheek in snatching the sword from the murderer, and upon my word of honour, you have been deceived upon every particular."

Sir Walter, when alone, took up the second volume of his history, which was in MS., and contemplating it, thought—"If I cannot believe my own eyes, how can I be assured of the truth of a tithe of the events which happened ages before I was born?" and he flung the manuscript into the fire[1].

Now I think that I can show that the story of William Tell and the apple is as fabulous as—what shall I say?—many another historical event.

It is almost too well known to need repetition.

In the year 1307, Gessler, Vogt of the Emperor Albert of Hapsburg, set a hat on a pole, as symbol of imperial power, and ordered every one who passed by to do obeisance towards it. A mountaineer of the name of Tell boldly traversed the space before it without saluting the abhorred symbol. By Gessler's command he was at once seized and brought before him. As Tell was known to be an expert archer, he was ordered, by

---

[1] This anecdote is taken from the *Journal de Paris*, May, 1787; which derived it from "Letters on Literature, by Robert Heron" (i. e. John Pinkerton, F.A.S.), 1785. But whence did Pinkerton obtain it?

way of punishment, to shoot an apple off the head of his own son. Finding remonstrance vain, he submitted. The apple was placed on the child's head, Tell bent his bow, the arrow sped, and apple and arrow fell together to the ground. But the Vogt noticed that Tell, before shooting, had stuck another arrow into his belt, and he inquired the reason.

"It was for you," replied the sturdy archer. "Had I shot my child, know that it would not have missed your heart."

This event, observe, took place in the beginning of the fourteenth century. But Saxo Grammaticus, a Danish writer of the twelfth century, tells the story of a hero of his own country, who lived in the tenth century. He relates the incident in horrible style as follows :—

"Nor ought what follows to be enveloped in silence. Toki, who had for some time been in the king's service, had by his deeds, surpassing those of his comrades, made enemies of his virtues. One day, when he had drunk too much, he boasted to those who sat at table with him, that his skill in archery was such, that with the first shot of an arrow he could hit the smallest apple set on the top of a stick at a considerable distance. His

detractors, hearing this, lost no time in conveying
what he had said to the king (Harald Bluetooth).
But the wickedness of this monarch soon transformed the confidence of the father to the jeopardy
of the son, for he ordered the dearest pledge of his
life to stand in place of the stick, from whom, if
the utterer of the boast did not at his first shot
strike down the apple, he should with his head pay
the penalty of having made an idle boast.   The
command of the king urged the soldier to do this
which was so much more than he had undertaken,
the detracting artifices of the others having taken
advantage of words spoken when he was hardly
sober.   As soon as the boy was led forth, Toki
carefully admonished him to receive the whir of
the arrow as calmly as possible, with attentive
ears, and without moving his head, lest by a slight
motion of the body he should frustrate the experience of his well-tried skill.   He also made him
stand with his back towards him, lest he should be
frightened at the sight of the arrow.   Then he
drew three arrows from his quiver, and the very
first he shot struck the proposed mark.   Toki
being asked by the king why he had taken so
many more arrows out of his quiver, when he
was to make but one trial with his bow; ' That I

might avenge on thee,' he replied, 'the error of the first, by the points of the others, lest my innocence might happen to be afflicted, and thy injustice go unpunished.'"

The same incident is told of Egil, brother of the mythical Velundr, in the Saga of Thidrik.

In Norwegian history also it appears with variations again and again. It is told of King Olaf the Saint (d. 1030), that, desiring the conversion of a brave heathen named Eindridi, he competed with him in various athletic sports; he swam with him, wrestled, and then shot with him. The king dared Eindridi to strike a writing-tablet from off his son's head with an arrow. Eindridi prepared to attempt the difficult shot. The king bade two men bind the eyes of the child and hold the napkin, so that he might not move when he heard the whistle of the arrow. The king aimed first, and the arrow grazed the lad's head. Eindridi then prepared to shoot, but the mother of the boy interfered, and persuaded the king to abandon this dangerous test of skill. In this version also, Eindridi is prepared to revenge himself on the king, should the child be injured.

But a closer approximation still to the Tell myth is found in the life of Hemingr, another Norse archer who was challenged by King Harald, Sigurd's son (d. 1066). The story is thus told :—

"The island was densely overgrown with wood, and the people went into the forest. The king took a spear and set it with its point in the soil, then he laid an arrow on the string and shot up into the air. The arrow turned in the air and came down upon the spear-shaft and stood up in it. Hemingr took another arrow and shot up ; his was lost to sight for some while, but it came back and pierced the nick of the king's arrow. . . . . Then the king took a knife and stuck it into an oak ; he next drew his bow and planted an arrow in the haft of the knife. Thereupon Hemingr took his arrows. The king stood by him and said, 'They are all inlaid with gold, you are a capital workman.' Hemingr answered, 'They are not my manufacture, but are presents.' He shot, and his arrow cleft the haft, and the point entered the socket of the blade.

"'We must have a keener contest,' said the king, taking an arrow and flushing with anger ; then he laid the arrow on the string and drew his bow to the farthest, so that the horns were nearly brought to meet. Away flashed the arrow, and pierced a tender twig. All said that this was a most astonishing feat of dexterity. But Hemingr shot from a greater distance, and split a hazel nut All were astonished to see this. Then said the king, 'Take a nut and set it on the head of your brother Bjorn, and aim at it from precisely the same distance. If you miss the mark, then your life goes.'

"Hemingr answered, 'Sire, my life is at your disposal, but I will not adventure that shot.' Then out spake Bjorn, 'Shoot, brother, rather than die yourself.' Hemingr said, 'Have you the pluck to stand quite still without shrinking?' 'I will do my best,' said Bjorn. 'Then let the king stand by,' said Hemingr, 'and let him see whether I touch the nut.'

"The king agreed, and bade Oddr Ufeig's son stand by Bjorn, and see that the shot was fair. Hemingr then went to the spot fixed for him by the king, and signed himself with the cross, saying, 'God be my witness that I had rather die myself than injure my brother Bjorn; let all the blame rest on King Harald.'

"Then Hemingr flung his spear. The spear went straight to the mark, and passed between the nut and the crown of the lad, who was not in the least injured. It flew further, and stopped not till it fell.

"Then the king came up and asked Oddr what he thought about the shot."

Years after, this risk was revenged upon the hard-hearted monarch. In the battle of Stamford-bridge an arrow from a skilled archer penetrated the windpipe of the king, and it is supposed to have sped, observes the Saga writer, from the bow of Hemingr, then in the service of the English monarch.

The story is related somewhat differently in the Faroe Isles, and is told of Geyti, Aslak's son. The same Harald asks his men if they know who is his match in strength. "Yes," they reply, "there is a peasant's son in the uplands, Geyti, son of Aslak, who is the strongest of men." Forth goes the king, and at last rides up to the house of Aslak. "And where is your youngest son?"

"Alas! alas! he lies under the green sod of Kolrin kirkgarth." "Come, then, and show me his corpse, old man, that I may judge whether he was as stout of limb as men say."

The father puts the king off with the excuse that among so many dead it would be hard to find his boy. So the king rides away over the heath. He meets a stately man returning from the chase, with a bow over his shoulder. "And who art thou, friend?" "Geyti, Aslak's son." The dead man, in short, alive and well. The king tells him he has heard of his prowess, and is come to match his strength with him. So Geyti and the king **try a** swimming-match.

The king swims well, but Geyti swims better, and in the end gives the monarch such a ducking, that he is borne to his house devoid of sense and motion. Harald swallows his anger, as he had swallowed the water, and bids Geyti shoot a hazel nut from off his brother's head. Aslak's son consents, and invites the king into the forest to witness his dexterity.

> " On the string the shaft he laid,
>   And God hath heard his prayer;
> He shot the little nut away,
>   Nor hurt the lad a hair."

Next day the king sends for the skilful bowman :

> " List thee, Geyti, Aslak's son,
>   And truly tell to me,
> Wherefore hadst thou arrows twain
>   In the wood yestreen with thee ?"

The bowman replies :

> " Therefore had I arrows twain
>   Yestreen in the wood with me,
> Had I but hurt my brother dear,
>   The other had pierced thee [2]."

---

[2] Oxonian in Iceland, p. 15.

A very similar tale is told also in the celebrated Malleus Maleficarum of a man named Puncher, with this difference, that a coin is placed on the lad's head instead of an apple or a nut. The person who had dared Puncher to the test of skill, inquires the use of the second arrow in his belt, and receives the usual answer, that if the first arrow had missed the coin, the second would have transfixed a certain heart which was destitute of natural feeling.

We have, moreover, our English version of the same story in the venerable ballad of William of Cloudsley.

The Finn ethnologist Castrén obtained the following tale in the Finnish village of Uhtuwa :—

A fight took place between some freebooters and the inhabitants of the village of Alajärwi. The robbers plundered every house, and carried off amongst their captives an old man. As they proceeded with their spoils along the strand of the lake, a lad of twelve years old appeared from among the reeds on the opposite bank, armed with a bow, and amply provided with arrows ; he threatened to shoot down the captors unless the old man, his father, were restored to him. The robbers mockingly replied, that the aged man would be given to him, if he could shoot an apple off his head. The boy accepted the challenge, and on successfully accomplishing it the surrender of the venerable captive was made.

Farid-Uddin Âttar was a Persian dealer in perfumes, born in the year 1119. He one day was so impressed with the sight of a dervish, that he sold his possessions and followed righteousness. He composed the poem Mantic Uttaïr, or the language of birds. Observe, the Persian Âttar lived at the same time as the Danish Saxo, and long before the birth of Tell. Curiously enough we find a trace of the Tell myth in the pages of his poem. According to him, however, the king shoots the apple from the head of a beloved page, and the lad dies from sheer fright, though the arrow does not even graze his skin.

The coincidence of finding so many versions of the same story scattered through countries as remote as Persia and Iceland, Switzerland and Denmark, proves I think that it can in no way be regarded as history, but is rather one of the numerous household myths common to the whole stock of Aryan nations. Probably, some one more acquainted with Sanskrit literature than myself, and with better access to its unpublished stores of

fable and legend, will some day light on an early
Indian tale corresponding to that so prevalent
among other branches of the same family. The
coincidence of the Tell myth being discovered
among the Finns is attributable to Russian or
Swedish influence. I do not regard it as a
primeval Turanian, but as an Aryan story, which,
like an erratic block, is found deposited on foreign
soil far from the mountain whence it was torn.

Mythologists will, I suppose, consider the myth
to represent the manifestation of some natural
phenomena, and the individuals of the story
to be impersonifications of natural forces. Most
primeval stories were thus constructed, and their
origin is traceable enough. In Thorn-rose, for
instance, who can fail to see the earth goddess represented by the sleeping beauty in her long winter
slumber, only returning to life when kissed by the
golden-haired sun-god Phœbus or Baldur? But the
Tell myth has not its signification thus painted on
the surface, and though it is possible that Gessler
or Harald may be the power of evil and darkness,
and the bold archer the storm-cloud with his
arrow of lightning and his iris bow, bent against
the sun, which is resting like a coin or a golden
apple on the edge of the horizon, yet we have no

guarantee that such an interpretation is not an overstraining of a theory.

In these pages and elsewhere I have shown how some of the ancient myths related by the whole Aryan family of nations are reducible to allegorical explanations of certain well-known natural phenomena ; but I must protest against the manner in which our German friends fasten rapaciously upon every atom of history, sacred and profane, and demonstrate all heroes to represent the sun, all villains to be the demons of night or winter ; all sticks and spears and arrows to be the lightning, all cows and sheep and dragons and swans to be clouds.

In a work on the superstition of Werewolves, I have entered into this subject with some fulness, and am quite prepared to admit the premises upon which mythologists construct their theories ; at the same time I am not disposed to run to the extravagant lengths reached by some of the most enthusiastic German scholars. A wholesome warning to these gentlemen was given some years ago by an ingenious French ecclesiastic, who wrote the following argument to prove that Napoleon Bonaparte was a mythological character. Archbishop Whately's "Historic Doubts" was grounded on a totally different line of argument; I subjoin the other, as a curiosity and as a caution.

Napoleon is, says the writer, an impersonification of the sun.

1. Between the name Napoleon and Apollo, or Apoleon, the god of the sun, there is but a trifling difference; indeed the seeming difference is lessened, if we take the spelling of his name from the column of the Place Vendôme, where it stands Néapoleó. But this syllable *Ne* prefixed to the name of the sun-god is of importance; like the rest of the name it is of Greek origin, and is νη or ναι, a particle of affirmation, as though indicating Napoleon as the very true Apollo, or sun.

His other name, Bonaparte, makes this apparent connexion between the French hero and the luminary of the firmament conclusively certain. The day has its two parts, the good and luminous portion, and that which is bad and dark. To the sun belongs the good part, to the moon and stars belongs the bad portion. It is therefore natural that Apollo or Né-Apoleón should receive the surname of *Bonaparte*.

2. Apollo was born in Delos, a Mediterranean island; Napoleon in Corsica, an island in the same

sea. According to Pausanias, Apollo was an Egyptian deity ; and in the mythological history of the fabulous Napoleon we find the hero in Egypt, regarded by the inhabitants with veneration, and receiving their homage.

3. The mother of Napoleon was said to be Letitia, which signifies joy, and is an impersonification of the dawn of light dispensing joy and gladness to all creation. Letitia is no other than the break of day, which in a manner brings the sun into the world, and "with rosy fingers opes the gates of Day." It is significant that the Greek name for the mother of Apollo was Leto. From this the Romans made the name Latona which they gave to his mother. But *Læto* is the unused form of the verb *lætor*, and signified to inspire joy ; it is from this unused form that the substantive *Letitia* is derived. The identity, then, of the mother of Napoleon with the Greek Leto and the Latin Latona, is established conclusively.

4. According to the popular story, this son of Letitia had three sisters, and was it not the same with the Greek deity, who had the three Graces ?

5. The modern Gallic Apollo had four brothers. It is impossible not to discern here the anthropomorphosis of the four seasons. But, it will be

objected, the seasons should be females. Here the French language interposes; for in French the seasons are masculine, with the exception of autumn, upon the gender of which grammarians are undecided, whilst Autumnus in Latin is not more feminine than the other seasons. This difficulty is therefore trifling, and what follows removes all shadow of doubt.

Of the four brothers of Napoleon, three are said to have been kings, and these of course are, Spring reigning over the flowers, Summer reigning over the harvest, Autumn holding sway over the fruits. And as these three seasons owe all to the powerful influence of the Sun, we are told in the popular myth that the three brothers of Napoleon drew their authority from him, and received from him their kingdoms. But if it be added that, of the four brothers of Napoleon, one was not a king, that was because he is the impersonification of Winter, which has no reign over any thing. If however it be asserted, in contradiction, that the winter has an empire, he will be given the principality over snows and frosts, which, in the dreary season of the year, whiten the face of the earth. Well! the fourth brother of Napoleon is thus invested by popular tradition, commonly called history, with a vain principality accorded to him *in the decline of the power of Napoleon.* The principality was that of Canino, a name derived from cani, or the whitened hairs of a frozen old age,—true emblem of winter. To the eyes of poets, the forests covering the hills are their hair, and when winter frosts them, they represent the snowy locks of a decrepit nature in the old age of the year:

" Cum gelidus crescit *canis* in montibus humor."

Consequently the Prince of Canino is an impersonification of winter;—winter whose reign begins when the kingdoms of the three fine seasons are passed from them, and when the sun is driven from his power by the children of the North, as the poets call the boreal winds. This is the origin of the fabulous invasion of France by the allied armies of the North. The story relates that these invaders—the northern gales—banished the many-coloured flag, and replaced it by a white standard. This too is a graceful, but, at the same time, purely fabulous account of the Northern winds driving all the brilliant colours from the face of the soil, to replace them by the snowy sheet.

6. Napoleon is said to have had two wives. It is well known that the classic fable gave two also to

Apollo. These two were the moon and the earth. Plutarch asserts that the Greeks gave the moon to Apollo for wife, whilst the Egyptians attributed to him the earth. By the moon he had no posterity, but by the other he had one son only, the little Horus. This is an Egyptian allegory representing the fruits of agriculture produced by the earth fertilized by the Sun. The pretended son of the fabulous Napoleon is said to have been born on the 20th of March, the season of the spring equinox, when agriculture is assuming its greatest period of activity.

7. Napoleon is said to have released France from the devastating scourge which terrorized over the country, the hydra of the revolution, as it was popularly called. Who cannot see in this a Gallic version of the Greek legend of Apollo releasing Hellas from the terrible Python? The very name *revolution*, derived from the Latin verb *revolvo*, is indicative of the coils of a serpent like the Python.

8. The famous hero of the 19th century had, it is asserted, twelve Marshals at the head of his armies, and four who were stationary and inactive. The twelve first, as may be seen at once, are the signs of the zodiac, marching under the orders of the sun Napoleon, and each commanding a division of

the innumerable host of stars, which are parted into twelve portions, corresponding to the twelve signs. As for the four stationary officers, immovable in the midst of general motion, they are the cardinal points.

9. It is currently reported that the chief of these brilliant armies, after having gloriously traversed the Southern kingdoms, penetrated the North, and was there unable to maintain his sway. This too represents the course of the Sun, which assumes its greatest power in the South, but after the spring equinox seeks to reach the North, and after a *three months'* march towards the boreal regions, is driven back upon his traces, following the sign of Cancer, a sign given to represent the retrogression of the sun in that portion of the sphere. It is on this that the story of the march of Napoleon towards Moscow, and his humbling retreat, is founded.

10. Finally, the sun rises in the East and sets in the Western sea. The poets picture him rising out of the waters in the East, and setting in the ocean after his twelve hours' reign in the sky. Such is the history of Napoleon coming from his Mediterranean isle, holding the reins of government for twelve years, and finally disappearing in the mysterious regions of the great Atlantic.

The Dog Gellert

HAVING demolished the story of the famous shot of William Tell, I proceed to the destruction of another article of popular belief.

Who that has visited Snowdon has not seen the grave of Llewellyn's faithful hound Gellert, and been told by the guide the touching story of the death of the noble animal? How can we doubt the facts, seeing that the place, Beth-Gellert, is named after the dog, and that the grave is still visible? But unfortunately for the truth of the legend, its pedigree can be traced with the utmost precision.

The story is as follows:—

The Welsh Prince Llewellyn had a noble deer-hound, Gellert, whom he trusted to watch the cradle of his baby son whilst he himself was absent.

One day, on his return, to his intense horror, he beheld the cradle empty and upset, the clothes dabbled with blood, and Gellert's mouth dripping with gore. Concluding hastily that the hound had proved unfaithful, had fallen on the child and devoured it,—in a paroxysm of rage the prince drew his sword and slew the dog. Next instant the cry of the babe from behind the cradle showed him that the child was uninjured, and, on looking further, Llewellyn discovered the body of a huge wolf, which had entered the house to seize and devour the child, but which had been kept off and killed by the brave dog Gellert.

In his self-reproach and grief, the prince erected a stately monument to Gellert, and called the place where he was buried after the poor hound's name.

Now, I find in Russia precisely the same story told, with just the same appearance of truth, of a Czar Piras. In Germany it appears with considerable variations. A man determines on slaying his old dog Sultan, and consults with his wife how this is to be effected. Sultan overhears the conversation, and complains bitterly to the wolf, who suggests an ingenious plan by which the master may be induced to spare his dog. Next day, when the man is going to his work, the wolf undertakes to carry off the child from its cradle.

Sultan is to attack him and rescue the infant. The plan succeeds admirably, and the dog spends his remaining years in comfort. (Grimm, K. M. 48.)

But there is a story in closer conformity to that of Gellert among the French collections of fabliaux made by Le Grand d'Aussy and Edéléstand du Méril. It became popular through the " Gesta Romanorum," a collection of tales made by the monks for harmless reading, in the fourteenth century.

In the " Gesta " the tale is told as follows :—

" Folliculus, a knight, was fond of hunting and tournaments. He had an only son, for whom three nurses were provided. Next to this child, he loved his falcon and his greyhound. It happened one day that he was called to a tournament, whither his wife and domestics went also, leaving the child in the cradle, the greyhound lying by him, and the falcon on his perch. A serpent that inhabited a hole near the castle, taking advantage of the profound silence that reigned, crept from his habitation, and advanced towards the cradle to devour the child. The falcon perceiving the danger, fluttered with his wings till he awoke the dog, who instantly attacked the invader, and after a fierce conflict, in which he was sorely wounded, killed him. He then lay down on the ground to lick and heal his wounds. When the nurses returned, they found the cradle overturned, the child thrown out, and the ground covered with blood, as was also the dog, who they immediately concluded had killed the child.

"Terrified at the idea of meeting the anger of the parents, they determined to escape; but in their flight fell in with their mistress, to whom they were compelled to relate the supposed murder of the child by the greyhound. The knight soon arrived to hear the sad story, and, maddened with fury, rushed forward to the spot. The poor wounded and faithful animal made an effort to rise and welcome his master with his accustomed fondness, but the enraged knight received him on the point of his sword, and he fell lifeless to the ground. On examination of the cradle, the infant was found alive, and unhurt, with the dead serpent lying by him. The knight now perceived what had happened, lamented bitterly over his faithful dog, and blamed himself for having too hastily depended on the words of his wife. Abandoning the profession of arms, he broke his lance in pieces, and vowed a pilgrimage to the Holy Land, where he spent the rest of his days in peace."

The monkish hit at the wife is amusing, and might have been supposed to have originated with those determined misogynists, as the gallant Welshmen lay all the blame on the man. But the good compilers of the "Gesta" wrote little of their own, except moral applications of the tales they relate, and the story of Folliculus and his dog, like many others in their collection, is drawn from a foreign source.

It occurs in the Seven Wise Masters, and in the "Calumnia Novercalis" as well, so that it must have been popular throughout Mediæval Europe. Now the tales of the Seven Wise Masters are translations from a Hebrew work, the Kalilah and Dimnah of Rabbi Joel, composed about A.D. 1250, or from Symeon Seth's Greek Kylile and Dimne, written in 1080. These Greek and Hebrew works were derived from kindred sources. That of Rabbi Joel was a translation from an Arabic version made by Nasr-Allah in the twelfth century, whilst Simeon Seth's was a translation of the Persian Kalilah and Dimnah. But the Persian Kalilah and Dimnah was not either an original work, it was in turn a translation from the Sanskrit Pantschatantra, made about A.D. 540.

In this ancient Indian book the story runs as follows—

A Brahmin named Devasaman had a wife, who gave birth to a son, and also to an ichneumon. She loved both her children dearly, giving them alike the breast, and anointing them alike with salves. But she feared the ichneumon might not love his brother.

One day, having laid her boy in bed, she took up the water jar, and said to her husband, " Hear me, master ! I am going to the tank to fetch water. Whilst I am absent watch the boy, lest he gets injured by the ichneumon." After she had left the house, the Brahmin went forth begging, leaving the house empty. In crept a black snake, and attempted to bite the child ; but the ichneumon rushed at it, and tore it in pieces. Then proud of its achievement, it sallied forth, all bloody, to meet its mother. She, seeing the creature stained with blood, concluded, with feminine precipitance, that it had fallen on the baby and killed it, and she flung her water jar at it and slew it. Only on her return home did she ascertain her mistake.

The same story is also told in the Hitopadesa (iv. 13), but the animal is an otter, not an ichneumon. In the Arabic version a weasel takes the place of the ichneumon.

The Buddist missionaries carried the story into

Mongolia, and in the Mongolian Uligerun, which is a translation of the Tibetian Dsanglun, the story reappears with the pole-cat as the brave and suffering defender of the child.

Stanislaus Julien, the great Chinese scholar, has discovered the same tale in the Chinese work entitled, "The Forest of Pearls from the Garden of the Law." This work dates from 668; and in it the creature is an ichneumon.

In the Persian Sindibad-nâmeh, is the same tale, but the faithful animal is a cat. In Sandabar and Syntipas it has become a dog. Through the influence of Sandabar on the Hebrew translation of the Kalilah and Dimnah, the ichneumon is also replaced by a dog.

Such is the history of the Gellert legend; it is an introduction into Europe from India, every step of its transmission being clearly demonstrable. From the Gesta Romanorum it passed into a popular tale throughout Europe, and in different countries it was, like the Tell myth, localized and individualized. Many a Welsh story, such as those contained in the Mabinogion, are as easily traced to an Eastern origin.

But every story has its root. The root of the Gellert tale is this: A man forms an alliance of friendship with a beast or bird.   The dumb animal renders him a signal service.   He misunderstands the act, and kills his preserver.

We have tracked this myth under the Gellert form from India to Wales; but under another form it is the property of the whole Aryan family, and forms a portion of the traditional lore of all nations sprung from that stock.

Thence arose the classic fable of the peasant, who, as he slept, was bitten by a fly.   He awoke, and in a rage killed the insect.   When too late he observed that the little creature had aroused him that he might avoid a snake which lay coiled up near his pillow.

In the Anvar-i-Suhaili is the following kindred tale.   A king had a falcon.   One day, whilst hunting, he filled a goblet with water dropping from a rock.   As he put the vessel to his lips, his falcon dashed upon it, and upset it with its wings. The king, in a fury, slew the bird, and then discovered that the water dripped from the jaws of a serpent of the most poisonous description.

This story, with some variations, occurs in Æsop, Ælian, and Apthonius.   In the Greek fable, a peasant liberates an eagle from the clutches of a dragon.   The dragon spirts poison into the water which the peasant is about to drink, without observing what the monster had done. The grateful eagle upsets the goblet with his wings.

The story appears in Egypt under a whimsical form. A Wali once smashed a pot full of herbs which a cook had prepared. The exasperated cook thrashed the well-intentioned but unfortunate Wali within an inch of his life, and when he returned, exhausted with his efforts at belabouring the man, to examine the broken pot, he discovered amongst the herbs a poisonous snake.

How many brothers, sisters, uncles, aunts, and cousins of all degrees a little story has! And how few of the tales we listen to can lay any claim to originality? There is scarcely a story which I hear, which I cannot connect with some family of myths, and whose pedigree I cannot ascertain with more or less precision. Shakespeare drew the plots of his plays from Boccaccio or Straparola; but these Italians did not invent the tales they lent to the English dramatist. King Lear does not originate with Geoffry of Monmouth, but comes from early Indian stores of fable, whence also are derived the Merchant of Venice and the pound of flesh, aye! and the very incident of the three caskets.

But who would credit it, were it not proved by

conclusive facts, that Johnny Sands is the inheritance of the whole Aryan family of nations, and that Peeping Tom of Coventry peeped in India and on the Tartar steppes ages before Lady Godiva was born?

If you listen to Traviata at the opera, you have set before you a tale which has lasted for centuries, and which was perhaps born in India.

If you read in classic fable of Orpheus charming woods and meadows, beasts and birds, with his magic lyre, you remember to have seen the same fable related in the Kalewala of the Finnish Wainomainen, and in the Kaleopoeg of the Esthonian Kalewa.

If you take up English history and read of William the Conqueror slipping as he landed on British soil, and kissing the earth, saying he had come to greet and claim his own, you remember that the same story is told of Napoleon in Egypt, of King Olaf Harald's son in Norway, and in classic history of Junius Brutus on his return from the oracle.

A little while ago I cut out of a Sussex newspaper, a story purporting to be the relation of a fact which had taken place at a fixed date in Lewes. This was the story. A tyrannical husband locked the door against his wife, who was out having tea with a neighbour, gossiping and scandal-mongering; when she applied for admittance, he pretended not to know her. She threatened to jump into the well unless he opened the door.

The man, not supposing that she would carry her threat into execution, declined, alleging that he was in bed, and the night was chilly; besides which he entirely disclaimed all acquaintance with the lady who besought admittance.

The wife then flung a log into a well, and secreted herself behind the door. The man hearing the splash, fancied that his good lady was really in the deeps, and forth he darted in his nocturnal costume, which was of the lightest, to ascertain whether his deliverance was complete. At once the lady darted into the house, locked the door, and on the husband pleading for admittance, she declared most solemnly from the window that she did not know *him*.

Now this story, I can positively assert, unless the events of this world move in a circle, did not happen in Lewes, or any other Sussex town.

It was told in the Gesta Romanorum six hundred years ago, and it was told, may be, as many hundred years before in India, for it is still to be found in Sanskrit collections of tales.

Tailed Men

I WELL remember having it impressed upon
me by a Devonshire nurse, as a little child,
that all Cornishmen were born with tails; and it
was long before I could overcome the prejudice
thus early implanted in my breast against my
Cornubian neighbours. I looked upon those who
dwelt across the Tamar as "uncanny," as being
scarcely to be classed with Christian people, and
certainly not to be freely associated with by tail-
less Devonians. I think my eyes were first opened
to the fact that I had been deceived, by a worthy
bookseller of L——, with whom I had contracted
a warm friendship, he having at sundry times contributed pictures to my scrap-book. I remember
one day resolving to broach the delicate subject

with my tailed friend, whom I liked, notwithstanding his caudal appendage.

"Mr. X——, is it true that you are a Cornishman?"

"Yes, my little man; born and bred in the
West country."

"I like you very much ;—but—have you really
got a tail?"

When the bookseller had recovered from the
astonishment which I had produced by my question, he stoutly repudiated the charge.

"But you are a Cornishman?"

"To be sure I am."

"And all Cornishmen have tails."

I believe I satisfied my own mind that the good
man had sat his off, and my nurse assured me that
such was the case with those of sedentary habits.

It is curious that Devonshire superstition should
attribute the tail to Cornishmen, for it was asserted
of certain men of Kent in olden times, and was
referred to Divine vengeance upon them for having
insulted S. Thomas à Becket, if we may believe
Polydore Vergil. "There were some," he says,
"to whom it seemed that the king's secret wish
was, that Thomas should be got rid of. He,
indeed, as one accounted to be an enemy of the

king's person, was already regarded with so little respect, nay, was treated with so much contempt, that when he came to Strood, which village is situated on the Medway, the river that washes Rochester, the inhabitants of the place, being eager to show some mark of contumely to the prelate in his disgrace, did not scruple to cut off the tail of the horse on which he was riding; but by this profane and inhospitable act they covered themselves with eternal reproach, for it so happened after this, by the will of God, that all the offspring born from the men who had done this thing, were born with tails like brute animals. But this mark of infamy, which formerly was every where notorious, has disappeared with the extinction of the race whose fathers perpetrated this deed."

John Bale, the zealous reformer, and Bishop of Ossory in Edward VI.'s time, refers to this story, and also mentions a variation of the scene and cause of this ignoble punishment. He writes, quoting his authorities, "John Capgrave and Alexander of Esseby sayth, that for castynge of fyshe tayles at thys Augustyne, Dorsettshyre men had tayles ever after. But Polydorus applieth it unto Kentish men at Stroud, by Rochester, for cutting of Thomas Becket's horse's tail. Thus hath

England in all other land a perpetual infamy of tayles by theye wrytten legendes of lyes, yet can they not well tell where to bestowe them truely." Bale, a fierce and unsparing reformer, and one who stinted not hard words, applying to the inventors of these legends an epithet more strong than elegant, says, "In the legends of their sanctified sorcerers they have diffamed the English posterity with tails, as has been showed afore. That an Englyshman now cannot travayle in another land by way of marchandyse or any other honest occupyinge, but it is most contumeliously thrown in his tethe that all Englyshmen have tails. That uncomely note and report have the nation gotten, without recover, by these laisy and idle lubbers, the monkes and the priestes, which could find no matters to advance their canonized gains by, or their saintes, as they call them, but manifest lies and knaveries [1]."

Andrew Marvel also makes mention of this strange judgment in his *Loyal Scot:*—

> "But who considers right will find indeed,
> 'Tis Holy Island parts us, not the Tweed.
> Nothing but clergy could us two seclude,
> No Scotch was ever like a bishop's feud.

---

[1] "Actes of English Votaries."

All Litanys in this have wanted faith,
There's no—*Deliver us from a Bishop's wrath.*
Never shall Calvin pardon'd be for sales,
Never for Burnet's sake, the Lauderdales ;
For Becket's sake, Kent always shall have tails."

Bailey in his Dictionary, under the head of "Kentish longtails," endeavours to shift the charge to Dorsetshire ; and Lambarde, in his "Perambulation of Kent," is equally sensitive on the subject. Vieyra, the famous Portuguese preacher, says that Satan was tail-less till his fall, when that appendage grew to him "as an outward and visible token that he had lost the rank of an angel, and was fallen to the level of a brute [2]."

It may be remembered that Lord Monboddo, a Scotch judge of last century, and a philosopher of some repute, though of great eccentricity, stoutly maintained the theory that man ought to have a tail, that the tail is a *desideratum*, and that the abrupt termination of the spine without caudal elongation is a sad blemish in the organization of man. The tail, the point in which man is inferior to the brute, what a delicate index of the mind it is ! how it expresses the passions of love and hate, how nicely it gives token of the feelings of joy or

[2] Quarterly Review, No. 244, p. 446.

fear which animate the soul! But Lord Monboddo did not consider that what the tail is to the
brute, that the eye is to man; the lack of one
member is supplied by the other. I can tell a
proud man by his eye just as truly as if he stalked
past one with erect tail, and anger is as plainly
depicted in the human eye as in the bottle-brush
tail of a cat. I know a sneak by his cowering
glance, though he has not a tail between his legs,
and pleasure is evident in the laughing eye, without
there being any necessity for a wagging brush to
express it.

Dr. Johnson paid a visit to the judge, and
knocked on the head his theory, that men ought to
have tails, and actually were born with them
occasionally, for, said he, "Of a standing fact, sir,
there ought to be no controversy; if there are men
with tails, catch a *homo caudatus*." And, "It is a
pity to see Lord Monboddo publish such notions
as he has done; a man of sense, and of so much
elegant learning. There would be little in a
fool doing it; we should only laugh; but, when a
wise man does it, we are sorry. Other people have
strange notions, but they conceal them. If they
have tails, they hide them; but Monboddo is as
jealous of his tail as a squirrel." And yet Johnson

seems to have been tickled with the idea, and to have been amused with the notion of an appendage like a tail being regarded as the complement of human perfection. It may be remembered how Johnson made the acquaintance of the young Laird of Col, during his Highland tour, and how pleased he was with him. "Col," says he, "is a noble animal. He is as complete an islander as the mind can figure. He is a farmer, a sailor, a hunter, a fisher : he will run you down a dog ; *if any man has a tail*, it is Col." And notwithstanding all his aversion to puns, the great Doctor was fain to yield to human weakness on one occasion, under the influence of the mirth which Monboddo's name seems to have excited. Johnson writes to Mrs. Thrale of a party he had met one night, which he thus enumerates ; "There were Smelt, and the Bishop of S. Asaph, who comes to every place ; and Sir Joshua, and Lord Monboddo, and ladies *out of tale*."

There is a Polish story of a witch who made a girdle of human skin and laid it across the threshold of a door where a marriage-feast was being held. On the bridal pair stepping across the girdle they were transformed into wolves. Three years after the witch sought them out, and cast over them dresses of fur with the hair turned outward, whereupon they recovered their human forms, but, unfortunately, the dress cast over the bridegroom was too scanty, and did not extend over his tail, so that, when he was restored to his former condition, he retained his lupine caudal appendage, and this became hereditary in his family; so that all Poles with tails are lineal descendants of the ancestor to whom this little misfortune happened. John Struys, a Dutch traveller, who visited the isle of Formosa in 1677, gives a curious story which is worth transcribing.

"Before I visited this island," he writes, "I had often heard tell that there were men who had long tails like brute beasts; but I had never been able to believe it, and I regarded it as a thing so alien to our nature, that I should now have difficulty in accepting it, if my own senses had not removed from me every pretence for doubting the fact, by the following strange adventure:—The inhabitants of Formosa being used to see us, were in the habit of receiving us on terms which left nothing to apprehend on either side; so that, although mere foreigners, we always believed ourselves in safety, and had grown familiar enough to ramble at large without an escort, when grave experience taught us that, in so doing, we were hazarding too much. As some of our party were one day taking a stroll, one of them had occasion to withdraw about a stone's throw from the rest, who being at the moment engaged in an eager conversation, proceeded without heeding the disappearance of their companion. After a while, however, his absence was observed, and the party paused, thinking he would rejoin them. They waited some time, but at last, tired of the delay, they returned in the direction of the spot where they remembered to have seen him last. Arriving there, they were horrified to find his mangled body lying on the ground, though the nature of the lacerations showed that he had not had to suffer long ere death released him. Whilst some remained to watch the dead body, others went off in search of the murderer, and these had not gone far, when they came upon a man of peculiar appearance, who, finding himself enclosed by the exploring party, so as to make escape from them impossible, began to foam with rage, and by cries and wild gesticulations to intimate that he would make any one repent the attempt who should venture to meddle with him. The fierceness of his desperation for a time kept our people at bay, but as his fury gradually subsided, they gathered more closely

round him, and at length seized him. He then soon
made them understand that it was he who had
killed their comrade, but they could not learn from
him any cause for this conduct. As the crime was
so atrocious, and, if allowed to pass with impunity,
might entail even more serious consequences, it was
determined to burn the man. He was tied up to a
stake, where he was kept for some hours before the
time of execution arrived. It was then that I
beheld what I had never thought to see. He had a
tail more than a foot long, covered with red hair,
and very like that of a cow. When he saw the
surprise that this discovery created among the
European spectators, he informed us that his tail
was the effect of climate, for that all the inhabitants
of the southern side of the island, where they then
were, were provided with like appendages [3]."

After Struys, Hornemann reported that, between
the Gulf of Benin and Abyssinia, were tailed an-
thropophagi, named by the natives *Niam-niams;*
and in 1849, M. Descouret, on his return from
Mecca, affirmed that such was a common report,
and added that they had long arms, low and
narrow foreheads, long and erect ears, and slim
legs.

[3] "Voyages de Jean Struys," An. 1650.

Mr. Harrison, in his "Highlands of Ethiopia," alludes to the common belief among the Abyssinians, in a pigmy race of this nature.

MM. Arnault and Vayssière, travellers in the same country, in 1850, brought the subject before the Academy of Sciences.

In 1851 M. de Castelnau gave additional details relative to an expedition against these tailed men. "The Niam-niams," he says, "were sleeping in the sun: the Haoussas approached, and, falling on them, massacred them to the last man. They had all of them tails forty centimetres long, and from two to three in diameter. This organ is smooth. Among the corpses were those of several women, who were deformed in the same manner. In all other particulars, the men were precisely like all other negroes. They are of a deep black, their teeth are polished, their bodies not tattooed. They are armed with clubs and javelins; in war they utter piercing cries. They cultivate rice, maize, and other grain. They are fine-looking men, and their hair is not frizzled."

M. d'Abbadie, another Abyssinian traveller, writing in 1852, gives the following account from the lips of an Abyssinian priest. "At the distance of fifteen days' journey south of Herrar, is a place where all the men have tails, the length of a palm, covered with hair, and situated at the extremity of the spine. The females of that country are very beautiful and are tailless. I have seen some fifteen of these people at Besberah, and I am positive that the tail is natural."

It will be observed that there is a discrepancy between the accounts of M. de Castelnau and M. d'Abbadie. The former accords tails to the ladies, whilst the latter denies them. According to the former the tail is smooth, according to the latter it is covered with hair.

Dr. Wolf has improved on this in his "Travels and Adventures," Vol. II. 1861. "There are men and women in Abyssinia with tails like dogs and horses."—"Wolf heard also from a great many Abyssinians and Armenians (and Wolf is convinced of the truth of it), that there are near Narea in Abyssinia, people—men and women—with large tails, with which they are able to knock down a horse, and there are also such people near China." And in a note, "In the College of Surgeons at Dublin may still be seen a human skeleton, with a tail seven inches long! There are many known instances of this elongation of the caudal vertebra, as in the Poonangs in Borneo."

But the most interesting and circumstantial account of the Niam-niams is that given by Dr. Hubsch, physician to the hospitals of Constantinople. "It was in 1852," says he, "that I saw for the first time a tailed negress. I was struck with this phenomenon, and I questioned her master, a slave dealer. I learned from him that there exists a tribe called Niam-niam, occupying the interior of Africa. All the members of this tribe bear the caudal appendage, and, as Oriental imagination is given to exaggeration, I was assured that the tails sometimes attained the length of two feet. That which I observed was smooth and hairless. It was about two inches long, and terminated in a point. This woman was as black as ebony, her hair was frizzled, her teeth white, large, and planted in sockets which inclined considerably outward; her four canine teeth were filed, her eyes bloodshot. She ate meat raw, her clothes fidgeted her, her intellect was on a par with that of others of her condition.

"Her master had been unable, during six months, to sell her, notwithstanding the low figure at which he would have disposed of her; the abhorrence with which she was regarded was not attributed to her tail, but to the partiality, which she was unable to conceal, for human flesh. Her tribe fed on the flesh of the prisoners taken from the neighbouring tribes, with whom they were constantly at war.

"As soon as one of the tribe dies, his relations, instead of burying him, cut him up and regale themselves upon his remains; consequently there are no cemeteries in this land. They do not all of them lead a wandering life, but many of them construct hovels of the branches of trees. They make for themselves weapons of war and of agriculture; they cultivate maize and wheat, and keep cattle. The Niam-niams have a language of their own, of an entirely primitive character, though containing an infusion of Arabic words.

"They live in a state of complete nudity, and seek only to satisfy their brute appetites. There is among them an utter disregard for morality, incest and adultery being common. The strongest among them becomes the chief of the tribe; and it is he who apportions the shares of the booty obtained in war. It is hard to say whether they have any religion; but in all probability they have none, as they readily adopt any one which they are taught.

"It is difficult to tame them altogether; their

instinct impelling them constantly to seek for human flesh; and instances are related of slaves who have massacred and eaten the children confided to their charge.

" I have seen a man of the same race, who had a tail an inch and a half long, covered with a few hairs. He appeared to be thirty-five years old; he was robust, well built, of an ebon blackness, and had the same peculiar formation of jaw noticed above, that is to say, the tooth sockets were inclined outwards. Their four canine teeth are filed down, to diminish their power of mastication.

" I know also, at Constantinople, the son of a physician, aged two years, who was born with a tail an inch long; he belonged to the white Caucasian race. One of his grandfathers possessed the same appendage. This phenomenon is regarded generally in the East as a sign of great brute force."

About ten years ago, a newspaper paragraph recorded the birth of a boy at Newcastle-on-Tyne, provided with a tail about an inch and a quarter long. It was asserted that the child when sucking wagged this stump as token of pleasure.

According to a North-American Indian tradition

all men were created originally with tails, tails
long-haired, sleek, and comely.   These tails were
their delight, and they adorned them with paint,
beads and wampum.   Then the world was at peace,
discord and wars were unknown.   Men became
proud and forgot' their Maker, and He found it
necessary to disturb their serenity by sending
them a scourge which might teach them humility,
and make them realize their dependence on the
Great Spirit.   Then He amputated their tails, and
out of these *dejecta membra* fashioned women—
who, say the Kikapoos, retain traces of their origin,
for we find them ever trailing after the men, frisky
and impulsive [4].

Yet, notwithstanding all this testimony in favour
of tailed men and women, I profess myself dubious;
and shall yield only when a *homo caudatus* has
been caught and shown to me.

[4] Atherne Jones, Trad. N. American Indians, iii. 175.

Antichrist and Pope Joan

FROM the earliest ages of the Church, the advent of the Man of Sin has been looked forward to with terror, and the passages of Scripture relating to him have been studied with solemn awe, lest that day of wrath should come upon the Church unawares. As events in the world's history took place which seemed to be indications of the approach of Antichrist, a great horror fell upon men's minds, and their imaginations conjured up myths which flew from mouth to mouth, and which were implicitly believed.

Before speaking of these strange tales which produced such an effect on the minds of men in the Middle Ages, it will be well briefly to examine the opinions of divines of the early ages on the passages of Scripture connected with the coming of the last great persecutor of the Church. Antichrist was believed by most ancient writers to be destined to arise out of the tribe of Dan, a belief founded on the prediction of Jacob, " Dan shall be a serpent by the way, an adder in the path " (conf. Jeremiah viii. 16), and on the exclamation of the dying patriarch, when looking on his son Dan, " I have waited for Thy Salvation, O Lord," as though the long-suffering of God had borne long with that tribe, but in vain, and it was to be extinguished without hope.   This, indeed, is implied in the sealing of the servants of God in their foreheads (Revelation vii.), when twelve thousand out of every tribe, except Dan, were seen by S. John to receive the seal of adoption, whilst of the tribe of Dan *not one* was sealed, as though it, to a man, had apostatized.

Opinions as to the nature of Antichrist were divided.   Some held that he was to be a devil in phantom body, and of this number was Hippolytus. Others again believed that he would be an incarnate demon, true man and true devil ; in fearful and diabolical parody of the Incarnation of our Lord. A third view was that he would be merely a desperately wicked man, acting upon diabolic inspirations, just as the saints act upon divine inspirations. S. John Damascene expressly asserts that he will not be an incarnate demon, but a devilish man, for he says, "Not as Christ assumed humanity, so will the devil become human, but the Man will receive all the inspiration of Satan, and will suffer the devil to take up his abode within him." In this manner, Antichrist could have many forerunners, and so S. Jerome and S. Augustine saw an Antichrist in Nero, not *the* Antichrist, but one of those of whom the Apostle speaks—"Even now are there many Antichrists." Thus also every enemy of the faith, such as Diocletian, Julian, and Mahomet, has been regarded as a precursor of the Arch-persecutor, who was expected to sum up in himself the cruelty of a Nero or Diocletian, the show of virtue of a Julian, and the spiritual pride of a Mahomet.

From infancy the evil one is to take possession of Antichrist, and to train him for his office, instilling into him cunning, cruelty, and pride. His doctrine will be—not downright infidelity, but a "show of godliness," whilst "denying the power thereof," i.e. the miraculous origin and divine authority of Christianity. He will sow doubts of our Lord's manifestation "in the flesh," he will allow Christ to be an excellent Man, capable of teaching the most exalted truths, and inculcating the purest morality, yet Himself fallible and carried away by fanaticism.

In the end, however, Antichrist will "exalt himself to sit as God in the temple of God," and become "the abomination of desolation standing in the holy place." At the same time there is to be an awful alliance struck between himself, the impersonification of the world-power, and the Church of God ; some high pontiff of which, or the episcopacy in general, will enter into league with the unbelieving State to oppress the very elect. It is a strange instance of religionary virulence which makes some detect the Pope of Rome in the Man of Sin, the Harlot, the Beast, and the Priest going before it. The Man of Sin and the Beast are unmistakably identical, and refer to an Antichristian world-power; whilst the Harlot and the Priest are symbols of an apostasy in the Church. There is nothing Roman in this, but something very much the opposite.

How the Abomination of Desolation can be considered as set up in a Church where every sanctuary is adorned with all that can draw the heart to the Crucified, and raise the thoughts to the imposing ritual of heaven, is a puzzle to me. To the man uninitiated in the law that Revelation is

to be interpreted by contraries, it would seem more
like the Abomination of Desolation in the Holy
Place if he entered a Scotch Presbyterian, or a
Dutch Calvinist, place of worship.   Rome does not
fight against the Daily Sacrifice, and endeavour to
abolish it ; that has been rather the labour of so-
called Church Reformers, who with the suppression
of the doctrine of Eucharistic Sacrifice and Sacra-
mental Adoration have well nigh obliterated all
notion of worship to be addressed to the God-Man.
Rome does not deny the power of the godliness of
which she makes show, but insists on that power
with no broken accents.   It is rather in other com-
munities, where authority is flung aside, and 'any
man is permitted to believe or reject what he likes,
that we must look for the leaven of the Antichristian spirit at work.   However, this is not a question into which we care to enter, our province is
myth not theology.

In the time of Antichrist, we are told by ancient
Commentators, the Church will be divided : one
portion will hold to the world-power, the other will
seek out the old paths, and cling to the only true
Guide.   The high places will be filled with unbelievers in the Incarnation, and the Church will
be in a condition of the utmost spiritual degrada-

tion, but enjoying the highest State patronage. The religion in favour will be one of morality, but not of dogma ; and the Man of Sin will be able to promulgate his doctrine, according to S. Anselm, through his great eloquence and wisdom, his vast learning and mightiness in the Holy Scriptures, which he will wrest to the overthrowing of dogma. He will be liberal in bribes, for he will be of un-bounded wealth ; he will be capable of performing great "signs and wonders," so as "to deceive—the very elect ;" and at the last, he will tear the moral veil from his countenance, and a monster of impiety and cruelty, he will inaugurate that awful persecu-tion, which is to last for three years and a half, and to excel in horror all the persecutions that have gone before.

In that terrible season of confusion faith will be all but extinguished. "When the Son of Man cometh shall He find faith on the earth ?" asks our Blessed Lord, as though expecting the answer, No ; and then, says Marchantius, the vessel of the Church will disappear in the foam of that boiling deep of infidelity, and be hidden in the blackness of that storm of destruction which sweeps over the earth. The sun shall " be darkened, and the moon shall not give her light, and the stars shall fall from heaven ;" the sun of faith shall have gone out ; the moon, the Church, shall not give her light, being turned into blood, through stress of persecution ; and the stars, the great ecclesiastical dignitaries, shall fall into apostasy. But still the Church will remain unwrecked, she will weather the storm ; still will she come forth "beautiful as the moon, terrible as an army with banners ;" for after the lapse of those three and a half years, Christ will descend to avenge the blood of the saints, by destroying Antichrist and the world-power.

Such is a brief sketch of the Scriptural doctrine of Antichrist as held by the Early and Mediæval Church. Let us now see to what Myths it gave rise among the vulgar and the imaginative. Rabanus Maurus, in his work on the life of Antichrist, gives a full account of the miracles he will perform ; he tells us that the Man-fiend will heal the sick, raise the dead, restore sight to the blind, hearing to the deaf, speech to the dumb ; he will raise storms and calm them, will remove mountains, make trees flourish or wither at a word. He will rebuild the temple at Jerusalem, and make the Holy City the great capital of the world. Popular opinion added that his vast wealth would be obtained from hidden treasures, which are now being concealed by the demons for his use. Various possessed persons, when interrogated, announced that such was the case, and that the amount of buried gold was vast.

"In the year 1599," says Canon Moreau, a contemporary historian, "a rumour circulated with prodigious rapidity through Europe, that Antichrist had been born at Babylon, and that already the Jews of that part were hurrying to receive and recognize him as their Messiah. The news came from Italy and Germany, and extended to Spain, England, and other Western kingdoms, troubling many people, even the most discreet; however the learned gave it no credence, saying that the signs predicted in Scripture to precede that event were not yet accomplished, and among other that the Roman empire was not yet abolished. . . . Others said that, as for the signs, the majority had already appeared to the best of their knowledge, and with regard to the rest, they might have taken place in distant regions without their having been made known to them; that the Roman empire existed but in name, and that the interpretation of the passage on which its destruction was predicted, might be incorrect: that for many centuries, the most learned and pious had believed in the near approach of Antichrist, some believing that he had

already come, on account of the persecutions which
had fallen on the Christians ; others on account of
fires, or eclipses, or earthquakes. . . . Every one
was in excitement ; some declared that the news
must be correct, others believed nothing about it,
and the agitation became so excessive, that Henry
IV., who was then on the throne, was compelled by
edict to forbid any mention of the subject."

The report spoken of by Moreau gained additional confirmation from the announcement made
by an exorcised demoniac, that in 1600, the Man of
Sin had been born in the neighbourhood of Paris
of a Jewess, named Blanchefleure, who had conceived by Satan. The child had been baptized at
the Sabbath of Sorcerers ; and a witch, under torture, acknowledged that she had rocked the infant
Antichrist on her knees, and she averred that he
had claws on his feet, wore no shoes, and spoke all
languages.

In 1623 appeared the following startling announcement, which obtained an immense circulation among the lower orders : " We, brothers of the
Order of S. John of Jerusalem, in the isle of Malta,
have received letters from our spies, who are engaged in our service in the country of Babylon,
now possessed by the Grand Turk ; by the which

letters we are advertised, that, on the 1st of May, in the year of our Lord 1623, a child was born in the town of Bourydot, otherwise called Calka, near Babylon, of the which child the mother is a very aged woman of race unknown, called Fort-Juda: of the father nothing is known.   The child is dusky, has pleasant mouth and eyes, teeth pointed like those of a cat, ears large, stature by no means exceeding that of other children ; the said child, incontinent on his birth, walked and talked perfectly well.   His speech is comprehended by every one, admonishing the people that he is the true Messiah, and the son of God, and that in him all must believe.   Our spies also swear and protest that they have seen the said child with their own eyes ; and they add, that, on the occasion of his nativity, there appeared marvellous signs in heaven, for at full noon the sun lost its brightness, and was for some time obscured." This is followed by a list of other signs appearing, the most remarkable being a swarm of flying serpents, and a shower of precious stones.

According to Sebastian Michaeliz, in his history of the possessed of Flanders, on the authority of the exorcised demons, we learn that Antichrist is to be a son of Beelzebub, who will accompany his offspring under the form of a bird, with four feet and a bull's head ; that he will torture Christians with the same tortures with which the lost souls are racked ; that he will be able to fly, speak all languages, and will have any number of names.

We find that Antichrist is known to the Mussulmans as well as to Christians. Lane, in his edition of the " Arabian Nights," gives some curious details on Moslem ideas regarding him. According to these, Antichrist will overrun the earth, mounted on an ass, and followed by 40,000 Jews ; his empire will last forty days, whereof the first day will be a year long, the duration of the second will be a month, that of the third a week, the others being of their usual length. He will devastate the whole world, leaving Mecca and Medina alone in security, as these holy cities will be guarded by angelic legions. Christ at last will descend to earth, and in a great battle will destroy the Man-devil.

Several writers of different denominations, no less superstitious than the common people, connected the apparition of Antichrist with the fable of Pope Joan, which obtained such general credence at one time, but which modern criticism has at length succeeded in excluding from history.

The earliest writer supposed to mention Pope
Joan is Anastasius the Librarian, a contemporary
(d. 886) ; next to him is Marianus Scotus, who in
his chronicle inserts the following passage : "A.D.
854, Lotharii 14, Joanna, a woman, succeeded Leo,
and reigned two years, five months, and four days."
Marianus Scotus died A.D. 1086.   The same story
is inserted in the valuable chronicle of Sigebert de
Gemblours (d. 5th Oct. 1112) : "It is reported that
this John was a female, and that she conceived by
one of her servants.   The Pope, becoming pregnant, gave birth to a child, wherefore some do not
number her among the Pontiffs."   Hence the story
spread among the mediæval chroniclers, who were
great plagiarists.   Otto of Frisingen and Gotfrid of
Viterbo mention the Lady-Pope in their histories,
and Martin Polonus gives details as follows : "After
Leo IV. John Anglus, a native of Metz, reigned two
years, five months, and four days. And the pontificate was vacant for a month.   He died in Rome.
He is related to have been a female, and, when a
girl, to have accompanied her sweetheart in male
costume to Athens ; there she advanced in various
sciences, and none could be found to equal her.
So, after having studied for three years in Rome,
she had great masters for her pupils and hearers.

And when there arose a high opinion in the city of her virtue and knowledge, she was unanimously elected Pope. But during her papacy she became in the family way by a familiar. Not knowing the time of birth, as she was on her way from S. Peter's to the Lateran she had a painful delivery, between the Coliseum and S. Clement's Church, in the street. Having died after, it is said that she was buried on the spot, and therefore the Lord Pope always turns aside from that way, and it is supposed by some, out of detestation for what happened there. Nor on that account is she placed in the catalogue of the Holy Pontiffs, not only on account of her sex, but also because of the horribleness of the circumstance."

Certainly a story at all scandalous *crescit eundo*.

William Ocham alludes to the story, Thomas de Elmham (1422) quaintly observes, "A.D. 855. Joannes. Iste non computatus. Fœmina fuit ;" and John Huss, only too happy to believe it, provides the lady with a name, and asserts that she was baptized Agnes, or, as he will have it with a strong aspirate, Hagnes. Others, however, insist upon her name having been Gilberta, and some stout Germans, not relishing the notion of her being a daughter of Fatherland, palm her off on England.

As soon as we arrive at Reformation times the German and French Protestants fasten on the story with the utmost avidity, and add sweet little touches of their own, and draw conclusions galling enough to the Roman See, illustrating their accounts with wood engravings vigorous and graphic, but hardly decent. One of these represents the event in a peculiarly startling manner. The procession of bishops with the Host and tapers is sweeping along, when suddenly the cross-bearer before the triple-crowned and vested Pope starts aside to witness the unexpected arrival. This engraving, which it is quite impossible for me to reproduce, is in a curious little book, entitled "Puerperium Johannis Papæ 8, 1530."

The following jingling record of the event is from the Rhythmical Vitæ Pontificum of Gulielmus Jacobus of Egmonden, a work never printed. This fragment is preserved in "Wolffii Lectionum Memorabilium centenarii, XVI. :"

> " Priusquàm reconditur Sergius, vocatur
>   Ad summam, qui dicitur Johannes, huic addatur
>   Anglicus, Moguntia iste procreatur.
>   Qui, ut dat sententia, fœminis aptatur
>   Sexu : quod sequentia monstrant, breviatur,
>   Hæc vox : nam prolixius chronica procedunt.
>   Ista, de qua brevius dicta minus lædunt.

Huic erat amasius, ut scriptores credunt.
Patria relinqvitur Moguntia, Græcorum
Studiosè petitur schola.   Pòst doctorum
Hæc doctrix efficitur Romæ legens : horum
Hæc auditu fungitur loquens.   Hinc prostrato
Summo hæc eligitur : sexu exaltato
Quandoque negligitur.   Fatur quòd hæc nato
Per servum conficitur.   Tempore gignendi
Ad processum equus scanditur, vice flendi,
Papa cadit, panditur improbis ridendi
Norma, puer nascitur in vico Clementis,
Colossœum jungitur.   Corpus parentis
In eodem traditur sepulturæ gentis,
Faturque scriptoribus, quòd Papa præfato,
Vico senioribus transiens amato
Congruo ductoribus sequitur negato
Loco, quo Ecclesia partu denigratur,
Quamvis inter spacia Pontificum ponatur,
Propter sexum."

Stephen Blanch, in his " Urbis Romæ Mirabilia,"
says that an angel of heaven appeared to Joan
before the event, and asked her to choose whether
she should prefer burning eternally in hell, or
having her confinement in public ; with sense which
does her credit, she chose the latter.   The Protestant writers were not satisfied that the father of
the unhappy baby should have been a servant :
some made him a Cardinal, and others the devil
himself.   According to an eminent Dutch minister,
it is immaterial whether the child be fathered on
Satan or a monk : at all events, the former took a

lively interest in the youthful Antichrist, and, on the occasion of his birth, was seen and heard fluttering overhead, crowing and chanting in an unmusical voice the Sibyline verses announcing the birth of the Arch-persecutor :—

> " Papa pater patrum, Papissæ pandito partum
> Et tibi tunc eadem de corpore quando recedam ! "

which lines, as being perhaps the only ones known to be of diabolic composition, are deserving of preservation.

The Reformers, in order to reconcile dates, were put to the somewhat perplexing necessity of moving Pope Joan to their own times, or else of giving to the youthful Antichrist an age of seven hundred years.

It must be allowed that the *accouchement* of a Pope in full pontificals, during a solemn procession, was a prodigy not likely to occur more than once in the world's history, and was certain to be of momentous import.

It will be seen by the curious woodcut reproduced as frontispiece from Baptista Mantuanus, that he consigned Pope Joan to the jaws of hell, notwithstanding her choice. The verses accompanying this picture are :

" Hic pendebat adhuc sexum mentita virile
Fœmina, cui triplici Phrygiam diademate mitram
Extollebat apex : et pontificalis adulter."

It need hardly be stated that the whole story of Pope Joan is fabulous, and rests on not the slightest historical foundation. It was probably a Greek invention to throw discredit on the papal hierarchy, first circulated more than two hundred years after the date of the supposed Pope. Even Martin Polonus (A.D. 1282), who is the first to give the details, does so merely on popular report.

The great champions of the myth were the Protestants of the sixteenth century, who were thoroughly unscrupulous in distorting history and suppressing facts, so long as they could make a point. A paper war was waged upon the subject, and finally the whole story was proved conclusively to be utterly destitute of historical truth. A melancholy example of the blindness of party feeling and prejudice is seen in Mosheim, who assumes the truth of the ridiculous story, and gravely inserts it in his "Ecclesiastical History." "Between Leo IV., who died 855, and Benedict III., a woman, who concealed her sex and assumed the name of John, it is said, opened her way to the Pontifical throne by her learning and genius, and governed the

Church for a time. She is commonly called the
Papess Joan. During the five subsequent centuries
the witnesses to this extraordinary event are without
number; nor did any one, prior to the Reformation by Luther, regard the thing as either incredible or disgraceful to the Church." Such are
Mosheim's words, and I give them as a specimen
of the credit which is due to his opinion. The
"Ecclesiastical History" he wrote is full of perver-
sions of the plainest facts, and that under our
notice is but one out of many. "During the five
centuries after her reign," he says, "the witnesses
to the story are innumerable." Now for two
centuries there is not an allusion to be found to
the events. The only passage which can be found
is a universally acknowledged interpolation of the
"Lives of the Popes," by Anastasius Bibliothecarius, and this interpolation is stated in the first
printed edition by Busæus, Mogunt. 1602, to be
only found in two MS. copies.

Mosheim is false again in asserting that no one
prior to the Reformation regarded the thing as
either incredible or disgraceful. This is but of a
piece with his disregard for truth, whenever he can
hit the Catholic Church hard. Bart. Platina, in
his "Lives of the Popes," written before Luther

was born, after relating the story, says, "These things which I relate are popular reports, but derived from uncertain and obscure authors, which I have therefore inserted briefly and baldly, lest I should seem to omit obstinately and pertinaciously what most people assert." Thus the facts were justly doubted by Platina on the legitimate grounds that they rested on popular gossip, and not on reliable history. Anastasius the Librarian, contemporary of the alleged circumstance, is the first cited as evidence to there having been a Papess. This testimony is however open to serious objection. The MSS. of the works of Anastasius do not uniformly contain the fable. Panvini, who wrote additions to Platina, *De vitis Romanorum Pontificum*, assures us that "in old books of the lives of the Popes, written by Damasus, by the Librarian, and by Pandulph de Pisa, there is no mention of this woman : only on the margin, betwixt Leo IV. and Benedict III., this fable has been found inserted by a later writer, in characters altogether distinct from the text."

Blondel, the great Protestant writer, who ruined the case of the Decretals, says that he examined a MS. of Anastasius in the Royal Library at Paris, and found the story of Pope Joan inserted in such

a manner as to convince him that it was a late
interpolation. He says [1], "Having read and re-
read it, I found that the elogium of the pretended
Papess is taken from the words of Martinus Polonus, penitenciary to Innocent IV., and Archbishop of Cosenza, an author four hundred years later
than Anastasius, and much more given to all these
kinds of fables."   His reasons for so thinking are,
that the style is not that of the Librarian, but
similar to that of Martin Polonus ; also that the insertion interferes with the text of the chronicle, and
bears evidence of clumsy piecing.   "In the elogiums
of Leo IV. and Benedict III., as given to us in the
manuscript of the Bibliothèque Royale, swelled with
the romance of the Papess, the same expressions occur
as in the Mayence edition ; whence it follows that
(according to the intention of Anastasius, violated
by the rashness of those who have mingled with it
their idle dreams) it is absolutely impossible that
any one could have been Pope between Leo IV.
and Benedict III., for he says ;—'After the prelate
Leo was withdrawn from this world, *at once* (mox)
all the clergy, the nobles, and people of Rome
hastened to elect Benedict ; and at once (illico)

---

[1] Familier éclaircissement de la question, &c.   Amsterdam, 1647-9.

they sought him, praying in the Titular Church of S. Callixtus, and having seated him on the pontifical throne, and signed the decree of his election, they sent him to the very-invincible Augusti Lothair and Louis, and the first of these died on 29 September, 855, just seventy-four days after the death of Pope Leo.'"

Bayle in his *Dictionnaire historique et critique*, under the article Papesse Jeanne, says : "Is it not true that if we found in a manuscript a statement that the Emperor Ferdinand II. died in the year 1637, and that at once he was succeeded by Ferdinand III., and that Charles VI. succeeded Ferdinand II., and held the throne for two years, after which Ferdinand III., was elected Emperor, we should say that the same writer could not have made both statements, and that we were necessitated to attribute to copyists without judgment the statements which do not correspond ? Would not the man be a fool who related that Innocent X. having died, he was promptly given as successor Alexander VII., and that Innocent XI. was Pope immediately after Innocent X., and sat for two years and more, and that Alexander VII. succeeded him ? Anastasius Bibliothecarius must have committed a like extravagance, if he was the author of what occurs in the MSS. of his work which mention the Papess.   We however conclude that the statement concerning this woman was an insertion of a later hand."

Sarran, a zealous and learned Protestant, formed the same opinion of the Pope-Joan fable, and he gives as his reason for believing it not to have stood in the original copies of Anastasius, that it is there inserted with the words, " It is said that," or "we are assured that," expressions inconsistent with the fact that Anastasius was a contemporary resident in Rome [2].

Marianus Scotus, the next authority cited for the story of Pope Joan, died in 1086.   He was a monk of S. Martin of Cologne, then of Fulda, and lastly, of S. Alban's, at Metz.   How could he have obtained reliable information, or seen documents upon which to ground the assertion ?   The words in which the tale is alluded to in his Chronicle vary in different MSS., in some the fact is asserted plainly ; in others, it is founded on an *ut asseritur;* and other MS. copies have not the passage in them at all.   This looks as though the Pope-Joan passage were an interpolation.   Next to Marianus Scotus comes Sigebert de Gemblours, who died

[2] Sarran, Epist. cii., Utrecht, 1697.

1112. We have evidence conclusive that his Chronicle has been tampered with in this particular. The Gemblours MS., which was either written by Sigebert himself, or was a copy made from his, does not allude to Pope Joan.   Several other early copies have not the passage.   Guillaume de Nangiac, who wrote a Chronicle to the year 1302, transcribed, and absorbed into his work, the more ancient chronicle of Sigebert.   The copy used by Guillaume de Nangiac must have been without the disputed paragraph, for it is not to be found in his work.   We are therefore reduced to Martin Polonus (d. 1279), placing more than four centuries between him and the event he records.

The historical discrepancies are sufficiently glaring to make the story more than questionable.

Leo IV. died on the 17th July, 855 ; and Benedict III. was consecrated on the 1st September in the same year ; so that it is impossible to insert between their pontificates a reign of two years, five months, and four days.   It is, however, true that there was an antipope elected upon the death of Leo, at the instance of the Emperor Louis, but his name was Anastasius.   This man possessed himself of the palace of the Popes, and obtained the incarceration of Benedict.   However, his supporters almost immediately deserted him, and Benedict assumed the pontificate. The reign of Benedict was only for two years and a half, so that Anastasius cannot be the supposed Joan ; nor do we hear of any charge brought against him to the effect of his being a woman. But the stout partisans of the Pope-Joan tale assert, on the authority of the "Annales Augustani [3]," and some other, but late authorities, that the female Pope was John VIII., who consecrated Louis II. of France, and Ethelwolf of England. Here again is confusion. Ethelwolf sent Alfred to Rome in 853, and the youth received regal unction from the hands of Leo IV. In 855 Ethelwolf visited Rome, it is true, but was not consecrated by the existing Pope, whilst Charles the Bald was anointed by John VIII. in 875. John VIII. was a Roman, son of Gundus, and an archdeacon of the Eternal City. He assumed the triple crown in 872, and reigned till December 18th, 882. John took an active part in the troubles of the Church under the incursions of the Sarasins, and 325 letters of his are extant, addressed to the princes and prelates of his day.

Any one desirous of pursuing this examination

---

[3] These Annals were written in 1135.

into the untenable nature of the story may find an excellent summary of the arguments used on both sides in Gieseler, "Lehrbuch," &c., Cunningham's trans., vol. ii. pp. 20, 21, or in Bayle, "Dictionnaire," tom. iii. art. Papesse.

The arguments in favour of the myth may be seen in Spanheim, "Exercit. de Papa Fœmina." Opp. tom. ii. p. 577, or in Lenfant, "Histoire de la Papesse Jeanne," La Haye, 1736, 2 vols. 12mo.

The arguments on the other side may be had in "Allatii Confutatio Fabulæ de Johanna Papissa," Colon. 1645; in Le Quien, "Oriens Christianus," tom. iii. p. 777; and in the pages of the Lutheran Hue-mann, "Sylloge Diss. Sacras." tom. i. par. ii. p. 352; and Blondel, "Familier éclaircissement de la question, si une femme a été assise au siège papal de Rome." Amsterdam, 1647-9.

The final development of this extraordinary story, under the delicate fingers of the German and French Protestant controversialists, may not prove uninteresting.

Joan was the daughter of an English missionary, who left England to preach the Gospel to the recently converted Saxons. She was born at Engelheim, and according to different authors she was christened Agnes, Gerberta, Joanna, Margaret,

Isabel, Dorothy, or Jutt—the last must have been a
nickname surely! She early distinguished herself for genius and love of letters. A young monk
of Fulda having conceived for her a violent passion,
which she returned with ardour, she deserted her
parents, dressed herself in male attire, and in the
sacred precincts of Fulda divided her affections between the youthful monk and the musty books of the
monastic library. Not satisfied with the restraints
of conventual life, nor finding the library sufficiently
well provided with books of abstruse science, she
eloped with her young man, and after visiting
England, France, and Italy, she brought him to
Athens, where she addicted herself with unflagging
devotion to her literary pursuits. Wearied out by
his journey, the monk expired in the arms of the
blue-stocking who had influenced his life for evil,
and the young lady of so many aliases was for a
while inconsolable. She left Athens and repaired
to Rome. There she opened a school, and acquired
such a reputation for learning and feigned sanctity
that, on the death of Leo IV., she was unanimously
elected Pope. For two years and five months,
under the name of John VIII., she filled the papal
chair with reputation, no one suspecting her sex.
But having taken a fancy to one of the cardinals,

by him she became pregnant. At length arrived the time of Rogation processions. Whilst passing the street between the amphitheatre and S. Clement's, she was seized with violent pains, fell to the ground amidst the crowd, and whilst her attendants ministered to her, was delivered of a son. Some say the child and mother died on the spot, some that she survived but was incarcerated, some that the child was spirited away to be the Antichrist of the last days. A marble monument representing the papess with her baby was erected on the spot, which was declared to be accursed to all ages.

I have little doubt myself that Pope Joan is an impersonification of the great whore of Revelation, seated on the seven hills, and is the popular expression of the idea prevalent from the twelfth to the sixteenth centuries, that the mystery of iniquity was somehow working in the papal court. The scandal of the Antipopes, the utter worldliness and pride of others, the spiritual fornication with the kings of the earth, along with the words of Revelation prophesying the advent of an adulterous woman who should rule over the imperial city, and her connexion with Antichrist, crystallized into this curious myth, much as the floating uncertainty as to the signification of our Lord's words, " There be

some standing here which shall not taste of death
till they see the kingdom of God," condensed into
the myth of the Wandering Jew.

The literature connected with Antichrist is
voluminous. I need only specify some of the most
curious works which have appeared on the subject.
S. Hippolytus and Rabanus Maurus have been
already alluded to. Commodianus wrote "Carmen
Apologeticum adversus Gentes," which has been
published by Dom Pitra in his "Spicilegium Soles-
mense," with an introduction containing Jewish and
Christian traditions relating to Antichrist. "De
Turpissima Conceptione, Nativitate, et aliis Præ-
sagiis Diaboliciis illius Turpissimi Hominis Anti-
christi," is the title of a strange little volume published by Lenoir in A.D. 1500, containing rude yet
characteristic woodcuts, representing the birth, life,
and death of the Man of Sin, each picture accompanied by French verses in explanation. An
equally remarkable illustrated work on Antichrist
is the famous "Liber de Antichristo," a blockbook
of an early date. It is in twenty-seven folios, and
is excessively rare. Dibdin has reproduced three
of the plates in his "Bibliotheca Spenseriana,"
and Falckenstein has given full details of the work
in his "Geschichte der Buchdruckerkunst."

There is an Easter miracle-play of the twelfth century, still extant, the subject of which is the "Life and Death of Antichrist." More curious still is the "Farce de l'Antéchrist et de trois femmes," a composition of the sixteenth century, when that mysterious personage occupied all brains. The farce consists in a scene at a fish-stall, with three good ladies quarrelling over some fish. Antichrist steps in—for no particular reason that one can see —upsets fish and fish-women, sets them fighting, and skips off the stage. The best book on Antichrist, and that most full of learning and judgment, is Malvenda's great work in two folio volumes, "De Antichristo, libri xii." Lyons, 1647.

For the fable of the Pope Joan, see J. Lenfant, "Histoire de la Papesse Jeanne." La Haye, 1736, 2 vols. 12mo. "Allatii Confutatio Fabulæ de Johanna Papissa." Colon. 1645.

The Man in the Moon

From L. Richter.

EVERY one knows that the moon is inhabited by a man with a bundle of sticks on his back, who has been exiled thither for many centuries, and who is so far off that he is beyond the reach of Death.

He has once visited this earth, if the nursery rhyme is to be credited, when it asserts that—

> " The Man in the Moon
> Came down too soon,
> And asked his way to Norwich ;"

but whether he ever reached that city, the same authority does not state.

The story as told by nurses is, that this man was found by Moses gathering sticks on a Sabbath, and that, for this crime, he was doomed to reside in the moon till the end of all things ; and they refer to Numbers xv. 32—36 :

"And while the children of Israel were in the wilderness, they found a man that gathered sticks upon the sabbath day. And they that found him gathering sticks brought him unto Moses and Aaron, and unto all the congregation. And they put him in ward, because it was not declared what should be done to him. And the Lord said unto Moses, The man shall be surely put to death : all the congregation shall stone him with stones without the camp. And all the congregation brought him without the camp, and stoned him with stones till he died."

Of course, in the sacred writings there is no allusion to the moon.

The German tale is as follows :—

Ages ago there went one Sunday morning an old man into the wood to hew sticks. He cut a faggot and slung it on a stout staff, cast it over his shoulder, and began to trudge home with his burden. On his way he met a handsome man in Sunday suit, walking towards the Church ; this man stopped and asked the faggot-bearer, "Do you know that this is Sunday on earth, when all must rest from their labours?"

"Sunday on earth, or Monday in heaven, it is all one to me!" laughed the wood-cutter.

"Then bear your bundle for ever," answered the stranger; "and as you value not Sunday on earth, yours shall be a perpetual Moon-day in heaven; and you shall stand for eternity in the moon, a warning to all Sabbath-breakers." Thereupon the stranger vanished, and the man was caught up with his stock and his faggot into the moon, where he stands yet.

The superstition seems to be old in Germany, for the full moon is spoken of as *wadel*, or *wedel*, a faggot. Tobler relates the story thus: "An arma mā ket alawel am Sonnti holz ufglesa. Do hedem der liebe Gott dwahl gloh, öb er lieber wött ider sonn verbrenna oder im mo verfrüra, do willer lieber inn mo ihi. Dromm siedma no jetz an ma im mo inna, wenns wedel ist. Er hed a püscheli uffem rogga[1]." That is to say, he was given the choice of burning in the sun, or of freezing in the moon; he chose the latter; and now at full moon he is to be

[1] Tobler, Appenz. Sprachsbuch, 20.

seen seated with his bundle of faggots on his back.

In Schaumburg-lippe [2], the story goes, that a man and a woman stand in the moon, the man because he strewed brambles and thorns on the church path, so as to hinder people from attending Mass on Sunday morning ; the woman because she made butter on that day. The man carries his bundle of thorns, the woman her butter-tub. A similar tale is told in Swabia and in Marken. Fischart [3] says that there "is to be seen in the moon a mannikin who stole wood," and Prætorius, in his description of the world [4], that "superstitious people assert that the black flecks in the moon are a man who gathered wood on a Sabbath, and is therefore turned into stone."

At the time when wishing was of avail, say the North Frisians, a man, one Christmas eve, stole cabbages from his neighbour's garden. When just in the act of walking off with his load, he was perceived by the people, who conjured him up into the moon. There he stands in the full moon to be seen by every body, bearing his load of cabbages to all eternity. Every Christmas eve

[2] Wolf, Zeitschrift für Deut. Myth. i. 168.
[3] Fischart, Garg. 130.   [4] Prætorius, i. 447.

he is said to turn round once.   Others say
that he stole willow bows, which he must bear for
ever.

In Silt, the story goes that he was a sheep-stealer,
who enticed sheep to him with a bundle of cabbages, until, as an everlasting warning to others,
he was placed in the moon, where he constantly
holds in his hand a bundle of these vegetables.

The people of Rantum say that he is a giant,
who at the time of the flow stands in a stooping
posture, because he is then taking up water, which
he pours out on the earth, and thereby causes high
tide ; but at the time of the ebb he stands erect,
and rests from his labour, when the water can sub-
side again[5].

The Dutch household myth is, that the unhappy
man was caught stealing vegetables.   Dante calls
him Cain :—

> ". . . Now doth Cain with fork of thorns confine,
>   On either hemisphere, touching the wave
>   Beneath the towers of Seville.   Yesternight
>   The moon was round."—*Hell*, cant. xx.

---

[5] Thorpe's "Mythology and Popular Traditions," vol. iii.
p. 57.

And again,

"... Tell, I pray thee, whence the gloomy spots
   Upon this body, which below on earth
   Give rise to talk of Cain in fabling quaint?"
                                  Paradise, cant. ii.

Chaucer, in the "Testament of Cresside," adverts to the man in the moon, and attributes to him the same idea of theft. Of Lady Cynthia, or the moon, he says :—

" Her gite was gray and full of spottis blake,
   And on her brest a chorle painted ful even,
   Bering a bush of thornis on his backe,
   Whiche for his theft might clime so ner the heaven."

Ritson, among his "Ancient Songs," gives one extracted from a manuscript attributed by Mr. Wright to the period of Edward I., on the Man in the Moon ; but in very obscure language. The first verse, altered into more modern orthography, runs as follows :—

" Man in the Moon stand and stit,
      On his bot-fork his burden he beareth,
   It is much wonder that he do na doun slit,
      For doubt lest he fall he shudd'reth and shivereth.
          *   *   *   *   *
" When the frost freezes must chill he bide,
      The thorns be keen his attire so teareth,
   Nis no wight in the world there wot when he syt,
      Ne bote it by the hedge what weeds he weareth."

Alexander Necham, or Nequam, a writer of the twelfth century, in commenting on the dispersed shadows in the moon, thus alludes to the vulgar belief:—"Nonne novisti quid vulgus vocet rusticum in luna portantem spinas? Unde quidam vulgariter loquens ait:—

> "Rusticus in Luna,
> Quem sarcina deprimit una
> Monstrat per opinas
> Nulli prodesse rapinas[6],"

which may be translated thus: "Do you know what they call the rustic in the moon, who carries the faggot of sticks? So that one vulgarly speaking says:—

> "See the rustic in the Moon,
> How his bundle weighs him down;
> Thus his sticks the truth reveal
> It never profits man to steal."

Shakspeare refers to the same individual in his "Midsummer Night's Dream." Quince the carpenter, giving directions for the performance of the play of "Pyramus and Thisbe," orders: "One must come in with a bush of thorns and a lantern, and say he comes in to disfigure, or to present, the person of Moonshine." And the enacter of this part says, "All I have to say is, to tell you that the

[6] Alex. Neckam, De Naturis Rerum. Ed. Wright, p. xviii.

lantern is the moon; I the man in the moon; this thorn-bush my thorn-bush; and this dog my dog."

Also "Tempest," Act 2, Scene 2 :—

"*Cal.* Hast thou not dropt from heav'n?
"*Steph.* Out o' th' moon, I do assure thee. I was the man in th' moon when time was.
"*Cal.* I have seen thee in her; and I do adore thee. My mistress show'd me thee, and thy dog, and thy bush."

The dog I have myself had pointed out to me by an old Devonshire crone. If popular superstition places a dog in the moon, it puts a lamb in the sun; for in the same county it is said that those who see the sun rise on Easter-day may behold in the orb the lamb and flag.

I believe this idea of locating animals in the two great luminaries of heaven to be very ancient, and to be a relic of a primeval superstition of the Aryan race.

There is an ancient pictorial representation of our friend the Sabbath-breaker in Gyffyn Church, near Conway. The roof of the chancel is divided into compartments, in four of which are the Evangelistic symbols, rudely, yet effectively painted. Besides these symbols is delineated in each compartment an orb of heaven. The sun, the moon, and two stars, are placed at the feet of the Angel, the Bull, the Lion, and the Eagle. The representation of the moon is as below; in the disk is the

conventional man with his bundle of sticks, but without the dog. There is also a curious seal appended to a deed preserved in the Record Office,

dated the 9th year of Edward the Third (1335), bearing the man in the moon as its device. The deed is one of conveyance of a messuage, barn, and four acres of ground, in the parish of Kingston-on-Thames, from Walter de Grendesse, clerk, to Margaret his mother. On the seal we see the man carrying his sticks, and the moon surrounds him. There are also a couple of stars added, perhaps to show that he is in the sky. The legend on the seal reads :—

> " Te Waltere docebo
> cur spinas phebo
> gero,"

which may be translated, " I will teach thee, Walter, why I carry thorns in the moon."

The carved wooden sign of the " Man in the Moon," in Wych Street, Strand, a rare example of the suspended signs now to be found built into the wall, must not pass unnoticed. Other items connected with lunar mythology must be only briefly alluded to. According to the classic tale the figure in the moon is probably Endymion, beloved of Selene, and held by her passionately to her bosom. The Egyptian representations of the moon with a figure in the disk, represent the little Horus in the womb of his mother Isis. Plutarch wrote a tract on the Face in the Moon.

Clemens Alexandrinus tells us the face is that of a Sibyl[7].

The general superstition with regard to the spots in the moon may briefly be summed up thus: A man is located in the moon; he is a thief or Sabbath-breaker; he has a pole over his shoulder, from which is suspended a bundle of sticks or thorns. In some places a woman is believed to accompany him, and she has a butter-tub with her; in other localities she is replaced by a dog.

The belief in the Moon-man seems to exist among the natives of British Columbia; for I read in one of Mr. Duncan's letters to the Church Missionary Society:—"One very dark night I was told that there was a moon to see on the beach. On going to see, there was an illuminated disk, with the figure of a man upon it. The water was then very low, and one of the conjuring parties had lit up this disk at the water's edge. They had made it of wax with great exactness, and presently it was at full. It was an imposing sight. Nothing could be seen around it; but the Indians suppose that

---

[7] Clemens Alex. Strom. I.

[8] Hebel, in his charming poem on the Man in the Moon in "Allemanische Gedichte," makes him both thief and Sabbath-breaker.

the medicine party are then holding converse with the man in the moon. . . . After a short time the moon waned away, and the conjuring party returned whooping to their house."

Now let us turn to Scandinavian mythology, and see what we learn from that source.

Måni, the moon, stole two children from their parents, and carried them up to heaven. Their names were Hjuki and Bil. They had been drawing water from the well Byrgir, in the bucket Sœgr, suspended from the pole Simul, which they bore upon their shoulders. These children, pole, and bucket, were placed in heaven, "where they could be seen from earth." This refers undoubtedly to the spots in the moon, and so the Swedish peasantry explain these spots to this day, as representing a boy and a girl bearing a pail of water between them. Are we not reminded at once of our nursery rhyme—

> " Jack and Jill went up a hill
>   To fetch a pail of water ;
> Jack fell down, and broke his crown,
>   And Jill came tumbling after ?"

This verse, which to us seems at first sight non-sense, I have no hesitation in saying has a high antiquity, and refers to the Eddaic Hjuki and Bil.

The names indicate as much. Hjuki, in Norse, would be pronounced Juki, which would readily become Jack ; and Bil, for the sake of euphony, and in order to give a female name to one of the children, would become Jill.

The fall of Jack, and the subsequent fall of Jill, simply represent the vanishing of one moon-spot after another, as the moon wanes.

But the old Norse myth had a deeper signification than merely an explanation of the moon-spots.

Hjuki is derived from the verb jakka, to heap or pile together, to assemble and increase ; and Bil from bila, to break up or dissolve. Hjuki and Bil, therefore, signify nothing more than the waxing and waning of the moon, and the water they are represented as bearing signifies the fact that the rainfall depends on the phases of the moon. Waxing and waning were individualized, and the meteorological fact of the connexion of the rain with the moon was represented by the children as water-bearers.

But though Jack and Jill became by degrees dissevered in the popular mind from the moon, the original myth went through a fresh phase, and exists still under a new form. The Norse superstition attributed *theft* to the moon and the vulgar soon began to believe that the figure they saw in the moon was the thief. The lunar specks certainly may be made to resemble one figure, but only a lively imagination can discern two. The girl soon dropped out of popular mythology, the boy oldened into a venerable man, he retained his pole, and the bucket was transformed into the thing he had stolen—sticks or vegetables. The theft was in some places exchanged for Sabbath-breaking, especially among those in Protestant countries who were acquainted with the Bible story of the stick-gatherer.

The Indian superstition is worth examining, because of the connexion existing between Indian and European mythology, on account of our belonging to the same Aryan stock.

According to a Buddhist legend, Sâkyamunni himself, in one of his earlier stages of existence, was a hare, and lived in friendship with a fox and an ape. In order to test the virtue of the Bodhisattwa, Indra came to the friends, in the form of an old man asking for food. Hare, ape, and fox went forth in quest of victuals for their guest. The two latter returned from their foraging expedition successful, but the hare had found nothing. Then, rather than that he should treat the old man with inhospitality, the hare had a fire kindled, and cast himself into the flames, that he might himself become food for his guest. In reward for this act of self-sacrifice, Indra carried the hare to heaven, and placed him in the moon [9].

Here we have an old man and a hare in connexion with the lunar planet, just as in Shakspeare we have a faggot-bearer and a dog.

The fable rests upon the name of the moon in Sanskrit, çaçin, or "that marked with the hare;" but whether the belief in the spots taking the shape of a hare gave the name çaçin to the moon, or the lunar name çaçin originated the belief, it is impossible for us to say.

Grounded upon this myth is the curious story of "The Hare and the Elephant," in the "Pantscha-tantra," an ancient collection of Sanskrit fables. It will be found as the first tale in the third book. I have room only for an outline of the story.

THE CRAFTY HARE.

In a certain forest lived a mighty elephant, king of a herd, Toothy by name. On a certain occasion

[9] "Mémoires . . . par Hjouen Thsang, traduits du Chinois par Stanislas Julien," i. 375. Upham, "Sacred Books of Ceylon," iii. 309.

there was a long drought, so that pools, tanks, swamps, and lakes were dried up. Then the elephants sent out exploring parties in search of water. A young one discovered an extensive lake surrounded with trees, and teeming with water-fowl. It went by the name of the Moon-lake. The elephants, delighted at the prospect of having an inexhaustible supply of water, marched off to the spot, and found their most sanguine hopes realized. Round about the lake, in the sandy soil, were innumerable hare warrens, and as the herd of elephants trampled on the ground, the hares were severely injured, their homes broken down, their heads, legs, and backs crushed beneath the ponderous feet of the monsters of the forest. As soon as the herd had withdrawn, the hares assembled, some halting, some dripping with blood, some bearing the corpses of their cherished infants, some with piteous tales of ruination in their houses, all with tears streaming from their eyes, and wailing forth, "Alas, we are lost! The elephant-herd will return, for there is no water elsewhere, and that will be the death of all of us."

But the wise and prudent Longear volunteered to drive the herd away, and he succeeded in this manner: Longear went to the elephants, and having singled out their king, he addressed him as follows :—

"Ha, ha! bad elephant! what brings you with such thoughtless frivolity to this strange lake? back with you at once!"

When the king of the elephants heard this, he asked in astonishment, "Pray who are you?"

"I," replied Longear, "I am Vidschajadatta by name, the hare who resides in the Moon. Now am I sent by his Excellency the Moon as an ambassador to you. I speak to you in the name of the Moon."

"Ahem! Hare," said the elephant, somewhat staggered, "and what message have you brought me from his Excellency the Moon?"

"You have this day injured several hares. Are you not aware that they are the subjects of me? If you value your life, venture not near the lake again. Break my command, and I shall withdraw my beams from you at night, and your bodies will be consumed with perpetual sun."

The elephant after a short meditation said, "Friend! it is true that I have acted against the rights of the excellent Majesty of the Moon. I should wish to make an apology; how can I do so?"

The hare replied, "Come along with me, and I will show you."

The elephant asked, "Where is his Excellency at present?"

The other replied, "He is now in the lake, hearing the complaints of the maimed hares."

"If that be the case," said the elephant humbly, "bring me to my lord, that I may tender him my submission."

So the hare conducted the king of the elephants to the edge of the lake, and showed him the reflexion of the moon in the water, saying, "There stands our lord in the midst of the water, plunged in meditation; reverence him with devotion, and then depart with speed."

Thereupon the elephant poked his proboscis into the water, and muttered a fervent prayer. By so doing he set the water in agitation, so that the reflection of the moon was all of a quiver.

"Look!" exclaimed the hare, "his Majesty is trembling with rage at you!"

"Why is his supreme Excellency enraged with me?" asked the elephant.

"Because you have set the water in motion. Worship him, and then be off!"

The elephant let his ears droop, bowed his great

head to the earth, and after having expressed in suitable terms his regret for having annoyed the Moon and the hare dwelling in it, he vowed never to trouble the Moon-lake again. Then he departed, and the hares have ever since lived there unmolested.

The Mountain of Venus

RAGGED, bald, and desolate, as though a curse rested upon it, rises the Hörselberg out of the rich and populous land between Eisenach and Gotha, looking, from a distance, like a huge stone sarcophagus—a sarcophagus in which rests in magical slumber, till the end of all things, a mysterious world of wonders.

High up on the north-west flank of the mountain, in a precipitous wall of rock, opens a cavern, called the Hörselloch, from the depths of which issues a muffled roar of water, as though a subterraneous stream were rushing over rapidly-whirling mill-wheels. "When I have stood alone on the ridge of the mountain," says Bechstein, "after having sought the chasm in vain, I have heard a mighty rush, like that of falling water, beneath my feet, and after scrambling down the scarp, have found

myself—how, I never knew—in front of the cave."
("Sagenschatz des Thüringes-landes," 1835.)

In ancient days, according to the Thüringian
Chronicles, bitter cries and long-drawn moans
were heard issuing from this cavern ; and at night
wild shrieks, and the burst of diabolical laughter
would ring out from it over the vale, and fill the
inhabitants with terror.   It was supposed that this
hole gave admittance to Purgatory ; and the
popular but faulty derivation of Hörsel was *Hore*,
die Seele, Hark, the Souls !

But another popular belief respecting this mountain was, that in it Venus, the pagan Goddess of
Love, held her court in all the pomp and revelry of
heathendom ; and there were not a few who
declared that they had seen fair forms of female
beauty beckoning them from the mouth of the
chasm, and that they had heard dulcet strains of
music well up from the abyss above the thunder of
the falling, unseen torrent.   Charmed by the music,
and allured by the spectral forms, various individuals had entered the cave, and none had returned
except the Tanhäuser, of whom more anon.   Still
does the Hörselberg go by the name of the Venusberg, a name frequently used in the Middle Ages,
but without its locality being always defined.

" In 1398, at mid-day, there appeared suddenly three great fires in the air, which presently ran together into one globe of flame, parted again and finally sank into the Hörselberg," says the Thüringian Chronicle.

And now for the story of Tanhäuser.

A French knight was riding over the beauteous meadows in the Hörsel vale on his way to Wartburg, where the Landgrave Hermann was holding a gathering of minstrels, who were to contend in song for a prize.

Tanhäuser was a famous minnesinger, and all his lays were of love and of women, for his heart was full of passion, and that not of the purest and noblest description.

It was towards dusk that he passed the cliff in which is the Hörselloch, and as he rode by, he saw a white glimmering figure of matchless beauty standing before him, and beckoning him to her. He knew her at once, by her attributes and by her superhuman perfection, to be none other than Venus. As she spake to him the sweetest strains of music floated in the air, a soft roseate light glowed around her, and nymphs of exquisite loveliness scattered roses at her feet. A thrill of passion ran through the veins of the minnesinger; and,

leaving his horse, he followed the apparition.   It
led him up the mountain to the cave, and as it
went flowers bloomed upon the soil, and a radiant
track was left for Tanhäuser to follow. He entered
the cavern, and descended to the palace of Venus
in the heart of the mountain.

Seven years of revelry and debauch were passed,
and the minstrel's heart began to feel a strange
void.   The beauty, the magnificence, the variety,
of the scenes in the pagan goddess's home, and all
its heathenish pleasures, palled upon him, and he
yearned for the pure fresh breezes of earth, one
look up at the dark night sky spangled with stars,
one glimpse of simple mountain flowers, one tinkle
of sheep-bells.   At the same time his conscience
began to reproach him, and he longed to make his
peace with God.   In vain did he entreat Venus to
permit him to depart, and it was only when in the
bitterness of his grief he called upon the Virgin-
Mother, that a rift in the mountain-side appeared
to him, and he stood again above ground.

How sweet was the morning air, balmy with the
scent of hay, as it rolled up the mountain to him,
and fanned his haggard cheek !   How delightful to
him was the cushion of moss and scanty grass after
the downy couches of the palace of revelry below !

He plucked the little heather-bells and held them before him; the tears rolled from his eyes, and moistened his thin and wasted hands. He looked up at the soft blue sky and the newly-risen sun, and his heart overflowed. What were the golden jewel-incrusted, lamp-lit vaults beneath to that pure dome of God's building!

The chime of a village church struck sweetly on his ear, satiated with Bacchanalian songs; and he hurried down the mountain to the church which called him. There he made his confession, but the priest, horror-struck at his recital, dared not give him absolution, but passed him on to another. And so he went from one to another, till at last he was referred to the Pope himself. To the Pope he went. Urban IV. then occupied the chair of S. Peter. To him Tanhäuser related the sickening story of his guilt, and prayed for absolution. Urban was a hard and stern man, and shocked at the immensity of the sin, he thrust the penitent indignantly from him, exclaiming, "Guilt such as thine can never, never be remitted. Sooner shall this staff in my hand grow green and blossom, than that God should pardon thee!"

Then Tanhäuser, full of despair, and with his soul darkened, went away, and returned to the

only asylum open to him, the Venusberg. But lo!
three days after he had gone, Urban discovered
that his pastoral staff had put forth buds, and had
burst into flower. Then he sent messengers after
Tanhäuser, and they reached the Hörsel vale to
hear that a wayworn man, with haggard brow and
bowed head, had just entered the Hörselloch.
Since then the Tanhäuser has not been seen[1].

Such is the sad yet beautiful story of Tanhäuser.
It is a very ancient myth Christianized, a wide-
spread tradition localized. Originally heathen, it
has been transformed, and has acquired new beauty
by an infusion of Christianity. Scattered over
Europe, it exists in various forms, but in none so
graceful as that attached to the Hörselberg. There
are, however, other Venusbergs in Germany: as,
for instance, in Swabia, near Waldsee; another
near Ufhausen, at no great distance from Freiburg
(the same story is told of this Venusberg as of the
Hörselberg); in Saxony there is a Venusberg not
far from Wolkenstein. Paracelsus speaks of a
Venusberg in Italy, referring to that in which
Æneas Sylvius (Ep. 16) says Venus or a Sibyl

[1] Prœtorius, Blocksberg, Leipzig, 1668. Grimm, Deutsche
Sagen, Berlin, 1866, I. p. 214. Bechstein, Thuringische
Märchenschatz, 1835.

resides, occupying a cavern, and assuming once a week the form of a serpent. Geiler v. Keysersperg, a quaint old preacher of the fifteenth century, speaks of the witches assembling on the Venus berg, but does not say where it is.

The story, either in prose or verse, has often been printed. Some of the earliest editions are the following :—

"Das Lied von dem Danhewser." Nürnberg, without date ; the same, Nürnberg, 1515.—"Das Lyedt v. d. Thanheuser." Leyptzk, 1520.—"Das Lied v. d. Danheüser," reprinted by Bechstein, 1835.—"Das Lied vom edlen Tanheuser, Mons Veneris." Frankfort, 1614 ; Leipzig, 1668.—"Twe lede volgen Dat erste vam Danhüsser." Without date.—"Van heer Danielken." Tantwerpen, 1544. —A Danish version in "Nyerup, Danske Viser," No. VIII.

Let us now see some of the forms which this remarkable myth assumed in other countries. Every popular tale has its root, a root which may be traced among different countries, and though the accidents of the story may vary, yet the substance remains unaltered. It has been said that the common people never invent new story-radicals any more than we invent new word-roots, and this is perfectly true. The same story-root remains, but it is varied according to the temperament of the narrator or the exigencies of localization. The story-root of the Venusberg is this :—

> The underground folk seek union with human beings.

a. A man is enticed into their abode, where he unites with a woman of the underground race.

β. He desires to revisit the earth, and escapes.

γ. He returns again to the region below.

Now there is scarcely a collection of folk-lore which does not contain a story founded on this root. It appears in every branch of the Aryan family, and examples might be quoted from Modern Greek, Albanian, Neapolitan, French, German, Danish, Norwegian and Swedish, Icelandic, Scotch, Welsh, and other collections of popular tales. I have only space to mention some.

There is a Norse Tháttr of a certain Helgi Thorir's son, which is, in its present form, a production of the fourteenth century. Helgi and his brother Thorstein went a cruise to Finnmark, or Lapland. They reached a ness, and found the land covered with forest. Helgi explored this forest, and lighted suddenly on a party of red-dressed women riding upon red horses. These ladies were beautiful and of Troll race. One surpassed the others in beauty, and she was their mistress. They erected a tent and prepared a feast. Helgi observed that all their vessels were of silver and gold. The lady, who named herself Ingibjorg, advanced towards the Norseman, and invited him to live with her. He feasted and lived with the Trolls for three days, and then returned to his ship, bringing with him two chests of silver and gold, which Ingibjorg had given him. He had been forbidden to mention where he had been and with whom, so he told no one whence he had obtained the chests. The ships sailed, and he returned home.

One winter's night Helgi was fetched away from home, in the midst of a furious storm, by two mysterious horsemen, and no one was able to ascertain for many years what had become of him, till the prayers of the king, Olaf, obtained his release, and then he was restored to his father and brother, but he was thenceforth blind. All the time of his absence he had been with the red-vested lady in her mysterious abode of Glœsisvellir.

The Scotch story of Thomas of Ercildoune is the

same story. Thomas met with a strange lady, of elfin race, beneath Eildon Tree, who led him into the underground land, where he remained with her for seven years. He then returned to earth, still, however, remaining bound to come to his royal mistress whenever she should summon him. Accordingly, while Thomas was making merry with his friends in the Tower of Ercildoune, a person came running in, and told, with marks of fear and astonishment, that a hart and a hind had left the neighbouring forest, and were parading the street of the village. Thomas instantly arose, left his house, and followed the animals into the forest, from which he never returned. According to popular belief, he still "drees his weird" in Fairy Land, and is one day expected to revisit earth. (Scott, "Minstrelsy of the Scottish Border.") Compare with this the ancient ballad of Tamlane.

Debes relates that "it happened a good while since, when the burghers of Bergen had the commerce of the Faroe Isles, that there was a man in Serraade, called Jonas Soideman, who was kept by the spirits in a mountain during the space of seven years, and at length came out, but lived afterwards in great distress and fear, lest they should again take him away; wherefore people were obliged to watch him in the night." The same author mentions another young man who had been carried away, and after his return was removed a second time, upon the eve of his marriage.

Gervase of Tilbury says that "in Catalonia there is a lofty mountain, named Cavagum, at the foot of which runs a river with golden sands, in the vicinity of which there are likewise silver mines. This mountain is steep, and almost inaccessible. On its top, which is always covered with ice and snow, is a black and bottomless lake, into which if a stone be cast, a tempest suddenly arises; and near this lake is the portal of the palace of demons." He then tells how a young damsel was spirited in there and spent seven years with the mountain spirits. On her return to earth she was thin and withered, with wandering eyes, and almost bereft of understanding.

A Swedish story is to this effect. A young man was on his way to his bride, when he was allured into a mountain by a beautiful elfin woman. With her he lived forty years, which passed as an hour; on his return to earth all his old friends and relations were dead, or had forgotten him, and finding no rest there, he returned to his mountain elf-land.

In Pomerania, a labourer's son, John Dietrich of

Rambin, is said to have spent twelve years in the underground land. When about eight years old he was sent to spend a summer with his uncle, a farmer in Rodenkirchen. Here John had to keep cows with other boys, and they used to drive them to graze about the Nine-hills. There was an old cowherd, Klas Starkwolt, who used to join the boys, and tell them stories of the underground people who dwelt in a glorious land beneath the Nine-hills. These tales John swallowed eagerly, and could think of little else. One Midsummer day he ran to the hills, and laid himself down on the top of one of them, where, according to Klas, the little people were wont to dance. John lay quite still from ten till twelve at night. At last a distant tower-clock tolled midnight. Instantly the hill was covered with the little people, dancing and tossing their caps about. One of these fell near John: he caught it, and set it on his head. By the acquisition of this cap he had obtained power over the elves. When the cock began to crow, a bright glass point appeared on the hill-top, and opened. John and the people descended, and he found himself in a land of wonder. He found that there were in that place the most beautiful walks, in which he might ramble along for miles in all directions with-

out ever finding an end of them, so immensely
large was the hill that the little people lived in;
and yet outwardly it seemed but a little hill, with
a few bushes and trees growing on it. It was
extraordinary that, between the meads and fields,
which were thick sown with hills and lakes and
islands, and ornamented with trees and flowers in
the greatest variety, there ran, as it were, small
lanes, through which, as through crystal rocks, one
was obliged to pass to come to any new place;
and the single meads and fields were often a mile
long, and the flowers were so brilliant and so fragrant,
and the song of the numerous birds so sweet, that
John had never seen any thing on earth at all like
it. There was a breeze, and yet one did not feel
the wind; it was quite clear and bright, and yet
there was no heat, no sun, no moon; the waves
dashed about, but there was no danger; and the
most beautiful little barks and canoes came, like
white swans, when one wanted to cross the water,
and went backwards and forwards of themselves.
Whence all this came no one knew, nor could his
servant tell any thing about it; but one thing John
saw plainly, which was, that the large carbuncles
and diamonds that were set in the roof and walls
gave light instead of the sun, moon, and stars.

Here John found a little maiden, Elizabeth Krabbin, daughter of the minister of Rambin, who had been spirited away by the little people a few years before. John and she soon formed an attachment, and were wont to walk together. On one of their strolls they must have approached the surface, for they heard the crowing of a cock. At the sound, the remembrance of earth returned to them, and they felt a desire once more to be on Christian land. "Every thing down here," said Elizabeth, "is beautiful, and the little folk are kind, but there is not pure pleasure here. Every night I dream of my father and mother, and of our churchyard; and I cannot go to the House of God, and worship Him as a Christian should; for this is no Christian life we lead down here, but a delusive, half-heathen one."

John, however, could not release Elizabeth from the power of the underground folk till he found a toad, the sight and smell of which was so repulsive to them, that they readily complied with every request of John, on condition he should bury the offensive reptile.

Then he and the girl escaped, taking with them gold and silver and jewels, to such an amount, that their fortune was made. They were, of course, married; and John bought up half the island of

Rügen, was ennobled, built and endowed the present church of Rambin, and became the founder of
a powerful family. To the altar of Rambin he gave
some of the cups and plates of gold made by the
underground people, and his own and Elizabeth's
glass shoes which they had worn in the mount.
But these were taken away in the time of Charles
XII. of Sweden, when the Russians came on the
island, and the Cossacks plundered the churches[2].

In the year 1520, there lived at Basle, in Switzerland, a tailor's son, named Leonard. He entered a
cave which penetrated far into the bowels of the
earth, holding a consecrated taper in his hand.
He came to an enchanted land, where was a beautiful woman wearing a golden crown, but from her
waist downwards she was a serpent. She gave
him gold and silver, and entreated him to kiss her
three times. He complied twice, but the writhing
of her tail so horrified him, that he fled without
giving her the third kiss. Afterwards he prowled
about the mountains, seeking the entrance to the
cave, filled with a craving for the society of the
lady, but he never could find it again[3].

---

[2] Keightley's Fairy Mythology, 1860, p. 178.
[3] Kornemann, Mons Veneris, c. 34. Prœtorius, Weltbe-
schreibung, p. 661.

There is a curious story told by Fordun in his "Scotichronicon," by Matthew of Westminster in his Chronicle, and by Roger of Wendover in his "Flowers of History," which has some interest in connexion with the legend of the Tanhäuser. They relate that in the year 1050, a youth of noble birth had been married in Rome, and during the nuptial feast, being engaged in a game of ball, he took off his wedding-ring, and placed it on the finger of a statue of Venus. When he wished to resume it, he found that the stony hand had become clenched, so that it was impossible to remove the ring. Thenceforth he was haunted by the Goddess Venus, who constantly whispered in his ear, "Embrace me; I am Venus, whom you have wedded; I will never restore your ring." However, by the assistance of a priest, she was at length forced to give it up to its rightful owner.

This story occurs also in Vincent of Beauvais, whose version will be found in the Appendix[4]. Cæsarius of Heisterboch has also a story bearing a relation to that of Venus and the ring. A certain Clerk Phillip, a great necromancer, took some Swabian and Bavarian youths to a

---

[4] Appendix B. Vincent. Bellov. I. 36, Spec. Historiale. Antonini Summa Histor. P. II., tit. 16.

lonely spot in a field, where, at their desire, he proceeded to perform incantations. First he drew a circle round them with his sword, and warned them on no consideration to leave the ring. Then retiring from them a little space he began his incantations, and suddenly there appeared around the youths a multitude of armed men, brandishing weapons, and daring them to fight. The demons, failing to draw them by this means from their enchanted circle, vanished, and then there was seen a company of beautiful damsels, dancing about the ring, and by their attitudes alluring the youths towards them. One of these, exceeding the others in beauty and grace, singled out a youth, and dancing before him, extended to him a ring of gold, casting languishing glances towards him, and by all means in her power endeavouring to attract his attention, and kindle his passion. The young man, unable any longer to resist, put forth his finger beyond the circle to the ring, and the apparition at once drew him towards her and vanished along with him. However, after much trouble, the necromancer was able to recover him from the embraces of the evil spirit[5].

[5] Cæsarius Heister. V. 4.

Another mediæval story is founded on the same myth, but purified and Christianized. A knight is playing at ball, and incommoded by his ring. He therefore removes it, and places it for safety on the finger of a statue of the Blessed Virgin Mary. On seeking it again he finds the hand of the figure clasped, and he is unable to recover his ring. Whereupon the knight renounces the world, and as the betrothed of the Virgin enters a monastery[6].

The incident of the ring in connexion with the ancient goddess is certainly taken from the old religion of the Teutonic and Scandinavian peoples. Freyja was represented in her temples holding a ring in her hand; so was Thorgerda Hörgabrúda. The Faereyinga Saga relates an event in the life of the Faroese hero, Sigmund Brestesson, which is to the point. "They (Earl Hakon and Sigmund) went to the temple, and the earl fell on the ground before her statue, and there he lay long. The statue was richly dressed, and had a heavy gold ring on the arm. And the earl stood up and touched the ring, and tried to remove it, but could not; and it seemed to Sigmund as though she frowned. Then the earl said, 'She is not pleased

[6] Wolf, Beiträge z. deut. Myth. Göttingen, 1857, II., p. 257.

with thee, Sigmund! and I do not know whether I shall be able to reconcile you; but that shall be the token of her favour, if she gives us the ring, which she has in her hand.' Then the earl took much silver, and laid it on the footstool before her; and again he flung himself prostrate before her, and Sigmund noticed that he wept profusely. And when he stood up he took the ring, and she let go of it. Then the earl gave it to Sigmund, and said, 'I give thee this ring to thy weal, never part with it.' And Sigmund promised he would not[7]." This ring is the death of the Faroese chief. In after years, King Olaf, who converts him to Christianity, knowing that this gold ring is a relic of Paganism, asks Sigmund to give it him. The chief refuses, and the king angrily pronounces a warning that it will be the cause of his death. And his word falls true, for Sigmund is murdered in his sleep for the sake of the ring.

Unquestionably the Venus of the Hörselberg, of Basle, of the Eildon Hill, that of whom Fordun, Vincent, and Cæsarius relate such weird tales, is the ancient goddess Holda, or Thorgerda; a con-

[7] Faereyinga Saga. Copenhagen, 1832, p. 103; and Fornmanna Sögur, II., cap. 184.

clusion to which the stories of the ring naturally lead us.

The classic legend of Ulysses held captive for eight years by the nymph Calypso in the island of Ogygia, and again for one year by the enchantress Circe, contains the root of the same story of the Tanhäuser.

What may have been the significance of the primeval story-radical it is impossible for us now to ascertain ; but the legend, as it shaped itself in the Middle Ages, is certainly indicative of the struggle between the new and the old faith.

We see thinly veiled in Tanhäuser, the story of a man, Christian in name, but heathen at heart, allured by the attractions of Paganism, which seems to satisfy his poetic instincts, and which gives full rein to his passions. But these excesses pall on him after a while, and the religion of sensuality leaves a great void in his breast.

He turns to Christianity, and at first it seems to promise all that he requires. But alas! he is repelled by its ministers. On all sides he is met by practice widely at variance with profession. Pride, worldliness, want of sympathy, exist among those who should be the foremost to guide, sustain, and receive him. All the warm springs which gushed up in his broken heart are choked, his softened spirit is hardened again, and he returns in despair to bury his sorrows, and drown his anxieties, in the debauchery of his former creed.

A sad picture, but doubtless one very true.

S. Patrick's Purgatory

IN that charming mediæval romance, Fortunatus
and his Sons, which, by the way, is a treasury
of Popular Mythology, is an account of a visit paid
by the favoured youth to that cave of mystery in
Lough Derg, the Purgatory of S. Patrick.

Fortunatus, we are told, had heard in his travels
of how two days' journey from the town, Valdric,
in Ireland, was a town, Vernic, where was the
entrance to the Purgatory; so thither he went with
many servants.   He found a great abbey, and
behind the altar of the church a door, which led
into the dark cave which is called the Purgatory
of S. Patrick.   In order to enter it, leave had to
be obtained from the abbot; consequently, Leopold, servant to Fortunatus, betook himself to that
worthy, and made known to him that a nobleman
from Cyprus desired to enter the mysterious cavern.

The abbot at once requested Leopold to bring his master to supper with him. Fortunatus bought a large jar of wine, and sent it as a present to the monastery, and followed at the meal time.

"Venerable sir!" said Fortunatus, " I understand the Purgatory of S. Patrick is here ; is it so ?"

The abbot replied, " It is so indeed. Many hundred years ago, this place, where stand the abbey and the town, was a howling wilderness. Not far off, however, lived a venerable hermit, Patrick by name, who often sought the desert for the purpose of therein exercising his austerities. One day he lighted on this cave, which is of vast extent. He entered it, and wandering on in the dark, lost his way, so that he could no more find how to return to the light of day. After long ramblings through the gloomy passages, he fell on his knees, and besought Almighty God, if it were His will, to deliver him from the great peril wherein he lay. Whilst Patrick thus prayed, he was ware of piteous cries issuing from the depths of the cave, just such as would be the wailings of souls in purgatory. The hermit rose from his orison, and by God's mercy found his way back to the surface, and from that day exercised greater austerities, and after his death he was numbered with the saints. Pious people, who had heard the story of Patrick's adventure in the cave, built this cloister on the site."

Then Fortunatus asked whether all who ventured into the place heard likewise the howls of the tormented souls.

The abbot replied, " Some have affirmed that they have heard a bitter crying and piping therein ; whilst others have heard and seen nothing. No one, however, has penetrated, as yet, to the furthest limits of the cavern."

Fortunatus then asked permission to enter, and the abbot cheerfully consented, only stipulating that his guest should keep near the entrance, and not ramble too far, as some who had ventured in had never returned.

Next day, early, Fortunatus received the Blessed Sacrament with his trusty Leopold ; the door of the Purgatory was unlocked, each was provided with a taper, and then with the blessing of the abbot they were left in total darkness, and the door bolted behind them. Both wandered on in the cave, hearing faintly the chanting of the monks in the church, till the sound died away. They traversed several passages, lost their way, their candles burned out, and they sat down in de-

spair on the ground, a prey to hunger, thirst, and
fear.

The monks waited in the church hour after hour;
and the visitors of the Purgatory had not returned.
Day declined, vespers were sung, and still there
was no sign of the two who in the morning had
passed from the church into the cave. Then the
servants of Fortunatus began to exhibit anger, and
to insist on their master being restored to them.
The abbot was frightened, and sent for an old man
who had once penetrated far into the cave, with a
ball of twine, the end attached to the door handle.
This man volunteered to seek Fortunatus, and pro-
videntially his search was successful. After this
the abbot refused permission to any one to visit
the cave.

In the reign of Henry II. lived Henry of Saltrey,
who wrote a history of the visit of a Knight Owen
to the Purgatory of S. Patrick, which gained immense popularity. Henry was a monk of the
Benedictine Abbey of Saltrey, in Huntingdonshire,
and received his story from Gilbert, Abbot of
Louth, who is said by some to have also published
a written account of the extraordinary visions of
Owen[1]. This account was soon translated into

[1] Biograph. Brit. Lit.; Anglo-Norm. Period, p. 321.

other languages, and spread the fable through mediæval Europe.   It was this work of Henry of Saltrey which first made known the virtues of the mysterious cave of Lough Derg.   Marie of France translated it into French metre, but hers was not the only version in that tongue ; in English there are two versions.   In one of these, " Owayne Miles," H. S. Cotton. Calig. A. ii., fol. 89, the origin of the purgatory is thus described :—

> " Holy byschoppes some tyme ther were,
>   That tawgte me of Goddes lore.
>   In Irlonde preched Seyn Patryke,
>   In that londe was non hym lyke :
>   He prechede Goddes worde full wyde,
>   And tolde men what shullde betyde.
>   Fyrste he preched of Heven blysse,
>   Who ever go thyder may ryght nowgt mysse :
>   Sethen he preched of Hell pyne,
>   Howe wo them ys that cometh therinne :
>   And then he preched of purgatory,
>   As he fonde in hisstory,
>   But yet the folke of the contré
>   Beleved not that hit mygth be ;
>   And seyed, but gyf hit were so,
>   That eny non myth hymself go,
>   And se alle that, and come ageyn,
>   Then wolde they beleve fayn."

Vexed at the obstinacy of his hearers, S. Patrick besought the Almighty to make the truth manifest to the unbelievers ; whereupon

" God spakke to Saynt Patryke tho
By nam, and badde hym with Hym go :
He ladde hym ynte a wyldernesse,
Wher was no reste more ne lesse,
And shewed that he might se
Inte the erthe a pryvé entré :
Hit was yn a depe dyches ende.
' What mon,' He sayde, ' that wylle hereyn wende,
And dwelle theryn a day and a nyght,
And hold his byleve and ryght,
And come ageyn that he ne dwelle,
Mony a mervayle he may of telle.
And alle tho that doth thys pylgrymage,
I shalle hem graunt for her wage,
Whether he be sqwyer or knave,
Other purgatorye shalle he non have.'"

Thereupon S. Patrick, "he ne stynte ner day ne night," till he had built there a "fayr abbey," and stocked it with pious canons. Then he made a door to the cave, and locked the door, and gave the key to the keeping of the prior[2]. The Knight Owain, who had served under King Stephen, had lived a life of violence and dissolution; but filled with repentance, he sought by way of penance S. Patrick's Purgatory. Fifteen days he spent in preliminary devotions and alms-deeds, and then he heard mass, was washed with holy water, received the Holy Sacrament, and followed the sacred relics

[2] Wright, S. Patrick's Purgatory, p. 65.

in procession, whilst the priests sang for him the Litany, "as lowde as they mygth crye." Then Sir Owain was locked in the cave, and he groped his way onward in darkness, till he reached a glimmering light; this brightened, and he came out into an underground land, where was a great hall and cloister, in which were men with shaven heads and white garments. These men informed the knight how he was to protect himself against the assaults of evil spirits. After having received this instruction, he heard "grete dynn," and

> " Then come ther develes on every syde,
> Wykked gostes, I wote, fro Helle,
> So mony that no tonge mygte telle :
> They fylled the hows yn two rowes ;
> Some grenned on hym and some mad mowes."

He then visits the different places of torment. In one, the souls are nailed to the ground with glowing hot brazen nails; in another, they are fastened to the soil by their hair, and are bitten by fiery reptiles. In another, again, they are hung over fires by those members which had sinned, whilst others are roasted on spits. In one place were pits in which were molten metals. In these pits were men and women, some up to their chins, others to their breasts, others to their hams. The knight was pushed by the devils into one of these pits, and was dreadfully scalded, but he cried to the Saviour, and escaped. Then he visited a lake where souls were tormented with great cold; and a river of pitch, which he crossed on a frail and narrow bridge. Beyond this bridge was a wall of glass, in which opened a beautiful gate, which conducted into Paradise. This place so delighted him that he would fain have remained in it had he been suffered, but he was bidden return to earth and finish there his penitence. He was put into a shorter and pleasanter way back to the cave than that by which he had come ; and the prior found the knight next morning at the door, waiting to be let out, and full of his adventures. He afterwards went on a pilgrimage to the Holy Land, and ended his life in piety. " Explycit Owayne[3]."

Marie's translation is in three thousand verses ; Legrand d'Aussy has given the analysis of it in his " Fabliaux," tom. iv.

Giraldus Cambrensis, in his topography of Ireland, alludes to the Purgatory. He places the island of Lough Derg among one of the marvels of the country. According to him it is divided into

[3] Wright, Op. cit., cap. iii.

two parts, whereof one is fair and agreeable, and
contains a church, whilst the other is rough and
uncultivated, and a favourite haunt of devils.   In
the latter part of the island, he adds, there were
nine caves, in any one of which, if a person were
bold enough to pass the night, he would be so
tormented by the demons, that he would be fortunate if he escaped with life; and he says, it is
reported that a night so spent relieved the sufferer
from having to undergo the torments of purgatory
hereafter[4].

In the ancient Office of S. Patrick occurred the
following verse :—

> " Hic est doctor benevolus,
> Hibernicorum apostolus,
> Cui loca purgatoria
> Ostendit Dei gratia."

Joscelin, in his life of the saint, repeats the fable.
Henry de Knyghton, in his history, however,
asserts that it was not the Apostle of Ireland, but
an abbot Patrick, to whom the revelation of purgatory was made; and John of Brompton says the
same.   Alexander Neckham calls it S. Brandan's
Purgatory.   Cæsar of Heisterbach, in the begin-

---

[4] Girald. Cambr. Topog. Hiberniæ, cap. v.

ning of the 13th century, says, " If any one doubt
of purgatory, let him go to Scotland (i. e. Ireland),
and enter the Purgatory of S. Patrick, and his
doubts will be dispelled[5]." "This recommendation," says Mr. Wright, in his interesting and all
but exhaustive essay on the myth, " was frequently
acted upon in that, and particularly in the following century, when pilgrims from all parts of Europe,
some of them men of rank and wealth, repaired to
this abode of superstition. On the patent rolls in
the Tower of London, under the year 1358, we
have an instance of testimonials given by the king
(Edward III.) on the same day, to two distinguished
foreigners, one a noble Hungarian, the other a
Lombard, Nicholas de Beccariis, of their having
faithfully performed this pilgrimage. And still
later, in 1397, we find King Richard II. granting
a safe conduct to visit the same place, to Raymond,
Viscount of Perilhos, knight of Rhodes, and chamberlain of the King of France, with twenty men
and thirty horses. Raymond de Perilhos, on his
return to his native country, wrote a narrative of
what he had seen, in the dialect of the Limousan,

[5] Cæsar. Heist. De Miraculis sui Temporis, lib. xii.,
cap. 38. Ap. Wright.

of which a Latin version was printed by O'Sulle-van, in his ' Historia Catholica Iberniæ[6].'"

This work is simply the story of Owain slightly altered.

Froissart tells us of a conversation he had with one Sir William Lisle, who had been in the Purga-tory. " I asked him of what sort was the cave that is in Ireland, called S. Patrick's Purgatory, and if that were true which was related of it. He replied that there certainly was such a cave, for he and another English knight had been there whilst the king was at Dublin, and said that they entered the cave, and were shut in as the sun set, and that they remained there all night, and left it next morning at sunrise. And then I asked if he had seen the strange sights and visions spoken of. Then he said that when he and his companion had passed the gate of the Purgatory of S. Patrick, that they had descended as though into a cellar, and that a hot vapour rose towards them, and so affected their heads, that they were obliged to sit down on the stone steps. And after sitting there awhile they felt heavy with sleep, and so fell asleep, and slept all night. Then I asked if they

[6] Wright, Op. cit., p. 135.

knew where they were in their sleep, and what sort of dreams they had had; he answered that they had been oppressed with many fancies and wonderful dreams, different from those they were accustomed to in their chambers; and in the morning when they went out, in a short while they had clean forgotten their dreams and visions; wherefore he concluded that the whole matter was fancy."

The next to give us an account of his descent into S. Patrick's Purgatory, is William Staunton of Durham, who went down into the cave on the Friday next after the feast of Holyrood, in the year 1409. Mr. Wright has quoted the greater portion of his vision from a manuscript in the British Museum; I have only room for a few extracts, which I shall modernize, as the original spelling is somewhat perplexing.

"I was put in by the Prior of S. Matthew, of the same Purgatory, with procession and devout prayers of the prior, and the convent gave me an orison to bless me with, and to write the first word in my forehead, the which prayer is this, 'Jhesu Christe, Fili Dei vivi, miserere mihi peccatori.' And the prior taught me to say this prayer when any spirit good or evil, appeared unto me, or when I heard any noise that I should be afraid of." When left in the cave, William fell asleep, and dreamed that he saw coming to him S. John of Bridlington and S. Ive, who undertook to conduct him through the scenes of mystery. After they had proceeded a while, William was found to be guilty of a trespass against Holy Church, of which he had to be purged before he could proceed much further. Of this trespass he was accused by his sister who appeared in the way. "I make my complaint unto you against my brother that here standeth; for this man that standeth hereby loved me, and I loved him, and either of us would have had the other according to God's law, as Holy Church teaches, and I should have gotten of me three souls to God, but my brother hindered us from marrying." S. John of Bridlington then turned to William, and asked him why he did not allow the two who loved one another to be married. "I tell thee there is no man that hindereth man or woman from being united in the bond of God, though the man be a shepherd and all his ancestors, and the woman be come of kings or of emperors, or if the man be come of never so high kin, and the woman of never so low kin, if they love one another, but he sinneth in Holy Church against God and his deed,

and therefore he shall have much pain and tribula-
tions." Being assoiled of this crying sin, S. John
takes William to a fire "grete and styngkyng," in
which he sees people burning in their gay clothes.
"I saw some with collars of gold about their necks,
and some of silver, and some men I saw with gay
girdles of silver and gold, and harnessed with horns
about their necks, some with no jagges on their
clothes, than whole cloth, others full of jingles and
bells of silver all over set, and some with long
pokes on their sleeves, and women with gowns
trailing behind them a long space, and some with
chaplets on their heads of gold and pearls and
other precious stones. And I looked on him that
I saw first in pain, and saw the collars, and gay
girdles, and baldrics burning, and the fiends dragging
him by two fingermits. And I saw the jagges that
men were clothed in turn all to adders, to dragons,
and to toads, and 'many other orrible bestes'
sucking them, and biting them, and stinging them
with all their might, and through every jingle I
saw fiends smite burning nails of fire into their
flesh. I also saw fiends drawing down the skin of
their shoulders like to pokes, and cutting them off,
and drawing them to the heads of those they cut
them from, all burning as fire. And then I saw

the women that had side trails behind them, and
the side trails cut off by the fiends and burned on
their head; and some took of the cutting all
burning and stopped therewith their mouths, their
noses, and their ears. I saw also their gay chaplets of gold and pearls and precious stones, turned
into nails of iron, burning, and fiends with burning
hammers smiting them into their heads." These
were proud and vain people. Then he saw another
fire, where the fiends were putting out people's
eyes, and pouring molten brass and lead into the
sockets, and tearing off their arms, and the nails of
their feet and hands, and soldering them on again.
This was the doom of swearers. William saw
other fires wherein the devils were executing tortures varied and horrible on their unfortunate
victims. We need follow him no further.

At the end of the fifteenth century the Purgatory in Lough Derg was destroyed, by orders of
the pope, on hearing the report of a monk of
Eymstadt in Holland, who had visited it, and had
satisfied himself that there was nothing in it more
remarkable than in any ordinary cavern. The
Purgatory was closed on S. Patrick's day, 1497;
but the belief in it was not so speedily banished
from popular superstition. Calderon made it the

subject of one of his dramas ; and it became the subject of numerous popular chap-books in France and Spain, where during last century it occupied in the religious belief of the people precisely the same position which is assumed by the marvellous visions of heaven and hell sold by hawkers in England at the present day, one of which, probably founded on the old S. Patrick's Purgatory legend, I purchased the other day, and found it to be a publication of very modern date.

Unquestionably, the story of S. Patrick's Purgatory is founded on the ancient Hell-descents prevalent in all heathen nations ; Herakles, Orpheus, Odysseus, in Greek Mythology, Æneas, in Roman, descend to the nether world, and behold sights very similar to those described in the Christian legends just quoted. Among the Finns, Wainomoinen goes down into Pohjola, the land of darkness and fear; and the Esths tell of Kalewa plunging into a mysterious cave which led him to the abode of the foul fiend, where he visited his various courts, and whence he ravished his daughters. A still more striking myth is that of the ancient Quiches, contained in their sacred book, the Popol-Vuh ; in which the land of Xibalba contains mansions nearly as unpleasant as the fields and lakes of S. Patrick's

Purgatory. One is the house of gloom, another of men with sharp swords, another of heat, one of cold, one of the mansions is haunted by blood-sucking bats, another is the den of ferocious tigers[7]. Odin, in Northern Mythology, has mansions of cold and heat[8]; and Hell's abode is thus described:— "In Niflheim she possesses a habitation protected by exceedingly high walls and strongly barred gates. Her hall is called Elvidnir; Hunger is her table; Starvation, her knife; Delay, her man; Slowness, her maid; Precipice, her threshold; Care, her bed; and Burning Anguish forms the hangings of her apartment[9]." Into this the author of the Solarliod, in the Elder Edda, is supposed to have descended. This curious poem is attributed by some to Soemund the Wise (d. 1131), and is certainly not later. The composition exhibits a strange mixture of Christianity and Heathenism, whence it would seem that the poet's own religion was in a transition state:—

[7] Popul-Vuh: Brasseur de Boubourg, Paris, 1861; lib. ii. 7—14.

[8] Hrolf's Saga Kráka, cap. 39; in Fornm. Sögur I., pp. 77—79.

[9] Prose Edda, c. 33.

" 39. The sun I saw, true star of day,
   Sink in its roaring home ; but Hell's grated doors
   On the other side I heard heavily creaking.
51. In the Norn's seat nine days sat I,
   Thence was I mounted on a horse :
   There the giantess's sun shone grimly
   Through the dripping clouds of heaven.
52. Without and within, I seemed to traverse
   All the seven nether worlds ; up and down,
   I sought an easier way
   Where I might have the readiest paths."

He comes to a torrent about which flew "scorched
birds, which were souls, numerous as flies." Then
the wind dies away, and he comes to a land where
the waters do not flow. There false-faced women
grind earth for food.

" 58. Gory stones these dark women
   Turned sorrowfully ; out of their breasts
   Hung bleeding hearts, faint with much affliction."

He saw men with faces bloody, and heathen
stars above their heads, painted with deadly characters ; men who had envied others had bloody
runes cut in their breasts. Covetous men went to
Castle Covetous dragging weights of lead, murderers were consumed by venomous serpents,
sabbath-breakers were nailed by their hands to

hot stones.   Proud men were wrapped in flame,
slanderers had their eyes plucked out by Hell's
ravens.

> " 68. All the horrors thou wilt not get to know
>   Which Hell's inmates suffer.
>   Pleasant sins end in painful penalties :
>   Pains ever follow pleasure[1]."

Among the Greeks a descent into the cave of
Trophonius occupied much the same place in their
popular Mysticism that the Purgatory of S. Patrick
assumed among Christians.   Lustral rites, somewhat similar, preceded the descent, and the results
were not unlike[2].

It is worthy of remark that the myth of S. Patrick's Purgatory originated among the Kelts, and
the reason is not far to seek.   In ancient Keltic
Mythology the nether world was divided into three
circles, corresponding with Purgatory, Hell, and
Heaven ; and over Hell was cast a bridge, very
narrow, which souls were obliged to traverse if
they hoped to reach the mansions of light.   This
was—

> " The Brig o' Dread, na brader than a thread."

And the Purgatory under consideration is a reflex

---

[1] Edda of Sœmund, tr. by Thorpe, Part I., p. 117.
[2] Pausanias, ix. c. 39—40, and Plutarch., De genio Socrat.

of old Druidic teaching. Thus in an ancient Breton ballad Tina passes through the lake of pain, on which float the dead, white robed, in little boats. She then wades through valleys of blood[3].

As this myth has been exhaustively treated by Mr. Thomas Wright (S. Patrick's Purgatory; by T. Wright, London, 1844), it shall detain us no longer. I differ from him, however, as to its origin. He attributes it to monkish greed; but I have no hesitation in asserting that it is an example of the persistency of heathen myths, colouring and influencing Mediæval Christianity. We will only refer the reader for additional information to the *Purgatoire de Saint Patrice; légende du xiii* *Siècle*, 1842; a reprint by M. Prosper Tarbé of a MS. in the library at Rheims; a Mémoire by M. Paul Lacroix in the *Mélanges historiques*, published by M. Champollion Figeac, vol. iii.; the poem of Marie de France in the edition of her works, Paris, 1820, vol. ii.; an *Histoire de la Vie et du Purgatoire de S. Patrice*, par R. P. François Bouillon, O. S. F., Paris, 1651, Rouen, 1696; and also *Le Monde Enchanté*, par M. Ferdinand Denys, Paris, 1845, pp. 157—174.

[3] Lehrbuch der Religionsgeschichte: Band III., Die Kelten, p. 29.

The Terrestrial Paradise

THE exact position of Eden, and its present condition, does not seem to have occupied the minds of our Anglo-Saxon ancestors, nor to have given rise among them to wild speculations.

The map of the tenth century in the British Museum, accompanying the Periegesis of Priscian, is far more correct than the generality of maps which we find in MSS. at a later period; and Paradise does not occupy the place of Cochin China, or the isles of Japan, as it did later, after that the fabulous voyage of S. Brandan had become popular in the eleventh century[1]. The

---

[1] S. Brandan was an Irish monk, living at the close of the sixth century; he founded the Monastery of Clonfert, and is commemorated on May 16. His voyage seems to be founded on that of Sinbad, and is full of absurdities. It has been republished by M. Jubinal from MSS. in the Bibliothèque du Roi, Paris, 8vo., 1836; the earliest printed English edition is that of Wynkyn de Worde, London, 1516.

site, however, had been already indicated by
Cosmas, who wrote in the seventh century, and
had been specified by him as occupying a continent east of China, beyond the ocean, and still
watered by the four great rivers Pison, Gihon,
Hiddekel, and Euphrates, which sprang from subterranean canals. In a map of the ninth century,
preserved in the Strasbourg Library, the terrestrial
Paradise is, however, on the Continent, placed at
the extreme east of Asia ; in fact, is situated in the
Celestial Empire. It occupies the same position
in a Turin MS., and also in a map accompanying
a commentary on the Apocalypse in the British
Museum.

According to the fictitious letter of Prester John
to the Emperor Emanuel Comnenus, Paradise was
situated close to—within three days' journey of—
his own territories, but where those territories were,
is not distinctly specified.

" The river Indus, which issues out of Paradise,"
writes the mythical king, " flows among the plains,
through a certain province, and it expands, embracing the whole province with its various windings : there are found emeralds, sapphires, carbuncles, topazes, chrysolites, onyx, beryl, sardius,
and many other precious stones. There too grows

the plant called Asbestos." A wonderful fountain, moreover, breaks out at the roots of Olympus, a mountain in Prester John's domain, and "from hour to hour, and day by day, the taste of this fountain varies; and its source is hardly three days' journey from Paradise, from which Adam was expelled. If any man drinks thrice of this spring, he will from that day feel no infirmity, and he will, as long as he lives, appear of the age of thirty." This Olympus is a corruption of Alumbo, which is no other than Columbo in Ceylon, as is abundantly evident from Sir John Mandeville's Travels, though this important fountain has escaped the observation of Sir Emmerson Tennant.

"Toward the heed of that forest (he writes) is the cytee of Polombe, and above the city is a great mountayne, also clept Polombe. And of that mount, the Cytee hathe his name. And at the foot of that Mount is a fayr welle and a gret, that hathe odour and savour of all spices; and at every hour of the day, he chaungethe his odour and his savour dyversely. And whoso drynkethe 3 times fasting of that watre of that welle, he is hool of alle maner sykenesse, that he hathe. And thei that duellen there and drynken often of that welle, thei nevere han sykenesse, and thei semen alle weys yonge. I have dronken there of 3 or 4 sithes; and zit, methinkethe, I fare the better. Some men clepen it the Welle of Youthe : for thei that often drynken thereat, semen alle weys yongly, and lyven withouten sykenesse. And men seyn, that that welle comethe out of Paradys : and therefore it is so vertuous."

Gautier de Metz, in his poem on the "Image du Monde," written in the thirteenth century, places the terrestrial Paradise in an unapproachable region of Asia, surrounded by flames, and having an armed angel to guard the only gate.

Lambertus Floridus, in a MS. of the twelfth century, preserved in the Imperial Library in Paris, describes it as " Paradisus insula in oceano in oriente :" and in the map accompanying it, Paradise is represented as an island, a little south east of Asia, surrounded by rays, and at some distance from the mainland ; and in another MS. of the same library—a mediæval encyclopædia— under the word Paradisus is a passage which states that in the centre of Paradise is a fountain which waters the garden—that in fact described by Prester John, and that of which story-telling Sir John Mandeville declared he had " dronken 3 or 4 sithes." Close to this fountain is the Tree of Life.

The temperature of the country is equable ; neither frosts nor burning heats destroy the vegetation. The four rivers already mentioned rise in it. Paradise is, however, inaccessible to the traveller, on account of the wall of fire which surrounds it.

Paludanus relates in his " Thesaurus Novus," of course on incontrovertible authority, that Alexander the Great was full of desire to see the terrestrial Paradise, and that he undertook his wars in the East for the express purpose of reaching it, and obtaining admission into it. He states that on his nearing Eden an old man was captured in a ravine by some of Alexander's soldiers, and they were about to conduct him to their monarch, when the venerable man said, " Go and announce to Alexander that it is in vain he seeks Paradise ; his efforts will be perfectly fruitless, for the way of Paradise is the way of humility, a way of which he knows nothing. Take this stone and give it to Alexander, and say to him, 'From this stone learn what you must think of yourself.' " Now this stone was of great value and excessively heavy, outweighing and excelling in value all other gems, but when reduced to powder it was as light as a tuft of hay, and as worthless. By which token the mysterious old man meant, that Alexander alive was the greatest of monarchs, but Alexander dead would be a thing of nought.

That strangest of mediæval preachers, Meffreth, who got into trouble by denying the Immaculate Conception of the Blessed Virgin, in his second sermon for the Third Sunday in Advent, discusses the locality of the terrestrial Paradise, and claims S. Basil and S. Ambrose as his authorities for stating that it is situated on the top of a very lofty mountain in Eastern Asia ; so lofty indeed is the mountain, that the waters of the four rivers fall in cascade down to a lake at its foot, with such a roar that the natives who live on the shores of the lake are stone-deaf. Meffreth also explains the escape of Paradise from submergence at the Deluge, on the same grounds as does the Master of Sentences (lib. 2, dist. 17, c. 5), by the mountain being so very high that the waters which rose over Ararat were only able to wash its base.

A manuscript in the British Museum tells us that "Paradise is neither in heaven nor on earth. The book says that Noah's flood was forty fathoms high, over the highest hills that are on earth ; and Paradise is forty fathoms higher than Noah's flood was, and it hangeth between heaven and earth wonderfully, as the ruler of all things made it.

And it is perfectly level both in length and breadth. There is neither hollow nor hill ; nor is there frost nor snow, hail nor rain; but there is fons vitæ, that is, the well of life. When the calends of January commence, then floweth the well so beautifully and so gently, and no deeper than man may wet his finger on the front, over all that land. And so likewise each month, once when the month comes in the well begins to flow. And there is the copse of wood, which is called Radion Saltus, where each tree is as straight as an arrow, and so high, that no earthly man ever saw so high, or can say of what kind they are. And there never falleth leaf off, for they are evergreen, beautiful, and pleasant, full of happiness. Paradise is upright on the eastern part of this world. There is neither heat nor hunger, nor is there ever night, but always day. The sun there shineth seven times brighter than on this earth. Therein dwell innumerable angels of God with the holy souls till doomsday. Therein dwelleth a beautiful bird called Phœnix ; he is large and grand, as the Mighty One formed him ; he is the lord over all birds."—(MS. Cotton. Vespas. D. xiv., fol. 163.)

The monk who incited S. Brandan to undertake his mythical voyage told him that he had sailed due east from Ireland, and had come at last to Paradise, which was an island full of joy and mirth, and the earth as bright as the sun, and it was a glorious sight ; and the half-year he was there slipped by as a few moments. On his return to the abbey, his garments were still fragrant with the odours of Paradise. Brandan also arrived at the same island, and with his companions traversed it for the space of forty days without meeting any one, till he came to a broad river, on the banks of which stood a young man, who told him that this stream divided the world in twain ; and that none living might cross it.

In a MS. volume in the library of Corpus Christi College, Cambridge, is a map of the world, dating from the twelfth century, whereon Paradise is figured as an island opposite the mouth of the Ganges, which flows into the ocean somewhere about where the Amour in reality empties itself.

The Anglo-Saxon poem, " De Phœnice," in the Exeter book, a translation of the work of the Pseudo-Lactantius, asserts :—

> " I have heard tell
> That there is far hence
> In eastern parts
> A land most noble,
> Amongst men renowned.

> That tract of earth is not
> Over mid earth
> Fellow to many
> Peopled lands ;
> But it is withdrawn
> Through the Creator's might
> From wicked doers.
> Beauteous is all the plain,
> With delights blessed,
> With the sweetest
> Of earth's odours."

And then it rambles on in description of its delights, which may be imagined without further quotation.

The Hereford map of the thirteenth century represents the terrestrial Paradise as a circular island near India, cut off from the continent not only by the sea, but also by a battlemented wall, with a gateway to the west.

Rupert of Duytz regards it as having been situated in Armenia. Radulphus Highden, in the thirteenth century, relying on the authority of S. Basil and S. Isidore of Seville, places Eden in an inaccessible region of Oriental Asia ; and this was also the opinion of Philostorgus. Hugo de S. Victor, in his book "De Situ Terrarum," expresses himself thus:—"Paradise is a spot in the Orient productive of all kinds of woods and pomiferous trees. It contains the Tree of Life : there is neither cold nor heat there, but perpetual equable temperature. It contains a fountain which flows forth in four rivers."

Rabanus Maurus, with more discretion, says :— "Many folk want to make out that the site of Paradise is in the east of the earth, though cut off by the longest intervening space of ocean or earth from all regions which man now inhabits. Consequently, the waters of the Deluge, which covered the highest points of the surface of our orb, were unable to reach it. However, whether it be there, or whether it be any where else, God knows ; but that there *was* such a spot once, and that it was on earth, that is certain."

Jacques de Vitry ("Historia Orientalis"), Gervais of Tilbury, in his "Otia Imperalia," and many others, hold the same views as to the site of Paradise that were entertained by Hugo de S. Victor.

Jourdain de Sèverac, monk and traveller in the beginning of the fourteenth century, places the terrestrial Paradise in the " Third India ;" that is to say, in trans-Gangic India.

Leonardo Dati, a Florentine poet of the fifteenth century, composed a geographical treatise in verse, entitled "Della Sfera;" and it is in Asia that he locates the garden :—

"Asia è le prima parte dove l' huomo
Sendo innocente stava in Paradiso."

But perhaps the most remarkable account of the terrestrial Paradise ever furnished, is that of the "Eireks Saga Vídförla," an Icelandic narrative of the fourteenth century, giving the adventures of a certain Norwegian, named Eirek, who had vowed, whilst a heathen, that he would explore the fabulous Deathless Land of pagan Scandinavian mythology. The romance is possibly a Christian recension of an ancient heathen myth ; and Paradise has taken the place in it of Glœsisvellir.

According to the majority of the MSS. the story purports to be nothing more than a religious novel; but one audacious copyist has ventured to assert that it is all fact, and that the details are taken down from the lips of those who heard them from Eirek himself.   The account is briefly this :—

Eirek was a son of Thrand, king of Drontheim, and having taken upon him a vow to explore the Deathless Land, he went to Denmark, where he picked up a friend of the same name as himself. They then went to Constantinople, and called upon the Emperor, who held a long conversation with them, which is duly reported, relative to the truths of Christianity and the site of the Deathless Land, which, he assures them, is nothing more nor less than Paradise.

"The world," said the monarch, who had not forgotten his geography since he left school, "is precisely 180,000 stages round (about 1,000,000 English miles), and it is not propped up on posts— not a bit!—it is supported by the power of God ; and the distance between earth and heaven is 100,045 miles (another MS. reads 9382 miles—the difference is immaterial) ; and round about the earth is a big sea called Ocean." "And what's to the south of the earth?" asked Eirek. "Oh! there is the end of the world, and that is India." "And pray where am I to find the Deathless Land ?" "Paradise, I suppose you mean,—lies slightly east of India."

Having obtained this information, the two Eireks started, furnished with letters from the Greek Emperor.

They traversed Syria, and took ship—probably at Balsora ; then, reaching India, they proceeded on their journey on horseback, till they came to a dense forest, the gloom of which was so great, through the interlacing of the boughs, that even by day the stars could be observed twinkling, as though they were seen from the bottom of a well.

On emerging from the forest, the two Eireks came upon a strait, separating them from a beautiful land, which was unmistakably Paradise ; and the Danish Eirek, intent on displaying his Scriptural knowledge, pronounced the strait to be the river Pison. This was crossed by a stone bridge, guarded by a dragon.

The Danish Eirek, deterred by the prospect of an encounter with this monster, refused to advance, and even endeavoured to persuade his friend to give up the attempt to enter Paradise as hopeless, after that they had come within sight of the favoured land. But the Norseman deliberately walked, sword in hand, into the maw of the dragon, and next moment, to his infinite surprise and delight, found himself liberated from the gloom of the monster's interior, and safely placed in Paradise.

" The land was most beautiful, and the grass as gorgeous as purple ; it was studded with flowers, and was traversed by honey rills. The land was extensive and level, so that there was not to be seen mountain or hill, and the sun shone cloudless without night and darkness ; the calm of the air was great, and there was but a feeble murmur of wind, and that which there was, breathed redolent with the odour of blossoms." After a short walk, Eirek observed what certainly must have been a remarkable object, namely, a tower or steeple self-suspended in the air, without any support whatever, though access might be had to it by means of a slender ladder. By this Eirek ascended into a loft of the tower, and found there an excellent cold collation prepared for him. After having partaken of this he went to sleep, and in vision beheld and conversed with his guardian angel, who promised to conduct him back to his fatherland, but to come for him again, and fetch him away from it for ever at the expiration of the tenth year after his return to Drontheim.

Eirek then retraced his steps to India, unmolested by the dragon, which did not affect any surprise at having to disgorge him, and, indeed, which seems to have been, notwithstanding his looks, but a harmless and passive dragon.

After a tedious journey of seven years, Eirek reached his native land, where he related his adventures, to the confusion of the heathen, and to the delight and edification of the faithful. "And in the tenth year, and at break of day, as Eirek went to prayer, God's Spirit caught him away, and he was never seen again in this world : so here ends all we have to say of him[2]."

The Saga, of which I have given the merest outline, is certainly striking, and contains some beautiful passages. It follows the commonly-received opinion which identified Paradise with Ceylon ; and, indeed, an earlier Icelandic work, the "Rymbegla," indicates the locality of the terrestrial Paradise as being near India, for it speaks of the Ganges as taking its rise in the mountains of Eden. It is not unlikely that the curious history of Eirek, is a translation, with modifications, of a Keltic romance. I form this opinion from the introduction of the bridge over which Eirek has to pass, and the marvelous house suspended in air, which is an item peculiar to the Paradise of Druidical Mythology.

Later than the fifteenth century, we find no theories propounded concerning the terrestrial Paradise, though there are many treatises on the presumed situation of the ancient Eden. At Madrid was published a poem on the subject, entitled "Patriana decas," in 1629. In 1662 G. C. Kirchmayer, a Wittemberg professor, composed a

---

[2] Compare with this the death of Sir Galahad in the " Morte d'Arthur" of Sir Thomas Malory.

thoughtful dissertation, " De Paradiso," which he inserted in his " Deliciæ Æstivæ." Fr. Arnoulx wrote a work on Paradise in 1665, full of the grossest absurdities. In 1666 appeared Carver's " Discourse on the Terrestrian Paradise." Bochart composed a tract on the subject ; Huet wrote on it also, and his work passed through seven editions, the last dated from Amsterdam, 1701. The Père Hardouin composed a " Nouveau Traité de la Situation du Paradis Terrestre," La Haye, 1730. An Armenian work on the rivers of Paradise was translated by M. Saint Martin in 1819 ; and in 1842 Sir W. Ouseley read a paper on the situation of Eden, before the Literary Society in London.

S. George

A MORE interesting task for the comparative mythologist can hardly be found, than the analysis of the legends attaching to this celebrated soldier-martyr ;—interesting, because these legends contain almost unaltered representative myths of the Semitic and Aryan peoples, and myths which may be traced with certainty to their respective roots.

The popular traditions current relating to the Cappadocian martyr are distinct in the East and the West, and are alike sacred myths of faded creeds, absorbed into the newer faith, and re-coloured. On dealing with these myths, we are necessarily drawn into the discussion as to whether such a person as S. George existed, and if he did exist, whether he were a Catholic or a heretic. Eusebius says (Eccl. Hist. B. viii. c. 5), "Immediately on the first promulgation of the edict (of Diocletian), a certain man of no mean origin, but highly esteemed for his temporal dignities, as soon as the decree was published against the Churches in Nicomedia, stimulated by a divine zeal, and excited by an ardent faith, took it as it was openly placed and posted up for public inspection, and tore it to pieces as a most profane and wicked act. This, too, was done when two of the Cæsars were in the city, the first of whom was the eldest and chief of all, and the other held the fourth grade of the imperial dignity after him. But this man, as the first that was distinguished there in this manner, after enduring what was likely to follow an act so daring, preserved his mind calm and serene until the moment when his spirit fled."

This martyr, whose name Eusebius does not give, has been generally supposed to be S. George, and if so, this is nearly all we know authentic concerning him. But popular as a saint he unquestionably was, from a very early age. He is believed to have suffered at Nicomedia in 303, and his worship was soon extended through Phœnicia, Palestine, and the whole East. In the seventh century he had two Churches in Rome; in Gaul he was honoured in the fifth century. In an article contributed to the

Transactions of the Royal Society of Literature[1],
Mr. Hogg speaks of a Greek inscription copied
from a very ancient church, originally a heathen
temple at Ezra, in Syria, dated A.D. 346, in which
S. George is spoken of as a holy martyr. This is
important testimony, as at this very time was
living the other George, the Alexandrian bishop,
(d. 362) with whom the Saint is sometimes confounded.

The earliest acts quoted by the Bollandists, are
in Greek, and belong to the sixth century; they are
fabulous. Beside these, are some Latin acts, said
to have been composed by Pasikrâs, the servant of
the martyr, which belong to the eighth century, and
which are certainly translations of an earlier work
than the Greek acts printed by the Bollandists.
These are also apocryphal. Consequently we
know of S. George little, except that there was such
a martyr, that he was a native of Lydda, but
brought up in Cappadocia, that he entered the
Roman army and suffered a cruel death for Christ.
That his death was one of great cruelty, is rendered
probable by the manner in which his biographers
dilate on his tortures, all agreeing to represent them
as excessive.

[1] Second Series, vol. vii. pt. i.

The first to question the reverence shown for S. George was Calvin, who says ' Nil eos Christo reliquum facere qui pro nihilo ducunt ejus intercessionem, nisi accedant Georgius aut Hippolitus, aut similes larvæ.' Dr. Reynolds follows in the wake, and identifies the martyr with the Arian Bishop of Alexandria. This man had been born in a fuller's mill at Epiphania, in Cilicia. He is first heard of as purveyor of provisions for the army at Constantinople, where he assumed the profession of Arianism ; from thence, having been detected in certain frauds, he was obliged to fly, and take refuge in Cappadocia. His Arian friends obtained his pardon, by payment of a fine, and he was sent to Alexandria, where his party elected him Bishop, in opposition to S. Athanasius, immediately after the death of the Arian prelate, Gregory. There, associating with himself Dracontius, master of the mint, and the Count Diodorus, he tyrannized alike over Catholics and heathens, till the latter rose against him and put him to death. Dr. Heylin levelled a lance in honour of the Patron of England[2]; but his historical character was again questioned in 1753, by Dr. John Pettingal in a work on the original of the

[2] Historie of that Most famous Saint and Soldier of Christ Jesus, S. George of Cappadocia, 1633.

equestrian statue of S. George ; and he was answered by Dr. Samuel Pegge, in 1777, in a paper
read before the Society of Antiquaries. Gibbon,
without much investigation into the ground of the
charge, assumes the identity of the Saint and the
Arian prelate. " The odious stranger, disguising
every circumstance of time and place, assumed the
mask of a martyr, a saint, and a Christian hero ;
and the infamous George of Cappadocia has been
transformed into the renowned S. George of England, the patron of arms, of chivalry, and of the
Garter [3]."

The great improbability of such a transformation
would lead one to question the assertion, even if on
no other ground. Arians and Catholics were too
bitterly hostile, for it to be possible that a partisan
of the former, and a persecutor, should be accepted
as a saint by the latter. The writings of S. Athanasius were sufficiently known to the Mediævals to
save them from falling into such an error, and
S. Athanasius paints his antagonist in no charming colours. I am disposed to believe that there
really was such a person as S. George, that he was
a martyr to the Catholic faith, and that the very

---

[3] Gibbon's Decline and Fall, chap. xxiii.

uncertainty which existed regarding him, tended to give the composers of his biography the opportunity of attaching to him popular heathen myths, which had been floating unadopted by any Christian hero. The number of warrior saints was not so very great; Sebastian's history was fixed, so were those of Maurice and Gereon, but George was unprovided with a history. The deficiency was soon supplied. We have a similar instance in the story of S. Hippolitus. The ancient tale of the son of Theseus torn by horses was deliberately transferred to a Christian of the same name.

The substance of the Greek acts is to this effect:

George was born of Christian parents in Cappadocia. His father suffered a martyr's death, and the mother with her child took refuge in Palestine. He early entered the army, and behaved with great courage and endurance. At the age of twenty he was bereaved of his mother, and by her death came in for a large fortune. He then went to the court of Diocletian, where he hoped to find advancement. On the breaking out of the persecution, he distributed his money among the poor, and declared himself, before the Emperor, to be a Christian. Having been ordered to sacrifice, he refused, and was condemned to death.

The first day, he was thrust with spears to prison, one of the spears snapped like straw when it touched him. He was then fastened by the feet and hands to posts, and a heavy stone was laid upon his breast.

The second day, he was bound to a wheel set with blades of knives and swords. Diocletian believed him to be dead; but an angel appearing, George courteously saluted him in military fashion, whereby the persecutor ascertained that the Saint was still living. On removing him from the wheel, it was discovered that all his wounds were healed. George was then cast into a pit of quicklime, which, however, did not cause his death. On the next day but one, the Emperor sent to have his limbs broken, and he was discovered on his knees perfectly whole.

He was next made to run in red-hot iron shoes. The following night and day he spent in prayer, and on the sixth day he appeared before Diocletian walking and unhurt. He was then scourged with thongs of hide till his flesh came off his back, but was well next day.

On the seventh day he drank two cups, whereof the one was prepared to make him mad, the other to poison him, without experiencing any ill effects.

He then performed some miracles, raised a dead man to life, and restored to life an ox which had been killed ;—miracles which resulted in numerous conversions.

That night George dreamed that the Saviour laid a golden crown on his head, and bade him prepare for Paradise. S. George at once called to him the servant who wrote these memoirs (*ὅστις καὶ τὰ ὑπὸ τὸν ἅγιον ὑπομνήματα σὺν ἀκριβείᾳ πάσῃ συνέταξεν*), and commanded him, after his death, to take his body and will to Palestine. On the eighth day, the saint, by the sign of the cross, forced the devil inhabiting the statue of Apollo to declare that he was a fallen angel ; then all the statues of the gods fell before him.

This miracle converted the Empress Alexandra ; and Diocletian was so exasperated against the truth, that he condemned her to instant death. George was then executed. The day of his martyrdom was the 23rd of April.

The Latin acts may be summed up as follows ; they, as already stated, are a translation from a Greek original :

The devil urges Dacian, Emperor of the Persians, king of the four quarters of heaven, having domi nion over seventy-two kings, to persecute the

Church.   At this time lived George of Cappadocia, a native of Melitena.   Melitena is also the scene of his martyrdom.   Here he lived with a holy widow.   He is subjected to numerous tortures, such as the rack, iron pincers, fire, a sword-spiked wheel, shoes nailed to his feet; he is put into an iron box set within with sharp nails, and flung down a precipice; he is beaten with sledge-hammers, a pillar is laid on him, a heavy stone dashed on to his head; he is stretched on a red-hot iron bed, melted lead is poured over him; he is cast into a well, transfixed with forty long nails, shut into a brazen bull over a fire, and cast into a well with a stone round his neck.   Each time he returns from a torment, he is restored to former vigour. His tortures continue through seven years.   His constancy and miracles are the means of converting 40,900 men, and the Empress Alexandra.   Dacian then orders the execution of George and his queen; and as they die, a whirlwind of fire carries off the persecutor.

These two acts are the source of all later Greek legends.

Papenbroech prints legends by Simeon Metaphrastes (d. 904), Andreas Hierosolymites, and Gregorios Kyprios (d. 1289).

Reinbot von Dorn (cent. xiii.), or the French author from whom he translated the life of S. George, thought fit to reduce the extravagance of the original to moderate proportions, the seventy-two kings were reduced to seven, the countless tortures to eight; George is bound, and has a weight laid on him, is beaten with sticks, starved, put on a wheel covered with blades, quartered and thrown into a pond, rolled down a hill in a brazen bull, his nails transfixed with poisoned thorns, and he is then executed with the sword.

Jacques de Voragine says that he was first attached to a cross, and torn with iron hooks till his bowels protruded, and that then he was washed with salt water. Next day he was given poison to drink without its affecting him. Then George was fastened to a wheel covered with razors and knives, but the wheel snapped. He was next cast into a caldron of molten lead. George was uninjured by the bath. Then, at his prayer, lightning fell and destroyed all the idols, whilst the earth, opening, swallowed up the priests. At the sight of this, the wife of Dacian, whom Jacques de Voragine makes proconsul under Diocletian, is converted, and she and George are decapitated.

Thereupon lightning strikes Dacian and his ministers.

S. George, then, according to the Oriental Christian story, suffers at least seven martyrdoms, and revives after each, the last excepted.

The Mussulmans revere him equally with the Christians, and tell a tale concerning him having a strong affinity to that recorded in the acts. Gherghis, or El Khoudi, as he is called by them, lived at the same time as the Prophet. He was sent by God to the king of El Mauçil with the command that he should accept the faith. This the king refused to do, and ordered the execution of Gherghis. The saint was slain, but God revived him, and sent him to the king again. A second time was he slain, and again did God restore him to life. A third time did he preach his mission. Then the persecutor had him burned, and his ashes scattered in the Tigris. But God restored him to life once more, and destroyed the king and all his subjects[4]. The Greek historian, John Kantakuzenos (d. 1380) remarks, that in his time there were several shrines erected to the memory of George, at which the Mohammedans paid their devotions; and the traveller Burck-

---

[4] Mas'ûdi, übers. von Sprenger, vol. i. p. 120.

hardt relates, that "the Turks pay great veneration to S. George;" Dean Stanley moreover noticed a Mussulman chapel on the sea-shore near Sarafend, the ancient Sarepta, dedicated to El Khouder, in which "there is no tomb inside, only hangings before a recess. This variation from the usual type of Mussulman sepulchres was, as we were told by peasants on the spot, because El Khouder is not yet dead, but flies round and round the world, and these chapels are built wherever he has appeared [5]." Ibn Wahshíya al Kasdani was the translator of the Book of Nabathæan Agriculture. "Towards the year 900 of our era, a descendant of those ancient Babylonian families who had fled to the marshes of Wasith and of Bassora, where their posterity still dwell, was struck with profound admiration for the works of his ancestors, whose language he understood, and probably spoke. Ibn Wahshíya al Kasdani, or the Chaldæan, was a Mussulman, but Islamism only dated in his family from the time of his great-grandfather; he hated the Arabs, and cherished the same feeling of national jealousy towards them as the Persians also entertained against their conquerors. A piece of good fortune threw

[5] Sinai and Palestine, p. 274.

S. George

into his hands a large collection of Nabathæan
writings, which had been rescued from Moslem
fanaticism. The zealous Chaldæan devoted his life
to their translation, and thus created a Nabathæo-
Arabic library, of which three complete works, to
say nothing of the fragments of a fourth, have
descended to our days[6]." One of these is the
Book of Nabathæan Agriculture, written by
Kuthāmi the Babylonian. In it we find the
following remarkable passage : "The contemporaries of Yanbūshādh assert that all the sekā'in
of the gods and all the images lamented over Yanbūshādh after his death, just as all the angels and
sekā'in lamented over Tammūzī. The images (of
the gods), they say, congregated from all parts of
the world to the temple in Babylon, and betook
themselves to the temple of the Sun, to the great
golden image that is suspended between heaven
and earth. The Sun image stood, they say, in
the midst of the temple, surrounded by all the
images of the world. Next to it stood the images
of the Sun in all countries ; then those of the
Moon ; next those of Mars ; after them, the
images of Mercury ; then those of Jupiter ; after

[6] Ernest Renan, Essay on the Age and Antiquity of the
Book of Nabathæan Agriculture, London, 1862, p. 5.

them, those of Venus ; and last of all, of Saturn.
Thereupon the image of the Sun began to bewail
Tammūzī, and the idols to weep ; and the image of
the Sun uttered a lament over Tammūz and nar-
rated his history, whilst the idols all wept from the
setting of the sun till its rising at the end of that
night. Then the idols flew away, returning to their
own countries. They say that the eyes of the idol
of Tehāma (in South Arabia), called the eagle, are
perpetually flowing with tears, and will so continue,
from the night wherein it lamented over Tammūz
along with the image of the Sun, because of the
peculiar share that it had in the story of Tammūz.
This idol, called Nesr, they say, is the one that
inspired the Arabs with the gift of divination, so
that they can tell what has not yet come to pass,
and can explain dreams before the dreamers state
what they are. They (the contemporaries of Yanbūshādh) tell that the idols in the land of Babel
bewailed Yanbūshādh singly in all their temples a
whole night long till morning. During this night
there was a great flood of rain, with violent thunder
and lightning, as also a furious earthquake (in the
district) from the borders of the mountain ridge of
Holwān to the banks of the Tigris near the city
Nebārwājā, on the eastern bank of that river. The

S. George
280

idols, they say, returned during this flood to their places, because they had been a little shaken. This flood was brought by the idols as a judgment upon the people of the land of Babel for having abandoned the dead body of Yanbūshādh, as it lay on the bare ground in the desert of Shāmās, so that the flood carried his dead body to the Wādī el-A'hfar, and then swept it from this wādī into the sea. Then there was drought and pestilence in the land of Babel for three months, so that the living were not sufficient to bury the dead. These tales (of Ṭammūz and Yanbūshādh) have been collected and are read in the temples after prayers, and the people weep and lament much thereupon. When I myself am present with the people in the temple, at the feast of Tammūz, which is in the month called after him, and they read his story and weep, I weep along with them always, out of friendly feeling towards them, and because I compassionate their weeping, not that I believe what they relate of him. But I believe in the story of Yanbūshādh, and when they read it and weep, I weep along with them, very differently from my weeping over Tammūzī. The reason is this, that the time of Yanbūshādh is nearer to our own than the time of Tammūz, and his story is, therefore, more certain and worthy of belief. It is possible that some portions of the story of Tammūz may be true, but I have my doubts concerning other parts of it, owing to the distance of his time from ours."

Thus writes Kūthāmī the Babylonian, and his translator adds :—

"Says Abū Bekr A'hmed ibn Wa'hshīya. This month is called Tammūz, according to what the Nabathæans say, as I have found it in their books, and is named after a man of whom a strange long story is told, and who was put to death, they relate, several times in succession in a most cruel manner. Each of their months is named after some excellent and learned man, who was one, in ancient times, of those Nabathæans that in-habited the land of Babel before the Chaldæans. This Tammūz was not one of the Chaldæans, nor of the Canaanites, nor of the Hebrews, nor of the Assyrians, but of the primeval Ianbānīs. . . All the Ssabians of our time, down to our own day, wail and weep over Tammūz in the month of that name, on the occasion of a festival in his honour, and make great lamentation over him ; especially the women, who all arise, both here (at Bagdad) and at 'Harrān, and wail and weep

over Tammūz. They tell a long and silly story
about him ; but, as I have clearly ascertained,
not one of either sect has any certain information
regarding Tammūz, or the reason of their lamenting over him. However, after I had translated
this book, I found in the course of my reading
the statement that Tammūz was a man concerning
whom there was a legend, and that he had been
put to death in a shameful manner. That was all ;
not another word about him. They knew nothing
more about him than to say, 'We found our ancestors weeping and wailing over him in this way at
this feast that is called after him Tammūzi.' My
own opinion is, that this festival which they hold
in commemoration of Tammūz is an ancient one,
and has maintained itself till now, whilst the story
connected with him has been forgotten, owing to
the remoteness of his age, so that no one of these
Ssabians at the present day knows what his story
was, nor why they lament over him." Ibn
Wa'hshīya then goes on to speak of a festival
celebrated by the Christians towards the end of
the month Nisan (April) in honour of S. George,
who is said to have been several times put to death
by a king to whom he had gone to preach Christianity, and each time he was restored to life

again, but at the last died. Then Ibn Wa'hshīya remarks that what is related of the blessed George is the same as that told of Tammūz, whose festival is celebrated in the month Tammūz; and he adds that besides what he found regarding Tammūz in the "Agriculture," he lit on another Nabathæan book, in which was related in full the legend of Tammūz;—"how he summoned a king to worship the seven (planets) and the twelve (signs), and how the king put him to death several times in a cruel manner, Tammūz coming to life again after each time, until at last he died; and behold! it was identical with the legend of S. George that is current among the Christians [7]."

Mohammed en Medūn in his Fihrist-el-U'lūm, says, "Tammūz (July). In the middle of this month is the Feast El Būgāt, that is, of the weeping women, which Feast is identical with that Feast of Tā-uz, which is celebrated in honour of the god Tā-uz. The women bewail him, because his Lord had him so cruelly martyred,

---

[7] Chwolson: über Tammūz. St. Petersburg, 1860, pp. 41—56. The translation is for the most part from the Christian Remembrancer, No. cxii., an article on Tammūz, with the conclusions of which I cannot altogether agree. My own conviction as to Tammūz will be seen in the sequel.

his bones being ground in a mill, and scattered to the winds[8]."

We have then the Eastern myth of S. George identified with that of Tammūz, by one who is impartial. What that myth of Tammūz was in its entirety we cannot say, but we have sufficient evidence in the statement of Ibn Wa'hshīya to conclude that the worship of S. George and its popularity in the East, is mainly due to the fact of his being a Christianized Tammūz.

Professor Chwolson insists on Tammūz having been a man, deified and worshipped; and the review below referred to confirms this theory. I believe this to be entirely erroneous. Tammūz stands to Chaldee mythology in precisely the same relation that the Ribhavas do to that of the Vedas. A French orientalist, M. Nève, wrote a learned work in 1847, on these ancient Indian deities, to prove that they were deified sages. But the careful study of the Vedic hymns to the Ribhus lead to an entirely opposite conclusion. They are the Summer breezes deified, which, in that they waft the smoke of the sacrifices to heaven, are addressed as assisting at the sacred offerings;

[8] Chwolson: Die Ssabier, ii. 27.

and in a later age, when their real signification was lost, they were anthropomorphized into a sacred caste of priests. A similar process has, I believe, taken place with Tammūz, who was the sun, regarded as a God and hero, dying at the close of each year, and reviving with the new one. In Kuthāmi's age the old deity was apparently misappreciated, and had suffered, in consequence, a reincarnation in Yanbūshādh, of whom a similar story was told, and who received similar worship, because he was in fact one with Tammūz. Almost exactly the same legend is related by the Jews of Abraham, who, they say, was cruelly tortured by Nimrod, and miraculously preserved by God [9].

The Phœnician Adonis was identical with Tammūz. S. Jerome in the Vulgate rendered the passage in Ezekiel (viii. 14), "He brought me to the door of the gate of the Lord's house, which was towards the north; and behold, there sat women weeping for Tammūz," by *ecce mulieres sedentes plangentes Adonidem;* and in his commentary on the passage says, "Whom we have interpreted Adonis, both the Hebrew and Syriac

[9] Leben Abrahams nach Ausfassung der Judischen Sage, v. Dr. B. Beer, Leipzig, 1859.

languages call Thamuz . . . and they call the month June by that name." He informs us also of a very important fact, that the solstice was the time when Tammūz was believed to have died, though the wailing for him took place in June. Consequently Tammūz's martyrdom took place at the end of December. Cyril of Alexandria also tells us of the identity existing between Adonis and Tammūz (in Isaiah, chap. xviii.).

The name Adonis is purely Semitic, and signifies the Lord. His worship was introduced to the Greeks by the Phœnicians through Crete.

Adonis is identified with the Sun in one of the Orphic hymns : "Thou shining and vanishing in the beauteous circle of the Horæ, dwelling at one time in gloomy Tartarus, at another elevating thyself to Olympus, giving ripeness to the fruits [1]!" According to Theocritus, this rising and setting, this continual coursing, is accomplished in twelve months : "In twelve months the silent pacing Horæ follow him from the nether-world to that above, the dwelling of the Cyprian goddess, and then he declines again to Acheron [2]." The cause of these wanderings, according to the fable,

[1] Orph. Hymn lv. 5, and 10, 11.
[2] Theocrit. Id. xv. 103, 104, 136.

was that two goddesses loved Adonis, Aphrodite, or more properly Astarte, and Persephone.
Aphrodite, the Syrian Baalti, loved him so tenderly
that the jealousy of Ares was aroused, and he
sent a wild boar to gore him in the chase. When
Adonis descended to the realm of darkness, Persephone was inflamed with passion for the comely
youth. Consequently a strife arose between her
and Aphrodite, which should possess him. The
quarrel was settled by Zeus dividing the year
into three portions, whereof one, from the summer
solstice to the autumn equinox, was to belong
to Adonis, the second was to be spent by
him with Aphrodite, and the third with Persephone. But Adonis voluntarily surrendered his
portion to the goddess of beauty [3]. Others say,
that Zeus decreed that he should spend six months
in the heavens with Aphrodite, and the other six
in the land of gloom with Persephone [4].

The worship of Adonis, who was the same as
Baal, was general in Syria and Phœnicia. The
devotion to Tammūz, we are told, was popular
from Antioch to Elymaïs [5]. It penetrated into

[3] Cyrill. Alex. in Isa.; Apollodor. lib. iii. c. 14.
[4] Schol. in Theocrit. Id. iii. v. 48, and xv. v. 103.
[5] Ammian. Marcell. xxii. 9. Œlian, Hist. animal. xii. 33.

Greece from Crete. Biblos in Phœnicia was the main seat of this worship.

Tammūz, or Adonis, was again identical with Osiris. This is stated by several ancient writers [6].

The myth relating to Osiris was very similar. The Egyptian sun-god was born at the summer solstice and died at the winter solstice, when processions went round the temple seeking him, seven times. Osiris in heaven was the beloved of Isis, in the land of darkness was embraced by Nepthys.

Typhon, as the Greeks call Seth or Bes, a monster represented in swine or boar shape, attacked Osiris, and slaying him, cut him up, and cast him into the sea. This took place on the 17th of the month Athor.

Then began the wailing for Osiris, which lasted four days; this was followed by the seeking, and this again by the finding of the God.

Under another form, the same myth, and its accompanying ceremonies, prevailed in Egypt, just as at Babylon that of Tammūz had its reflection in the more modern *cultus* of Yanbūshādh. The soul of the deceased Osiris was supposed to be incarnate in Apis; and, in process of mythologic degradation, the legend of Osiris passed over to Apis, and with

[6] Lucian. de dea Syria. n. 7. Steph. de Urb. v.

it the significant ceremonial. Thus Herodotus tells us how that at Memphis the death of the sacred bull was a cause of general wailing, and its discovery one of exultation. When Cambyses was in Egypt, and the land groaned under foreign sway, no Apis appeared; but when his two armies were destroyed, and he came to Memphis, Apis had appeared; and he found the conquered people manifesting their joy in dances, and with feasting and gay raiment [7].

We have, it will be seen, among Phœnicians, Syrians, Egyptians, and Nabathæans, all Semitic nations, peculiar myths, with symbolic ceremonies bearing such a close resemblance to one another, that we are constrained to acknowledge them as forms, slightly varied, of some primæval myth.

We find also among the Arabs, another Semitic nation, a myth identical with that of the Babylonian Tammūz, prevalent among them not long after their adoption of Islamism. How shall we account for this? My answer is, that the pre-Mohammedan Arabs had a worship very similar to that of Tammūz, Baal, Adonis, or Osiris, and that, on their conversion to the faith of the prophet, they retained the ancient legend, adapting it to El Koudir, whom

[7] Thalia. c. 27.

they identified with S. George, because they found
that the Christians had already adopted this course,
and had fixed the ancient myth on the martyr of
Nicomedia. In Babylonia it had already passed to
Yanbūshādh; and it was made to pass further to
Gherghis, much as in Greece the story of Apollo
and Python was transferred to Perseus and the sea-
monster, and, as we shall see presently, was adopted
into Christian mythology, and attributed to the
subject of this paper. And indeed the process
was perhaps facilitated by the fact that one
of the names of this solar god was Giggras; he
was so called after the pipes used in wailing for
him.

The circumstances of the death of Tammūz vary
in the different Semitic creeds.

Let me place them briefly in apposition.

Nabathæan myth. Tammūz.

A great hero, and prophet; is cruelly put to
death several times, but revives after each martyrdom. His death a subject of wailing.

Phœnician myth. Adon or Baal.

A beautiful deity, killed by the furious Boar god.
Revived and sent to heaven. Divides his time
between heaven and hell, subject of wailing,
seeking, and finding.

Syrian myth.   Baal.

Identical with the Phœnician.

Egyptian myth.   Osiris.

A glorious god and great hero, killed by the evil god.   Passes half his time in heaven, and half in the nether world.   Subject of wailing, seeking, and finding.

Arabian myth.   El Khouder, original name Ta'uz.

A prophet, killed by a wicked king several times and revived each time.

Oriental Christian myth.   S. George.

A soldier, killed by a wicked king, undergoes numerous torments, but revives after each.   On earth lives with a widow.   Takes to the other world with him the queen.   Wailing and seeking fall away, and the festival alone remains.

From this tabular view of the legends it is, I think, impossible not to see that S. George, in his mythical character, is a Semitic god Christianized. In order to undergo the process of conversion, a few little arrangements were rendered necessary, to divest the story of its sensuous character, and purify it.   Astarte or Aphrodite had to be got out of the way somehow.   She was made into a pious widow, in whose house the youthful saint lodged.

Then Persephone, the queen of Hades, had to be

accounted for. She was turned into a martyr, Alexandra ; and just as Persephone was the wife of the ruthless monarch of the nether world, so was Alexandra represented as the queen of Diocletian or Datian, and accompanied George to the unseen world. Consequently in the land of light, George was with the widow; in that of gloom, with Alexandra : just as Osiris spent his year between Isis and Nepthys, and Adonis between Aphrodite and Persephone. According to the ancient Christian legend, the body of George travelled from the place of his martyrdom to that of his nativity ; this resembles the journey of the body of Osiris, down the Nile, over the waves to Biblos, where Isis found him again.

The influence of Persian mythology is also perceptible in the legend. El Nedim says that Tammūz was brayed in a mill ; this feature in his martyrdom is adopted from the Iranian tradition of Hom, the Indian Soma, or the divine drink of sacrifice, which was anthropomorphized, and the history of the composition of the liquor was transformed into the fable of the hero. The Hom was pounded in a mortar, and the juice was poured on the sacrificial flames, and thus carried up into heaven in fire ; in the legend of the demigod, Hom was a martyr who was cruelly bruised and broken in a mortar, but who revived, and ascended to the skies. In the tale of George there is another indication of the absorption into it of a foreign myth. George revives the dead cow of the peasant Glycerius ; the same story is told of Abbot William of Villiers, of S. Germanus, of S. Garmon, and of S. Mochua. Thor also brought to life goats which had been killed and eaten. The same is told in the Rigveda of the Ribhus : "O sons of Sudharvān, out of the hide have you made the cow to arise ; by your songs the old have you made young, and from one horse have you made another horse[8]."

The numbers in the legend of the soldier-saint have a solar look about them. The torments of S. George last seven years, or, according to the Greek acts, seven days ; the tyrant reigns over the four quarters of heaven, and seven kings ; in the Nabathæan story, Tammūz preaches the worship of the seven planets, and the twelve signs of the Zodiac. Osiris is sought seven days. The seven winter months are features in all mythologies.

The manner in which S. George dies repeatedly represents the different ways in which the sun dies

[8] See my note in Appendix to " The Folklore of the N. Counties of England," London, 1866. pp. 321-4.

each day. The Greeks, and, indeed, most nations, regarded the close of day as the expiration of the solar deity, and framed myths to account for his decease. In Greek mythology the solar gods are many, and the stories of their deaths are distributed so as to provide each with his exit from the world; but in Semitic mythology it is not so, the sun-god is one, and all kinds of deaths are attributed to him alone, or, if he suffers anthropomorphism, to his representative.

Phaethon is a solar deity; he falls into the western seas. Herakles is another; he expires in flames, rending the poisoned garment given him by Dejanira. Phaethon's death represents the rapid descent of the sun in the west; that of Herakles, the setting orb in a flaming western sky rending the fire-lined clouds, which wrap his body. The same blaze, wherein sank the sun, was also supposed to be a funeral pyre, on which lay Memnon; and the clouds fleeting about it, some falling into the fire, and some scudding over the darkling sky, were the birds which escaped from the funeral pyre. Achilles, a humanized sun-god, was vulnerable in his heel, just as the Teutonic Sigfried could only be wounded in his back: this represents the sun as retiring from the heavens with his back turned, struck by the weapon of darkness, just as Ares, the blind God, with his tusk slew Adonis, or sightless Hodr with his mistletoe shaft smote Baldur.

In the S. George fable, we have the martyr, like Memnon or Herakles, on the fire, and transfixed, like Achilles and Ajax ; exposed in a brazen bull on a fire, that is, hung in the full rain-cloud over the western blaze ; cast down a hill, like Phaethon ; plunged into boiling metal, a representation of the lurid vapours of the west.

Having identified S. George or Tammūz with the sun, we shall have little difficulty in seeing that Aphrodite or Isis is the moon when visible, and Persephone or Nepthys the waned moon ; Persephone is in fact no other than Aphrodite in the region of gloom, where, according to the decree of Zeus, she was to spend six months with Aidoneus, and six months in heaven.

But it is time for us to turn to the Western myth, that of the fight of S. George with the dragon ; in this, again, we shall find sacred beliefs of antiquity reappearing in Christian form.

The story of S. George and the dragon first presents itself in the Legenda Aurea of Jacques de Voragine. It was accepted by the unquestioning clerks and laity of the middle ages, so that it found its way into the office-books of the Church.

> O Georgi Martyr inclyte,
> Te decet laus et gloria,
> Predotatum militia;
> Per quem puella regia,
> Existens in tristitia,
> Coram Dracone pessimo,
> Salvata est. Ex animo
> Te rogamus corde intimo,
> Ut cunctis cum fidelibus
> Cœli jungamur civibus
> Nostris ablatis sordibus:
> Et simul cum lætitia
> Tecum simus in gloria;
> Nostraque reddant labia
> Laudes Christo cum gratia,
> Cui sit honos in secula.

Thus sang the clerks from the Sarum "Horæ B. Mariæ," on S. George's day, till the reformation of the Missals and Breviaries by Pope Clement VII., when the story of the dragon was cut out, and S. George was simply acknowledged as a martyr, reigning with Christ. His introit was from Ps. lxiii. The Collect, "God, who makest us glad through the merits and intercession of blessed George the martyr, mercifully grant that we who ask through him Thy good things may obtain the gift of Thy grace." The Epistle,

2 Tim. ii. 8—11, and iii. 10—13 ; and the Gospel,
S. John xv. 1—8.

The legend, as told by Voragine, is this :—

George, a tribune, was born in Cappadocia, and
came to Lybia, to the town called Silene, near
which was a pond infested by a monster, which
had many times driven back an armed host that
had come to destroy him. He even approached the
walls of the city, and with his exhalations poisoned
all who were near. To avoid such visits, he was
furnished each day with two sheep, to satisfy his
voracity. If these were not given, he so attacked
the walls of the town, that his envenomed breath
infected the air, and many of the inhabitants died.
He was supplied with sheep, till they were exhausted, and it was impossible to procure the
necessary number. Then the citizens held counsel, and it was decided that each day a man and
a beast should be offered, so that at last they gave
up their children, sons and daughters, and none
were spared. The lot fell one day on the princess.
The monarch, horror-struck, offered in exchange
for her his gold, his silver, and half his realm, only
desiring to save his daughter from this frightful
death. But the people insisted on the sacrifice of
the maiden, and all the poor father could obtain,

was a delay of eight days, in which to bewail the fate of the damsel. At the expiration of this time, the people returned to the palace, and said, "Why do you sacrifice your subjects for your daughter? We are all dying before the breath of this monster!" The king felt that he must resolve on parting with his child. He covered her with royal clothes, embraced her, and said, "Alas! dear daughter, I thought to have seen myself re-born in your offspring. I hoped to have invited princes to your wedding, to have adorned you with royal garments, and accompanied you with flutes, tambourins, and all kinds of music; but you are to be devoured by this monster! Why did not I die before you?"

Then she fell at her father's feet and besought his blessing. He accorded it her, weeping, and he clasped her tenderly in his arms; then she went to the lake. George, who passed that way, saw her weeping, and asked the cause of her tears. She replied :—"Good youth! quickly mount your horse and fly, lest you perish with me." But George said to her :—"Do not fear; tell me what you await, and why all this multitude look on." She answered :—"I see that you have a great and noble heart; yet, fly!" "I shall not go without knowing the cause," he replied. Then she explained all to him ; whereupon he exclaimed :— "Fear nothing ! in the name of Jesus Christ, I will assist you." "Brave knight !" said she ; "do not seek to die with me ; enough that I should perish ; for you can neither assist nor deliver me, and you will only die with me."

At this moment the monster rose above the surface of the water. And the virgin said, all trembling, "Fly, fly, sir knight !"

His only answer was the sign of the cross. Then he advanced to meet the monster, recommending himself to God.

He brandished his lance with such force, that he transfixed it, and cast it to the ground. Then, addressing the princess, he bade her pass her girdle round it, and fear nothing. When this was done, the monster followed like a docile hound. When they had brought it into the town, the people fled before it ; but George recalled them, bidding them put aside all fear, for the Lord had sent him to deliver them from the dragon. Then the king and all his people, twenty thousand men, without counting women and children, were baptized, and George smote off the head of the monster.

Other versions of the story are to the effect that
the princess was shut up in a castle, and that
all within were perishing for want of water,
which could only be obtained from a fountain
at the base of a hill, and this was guarded by
the "laidly worm," from which George delivered
them.

> " The hero won his well-earn'd place
>   Amid the saints, in death's dread hour;
> And still the peasant seeks his grace,
>   And next to God, reveres his power.
> In many a church his form is seen
> ,With sword, and shield, and helmet sheen :
> Ye know him by his steed of pride,
> And by the dragon at his side."

CHR. SCHMID.

The same story has attached itself to other saints
and heroes of the middle ages, as S. Secundus of
Asti, S. Victor, Gozo of Rhodes, Raimond of S.
Sulpice, Struth von Winkelried, the Count Aymon,
Moor of Moorhall, "who slew the dragon of Want-
ley," Conyers of Sockburn, and the Knight of
Lambton, "John that slew ye Worme." Ariosto
adopted it into his Orlando Furioso, and made
his hero deliver Angelica from Orca, in the true
mythic style of George[9]; and it appears again in

---

[9] Orland. Fur. c. xi.

the tale of Chederles [1]. The cause of the legend attaching itself to our hero, was possibly a mis-understanding of an encomium, made in memory of S. George, by Metaphrastes, which concludes thus : "Licebat igitur videre astutissimum Draconem, adversus carnem et sanguinem gloriari solitum, elatumque, et sese efferentem, a juvene uno illu-sum, et ita dispectum atque confusum, ut quid ageret non haberet." Another writer, summing up the acts of S. George, says : "Secundo quod Dra-conem vicit qui significat Diabolum ;" and Hos-pinian, relating the sufferings of the martyr, affirms distinctly that his constancy was the occasion of the creation of the legend by Voragine [2].

If we look at the story of Perseus and Andro-meda, we shall find that in all essential particulars it is the same as that of the Cappadocian Saint.

Cassiope having boasted herself to be fairer than Hera, Poseidon sent a flood and a sea-monster to ravage the country belonging to her husband Cepheus. The oracle of Ammon having been consulted, it was ascertained that nothing would stop the resentment of the gods except the ex-posure of the king's daughter, Andromeda, on a

---

[1] Noël: Dict. de la Fable; art. Chederles.
[2] Christian Remembrancer, vol. xlv. p. 320.

rock, to be devoured by the monster. At the moment that the dragon approached the maiden, Perseus appeared, and learning her peril, engaged the monster and slew him.

The scene of this conflict was near Joppa, where in the days of S. Jerome the bones of the huge reptile were exhibited, and Josephus pretends to have seen there the chains which attached the princess to the rock[3]. It was at Berytus (Beyrut) that the fight of S. George with the dragon took place.

Similar stories were prevalent in Greece. In the isle of Salamis, Cenchrius, a son of Poseidon, relieved the inhabitants from the scourge of a similar monster, who devastated the island. At Thespia, a dragon ravaged the country round the city; Zeus ordered the inhabitants to give the monster their children by lot. One year it fell on Cleostratus. Menestratus determined to save him. He armed himself with a suit covered with hooks, and was devoured by the dragon, which perished in killing him. Pherecydes killed a great serpent in Caulonia, an adventure afterwards related of Pythagoras, with the scene shifted to Sybaris; and Herakles, as is well known, slew Hydra. But these are all ver-

---

[3] Hieron. Epist. 108. Joseph. Bell. Jud. iii. c. 7.

sions—echoes—of the principal myth of Apollo and Python.

The monster Python was sent by Hera to persecute Leto, when pregnant. Apollo, the moment that he was born, attacked the hideous beast and pierced him with his arrows. And from the place where the serpent died, there burst forth a torrent.

A similar myth is found among the Scandinavian and Teutonic nations. In these Northern mythologies Apollo is replaced by Sigurd, Sigfried, and Beowulf.

The dragon with which Sigurd fights is Fafnir, who keeps guard over a treasure of gold. Sigfried, in like manner, in the Nibelungen Lied, fights and overcomes a mighty dragon, and despoils him of a vast treasure. The Anglo-Saxon poem of Beowulf contains a similar engagement. A monster Grendel haunts a marsh near a town on the North Sea. At night the evil spirit rises from the swamp, and flies to the mountains, attacking the armed men, and slaying them. Beowulf awakes, fights him, and puts him to flight. But next night Grendel again attacks him, but is killed by the hero with an enchanted sword. He fights a dragon some years later, and robs it of an incalculable store of gold. The Icelandic Sagas teem with similar stories; and they abound in all European household tales.

In the Rigveda we have the same story. Indra fights with the hideous serpent Ahi, or Vrita, who keeps guard over the fountain of rains. In Iranian mythology, the same battle is waged between Mithra and the dæmon Ahriman.

It seems, then, that the fight with the dragon is a myth common to all Aryan peoples.

Its signification is this:—

The maiden which the dragon attemps to devour is the earth. The monster is the storm-cloud. The hero who fights it is the sun, with his glorious sword, the lightning-flash. By his victory the earth is relieved from her peril. The fable has been varied to suit the atmospheric peculiarities of different climes in which the Aryans found themselves. In India, Vrita is coiled about the source of water, and the earth is perishing for want of rain, till pierced by the sword of Indra, when the streams descend. "I will sing," says the Rigveda, "the ancient exploits by which flashing Indra is distinguished. He has struck Ahi, he has scattered the waters on the earth, he has unlocked the torrents of the heavenly mountains (i. e., the clouds). He has struck Ahi, who lurked in the bosom of the celestial mountain, he has struck him with that sounding weapon wrought for him by Twachtri ; and the waters, like cattle rushing to their stable, have poured down on the earth[4]." And again :—

"O Indra, thou hast killed the violent Ahi, who withheld the waters !"

"O Indra, thou hast struck Ahi, sleeping guardian of the waters, and thou hast precipitated them into the sea ; thou hast pierced the compact scale of the cloud ; thou hast given vent to the streams, which burst forth on all sides[5]."

Among the ancient Iranians the same myth prevailed, but was sublimated into a conflict between good and evil. Ahriman represents Ahi, and is the principle of evil ; corrupted into Kharaman, it became the Armenian name for a serpent and the devil. Ahriman entered heaven in the shape of a dragon, was met by Mithra, conquered, and like the old serpent of Apocalyptic vision, "he

---

[4] Rigveda, sect. i. lec. 2. p. xiii. Ed. Langlois, iii. p. 329.

[5] Ibid. vol. i. p. 44 ; ii. p. 447. In the Katha Sarit Sagara, a hero fights a dæmon monster, and releases a beautiful woman from his thraldom. The story as told by Soma Deva has already progressed and assumed a form very similar to that of Perseus and Andromeda. Katha Sarit Sagara, book vii. c. 42.

shall be bound for three thousand years, and burned at the end of the world in melted metals [6]," Aschmogh (Asmodeus) is also the infernal serpent of the books of the Avesta ; he is but another form of Ahriman. This fable rapidly followed in Persia the same process of application to known historical individuals that it pursued in Europe. In the ninth hymn of the Yaçna, Zoroaster asks Hōma who were the first of mortals to honour him, and Hōma replies : " The first of mortals to whom I manifested myself was Vivanghvat, father of Yima, under whom flourished the blessed age which knew not cold of winter, or scorching heat of summer, old age or death, or the hatred produced by the Devas. The second was Athwya, father of Thraetana, the conqueror of the dragon Dahak, with three heads, and three throats, and six eyes, and a thousand strengths." This Thraetana, in the Shahnāmeh, has become Feridun, who overcomes the great dragon Zohak.

In northern mythology, the serpent is probably the winter cloud, which broods over and keeps from mortals the gold of the sun's light and heat, till in the spring the bright orb overcomes the powers of darkness and tempest, and scatters his gold

[6] Boundehesch, ii. 351. 416.

over the face of the earth. In the ancient Sagas
of Iceland, the myth has assumed .a very peculiar
form, which, if it would not have protracted this
article to an undue length, I should have been glad
to have followed out. The hero descends into
a tomb, where he fights a vampire, who has
possession of a glorious sword, and much gold and
silver. After a desperate struggle, the hero overcomes, and rises with the treasures to the surface
of the earth. This too, represents the sun in the
northern realms, descending into the tomb of winter,
and there overcoming the power of darkness, from
whom he takes the sword of the lightning, and the
treasures of fertility, wherewith the earth is blessed
on the return of the sun to the skies in summer.·

This is probably the ancient form of the Scandinavian myth, and the King of gloom reigning over
his gold in the cairn, was only dragonized when the
Norse became acquainted with the dragon myths of
other nations. In the Saga of Hromund Greipson,
the hero is let down by a rope into a barrow, into
which he had been digging for six days. He found
below the old king Thrain the Viking, with a kettle
of quivering red flames suspended from the roof of
the vault above him. This king, years before, had
gathered all the treasures that he had obtained in

a long life of piracy, and had suffered himself to be buried alive with his ill-gotten wealth. Hromund found him seated on a throne in full armour, girded with his sword, crowned, and with his feet resting on three boxes containing silver. We have the same story in the Gretla; only there the dead king is Karr the old; Grettir is led to open his cairn, by seeing flames dancing on the mound at night. In the struggle underground, Grettir and the vampire stumble over the bones of the old king's horse, and thereby Grettir is able to get the upper hand.

Similar stories occur in the Flóamanna Saga, the younger Saga of Olaf the saint (cap. 16), the elder Olaf Saga (3—4), the history of Olaf Geirstafaalp, the Holmverja Saga, and the Bârda Saga. The last of these is strongly impressed with Christian influence, and gives indications of the transformation of the evil being into a dragon. Gest visited an island off the coast of Helluland (Labrador), where lay buried a grimly dæmon king Raknar. He took with him a priest with holy water and a crucifix. They had to dig fifty fathoms before they reached the chamber of the dead. Into this Gest descended by a rope, holding a sword in one hand, and a taper in the other. He saw below a great dragon-ship, in which sat five hundred men, champions of the old king, who were buried with him. They did not stir, but gazed with blank eyes at the taper flame, and snorted vapour from their nostrils. Gest despoiled the old king of all his gold and armour, and was about to rob him of his sword, when the taper expired. Then, at once, the five hundred rose from the dragon-ship, and the dæmon king rushed at him; they grappled and fought. In his need, Gest invoked S. Olaf, who appeared with light streaming from his body, and illumining the interior of the cairn. Before this light, the power of the dead men failed, and Gest completed his work in the vault[7]. In the story of Sigurd and Fafnir, the dragon is more than half man; but in the battle of Gull-Thorir the creature is scaled and winged in the most approved Oriental style[8].

Let me place in apposition a few of the Aryan myths relating to the strife between the sun and the dæmon of darkness, or storm.

Indian myth. Indra fights Ahi.

Indra kills Ahi, who is identified with the storm-cloud, and releases from him the pent-up waters, for want of which the earth is perishing. Ahi a serpent.

---

[7] Bårdar S. Snæfellsass. Kjobnhavn. 1860. pp. 41—43.
[8] Gull-Thoris Saga. Leipzig, 1858. c. iv.

Persian myth.　Mithra and Ahriman.

Mithra is clearly identical with the sun, and Ahriman with darkness.　Ahriman a dragon.

Greek myth.　Apollo and Python ; Perseus and the sea-monster.

Apollo identical with the sun, Python the storm-cloud.　Apollo delivers his mother from the assault of the dragon.

Perseus delivers Andromeda from the water-born serpent.　In other Greek fables it is the earth which is saved from destruction by the victory of the hero.

Teutonic myth.　Sigfried and the dragon.

Sigfried conquers the dragon who keeps guard over a hidden treasure, the hero kills the dragon and brings to light the treasure.

Scandinavian myth.　Sigurd and Fafnir.

Like the myth of Sigfried.　Other, and perhaps earlier form, the dragon is a king of Hades, who cannot endure light, and who has robbed the earth of its gold.　The hero descends to his realm, fights, overcomes him, and despoils him of his treasures.

Christian myth.　S. George and dragon.

S. George delivers a princess from a monster, who is about to devour her.　According to another version, the dragon guards the spring of water, and the country is languishing for want of water ; S. George restores to the land the use of the spring by slaying the dragon.

This table might have been considerably extended by including Keltic and Sclavonic fables, but it is sufficiently complete to show that the legend of S. George and the dragon forms part of one of the sacred myths of the Aryan family, and it is impossible not to grasp its signification in the light cast upon it by the Vedic poems.

And when we perceive how popular this venerable myth was in heathen nations of Europe, it is not surprising that it should perpetuate itself under Christianity, and that, when once transferred to a hero of the new creed, it should make that hero one of the most venerated and popular of all the saints in the calendar.

In the reign of Constantine the Great, there existed a great and beautiful church between Ramula, the ancient Arimathæa, and Lydda or Decapolis, dedicated by the Emperor to S. George, over his tomb. Ramula also bore the name of Georgia, and the inhabitants pretended that the warrior saint was a native of their town. A temple of Juno at Constantinople was converted into a church, with the same dedication, by the first Christian Emperor, and according to one tradition, the bones of the martyr were translated from his tomb near Lydda, to the church in the great city of Constantine. At an early date his head was in Rome, or at all events one of his heads, for another found its way to the church of Mares-Moutier, in Picardy, after the capture of Byzantium by the Turks, when it was taken from a church erected by Constantine Monomachus, dedicated to the saint. The Roman head, long forgotten, was rediscovered in 751, with an inscription on it which identified it with S. George. In 1600 it was given to the church of Ferrara. In Rome, at Palermo, and at Naples there were churches at a very early date, consecrated to the martyr. In 509 Clotilda founded a nunnery at Chelles in his honour; and Clovis II. placed a convent at Barala under his invocation. In this religious house was preserved an arm of S. George, which in the ninth century was transported to Cambray; and fifty years later S. Germain dedicated an altar in Paris to the champion. In the sixth century a church was erected to his honour at Mayence; Clothaire in the following century dedicated one at Nimègue, and his brother another in Alsace. George had a

monastery dedicated to him at Thetford, founded
in the reign of Canute; a collegiate church in
Oxford placed under his invocation in the reign
of the Conqueror. S. George's, Southwark, dates
from before the Norman invasion. The priory
church of Griesly in Derbyshire was dedicated
to SS. Mary and George, in the reign of Henry I.
The Crusades gave an impetus to the worship
of our patron. He appeared in light on the walls
of Jerusalem, waving his sword, and led the
victorious assault on the Holy City. Unob-
trusively he and S. Michael slipped into the
offices, and exercised the functions, of the Dioscuri.
Robert of Flanders, on his return from the Holy
Land, presented part of an arm of the saint to
the city of Toulouse, and other portions to the
Countess Matilda and to the abbey of Auchin.
Another arm of S. George fell miraculously from
heaven upon the altar of S. Pantaleon at Cologne,
and in honour of it Bishop Anno founded a church.

The church of Villers-Saint-Leu contains relics
of the saint, which were given to it in 1101 by
Alexander, chaplain of Count Ernest, who had
received them from Baldwin at Jerusalem.

The enthusiasm of the Crusaders for the Eastern
soldier-saint who led them to battle, soon raised S.

George to the highest pitch of popularity among the nobles and fighting-men of Europe. England, Aragon, and Portugal assumed him as their patron, as well as most chivalrous orders founded at the date of these wars. In 1245, on S. George's day, Frederic of Austria instituted an order of knighthood under his patronage; and its banner, white charged with a blood-red cross, in battle floated alongside of that of the empire. When the emperor entered the castle of S. Angelo at Rome, these two banners were carried before him. The custody of the sacred standard of S. George was confided to the Swabian knights. In the early part of the thirteenth century there existed a military order under the protection of S. George at Genoa, and in 1201 an order was founded in Aragon, with the title of knights of S. George of Alfama.

In 1348 King Edward III. founded S. George's Chapel, Windsor. In the following year he was besieging Calais. Moved by a sudden impulse, says Thomas of Walsingham, he drew his sword with the exclamation "Ha! Saint Edward! Ha! Saint George!" The words and action communicated spirit to his soldiers : they fell with vigour on the French, and routed them with a slaughter of two hundred soldiers. From that time S. George replaced Edward the Confessor as patron of England. In 1350 the celebrated order was instituted. In 1415, by the Constitutions of Archbishop Chichely, S. George's Day was made a major double feast, and ordered to be observed the same as Christmas Day, all labour ceasing; and he received the title of spiritual patron of the English soldiery.

In 1545 S. George's Day was observed as a red letter day, with proper Collect, Epistle, and Gospel; but in the reign of Edward VI. it was swept away, and the holding of the chapter of the Garter on S. George's Day was transferred to Whitsun Eve, Whitsun Day, and Whitsun Monday. Next year, the first of Queen Mary, the enactment was reversed, and since then the ancient custom has obtained, and the chapter is held annually on the feast of the patron.

In concluding this paper, it remains only to point out the graceful allegory which lies beneath the Western fable. S. George is any Christian who is sealed at his baptism to be "Christ's faithful soldier and servant unto his life's end," and armed with the breastplate of righteousness, the shield of the faith, marked with its blood-red cross, the helmet of salvation, and the sword of the Spirit, which is the word or power of God.

The hideous monster against whom the Christian soldier is called to fight is that "old serpent, the devil," who withholds or poisons the streams of grace, and who seeks to rend and devour the virgin soul, in whose defence the champion fights.

If the warfare symbolized by this legend be carried out in life, then, in Spenser's words—

"Thou, amongst those saints whom thou doest see,
Shall be a saint, and thine owne nations frend
And patrone: thou Saint George shalt called bee,
Saint George of mery England, the sign of victoree."

𝔖. 𝔘rsula and the 𝔈leven 𝔗housand 𝔙irgins

IN reading the Germania of Tacitus, with a view to the study of Teutonic mythology, I lit upon a passage so perplexing, that I resolved to minutely investigate it, and trace its connexion with other statements, and examine its bearings, little knowing whither it would lead. That passage shall be quoted in the sequel. Suffice it to say here, that it guided me to the legend of S. Ursula and her virgin company of martyrs.

At this point I became acquainted with the masterly treatise of Dr. Oskar Schade, of Bonn, on the story of S. Ursula [1], and was agreeably surprised to find that, proceeding from the point at which I had arrived, he had been guided by sure stages to that from which I had started.

---

[1] Die Sage von der Heiligen Ursula, von Oskar Schade. Hanover, 1854.

As my object in these pages is the analysis of a Christian myth, I shall follow the Doctor's course rather than my own. The fable of S. Ursula is too important to be omitted from this collection of Myths, because of the extravagance of its details, the devotion which it excited, the persistency with which the Church clings to it, setting all her scenery in motion to present the tragedy in its most imposing and probable aspect. It may not be omitted also because it is a specimen of the manner in which saintly legends were developed in the Middle Ages, the process of the development being unusually evident; a specimen, lastly, of the manner in which they were generated out of worse than nothing; a process which is also, in this case, singularly apparent.

The legends of the Middle Ages were some beautiful, some grotesque, some revolting. The two latter classes we put aside at once, but for the first we profess a lingering affection. Alas! too often they are but apples of Sodom, fair cheeked, but containing the dust and ashes of heathenism.

Ursula and the eleven thousand British virgins are said to have suffered martyrdom at Cologne, on October 21st, 237; for in 1837 was celebrated with splendor the 16th centenary jubilee of their passion. They suffered under the Huns, on their return from their defeat at Chalons by Aëtius in 451; so that the anachronism is considerable. The early martyrology of Jerome, published by d'Achery, makes no mention of S. Ursula; neither does that of the Venerable Bede, who was born in 672. Bede states that he has included all the names of which he read: as Ursula was a British lady of rank, and was accompanied to martyrdom by the enormous number of eleven thousand damsels, who shared with her the martyr's crown and palm, it is singular and significant that Bede should not allude to this goodly company. The Martyrologium Gallinense, a compilation made in 804, does not include her; nor does the Vetus Calendarium Corbeiense, composed in or about 831. Neither is she mentioned in the Martyrology of Rabanus Maurus, who died in 856. Usardus, who wrote about 875, does not speak of her, though under the 20th October he inserts the passion of the holy virgins, Martha and Saula, with many others in the city of Cologne. S. Ado wrote a martyrology in 880, but makes no mention of Ursula and the other virgins; nor does Notker of S. Gall, who died in 912; nor, again, does the Corbey martyrology of 900; neither do the two of uncertain date called after Labbe and Richenove. We see that up to the tenth century, for either 650 or 450 years after the martyrdom, there is no mention of S. Ursula by name, and only one reference to virgin martyrs at Cologne. Usardus, who mentions these, gives the names of Martha and Saula. An old calendar in the Dusseldorf town library, belonging to the tenth century, copies Usardus, merely transferring the saints to the 21st October. A litany of the following century, in the Darmstadt library, invokes five, in this order: Martha, Saula, Paula, Brittola, Ursula. Another litany in the same collection raises their number to eight, and gives a different succession: Brittola, Martha, Saula, Sambatia, Saturnina, Gregoria, Pinnosa, Palladia. Another litany, in the Dusseldorf library, extends the number to eleven: Ursula, Sencia, Gregoria, Pinnosa, Martha, Saula, Brittola, Saturnina, Rabacia, Saturia, Palladia. And, again, another gives eleven, but in different order: Martha, Saula, Brittola, Gregoria, Saturnina, Sabatia, Pinnosa, Ursula, Sentia, Palladia, Saturia.

A calendar in a Freisingen Codex, published in Eckhart's Francia Orientalis, notices them as *SS. M. XI. Virginum.* And, lastly, in the twelfth century the chronicle of Rodulf (written 1117) reckons the virgin martyrs as twelve.

But S. Cunibert (d. 663) is related, in a legend of the ninth century, to have been celebrating in the church of the Blessed Virgins, when a white dove appeared, and indicated the spot where lay the relics of one of the martyrs : these were, of course at once exhumed.

In the ninth century there was a cloister of the blessed virgins at Cologne : this is also alluded to in the tenth and following centuries. The first, however, to develope the number of martyrs to any very considerable extent, was Wandalbert, in his metrical list of saints. This was written about 851. He does not mention Ursula by name, but reckons the virgins who suffered as " thousands."

> " Tunc numerosa simul Rheni per littora fulgent
> Christo virgineis erecta trophæa maniplis
> Agrippinæ urbi, quarum furor impius olim
> Millia mactavit ductricibus inclyta sanctis."

The authenticity of these lines has, however, been questioned by critics.

The next mention of the virgins as very numerous is in a calendar of the latter end of the ninth century, in which, under October 21st, are commemorated S. Hilario and the eleven thousand virgins. Archbishop Hermann of Cologne, in 922, also speaks of this number. In 927 and 941 Archbishop Wichfried reckons them at eleven thousand, and from that time the belief in the virgin saints having numbered eleven thousand spread gradually through Europe.

Various suggestions have been made to account for this extraordinary number. By some it has been supposed that Undecimilla was the name of one of the martyrs, and that the entry in the ancient calendars of *Ursula et Undecimilla Virg. Mart.*, originated the misconception; and, in fact, one missal, supposed to be old, has a similar commemoration; whilst an inscription at Spiers, according to Rettberg, mentions Ursula et Decumilia. Johann Sprenz believed that the mistake arose from the use, in the old MSS. martyrologies and calendars, of the Teutonic Gimartarôt, or Kimartrôt (passus), which, standing S. Ursula Ximartor, might have led later writers to have taken the entry to signify S. Ursula, et XI. Martor. Or, again, if the number of the virgins were eleven, they may have been entered as SS. XI. M. Virgines, or the eleven martyr-virgins, and the M. have been mistaken in a later age for a numeral. Against this it is urged that in no ancient calendar does the M. precede the Virg.; the usual manner of describing these saints being SS. M. XI. Virg., till the number rose at a leap to eleven thousand.

As yet we have had no circumstances relating to these ladies, but with the tenth century they begin to appear. Sigebert of Gemblours (d. 1112) is the first author to narrate them. Under the date 453, he reports the glorious victory of the Virgin Ursula. She was the only daughter of Nothus, an illustrious and wealthy British prince, and was sought in marriage by the son of a "certain most ferocious tyrant." Ursula had, however, dedicated herself to celibacy, and her father was in great fear of offending God by consenting to the union, and of exasperating the king by refusing it. However, the damsel solved the difficulty : by Divine inspiration, she persuaded her father to agree to the proposal of the tyrant, but only subject to the condition that her father and the king should choose ten virgins of beauty and proper age, and should give them to her, and that she and they should each have a thousand damsels under them, and that on eleven triremes they should be suffered to cruize about for three years in the sanctity of unsullied virginity. Ursula made this condition in the hopes that the difficulty of fulfilling it would prove insurmountable, or that she might be able, should it be overcome, to persuade a vast host of maidens to devote themselves to the Almighty.

The tyrant succeeded in mustering the desired number, and then presented them to Ursula, together with eleven elegantly furnished galleys. For three years these damsels sailed the blue seas. One day the wind drove them into the port of Tiela, in Gaul, and thence up the Rhine to Cologne. Thence they pursued their course to Basle, where they left their ships, and crossed the Alps on foot, descended into Italy, and visited the tombs of the Apostles at Rome. In like manner they returned, but, falling in with the Huns at Cologne, they were every one martyred by the barbarians.

This story bears evidence of being an addition to the original text of Sigebert's Chronicle, for it is not to be found in the original MS. in the handwriting of the author, though marks of stitches at the side of the page indicate that an additional item had been appended, but by whom, or when, is not clear, as the strip of parchment which had been tacked on is lost.

Otto of Freisingen (d. 1158) mentions the legend in his Chronicle ; for he says, " This army (of the Huns) when overrunning the earth, crowned with martyrdom the eleven thousand virgins at Cologne."

A legend of the twelfth century, given by Surius, invests the story with all the colours of a romance. In the same century it appears in the marvellous history of Geoffrey of Monmouth (d. 1154). Whether this legend was in the Welsh book of Walter the Archdeacon, from which the good Bishop of S. Asaph derived so much of his history, does not appear. The story, as told by him, differs materially from that received in Germany. He relates that the Emperor Maximian, having depopulated Northern Gaul, sent to Britain for colonies wherewith to re-people the waste country. Thus out of Armorica he made a second Britain, which he put under the control of Conan Meriadoc. He then turned his arms eastward, and, having established himself at Treves, commenced hostilities against the emperors Gratian and Valentinian, who disputed with him the imperial purple. In the meanwhile Conan was defending Brittany against the incursions of the neighbouring Gauls, but, finding that his troops would not settle without wives, he sent to Britain for a cargo of damsels, who might become the spouses of his soldiers, and raise up another generation of fighting men to continue the war with the Gauls. At this time there reigned in Cornwall a king, Dionotus by name, who had succeeded his brother Caradoc on the throne. He was blessed with a daughter of singular beauty, named Ursula, whose hand Conan desired to obtain. Dionotus, having received a message from the prince of Armorica stating his difficulties, at once collected a body of eleven thousand girls of noble rank, and sixty thousand of low birth, and shipped them on the Thames for the Armorican colony of expectant husbands.

No sooner, however, had the fleet left the mouth of the Thames, than it was scattered by the winds, and, some of the vessels having been driven ashore on barbarous island coasts, the damsels were either killed or enslaved; some became the prey of the execrable army of Guanius and Melga, kings of the Huns and Picts, who, falling upon the band of luckless virgins, massacred them without compunction.

It is evident that Geoffrey did not regard this legend as invested with sanctity, and he tells it as an historical, and not a hagiological fact.

In 1106 Cologne was besieged, and the walls in several places were battered down. Directly the enemy were gone, the inhabitants began to rebuild them; and, as the foundations had suffered, they were compelled to relay them.

Now it happened that the old walls ran across the ancient cemetery of the Roman settlement of Colonia Agrippina. Consequently in redigging the foundations a number of bones were discovered, especially at one spot. Thereupon some ecstatic or excitable visionary beheld two females in a halo of light, who indicated the bones as those of the virgin martyrs. Immediately enthusiasm was aroused, and the cemetery was examined. Innumerable bones were found, together with urns, arms, stone cists, and monumental inscriptions. The old Roman cemetery became a quarry of relics, apparently inexhaustible. But in the midst of the religious enthusiasm of the clergy and devotees of Cologne, a sudden difficulty occurred, which produced bewilderment in the faithful, and mockery in the unbelieving. A large number of bones and inscriptions belonging to men were discovered; thus a Simplicius, a Pantulus, an Aetherius, were commemorated on the slabs exhumed, and the great size of some of the tibia rendered it certain that they had never belonged to slender virgins.

In the midst of the dismay reigning in the breasts of the good Catholics at this untoward discovery, appeared, most opportunely, an ecstatic nun, Elizabeth by name, who resided in the convent of

Schönau. This visionary solved the difficulty, to the great edification of the faithful. She fell into trances, during which she was vouchsafed wondrous revelations, which she detailed in Latin to her brother Egbert, who alone was suffered to be present during her ecstasies. According to her account, the Pope Cyriacus, the cardinals of Rome, several bishops, priests, and monks, had been so edified at the sight of the holy virgins in Rome, that they had followed them on their return as far as Cologne, where they, as well as the damsels, had won the martyr's palm.

Thus, in a most satisfactory way, the presence of these male bones was accounted for, and no scandal attached to the chaste troop of male and female celibates which had crossed the Alps, and descended the Rhine, to fall before the sword of the barbarian. Simplicius was ascertained to have been Archbishop of Ravenna, Pantulus to have been Bishop of Basle, and Aetherius proved to have been the bridegroom elect of Ursula, who had been converted to Christianity, and had come up the Rhine to meet his saintly betrothed.

A little difficulty occurred on another point. How was it that the martyrs were provided with stone coffins and sepulchral slabs?

In order to explain this, another incident was added to the legend by the vision-seeing nun.

Jacobus, Archbishop of Antioch, a Briton by birth, had gone to Rome to visit Cyriacus the Pope, but had learned, on his arrival, that his holiness had been last seen clambering the Alps in the train of eleven thousand virgins of entrancing beauty. The Eastern patriarch at once followed the successor of S. Peter, and reached Cologne on the morrow of the great massacre. He thereupon cut the names and titles of many of the deceased on stone—how he ascertained their names is not stated; but, before he had accomplished his task, the Huns discovered him engaged in his pious work, and dispatched him.

Doubt and disbelief were now silenced, and the ecstatic nun, having finished her revelations concerning the eleven thousand, died in the odour of sanctity.

Scarcely was she dead before fresh discoveries in the old cemetery reopened the scandal.

A considerable number of children's bones were exhumed, and some of these belonged to infants but a few months old. This was a startling and awkward discovery, seriously compromising to the memories of the Pope, cardinals, and prelates who had accompanied the young ladies from Rome, and arousing a suspicion that the damsels had not been the sole managers of their vessels on the high seas, as the early legends had stated.

The nun, Elizabeth of Schönau, was dead. Who was there then to clear the characters of these glorious martyrs?

Fortunately, an old Præmonstratine mcnk, named Richard, an Englishman, lived in the diocese of Cologne, in the abbey of Arnsberg. He was keenly alive to the slur cast upon the fair fame of his national saints, and, by means of visions, laboured effectively to vindicate it. He declared that the eleven thousand had excited such enthusiasm in England, that their married relations had accompanied them in the vessels, with their children of all ages, and that all together had received the martyr's crown. Richard added that a Sicilian princess, Gerasina, had accompanied the pilgrims, together with her four daughters and baby son; also that an empress of the Eastern empire, Constantia by name, had suffered with them. Kings, princes, and princesses, of Norway, Sweden, Ireland, Flanders, Normandy, Brabant, Friesland, Denmark —in a word, of all lands with which a geographer of the twelfth century was acquainted—had joined the expedition, in their desire to testify their admiration of the chastity and piety of Ursula and her companions. Holofernes, bridegroom elect of Ursula, notwithstanding his father's opposition, insisted on taking command of the fleet. Under him were three hundred sailors who manned the vessels.

Such is the history of the expansion and final development of this curious fable. It exhibits a series of misconceptions and impostures, we should hope, unparalleled. To this day the church of S. Ursula at Cologne is visited by thousands who rely on the intercession of a saint who never existed, and believe in the miraculous virtues of relics which are those of pagans.

But something worse remains to be told.

Ursula is no other than the Swabian goddess Ursel or Hörsel transformed into a saint of the Christian calendar.

"A part of the Suevi sacrifice to Isis," says Tacitus, in his Germania. This Isis has been identified by Grimm with a goddess Ziza, who was worshipped by the inhabitants of the parts about Augsburg. Küchlen, an Augsburg poet of the fourteenth century, sings—

"They built a great temple therein,
  To the honour of Zise the heathen goddess,

> Whom they after heathen customs
> Worshipped at that time :
> The city was named eke Zisaris,
> After the heathen goddess ; that was its glory.
> The temple long stood entire,
> Until its fall was caused by age."

But it may be questioned whether Tacitus called the goddess worshipped by the Suevi, Isis, because the name resembled that of the German deity, or whether he so termed her because he traced a similarity in the myths and worship of the two goddesses. I believe the latter to have been the case. The entire passage reads, "They chiefly worship Mercury, to whom on certain days they sacrifice human beings. They appease Hercules and Mars with beasts, and part of the Suevi sacrifice to Isis. Whence the cause and origin of the foreign rite I have not ascertained, except that the symbol itself, in shape of a Liburnian ship, indicates that the religion was brought from abroad [2]."

Here, in the same sentence, three of the German gods are called by Roman names. Mercury is Woden : Hercules, or Mars, is Thorr. It is, therefore, probable that the fourth, Isis, is named from a resemblance of attributes, rather than identity of name. Again, in connexion with the mention of

[2] Tacitus, Germania, ix.

Isis, he alludes to a rite observed by the Suevi of carrying about a ship in her honour. Now, in Rome, the 5th March (III. Non. Mart.) was called, in the Kalendarium Rusticum, the day of the *Isidis navigium*. This is referred to by Apulëius in his Metamorphoses. The goddess appeared to the poor ass, and said, "The morrow that from the present night will have its birth is a day that eternal religion hath appointed as a holy festival, at a period when, the tempests of winter having subsided, the waves of the stormy sea abated, and the surface of the ocean become navigable, my priests dedicate to me a new ship, laden with the first-fruits of spring, at the opening of the navigation" (Lib. xi.). To this alludes also Lactantius[3].

The myth of Isis and her wanderings is too well known to be related. Now it is certain that in parts of Germany the custom of carrying about a ship existed through the Middle Ages to the present day, and was denounced by the Church as idolatrous. Grimm[4] mentions a very curious passage in the Chronicle of Rodulph, wherein it is related that, in 1133, a ship was secretly constructed in a forest at Inda, and was placed on

[3] Lactant. Instit. i. 27.
[4] Deutsche Myth. i. 237.

wheels, and rolled by the weavers to Aix, then to Maestricht, and elsewhere, amidst dances, and music, and scenes which the pious chronicler refrains from describing. That it was regarded with abhorrence by the clergy, is evident from the epithets employed in describing it : navim infausto omine compactum—gentilitatis studium—profanas simulacri excubias—maligni spiritus qui in illa ferebantur—infausti ominis monstrum; and the like.

At Ulm, in Swabia, in 1530, the people were forbidden the carrying about of ploughs and ships on Shrove Tuesday. A like prohibition was decreed at Tübingen on the 5th March, 1584, against a similar practice. I have myself, on two occasions, seen ships dragged through the streets on wheels, upon Shrove Tuesday, at Mannheim on the Rhine. In Brussels is celebrated, I believe to this day, a festival called the Ommegank, in which a ship is drawn through the town by horses, with an image of the Blessed Virgin upon it, in commemoration of a miraculous figure of our Lady which came in a boat from Antwerp to Brussels.

Sometimes the ship was replaced by a plough, and the rustic ceremony of Plough Monday in England is a relic of the same religious rite performed in honour of the Teutonic Isis.

This great goddess was known by different names among the various peoples of Germany. She may have been the same as Zisca, but, as we know absolutely nothing of the myth and attributes of that deity, we cannot decide with certainty. More probably she was the Holda, or Holle, who still holds sway over the imagination of the German peasantry.

Now Holda is the great pale lady who glides through the sky at night, in whose dark courts are many thousand bright-eyed damsels, all, like her, pure ; all, with her, suffering eclipse.

"Siderum regina bicornis audi
    Luna puellas.
  O Ursula!   Princess among thy thousands of virgins,
                    Pray for us !"

Holda, or the Moon, is the wandering Isis, or Ursula, whom German poets love still to regard as sailing over heaven's deep in her silver boat. As—

"Seh' ziehen die Wolke mit der Brust voll Segen,
  Des Mondes Kahn im Meer der Nächte prangen."
                                    ANAST. GRÜN.

Or—

    "Es schimmert, wie der Silberkahn,
      Der dort am Himmel strahlt."
                            VON STOLBERG.

Holda, in Teutonic mythology, is a gentle lady

with a sad smile on her countenance, ever accompanied by the souls of maidens and children, which are under her care. She sits in a mountain of crystal, surrounded by her bright-eyed maidens, and comes forth to scatter on earth the winter snow, or to revive the spring earth, or bless the fruits of autumn. This company of virgins surrounding her in the crystal vault of heaven is that described by Æschylus : ʼΑστρων κάτοιδα νυκτέρων ὁμήγυριν (Agam. v. 4).

The kindly Holda was in other parts called Gôde, under which name she resembled Artemis, as the heavenly huntress accompanied by her maidens. In Austria and Bavaria she was called Perchta, or Bertha (the shining), and was supposed to have horns like Isis or Io, other lunar goddesses But in Swabia and Thuringia she was represented by Hörsel or Ursul.

This Hörsel, in other places called the night bird Tutösel, haunted the Venusberg into which Tanhäuser plunged. She lived there in the midst of her numerous troop of damsels, to assist the laborious farmer and bless faithful lovers, or to allure to herself those souls which still clung to the ancient faith. A beautiful and benignant goddess the peasantry ever regarded her, little

heeding the brand put upon her pure brow by
an indignant clergy, who saw in her only the
Roman Venus in her grossest character, and not
Aphrodite, the foam-begotten moon, rising silvery
above the frothing sea.

Further this legend shall not lead us.   Its
history is painful.

That ancient myths should have penetrated and
coloured Mediæval Christianity is not to be wondered at, for old convictions are not eradicated in
the course of centuries.   I shall, in this book,
instance several cases in which they have left their
impress on modern Protestant mythology.   But
it is sad that the Church should have lent herself
to establish this fable by the aid of fictitious
miracles and feigned revelations.   And now, when
minds weary with groping after truth, and not
finding it in science, philosophy, and metaphysics,
turn to the Church with yearning look, why should
she repel them from clasping the Cross, which, in
spite of all fables, "will stand whilst the world
rolls," by her tenacity in clinging to these idle
and foolish tales, founded on paganism, and but-
tressed with fraud ?

Is this cultus of Ursula and her eleven thousand
nothing but a "pious belief"?   A pious belief,

which can trust in the moon and the myriad stars, and invoke them as saints in Paradise! "If I beheld . . . the moon walking in brightness; and my heart hath been secretly enticed, or my mouth hath kissed my hand: this also were an iniquity to be punished by the judge: for I should have denied the God that is above" (Job xxxi. 26—28).

It is Truth which men yearn for now; and sacred Truth, when taught by a mouth which lends itself to utter cunningly devised fables, is not listened to.

If the Catholic Church abroad would only purge herself of these, her grand eternal doctrines would be embraced by thousands. But the fathers have eaten sour grapes, and the children's teeth are set on edge.

The bibliography of the legend must be briefly discussed. It is not of remarkable interest.

The revelations of Elizabeth of Schönau, and those of Hermann, Joseph of Steinfeld, will be found in Surius, "Vita Sanctorum," under October 21st.

"Epistola ad virgines Christi univ. super hystoria nova undecim milimum (sic!) virginum," without place and date, but belonging to the latter end of the fifteenth century, is very rare: I have not seen it.

" Hjstoria vndecim milium virginum breviori atque faciliori modo pulcerrime collecta." Colon. 1509, 4to. Very scarce also.

"De Legende, vn hystorie der XI dusent jonferen, s. l. et a." (circ. 1490), a curious Low German legend, illustrated with quaint engravings, forty in number.

De S. Lory, "Sainte Ursule triomphante des cœurs, de l'enfer, de l'empire, Patrone du célèbre collége de Sorbonne," Paris, 1666, 4to. The legend has been carefully analyzed by Rettberg, in his "Deutschlands Kirchengeschichte," i. pp. 111—123.

Crombach broke a lance in honour of the eleven thousand in 1647: his work, "Ursula Vindicata," Colon. 1647, fol., with three maps, is interesting as containing documentary evidence ; but it is disfigured by the superstition of the writer.

Leo, J. G., " ἀποσκίασμα hist.-antiquarium de 11,000 virginibus." Leucopetræ, 1721, 4to. Reischert, L., "Lebens-Geschichte u. Märtyrtod der N. Ursula." Cologne, 1837, 8vo.

Heinen, E. M. J., "Leben, Fahrt, u. Märtyrtod der h. Ursula." Cologne, 1838, 8vo. Scheben, A., "Leben der h. Ursula." Cologne, 1850, 8vo.

Schade, Oskar, " Die Sage v. der h. Ursula,"

Hanover, 1854, 8vo. Also a beautiful series of illustrations of the legend copied from the interesting paintings in the church at Cologne, published by Kellerhoven, " La légende de S. Ursula." Leipzig 1861.

Some curious stories of the appearances of the sacred virgin companions of Ursula, and of the marvels wrought by their bones, occur in Cæsarius of Heisterbach's gossiping Dialogue of Miracles.

The Legend of the Cross

Ὦ ξύλον, ᾧ μακαριστόν, ἐφ᾽ ᾧ Θεὸς ἐξετανύσθη.
Sibyll. vi. 26.

IN the year 1850 chance led me to the discovery of a Gallo-Roman palace at Pont d'Oli (Pons Aulæ), near Pau, in the south of France. I was able to exhume the whole of the ruins, and to bring to light one of the most extensive series of mosaic pavements extant.

The remains consisted of a mansion two hundred feet long, paved throughout with mosaic : it was divided into summer and winter apartments ; the latter heated by means of hypocausts, and of small size ; the former very large, and opening on to a corridor above the river, once adorned with white marble pillars, having capitals of the Corinthian order. One of the first portions of the palace to be examined was the atrium, out of which, on the west, opened the tablinum, a semi-circular chamber panelled with alabaster and painted.

The atrium contained a large quadrangular tank or impluvium, the dwarf walls of which were encased in variegated Pyrenean marbles.   On the west side of the impluvium, below the step of the tablinum, the pavement represented five rows of squares. The squares in the first, third, and fifth rows were filled with a graceful pattern composed of curves. In the second and fourth rows, however, every fourth square contained a distinctly characterized red cross on white ground, with a delicate white spine down the middle (Fig. 2).   Some few ot these crosses had a black floriation in the angles, much resembling that met with in Gothic crosses (Fig. 4).   Immediately in front of the tablinum, on the dwarf wall of the impluvium, stood the altar to the Penates, which was found.   The corresponding pavement on the east of the impluvium was similar in design to the other, but the S. George's crosses were replaced by those of S. Andrew, each limb terminating either in a heart-shaped leaf or a trefoil (Figs. 1, 5).   The design on the north and south was different, and contained no crosses.   The excavations to the north led to the summer apartment.   The most northerly chamber measured 26

feet by 22 feet; it was not only the largest, but
evidently the principal room of the mansion, for
the pavement was the most elaborate and beautiful.
It was bordered by an exquisite running pattern of
vines and grape bunches, springing from four drinking vessels in the centres of the north, south, east,
and west sides. The pattern within this border
was of circles, containing conventional roses alter-
nately folded and expanded. This design was,
however, rudely interrupted by a monstrous cross

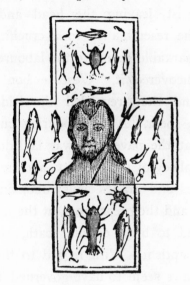

measuring 19 feet 8 inches by 13 feet, with its head
towards the south, and its foot at the head of a
flight of marble steps descending into what we were

unable to decide whether it was a bath or a vestibule. The ground of the cross was white ; the limbs were filled with cuttle, lobsters, eels, oysters, and fish, swimming as though in their natural element ; but the centre, where the arms intersected, was occupied by a gigantic bust of Neptune with his trident. The flesh was represented red; the hair, and beard, and trident were a blue-black. The arms of the figure did not show : a line joining the lower edge of the transverse limbs of the cross cut the figure at the breast, leaving the head and shoulders above. The resemblance to a crucifix was sufficiently remarkable to make the labourers exclaim, as they uncovered it, " C'est le bon Dieu, c'est Jésus !" and they regarded the trident as the centurion's spear. A neighbouring curé satisfied himself that the pavement was laid down in conscious prophecy of Christianity, and he pointed to the chalices and grapes as symbolizing the holy Eucharist, and the great cross, at the head of what we believed to be a circular bath, as typical of Christian baptism. With regard to the cross, the following laws seem to have governed its representation in the Gallo-Roman villa :—

The S. George's cross occupied the place of honour in the chief room, and at the head of this

room, not in the middle, but near the bath or porch. Again, in the atrium this cross was repeated twenty times in the principal place before the tablinum and altar of the household divinities, and again in connexion with water. Its colour was always red or white.

Six varieties of crosses occurred in the villa (Figs. 1—5) : the S. George's cross plain ; the same with foliations in the angles ; the same inhabited by fish, and bust of Neptune : the Maltese cross : the S. Andrew's cross with trefoiled ends ; the same with heart-shaped ends.

On the discovery of the villa, several theories were propounded to explain the prominence given to the cross in the mosaics.

It was conjectured by some that the Neptune crucifix was a satire upon the Christians. To this it was objected that the figure was too large and solemn, and was made too prominent, to be so taken ; that to the cross was assigned the place of honour; and that, independently of the bust of the sea-god, it was connected by the artists with the presence of water.

It was supposed by others that the villa had belonged to a Christian, and that the execution of

his design in the pavement had been entrusted
to pagans, who, through ignorance, had sub-
stituted the head of Neptune for that of the
Saviour.

Such a solution, though possible, is barely
probable.

My own belief is, that the cross was a
sacred sign among the Gaulish Kelts, and
that the villa at Pau had belonged to a Gallo-
Roman, who introduced into it the symbol of
the water-god of his national religion, and combined it with the representation of the marine
deity of the conquerors' creed.

My reasons for believing the cross to have
been a Gaulish sign are these:—

The most ancient coins of the Gauls were
circular, with a cross in the middle; little wheels,
as it were, with four large perforations (Figs. 6, 7,
8). That these *rouelles* were not designed to
represent wheels is apparent from there being
only four spokes, placed at right angles. Moreover, when the coins of the Greek type took
their place, the cross was continued as the orna-
mentation of the coin. The gold and silver
Greek pieces circulating at Marseilles were the
cause of the abandonment of the primitive type;

and rude copies of the Greek coins were made by the Keltic inhabitants of Gaul. In copying the foreign pieces, they retained their own symbolic cross.

The reverse of the coins of the Volcæ Tectosages, who inhabited the greater portion of Languedoc, was impressed with crosses, their angles filled with pellets, so like those on the silver coins of the Edwards, that, were it not for the quality of the metal, one would take these Gaulish coins to be the production of the Middle Ages. The Leuci, who inhabited the country round the modern Toul, had similar coins. One of their pieces has been figured by M. de Saulcy[1]. It represents a circle containing a cross, the angles between the arms occupied by a chevron. Some of the crosses have bezants, or pearls, forming a ring about them, or occupying the spaces between their limbs. Near Paris, at Choisy-le-Roy, was discovered a Gaulish coin representing a head, in barbarous imitation of that on a Greek medal, and the reverse occupied by a serpent coiled round the circumference, and enclosing two birds.

[1] Revue de Numismatique, 1836.

Between these birds is a cross, with pellets at
the end of each limb, and a pellet in each
angle.

A similar coin has been found in numbers
near Arthenay, in Loïret, as well as others of
analogous type. Other Gaulish coins bear the
cross on both obverse and reverse. About two
hundred pieces of this description were found
in 1835, in the village of Cremiat-sur-Yen, near
Quimper, in a brown earthen urn, with ashes
and charcoal, in a rude kistvaen of stone
blocks ; proving that the cross was used on the
coins in Armorica, at the time when increma-
tion was practised. This cross with pellets, a
characteristic of Gaulish coins, became in time
the recognized reverse of early French pieces,
and introduced itself into England with the Anglo-
Norman kings.

We unfortunately know too little of the iconography of the Gauls, to be able to decide whether
the cross was with them the symbol of a water
deity; but I think it probable, and for this
reason, that it is the sign of gods connected, more
or less remotely, with water in other religions.
That it was symbolic among the Irish and British
Kelts is more than probable. The temple in the

tumulus of Newgrange is in the shape of a cross with rounded arms (Fig. 9). Curiously enough, the so-called Phœnician ruin of Giganteia, in Gozzo, resembles it in shape. The shamrock of Ireland derives its sacredness from its affecting the same form. In the mysticism of the Druids the stalk or long arm of the cross represented the way of life, and the three lobes of the clover-leaf, or the short arms of the cross, symbolized the three conditions of the spirit-world, Heaven, Purgatory, and Hell.

Let us turn to the Scandinavians. Their god Thorr was the thunder, and the hammer was his symbol. It was with this hammer that Thorr crushed the head of the great Mitgard serpent, that he destroyed the giants, that he restored the dead goats to life which drew his car, that he consecrated the pyre of Baldur. This hammer was a cross.

Just as the S. George's cross appears on the Gaulish coins, so does the cross cramponnée, or Thorr's hammer (Fig. 11), appear on the Scandinavian moneys.

In ploughing a field near Bornholm, in Fyen, in 1835, a discovery was made of several gold coins and ornaments belonging to ancient Danish

civilization.   The collection consisted of personal
ornaments, such as brooches, fibulæ, and torques,
and also of pieces of money, to which were fastened
rings in order that they might be strung on a necklace.   Among these were two rude copies of coins
of the successors of Constantine ; but the others
were of a class very common in the North.   They
were impressed with a four-footed horned beast,
girthed, and mounted by a monstrous human head,
intended, in barbarous fashion, to represent the
rider.   In front of the head was the sign of Thorr's
hammer, a cross cramponnée.   Four of the specimens
bearing this symbol exhibited likewise the name of
Thorr in runes.   A still ruder coin, discovered with
the others, was deficient in the cross, whose place
was occupied by a four-point star[2].

Among the flint weapons discovered in Denmark
are stone cruciform hammers, with a hole at the
intersection of the arms for the insertion of the
haft (Fig. 10).   As the lateral limbs could have
been of little or no use, it is probable that these
cruciform hammers were those used in conse-
crating victims in Thorr's worship.

The cross of Thorr is still used in Iceland as a

[2] Transactions of the Society of Northern Antiquaries for
1836.

magical sign in connexion with storms of wind and rain.

King Olaf, Longfellow tells us, when keeping Christmas at Drontheim—

> " O'er his drinking-horn, the sign
> He made of the Cross Divine,
>   As he drank, and mutter'd his prayers ;
> But the Berserks evermore
> Made the sign of the Hammer of Thorr
>   Over theirs."

Actually they both made the same symbol.

This we are told by Snorro Sturleson, in the Heimskringla[3], when he describes the sacrifice at Lade, at which King Hakon, Athelstan's foster-son was present : " Now, when the first full goblet was filled, Earl Sigurd spoke some words over it, and blessed it in Odin's name, and drank to the king out of the horn ; and the king then took it, and made the sign of the cross over it. Then said Kaare of Greyting, 'What does the king mean by doing so ? will he not sacrifice ?' But Earl Sigurd replied, 'The king is doing what all of you do who trust in your power and strength ; for he is blessing the full goblet in the name of Thorr, by making the sign of his hammer over it before he drinks it.'"

[3] Heimskringla, Saga iv., c. 18.

Bells were rung in the Middle Ages to drive away thunder. Among the German peasantry the sign of the cross is used to dispel a thunder-storm. The cross is used because it resembles Thorr's hammer, and Thorr is the Thunderer: for the same reason bells were often marked with the "fylfot," or cross of Thorr (Fig. 11), especially where the Norse settled, as in Lincolnshire and Yorkshire. Thorr's cross is on the bells of Appleby, and Scotherne, Waddingham, Bishop's Norton, and West Barkwith,, in Lincolnshire, on those of Hathersage in Derbyshire, Mexborough in Yorkshire, and many more.

The fylfot is curiously enough the sacred Swaslika of the Buddhist; and the symbol of Buddha on the reverse of a coin found at Ugain is a cross of equal arms, with a circle at the extremity of each, and the fylfot in each circle.

The same peculiar figure occurs on coins of Syracuse, Corinth, and Chalcedon, and is frequently employed on Etruscan cinerary urns. It curiously enough appears on the dress of a fossor, as a sort of badge of his office, on one of the paintings in the Roman catacombs.

But, leaving the cross cramponnée, let us examine some other crosses.

Sozomen, the ecclesiastical historian, says that, on the destruction of the Serapium in Egypt, "there were found sculptured on the stones certain characters regarded as sacred, resembling the sign of the cross. This representation, interpreted by those who knew the meaning, signified 'The Life to come.' This was the occasion of a great number of pagans embracing Christianity, the more so because other characters announced that the temple would be destroyed when this character came to light [4]." Socrates gives further particulars : "Whilst they were demolishing and despoiling the temple of Serapis, they found characters, engraved on the stone, of the kind called hieroglyphics, the which characters had the figure of the cross. When the Christians and the Greeks [i. e. heathen] saw this, they referred the signs to their own religions. The Christians, who regarded the cross as the symbol of the salutary passion of Christ, thought that this character was their own. But the Greeks said it was common to Christ and Serapis ; though this cruciform character is, in fact, one thing to the Christians, and another to the Greeks. A controversy having arisen,

---

[4] Sozomen, Hist. Eccles. vii., c. 14.

some of the Greeks [heathen] converted to Christianity, who understood the hieroglyphics, interpreted this cross-like figure to signify 'The Life to come.' The Christians, seizing on this as in favour of their religion, gathered boldness and assurance ; and as it was shown by other sacred characters that the temple of Serapis was to have an end when was brought to light this cruciform character, signifying 'The Life to come,' a great number were converted and were baptized, confessing their sins [5]."

Rufinus, who tells the story also, says that this took place at the destruction of the Serapium at Canopus [6]; but Socrates and Sozomen probably followed Sophronius, who wrote a book on the destruction of the Serapium, and locate the event in Alexandria [7].

Rufinus says, "The Egyptians are said to have the sign of the Lord's cross among those letters which are called sacerdotal—of which letter or figure this, they say, is the interpretation : 'The Life to come.'"

[5] Socrat. Hist. Eccles. v., c. 17,

[6] Rufin. Hist. Eccles. ii., c. 29.

[7] " Sophronius, vir apprime eruditus, laudes Bethleem adhuc puer, et nuper de subversione Serapis insignem librum composuit."—Hieronym. Vit. Illust.

There is some slight difficulty as to fixing the date of the destruction of the Serapium. Marcellinus refers it to the year 389, but some chronologists have moved it to 391. It was certainly overthrown in the reign of Theodosius I.

There can be little doubt that the cross in the Serapium was the *Crux ansata* (Fig. 12), the S. Anthony's cross, or Tau with a handle. The antiquaries of last century supposed it to be a Nile key or a phallus, significations purely hypothetical and false, as were all those they attributed to Egyptian hieroglyphs. As Sir Gardner Wilkinson remarks, it is precisely the god Nilus who is least often represented with this symbol in his hand[8], and the Nile key is an ascertained figure of different shape. Now it is known for certain that the symbol is that of life. Among other indications, we have only to cite the Rosetta stone, on which it is employed to translate the title αἰωνόβιος given to Ptolemy Epiphanius.

The Christians of Egypt gladly accepted this witness to the cross, and reproduced it in their churches and elsewhere, making it precede, follow, or accompany their inscriptions. Thus, beside

[8] Manners and Customs of the Ancient Egyptians, iv. p. 341.

one of the Christian inscriptions at Phile is seen
both a Maltese cross and a crux ansata. In a
painting covering the end of a church in the
cemetery of El-Khargeh, in the Great Oasis, are
three handled crosses around the principal subject, which seems to have been a figure of a
saint [9].

Not less manifest is the intention in an inscription in a Christian church to the east of the
Nile in the desert.   It is this :—

KAΘO✠ΛIKH✝EKKΛH✠CIA.

Beside, or in the hand of, the Egyptian gods, this
symbol is generally to be seen : it is held in the
right hand, by the loop, and indicates the Eternity of Life which is the attribute of divinity.
When Osiris is represented holding out the crux
ansata to a mortal, it means that the person to
whom he presents it has put off mortality, and
entered on the life to come.

Several theories have been started to account
for the shape.   The Phallic theory is monstrous,
and devoid of evidence.   It has also been suggested that the Tau (T) represents a table or altar,

---

[9] Hoskins, Visit to the Great Oasis, Lond. 1837, plate
xii.

and that the loop symbolizes a vase [1] or an egg [2] upon that altar.

These explanations are untenable when brought into contact with the monuments of Egypt. The ovoid form of the upper member is certainly a handle, and is so used (Fig. 13). No one knows, and probably no one ever will know, what originated the use of this sign, and gave it such significance.

The Greek cross is also found on Egyptian monuments, but less frequently than the cross of S. Anthony. A figure of a Shari (Fig. 14), from Sir Gardner Wilkinson's book, has a necklace round his throat, from which depends a pectoral cross. A similar ornament hangs on the breast of Tiglath Pileser, in the colossal tablet from Nimroud, now in the British Museum (Fig. 15). Another king from the ruins of Nineveh wears a Maltese cross on his bosom. And another, from the hall of Nisroch, carries an emblematic necklace, consisting of the sun surrounded by a ring, the moon, a Maltese

[1] " Hieroglyphica ejusdem (vocis) figura formam exhibet mensæ sacræ fulcro innixæ cui vas quoddam religionis indicium superpositum est."—P. Ungarelli, Interpretat. Obeliscorum Urbis, p. 5.

[2] Dognée, Les Symboles Antiques, L'Œuf. Bruxelles, 1865.

cross likewise in a ring, a three-horned cap, and a symbol like two horns [3].

A third Egyptian cross is that represented Fig. 16, which apparently is intended for a Latin cross rising out of a heart, like the mediæval emblem of " Cor in Cruce, Crux in Corde : " it is the hieroglyph of goodness [4].

The handled cross was certainly a sacred symbol among the Babylonians. It occurs repeatedly on their cylinders, bricks, and gems.

On a cylinder in the Paris Cabinet of Antiquities, published by Münter [5], are four figures, the first winged, the second armed with what seems to be thunderbolts. Beside him is the crux ansata, with a hawk sitting on the oval handle. The other figures are a woman and a child. This cross is half the height of the deity.

Another cylinder in the same Cabinet represents three personages. Between two with tiaras is the same symbol. A third in the same collection bears the same three principal figures as the first. The winged deity holds a spear ; the central god

---

[3] Bonomi, Nineveh and its Palaces, pp. 303, 333, 414.

[4] H. W. Westrop, in Gentleman's Magazine, N. S., vol. xv., p. 80.

[5] Münter, Religion d. Babylonier, Taf. i.

is armed with a bundle of thunderbolts and a dart, and is accompanied by the cross; the third, a female, bears a flower. On another and still more curious cylinder is a monarch or god, behind whom stands a servant holding up the symbol (Fig. 17). The god is between two handled crosses, and behind the servant is a Maltese cross. Some way above is a bird with expanded wings. Again, on another the winged figure is accompanied by the cross. A remarkable specimen, from which I have copied the principal figure (Fig. 18), represents a god holding the sacred sign by the long arm, whilst a priest offers him a gazelle.

An oval seal, of white chalcedony, engraved in the Mémoires de l'Académie royale des Inscriptions et Belles Lettres (vol. xvi.), has as subject a standing figure between two stars, beneath which are handled crosses. Above the head of the deity is the triangle, or symbol of the Trinity.

This seal is of uncertain origin : it is supposed not to be Babylonish, but Phœnician. The Phœnicians also regarded the cross as a sacred sign. The goddess Astarte, the moon, the presiding divinity over the watery element, is represented on the coins of Byblos holding a long staff surmounted by a cross, and resting her foot on the prow of a galley, and not unlike the familiar figures of Faith on the Christian Knowledge Society books.

The cyclopean temple at Gozzo, the island adjacent to Malta, has been supposed to be a shrine of the Phœnicians to Mylitta or Astarte. It is of a cruciform shape (Fig. 9). A superb medal of Cilicia, bearing a Phœnician legend, and struck under the Persian domination, has on one side a figure of this goddess with a crux ansata by her side, the lower member split.

Another form of the cross (Figs. 19, 20) is repeated frequently and prominently on coins of Asia Minor. It occurs as the reverse of a silver coin supposed to be of Cyprus, on several Cilician coins: it is placed beneath the throne of Baal of Tarsus, on a Phœnician coin of that town, bearing the legend בעל תרז (Baal Tharz). A medal, possibly of the same place, with partially obliterated Phœnician characters, has the cross occupying the entire field of the reverse side. Several, with inscriptions in unknown characters, have a ram on one side, and the cross and ring on the other. Another has the sacred bull accompanied by this symbol; others have a lion's head on obverse, and the cross and circle on the reverse.

A beautiful Sicilian medal of Camarina bears a

swan and altar, and beneath the altar is one of these crosses with a ring attached to it [6].

As in Phœnician iconography this cross generally accompanies a deity, in the same manner as the handled cross is associated with the Persepolitan, Babylonish, and Egyptian gods, we may conclude that it had with the Phœnicians the same signification of life eternal. That it also symbolized regeneration through water, I also believe. On Babylonish cylinders it is generally employed in conjunction with the hawk or eagle, either seated on it, or flying above it. This eagle is Nisroch, whose eyes are always flowing with tears for the death of Tammūz. Nesr, or Nisroch, is certainly the rain-cloud. In Greek iconography Zeus, the heaven, is accompanied by the eagle to symbolize the cloud. On several Phœnician or uncertain coins of Asia Minor the eagle and the cross go together. Therefore I think that the cross may symbolize life restored by rain.

An inscription in Thessaly, **ΕΡΜΑΩ ΧΘΟΝΙΟΥ**, is accompanied by a Calvary cross (Fig. 21); and Greek crosses of equal arms adorn the tomb of

---

[6] These medals are engraved to accompany the article of M. Raoul-Rochette on the Croix ansée, in the Mém. de l'Académie des Inscr. et Belles Lettres, tom. xvi.

Midas, in Phrygia. Crosses of different shapes, chiefly like Figs. 2 and 11, are common on ancient cinerary urns in Italy. These two forms occur on sepulchral vessels found under a bed of volcanic tufa on the Alban mount, and of remote antiquity.

It is curious that the **T** should have been used on the roll of the Roman soldiery as the sign of life, whilst the **Θ** designated death [7].

But, long before the Romans, long before the Etruscans, there lived in the plains of Northern Italy a people to whom the cross was a religious symbol, the sign beneath which they laid their dead to rest; a people of whom history tells nothing, knowing not their name; but of whom antiquarian research has learned this, that they lived in ignorance of the arts of civilization, that they dwelt in villages built on platforms over lakes, and that they trusted in the cross to guard, and may be to revive, their loved ones whom they committed to the dust. Throughout Emilia are found remains of these people; these remains form quarries whence manure is dug by the peasants of the present day. These quarries

[7] Isidor. Origin. i., c. 23. "**T** nota in capite versiculi supposita superstitem designat." Persius, Sat. iv. 13. Rufin. in Hieronym. ap. Casaubon ad Pers.

go by the name of *terramares*. They are vast accumulations of cinders, charcoal, bones, fragments of pottery, and other remains of human industry. As this earth is very rich in phosphates, it is much appreciated by the agriculturists as a dressing for their land. In these terramares there are no human bones. The fragments of earthenware belong to articles of domestic use; with them are found querns, moulds for metal, portions of cabin floors and walls, and great quantities of kitchen refuse. They are deposits analogous to those which have been discovered in Denmark and in Switzerland. The metal discovered in the majority of these terramares is bronze. The remains belong to three distinct ages. In the first none of the fictile ware was turned on the wheel or fire-baked. Sometimes these deposits exhibit an advance of civilization. Iron came into use, and with it the potter's wheel was discovered, and the earthenware was put in the furnace.

When in the same quarry these two epochs are found, the remains of the second age are always superposed over those of the bronze age.

A third period is occasionally met with, but only occasionally. A period when a rude art introduced itself, and representations of animals or human beings adorned the pottery. Among the remains of this period is found the first trace of money, the æs rude, little bronze fragments without shape.

According to the calculations of M. Des Vergers, the great development of Etruscan civilization took place about 290 years before the foundation of Rome, more than 1040 years before our era. The age of the terramares must be long antecedent to the time of Etruscan civilization. The remote antiquity of these remains may be gathered from the amount of accumulation over them. A section of the deposit in Parma, where was one of these lacustrine villages is as follows :—

	ft.	in.
Roman and later remains . . . . . . a depth of	4	1
Midden of ancient inhabitants, three deposits separated by thin layers of red earth or ashes	6	8
Latest bed of lake containing piles	7	0
Secondary bed containing piles	3	3
Original bed of lake containing piles	21	0

Twice had the accumulation risen so as to necessitate the re-driving of piles, and over the last, the deposits had reached the height of 6 feet 8 inches. Since the age when these people vanished, earth has accumulated to the depth of 4 feet.

At Castione, not far from the station of Borgo S. Donino, on the line between Parma and Placenza, is a convent built on a mound. Where that mound rises there was originally a lake, and the foundations of the building are laid in the ruins of an ancient population which filled the lake, and converted it into a hill of refuse.

From the broken bones in the middens, we learn that the roebuck, the stag, the wild boar, then ranged the forests, that cattle, pigs, sheep, goats, and dogs were domesticated; that these people had two kinds of horses, one a powerful animal, the other small-boned, and that horseflesh was eaten by the inhabitants of the terramares.

Wheat, barley, millet, and beans have been found about the piles, together with the stones of wild plums, sloes, and cherries, also crab-apple pips.

A bronze dagger was found at Castione, a spear-head of the same metal in the deposit of Bargone di Salso. A hatchet came from the terramare of Noceto ; quantities of little wheels, of unknown use, have been discovered, also hair-pins and combs. One, for a lady's back-hair, ornamented, and of stag's horn, came from the terramare of Fodico di Poviglio. The pottery found is mostly in fragments. Sometimes the bottoms of the vessels were rudely engraved with crosses (Figs. 22, 23, 24).

At Villanova, in the Commune of S. Maria delle

Caselle, near Bologna, has been discovered a cemetery of this ancient people. The graves cover a
space measuring about 73 yards by 36 yards. One
hundred and thirty-three tombs have been examined.
They were constructed of great boulders, rect-
angular, somewhat cylindrical, and slightly conical.
Earth had accumulated over them, and they were
buried. They were about four feet deep. The cist
was floored with slabs of freestone, the sides were
built up of boulders ; other cists were constructed of
slabs, and cubical in shape. A hundred and seventy-
nine of the bodies had been burnt. Each tomb
contained a cinerary urn containing the calcined
human remains. The urns were of a peculiar shape,
and appeared to have been made for the purpose.
They resembled a dice-box, and consisted of a
couple of inverted cones with a partition at their
bases, where they were united. Half-melted remains
of ornaments were found with some of the human
ashes. In one vessel was a charred fragment of a
horse's rib. Therefore it is likely that the favourite
horse was sacrificed and consumed with his master.

The mouth of the urn which contained the ashes
of the deceased was closed with a little vessel or
saucer. Near the remains of the dead were found
curious solid double cones with rounded ends; these

ends were elaborately engraved with crosses (Figs. 23. 25. 27). In the ossuaries made of double cones, around the diaphragm ran a line of circles containing crosses (Fig. 26).

Another cemetery of the same people exists at Golasecca, on the plateau of Somma, at the extremity of the Lago Maggiore. A vast number of sepulchres have there been opened. They belong to the same period as those of Villanova, the age of lacustrine habitations.

"That which characterizes the sepulchres of Golasecca, and gives them their highest interest," says M. de Mortillet, who investigated them, "is this, —first, the entire absence of all organic representations ; we only found three, and they were exceptional, in tombs not belonging to the plateau ;— secondly, the almost invariable presence of the cross under the vases in the tombs. When one reverses the ossuaries, the saucer-lids, or the accessory vases, one saw almost always, if in good preservation, a cross traced thereon. . . . The examination of the tombs of Golasecca proves in a most convincing, positive, and precise manner, that which the terramares of Emilia had only indicated, but which had been confirmed by the cemetery of Villanova ; that above a thousand years before

Christ, the cross was already a religious emblem of frequent employment [8]."

It may be objected to this, that the cross is a sign so easily made, that it was naturally the first attempted by a rude people. There are, however, so many varieties of crosses among the urns of Golasecca, and ingenuity seems to have been so largely exercised in diversifying this one sign, without recurring to others, that I cannot but believe the sign itself had a religious signification.

On the other side of the Alps, at the same period, lived a people in a similar state of civilization, whose palustrine habitations and remains have been carefully explored. Among the Swiss potteries, however, the cross is very rarely found.

In the depths of the forests of Central America, is a ruined city. It was not inhabited at the time of the conquest of Mexico by the Spaniards. They discovered the temples and palaces of Chiapa, but of Palenque they knew nothing. According to tradition it was founded by Votan

---

[8] De Mortillet, Le signe de la Croix avant le Christianisme. Paris, 1866. The title of this book is deceptive. The subject is the excavations of pre-historic remains in Northern Italy, and pre-Christian crosses are only casually and cursorily dealt with.

in the ninth century before the Christian era. The principal building in Palenque is the palace, 228 feet long, by 180 feet, and 40 feet high. The Eastern façade has fourteen doors opening on a terrace, with bas-reliefs between them. A noble tower rises above the courtyard in the centre. In this building are several small temples or chapels, with altars standing. At the back of one of these altars is a slab of gypsum, on which are sculptured two figures standing, one on each side of a cross (Fig. 28), to which one is extending his hands with an offering of a baby or a monkey. The cross is surrounded with rich feather-work, and ornamental chains [9].

The style of sculpture, and the accompanying hieroglyphic inscriptions leave no room for doubting it to be a heathen representation. Above the cross is a bird of peculiar character, perched, as we saw the eagle Nisroch on a cross upon a Babylonish cylinder. The same cross is represented on old pre-Mexican MSS., as in the Dresden Codex, and that in the possession of Herr Fejérváry, at the end of which is a colossal cross, in the midst of which is represented a bleeding deity, and figures

[9] Stephens, Central America. London, 1842. Vol. ii. p. 346

stand round a Tau cross, upon which is perched
the sacred bird [1].

The cross was also used in the north of Mexico.
It occurs amongst the Mixtecas and in Queredaro.
Siguenza speaks of an Indian cross which was found
in the cave of Mixteca Baja.   Among the ruins on
the island of Zaputero in Lake Nicaragua were also
found old crosses reverenced by the Indians.   White
marble crosses were found on the island of S. Ulloa,
on its discovery.   In the state of Oaxaca, the
Spaniards found that wooden crosses were erected
as sacred symbols, so also in Aguatolco, and among
the Zapatecas.   The cross was venerated as far as
Florida on one side, and Cibola on the other.   In South
America, the same sign was considered symbolical
and   sacred.   It   was   revered   in   Paraguay.   In
Peru the Incas honoured a cross made out of a
single piece of jasper, it was an emblem belonging to a former civilization.

Among the Muyscas at Cumana the cross was regarded with devotion, and was believed to be endued
with power to drive away evil spirits; consequently
new-born children were placed under the sign [2].

[1] Klemm, Kulturgeschichte, v. 142, 143.
[2] See list of authorities in Müller, Geschichte der Amerikanischen Urreligionen.   Basel, 1855, pp. 371. 421. 498, 499.

Probably all these crosses, certainly those of Central America, were symbols of the Rain-god. This we are told by the conquerors, of the crosses on the island of Cozumel. The cross was not an original symbol of the Azteks and Tolteks, but of the Maya race, who inhabited Mexico, Guatemala, and Yucatan. The Mayas were subdivided into the tribes of Totonacs, Othomi, Huasteks, Tzendales, &c., and were conquered by a Nahual race from the North, called Azteks and Tolteks, who founded the great Mexican empire with which Cortez and his Spaniards were brought in collision[3]. This Maya stock was said to have been highly civilized, and the conquered to have influenced their conquerors.

The Maya race invaded Central America, coming from the Antilles, when the country was peopled by the Quinamies, to whom the Cyclopean erections still extant are attributed. They were overthrown by Votan, B.C. 800. The cross was adopted by the Azteks, from the conquered Mayas. It was the emblem of Quiateot, the god of Rain. In order to obtain rain

---

[3] It is exceedingly difficult to classify these races, and arrive at any exact conclusions with regard to their history. The Tzendales were probably never conquered.

little boys and girls were sacrificed to him, and their flesh was devoured at a sacred banquet by the chiefs.   Among the Mexicans, the showery month Quiahuitl received its name from him.   In Cibola, water as the generator was honoured under this symbol ; in Cozumel, the sacred cross in the temples was of wood or stone, ten palms high, and to it were offered incense and quails.   To obtain showers, the people bore it in procession.

The Tolteks said that their national deity Quetzalcoatl had introduced the sign and ritual of the cross, and it was their God of Rain and Health, and was called the Tree of Nutriment, or Tree of Life. On this account also was the mantle of the Toltek atmospheric god covered with red crosses.

The cross was again a symbol of mysterious significance in Brahminical iconography.   In the Cave of Elephanta, in India, over the head of a figure engaged in massacring infants, is to be seen the cross.   It is placed by Müller, in his " Glauben, Wissen, und Kunst der alten Hindus," in the hands of Seva, Brahma, Vishnu, Tvashtri (Fig. 29).   This cross has a wheel in the centre, and is called Kiakra or Tschakra.   When held by Vishnu, the world-sustaining principle, it signifies his power to penetrate heaven and earth, and bring to naught the powers of evil.   It symbolizes the eternal governance of the world, and to it the worshipper of Vishnu attributes as many virtues as does the devout Catholic to the Christian cross. Fra Paolino tells us it was used by the ancient kings of India as a sceptre.

In a curious Indian painting reproduced by Müller (Tab. i., fig. 2), Brahma is represented crowned with clouds, with lilies for eyes, with four hands—one holding the necklace of creation; another the Veda ; a third, the chalice of the source of life ; the fourth, the fiery cross. Another painting (Tab. i., fig. 78) represents Krishna in the centre of the world as its sustaining principle, with six arms, three of which hold the cross, one a sceptre of dominion, another a flute, a third a sword. Another (Tab. ii., fig. 61) gives Jama, the judge of the nether world, with spear, sword, scales, torch, and cross. Tab. ii., fig. 140, gives Brawani, the female earth principle, holding a lily, a flame, a sword, and a cross. The list of representations might be greatly extended.

It was only natural that the early and mediæval Christians, finding the cross a symbol of life among the nations of antiquity, should look curiously into the Old Testament, to see whether there were not foreshadowings in it of "the wood whereby righteousness cometh."

They found it in the blood struck on the lintel and the door-posts of the houses of the Israelites in Egypt. They supposed the rod of Moses to have been headed with the Egyptian Crux ansata, in which case its employment in producing the storm of rain and hail, in dividing the Red Sea, in bringing streams of water from the rock, testify to its symbolic character with reference to water. They saw it in Moses with arms expanded on the Mount, in the pole with transverse bar upon which was wreathed the brazen serpent, and in the two sticks gathered by the Widow of Sarepta. But especially was it seen in the passage of Ezekiel (ix. 4. 6), "The Lord said unto him, Go through the midst of the city, through the midst of Jerusalem, and set a mark upon the foreheads of the men that sigh and that cry for all the abominations that be done in the midst thereof. Slay utterly old and young, both maids, and little children, and women : but come not near any man upon whom is the mark ; and begin at My sanctuary." In the Vulgate, it stands : " Et signa Thau super frontes vivorum gementium." There is some doubt as to whether the sign Thau should be inserted or not. The Septuagint does not give it. It simply says δὸς σημεῖον. S. Jerome testifies that the versions of

Aquila and Symmachus, written, the one under Adrian, the other under Marcus Aurelius, were without it, and that it was only in the version of Theodotion, made under Septimius Severus, that the T was inserted. Nevertheless S. Jerome adopted it in his translation.

On the other hand Tertullian saw the cross in this passage[4]. The Thau was the old Hebrew character, which the Samaritan resembled, and which was shaped like a cross. S. Jerome probably did not adopt his rendering without foundation, for he was well skilled in Hebrew, and he refers again and again to this passage of Ezekiel[5]. The Epistle of S. Barnabas seems to allude to it[6]; so do S. Cyprian, S. Augustine, Origen, and S. Isidore[7]. Bishop Lowth was disposed to accept the Thau, so was Dr. Münter, the Protestant bishop of Zeeland. But, indeed, there need be little doubt as to the passage. The

---

[4] Adv. Marcion. iii. 22 : "Est enim littera, Græcorum Thau, nostra autem T, species crucis quam portendebant futuram in frontibus nostris apud veram et catholicam Hierusalem."

[5] In Ezech. ix. 4.   Epistol. ad Fabiol.   In Isaia c. lxvi.

[6] Epist. ch. ix. : Σταυρὸς ἐν τῷ T ἔμελλεν ἔχειν τὴν χάριν.

[7] Cypr. Testimon. adv. Jud. ii. c. 27.   August. de Alterc Synag. et Eccles.

word for *sign* used by the prophet is תָּו *Tau*, meaning, as Gesenius says in his Lexicon, *signum cruciforme;* and he adds, "The Hebrews on their coins adopted the most ancient cruciform sign +."

The Mediævals went further still, they desired to see the cross still stronger characterized in the history of the Jewish Church, and as the records of the Old Covenant were deficient on that point, they supplemented them with fable.

That fable is the romance or Legend of the Cross, a legend of immense popularity in the Middle Ages, if we may judge by the numerous representations of its leading incidents, which meet us in stained glass and fresco.

In the churches of Troyes alone, it appears on the windows of S. Martin-ès-Vignes, of S. Pantaléon, S. Madeleine, and S. Nizier[8].

It is frescoed along the walls of the choir of the church of S. Croce at Florence, by the hand of Agnolo Gaddi. Pietro della Francesca also dedicated his pencil to the history of the Cross in a series of frescoes in the Chapel of the Bacci, in the church of S. Francesco at Arezzo. It occurs as a predella painting among the specimens of early art

---

[8] Curiosités de la Champagne.   Paris, 1860.

in the Academia delle Belle Arti at Venice, and is the subject of a picture by Beham in the Munich Gallery[9]. The legend is told in full in the Vita Christi, printed at Troyes in 1517, in the Legenda Aurea of Jacques de Voragine, in an old Dutch work, "Gerschiedenis van det heylighe Cruys," in a French MS. of the thirteenth century in the British Museum. Gervase of Tilbury relates a portion of it in his Otia Imperialia[1], quoting from Comestor; it appears also in the Speculum Historiale, in Gottfried von Viterbo, in the Chronicon Engelhusii, and elsewhere.

Gottfried introduces a Hiontus in the place of Seth in the following story; Hiontus is corrupted from Ionicus or Ionithus.

The story is as follows:—

When our first father was banished Paradise, he lived in penitence, striving to recompense for the past by prayer and toil. When he reached a great age and felt death approach, he summoned Seth to his side, and said, "Go, my son, to the terrestrial Paradise, and ask the Archangel who keeps the gate to give me a balsam which will

[9] Lady Eastlake's History of our Lord. Lond. 1865, ii. p. 390.

[1] Tertia Decisio, c. liv.; ed. Liebrecht, p. 25.

save me from death. You will easily find the way, because my footprints scorched the soil as I left Paradise. Follow my blackened traces, and they will conduct you to the gate whence I was expelled."
Seth hastened to Paradise. The way was barren, vegetation was scanty and of sombre colours; over all lay the black prints of his father's and mother's feet. Presently the walls surrounding Paradise appeared. Around them nature revived, the earth was covered with verdure and dappled with flowers. The air vibrated with exquisite music. Seth was dazzled with the beauty which surrounded him, and he walked on forgetful of his mission. Suddenly there flashed before him a wavering line of fire, upright, like a serpent of light continuously quivering. It was the flaming sword in the hand of the Cherub who guarded the gate. As Seth drew nigh, he saw that the angel's wings were expanded so as to block the door. He prostrated himself before the Cherub, unable to utter a word. But the celestial being read in his soul, better than a mortal can read a book, the words which were there impressed, and he said, " The time of pardon is not yet come. Four thousand years must roll away ere the Redeemer shall open the gate to Adam, closed by his disobedience.

But as a token of future pardon, the wood whereon redemption shall be won shall grow from the tomb of thy father. Behold what he lost by his transgression!"

At these words the angel swung open the great portal of gold and fire, and Seth looked in.

He beheld a fountain, clear as crystal, sparkling like silver dust, playing in the midst of the garden, and gushing forth in four living streams. Before this mystic fountain grew a mighty tree, with a trunk of vast bulk, and thickly branched, but destitute of bark and foliage. Around the bole was wreathed a frightful serpent or caterpillar, which had scorched the bark and devoured the leaves. Beneath the tree was a precipice. Seth beheld the roots of the tree in Hell. There Cain was endeavouring to grasp the roots, and clamber up them into Paradise; but they laced themselves around the body and limbs of the fratricide, as the threads of a spider's web entangle a fly, and the fibres of the tree penetrated the body of Cain as though they were endued with life.

Horror-struck at this appalling spectacle, Seth raised his eyes to the summit of the tree. Now all was changed. The tree had grown till its branches reached heaven. The boughs were co-

vered with leaves, flowers, and fruit.   But the fairest
fruit was a little babe, a living sun, who seemed to
be listening to the songs of seven white doves
who circled round his head.   A woman, more
lovely than the moon, bore the child in her
arms.

Then the Cherub shut the door, and said, " I give
thee now three seeds taken from that tree.   When
Adam is dead, place these three seeds in thy father's
mouth, and bury him."

So Seth took the seeds and returned to his
father.   Adam was glad to hear what his son told
him, and he praised God.   On the third day after
the return of Seth he died.   Then his son buried
him in the skins of beasts which God had given him
for a covering, and his sepulchre was on Golgotha.
In course of time three trees grew from the seeds
brought from Paradise : one was a cedar, another a
cypress, and the third a pine.   They grew with prodigious force, thrusting their boughs to right and
left.   It was with one of these boughs that Moses
performed his miracles in Egypt, brought water out
of the rock, and healed those whom the serpents
slew in the desert.

After a while the three trees touched one another,
then began to incorporate and confound their

several natures in a single trunk. It was beneath this tree that David sat when he bewailed his sins.

In the time of Solomon, this was the noblest of the trees of Lebanon ; it surpassed all in the forests of King Hiram, as a monarch surpasses those who crouch at his feet. Now, when the son of David erected his palace, he cut down this tree to convert it into the main pillar supporting his roof. But all in vain. The column refused to answer the purpose : it was at one time too long, at another too short. Surprised at this resistance, Solomon lowered the walls of his palace, to suit the beam, but at once it shot up and pierced the roof, like an arrow driven through a piece of canvas, or a bird recovering its liberty. Solomon, enraged, cast the tree over Cedron, that all might trample on it as they crossed the brook.

There the Queen of Sheba found it, and she, recognizing its virtue, had it raised. Solomon then buried it. Some while after, the king dug the pool of Bethesda on the spot. This pond at once acquired miraculous properties, and healed the sick who flocked to it. The water owed its virtues to the beam which lay beneath it.

When the time of the Crucifixion of Christ drew

nigh, this wood rose to the surface, and was brought out of the water. The executioners, when seeking a suitable beam to serve for the cross, found it, and of it made the instrument of the death of the Saviour. After the Crucifixion it was buried on Calvary, but it was found by the Empress Helena, mother of Constantine the Great, deep in the ground with two others, May 3, 328 ; Christ's was distinguished from those of the thieves by a sick woman being cured by touching it. This same event is, however, ascribed by a Syriac MS. in the British Museum, unquestionably of the 5th century, to Protonice, wife of the Emperor Claudius. It was carried away by Chosroes, king of Persia, on the plundering of Jerusalem ; but was recovered by Heraclius, who defeated him in battle, Sept. 14, 615 ; a day that has ever since been commemorated as the Feast of the Exaltation of the Cross.

Such is the Legend of the Cross, one of the wildest of mediæval fancies. It is founded, though unconsciously, on this truth, that the Cross was a sacred sign long before Christ died upon it.

And how account for this ?

For my own part, I see no difficulty in believing that it formed a portion of the primæval religion, traces of which exist over the whole world, among every people ; that trust in the Cross was a part of the ancient faith which taught men to believe in a Trinity, in a War in Heaven, a Paradise from which man fell, a Flood, and a Babel ; a faith which was deeply impressed with a conviction that a Virgin should conceive and bear a son, that the Dragon's head should be bruised, and that through Shedding of blood should come Remission. The use of the cross, as a symbol of life and regeneration through water, is as widely spread over the world as the belief in the ark of Noah. May be, the shadow of the Cross was cast further back into the night of ages, and fell on a wider range of country, than we are aware of.

It is more than a coincidence that Osiris by the cross should give life eternal to the Spirits of the Just ; that with the cross Thorr should smite the head of the Great Serpent, and bring to life those who were slain ; that beneath the cross the Muysca mothers should lay their babes, trusting by that sign to secure them from the power of evil spirits ; that with that symbol to protect them, the ancient people of Northern Italy should lay them down in the dust [2].

[2] Appendix C.

Schamir

IT will be remembered that, on the giving of the law from Sinai, Moses was bidden erect to God an altar: "Thou shalt not build it of hewn stone, for if thou lift up thy tool upon it, thou hast polluted it" (Exod. xx. 25). And later: "There shalt thou build an altar unto the Lord thy God, an altar of stones: thou shalt not lift up any iron tool upon them" (Deut. xxvii. 6). Such an altar was raised by Joshua after the passage of Jordan: "An altar of whole stones, over which no man hath lift up any iron" (Joshua viii. 31).

When King Solomon erected his glorious temple, "the house, when it was in building, was built of stone made ready before it was brought thither: so that there was neither hammer, nor axe, nor any tool of iron, heard in the house while it was in building" (1 Kings vi. 7). And the reason of the prohibition of iron in the construction of the altar is given in the Mischna—iron is used to shorten life, the altar to prolong it (Middoth 3, 4). Iron is the metal used in war; with it, says Pliny, we do the best and worst acts: we plough fields, we build houses, we cleave rocks; but with it, also, come strife, and bloodshed, and rapine. The altar was the symbol of peace made between God and man, and therefore the metal employed in war was forbidden to be used in its erection. The idea was extended by Solomon to the whole temple. It is not said that iron was not used in the preparation of the building stones, but that no tool was heard in the fitting together of the parts.

That temple symbolized the Church triumphant in heaven when the stones, hewn afar off in the quarries of this world, are laid noiselessly in their proper place, so that the whole, "fitly framed together, groweth unto a holy temple in the Lord;" an idea well expressed in the ancient hymn "Angulare fundamentum:"—

> "Many a blow and biting sculpture
> Polish'd well those stones elect,
> In their places well compacted
> By the heavenly Architect."

Nothing in the sacred narrative implies any

miraculous act having been accomplished in this erecting a temple of stones hewn at a distance; and in the account of the building of the temple in the Book of Chronicles no reference is made to the circumstance, which would have been the case had any marvel attended it.

The Septuagint renders the passage, ὁ οἶκος λίθοις ἀκροτόμοις ἀργοῖς ᾠκοδομήθη. The word ἀκρότομος is used by the LXX in three places, for חַלָּמִישׁ, which is rough, hard, unhewn stone. Where it says in Deuteronomy (viii. 15), "Who brought thee forth water out of the rock of flint," the LXX use ἀκρότομος. Where the Psalmist says, " Who turned the flint-stone into a springing well" (Ps. cxiv. 8), and Job, " He putteth His hand upon the rock " (xxviii. 9), they employ ἀκρότομος. So, too, in the Book of Wisdom (xi. 4), "Water was given them out of the flinty rock," ἐκ πέτρας ἀκροτόμου, which is paralleled by "the hard stone," λίθος σκληρός. And in Ecclesiasticus, Ezekias is said to have " digged the hard rock with iron," ὤρυξε σιδήρῳ ἀκρότομον (xlviii. 17).

Λίθος ἀκρότομος is, therefore, not a hewn stone, but one with natural angles, unhewn. Thus Suidas uses the expression, σκληρὰ καὶ ἄτμητος, and Theodotion calls the sharp stone used by Zipporah in circumcising her son, ἀκρότομος. The ἀργοῖς of the LXX signifies also the rough natural condition of the stones. Thus Pausanias speaks of gold and silver in unfused, rough lumps as ἄργυρος καὶ χρυσὸς ἀργός. Apparently, then, the LXX, in saying that the temple was erected of ἀκροτόμοις ἀργοῖς, express their meaning that the stones were unhewn and in their natural condition, so that the skill of Solomon was exhibited in putting together stones which had never been subjected to the tool. This is also the opinion of Josephus, who says, "The whole edifice of the temple is, with great art, compacted of rough stones, ἐκ λίθων ἀκροτόμων, which have been fitted into one another quite harmoniously, without the work of hammer or any other builder's tool being observable, but the whole fits together without the use of these, and the fitting seems to be rather one of free will than of force through mechanical means." And therein lay the skill of the king, for the un-shapen blocks were pieced together as though they had been carefully wrought to their positions. And Procopius says that the temple was erected of unhewn stones, as it was forbidden of God to lift iron upon them, but that, nevertheless, they all fitted into one another. We see in these passages tokens of the marvellous having been supposed to attach to a work which was free from any miraculous interposition. But at this point fable did not stop. Upon the carrying away of the Jews to Babylon, they were brought into contact with a flood of Iranian as well as Chaldæan myths, and adopted them without hesitation.

Around Solomon accumulated the fables which were related of Dschemschid and other Persian heroes, and were adopted by the Jews as legends of native production. It was not sufficient that Solomon should have skilfully pieced together the rough stones : he was supposed to have hewn them by supernatural means, without the tool of iron.

As Solomon, thus ran the tale, was about to build the temple without the use of iron, his wise men drew his attention to the stones of the high priest's breastplate, which had been cut and polished by something harder than themselves. This was schamir, which was able to cut where iron would not bite. Thereupon Solomon summoned the spirits to inform him of the whereabouts of this substance. They told him schamir was a worm of the size of a barley corn, but so powerful that the hardest flint could not resist him. The spirits advised Solomon to seek Asmodeus, king of the devils, who could give him further information. When Solomon inquired where Asmodeus was to be met with, they replied that, on a distant mountain, he had dug a huge cistern, out of which he daily drank. Solomon then sent Benaiah with a chain, on which was written the magic word "schem hammphorasch," a fleece of wool and a skin of wine. Benaiah, having arrived at the cistern of Asmodeus, undermined it, and let the water off by a little hole, which he then plugged up with the wool; after which he filled the pit with wine. The evil spirit came, as was his wont, to the cistern, and scented the wine. Suspecting treachery, he refused to drink, and retired; but at length, impelled by thirst, he drank, and, becoming intoxicated, was chained by Benaiah and carried away. Benaiah had no willing prisoner to conduct: Asmodeus plunged and kicked, upsetting trees and houses. In this manner he came near a hut in which lived a widow, and when she besought him not to injure her poor little cot, he turned aside, and, in so doing, broke his leg. "Rightly," said the devil, "is it written: 'a soft tongue breaketh the bone!'" (Prov. xxv. 15). And a *diable boiteux* he has ever remained. When in the presence of Solomon,

Asmodeus was constrained to behave with greater decorum. Schamir, he told Solomon, was the property of the Prince of the Sea, and that prince entrusted none with the mysterious worm except the moor-hen, which had taken an oath of fidelity to him. The moor-hen takes the schamir with her to the tops of the mountains, splits them, and injects seeds, which grow and cover the naked rocks. Wherefore the bird is called Naggar Tura, the mountain-carver. If Solomon desired to possess himself of the worm, he must find the nest of the moor-hen, and cover it with a plate of glass, so that the mother bird could not get at her young without breaking the glass. She would seek schamir for the purpose, and the worm must be obtained from her.

Accordingly, Benaiah, son of Jehoiada, sought the nest of the bird, and laid over it a piece of glass. When the moor-hen came, and could not reach her young, she flew away and fetched schamir, and placed it on the glass. Then Benaiah shouted, and so terrified the bird, that she dropped the worm and flew away. Benaiah by this means obtained possession of the coveted schamir, and bore it to Solomon. But the moor-hen was so distressed at having broken her oath to the Prince

of the Sea that she slew herself[1]. According to
another version, Solomon went to his fountain,
where he found the dæmon Sackar, whom he
captured by a ruse, and chained down. Solomon pressed his ring to the chains, and Sackar
uttered a cry so shrill that the earth quaked.

Quoth Solomon, "Fear not; I shall restore you
to liberty if you will tell me how to burrow noiselessly after minerals and metals."

"I know not how to do so," answered the Jin;
"but the raven can tell you: place over her eggs
a sheet of crystal, and you shall see how the
mother will break it."

Solomon did so, and the mother brought a stone
and shattered the crystal. "Whence got you that
stone?" asked Solomon.

"It is the stone Samur," answered the raven;
"it comes from a desert in the uttermost east."
So the monarch sent some giants to follow the
raven, and bring him a suitable number of stones[2]."

According to a third version, the bird is an eagle,
and schamir is the Stone of Wisdom.

---

[1] Gittin, lxviii. Eisenmenger : Neu-entdecktes Judenthum.
Königsberg, 1711, i. p. 351.
[2] Collin de Plancy : Légendes de l'Ancien Test. Paris,
1861, p. 280.

Possessed of this schamir, Solomon wrought the stones for his temple.

Rabbinical fantasy has developed other myths concerning this mysterious force, resident in worm or stone. On the second day of Creation were created the well by which Jacob met Rebecca, the manna which fed the Israelites, the wonder-working rod of Moses, the ass which spake to Balaam, and schamir, the means whereby without iron tool Solomon was to build the House of God. Schamir is not in early rabbinical fable a worm; the treatise Sota gives the first indication of its being regarded as something more than a stone, by terming it a "creature," ברייתא. "Our Rabbis have taught us that schamir is a creature as big as a barley-corn, created in the hexameron, and that nothing can resist it. How is it preserved? It is wrapped in a wisp of wool, and kept in a leaden box full of small grains like barley-meal[3]." After the building of the temple schamir vanished.

The story passed to the Greeks. Ælian relates of the ἔποψ or hoopoe, that a bird had once a nest in an old wall, in which there was a rent. The proprietor plastered over this crack. The hoopoe find-

---

[3] Sota, xlviii. 8.

ing that she could not get to her young, flew away
in quest of a plant πόα, which she brought, and
applied to the plaster, which at once gave way,
and admitted her to her young. Then she went
forth to seek food, and the man again stopped up
the hole, but once more the hoopoe removed the
obstacle by the same means. And this took place
a third time again[4]. What Ælian relates of the
hoopoe, Pliny tells of the woodpecker. This bird,
he says, brings up its young in holes; and if the
entrance to them be plugged up never so tight, the
bird is able to make the plug burst out.

In the English Gesta Romanorum is the following story. There lived in Rome a noble emperor,
Diocletian by name, who loved the virtue of compassion above every thing. Therefore he desired
to know which of all the birds was most kindly
affectioned towards its young. One day, the
Emperor was wandering in the forest, when he lit
upon the nest of a great bird called ostrich, in
which was the mother with her young. The king
took the nest along with the poults to his palace,
and put it into a glass vessel. This the mother-
bird saw, and, unable to reach her little ones, she

[4] Ælian, Hist. Animal. iii. 26.

returned into the wood, and after an absence of three days came back with a worm in her beak, called thumare. This she dropped on the glass, and by the power of the worm, the glass was shivered, and the young flew away after their mother. When the Emperor saw this, he highly commended both the affection and the sagacity of the ostrich. On which we may remark, that a portion of that sagacity was wanting to those who applied the myth to that bird which of all others is singularly deficient in the qualities with which Diocletian credited it. Similar stories are told by Vincent of Beauvais in his "Historical Mirror [5]," and by gossiping, fable-loving, and delightful Gervase of Tilbury [6]. The latter says that Solomon cut the stones of the temple with the blood of a little worm called thamir, which when sprinkled on the marble, made it easy to split. And the way in which Solomon obtained the worm was this. He had an ostrich, whose chick he put in a glass bottle. Seeing this, the ostrich ran to the desert, and brought the worm, and with its blood fractured the vessel. "And in our time, in the reign of Pope Alexander III.,

---

[5] Vincent Bellov., Spec. Nat. 20, 170.

[6] Gervasii Tilberiensis Otia Imp., ed. Liebrecht. Hanov. 1856, p. 48.

when I was a boy, there was found at Rome, a
vial full of milky liquid, which, when sprinkled on
any kinds of stone, made them receive such sculpture as the hand of the graver was wont to execute.
It was a vial discovered in a most ancient palace,
the matter and art of which was a subject of
wonder to the Roman people."

Gervase drew from Comestor (Regum lib. iii.
c. 5).

"If you wish to burst chains," says Albertus
Magnus[7], "go into the wood, and look for a woodpecker's nest, where there are young; climb the
tree, and choke the mouth of the nest with any thing
you like. As soon as she sees you do this, she flies
off for a plant, which she lays on the stoppage; this
bursts, and the plant falls to the ground under the
tree, where you must have a cloth spread for receiving it." But then, says Albertus, this is a fancy
of the Jews[8].

Conrad von Megenburg relates: "There is a bird
which in Latin is called merops, but which we in
German term Bömheckel (i.e. Baumhacker), which
nests in high trees, and when one covers its children
with something to impede the approach of the bird,

[7] De Mirab. Mundi. Argent. 1601, p. 225.
[8] De Animalibus. Mantua, 1479, ult. pag.

it brings a herb, and holds it over the obstacle, and it gives way.   The plant is called *herba meropis*, or woodpecker-plant, and is called in magical books *chora* [9]."

In Normandy, the swallow knows how to find upon the sea-beach a pebble which has the marvellous power of restoring sight to the blind.   The peasants tell of a certain way of obtaining possession of this stone.   You must put out the eyes of a swallow's young, whereupon the mother-bird will immediately go in quest of the stone.   When she has found it and applied it, she will endeavour to make away with the talisman, that none may discover it.   But if one has taken the precaution to spread a piece of scarlet cloth below the nest, the swallow, mistaking it for fire, will drop the stone upon it.

I met with the story in Iceland.   There the natives tell that there is a stone of such wondrous power, that the possessor can walk invisible, can, at a wish, provide himself with as much stock-fish and corn-brandy as he may desire, can raise the dead, cure disease, and break bolts and bars.   In order to obtain this prize, one must hard-boil an egg from

---

[9] Apud Mone, Anzeiger, viii. p. 614.

the raven's nest, then replace it, and secrete oneself till the mother-bird, finding one of her eggs resist all her endeavours to infuse warmth into it, flies off and brings a black pebble in her beak, with which she touches the boiled egg, and restores it to its former condition. At this moment she must be shot, and the stone be secured.

In this form of the superstition schamir has the power of giving life. This probably connects it with those stories, so rife in the middle ages, of birds or weasels, which were able to restore the dead to life by means of a mysterious plant. Avicenna relates in his eighth book, "Of Animals," that it was related to him by a faithful old man, that he had seen two little birds squabbling, and that one was overcome ; it therefore retired and ate of a certain herb, then it returned to the onslaught ; which when the old man observed frequently, he took away the herb, and when the bird came and found the plant gone, it set up a great cry and died. And this plant was *lactua agrestis*.

In Fouqué's "Sir Elidoc," a little boy Amyot is watching by a dead lady laid out in the church, when "suddenly I heard a loud cry from the child. I looked up, a little creature glided by me ; the shepherd's staff of the boy flew after it ; the creature

lay dead, stretched on the ground by the blow.   It
was a weasel. . . . Presently there came a
second weasel, as if to seek his comrade, and when
he found him dead, a mournful scene began ; he
touched him as if to say, 'Wake up, wake up,
let us play together !'   And when the other little
animal lay dead and motionless, the living one
sprang back from him in terror, and then repeated
the attempt again and again, many times.   Its
bright little eyes shone sadly, as if they were full of
tears.   The sorrowful creature seemed as though it
suddenly bethought itself of something.   It erected
its ears, it looked round with its bright eyes, and
then swiftly darted away.   And before Amyot and
I could ask each other of the strange sight, the little
animal returned again, bearing in its mouth a root,
a root to which grew a red flower ; I had never
before seen such a flower blowing ; I made a sign
to Amyot, and we both remained motionless.   The
weasel came up quickly, and laid the root and the
flower gently on its companion's mouth ; the creature, but now stiff in death, stretched itself, and
suddenly sprang up, with the root still in its mouth.
I called to Amyot, ' The root ! take it, take it, but
do not kill !'   Again he flung his staff, but so dexter-
ously that he killed neither of the weasels, nor even

hurt them. The root of life and the red blossoms lay on the ground before me, and in my power." With this, naturally enough, the lady who is speaking restores the corpse to life. Sir Eliduc is founded on a Breton legend, the Lai d'Eliduc of Marie de France; but another tale from the same country makes the flower yellow; it is a marigold, which, when touched on a certain morning by the bare foot of one who has a pure heart, gives the power to understand the language of birds [1]. This is the same story as that of Polyidus and Glaucus. Polyidus observed a serpent stealing towards the corpse of the young prince. He slew it; then came another serpent, and finding its companion dead, it fetched a root by which it restored life to the dead serpent. Polyidus obtained possession of the plant, and therewith revived Glaucus [2]. In the Greek romance of Rhodante and Dosicles is an incident of similar character. Rhodante swallows a poisoned goblet of wine, and lies as one dead, deprived of sense and motion. In the meanwhile, Dosicles and Cratander are chasing wild beasts in the forest. There they find a wounded bear, which seeks a certain plant, and, rolling upon it, recovers health

[1] Bode, Volksmährchen a. d. Bretagne. Leipz. 1847, p. 6.
[2] Apollodorus, ii. 3.

and vigour instantaneously. The root of this herb was white, its flowers of a rosy hue, attached to a stalk of purplish tinge. Dosicles picked the herb, and with it returned to the house where he found Rhodante apparently dead; with the wondrous plant he, however, was able to restore her. The same story is told in Germany, in Lithuania, among the modern Greeks and ancient Scandinavians.

Germany teems with stories of the marvellous properties of the Luckflower.

A man chances to pluck a beautiful flower, which in most instances is blue, and this he puts in his breast, or in his hat. Passing along a mountain side, he sees the rocks gape before him, and entering, he sees a beautiful lady, who bids him help himself freely to the gold which is scattered on all sides in profusion. He crams the glittering nuggets into his pockets, and is about to leave, when she calls after him, "Forget not the best!" Thinking that she means him to take more, he feels his crammed pockets, and finding that he has nothing to reproach himself with in that respect, he seeks the light of day, entirely forgetting the precious blue flower which had opened to him the rocks, and which has dropped on the ground.

As he hurries through the doorway, the rocks

close upon him with a thunder-crash and cut off his heel. The mountain-side is thenceforth closed to him for ever.

Once upon a time a shepherd was driving his flock over the Ilsenstein, when, wearied with his tramp, he leaned upon his staff. Instantly the mountain opened, for in that staff was the "Spring-wort." Within he saw the Princess Ilse, who bade him fill his pockets with gold. The shepherd obeyed, and was going away, when the princess exclaimed, "Forget not the best!" alluding to his staff, which lay against the wall. But he, misunderstanding her, took more gold, and the mountain clashing together, severed him in twain. In some versions of the story, it is the pale blue flower—

> "The blue flower, which—Bramins say—
> Blooms nowhere but in Paradise"—
>
> (*Lalla Rookh*)

which exclaims in feeble, piteous tone, "Forget-me-not!" but its little cry is unheeded.

Thus originated the name of the beautiful little flower. When this story was forgotten, a romantic fable was invented to account for the peculiar appellation.

In the story of Ali Baba and the Forty Thieves,

it is a word, "sesame," which makes the rocks part, and gives admission to the treasures within; and it is oblivion of the magic word which brings destruction upon the luckless wretch within. But sesame is the name of a well-known eastern plant, *sesamum orientale;* so that probably in the original form of the Persian tale absorbed into the Arabian Nights, a flower was employed to give admission to the mountain. But classic antiquity has also its rock-breaking plant, the *saxifraga,* whose tender rootlets penetrate and dissolve the hardest stones with a force for which the Ancients were unable to account.

Isaiah, describing the desolation of the vineyard of Zion, says that "There shall come up briars and thorns" (v. 6), לשמיר ולשית יהיה (vii. 23 : cf. also ix. 17; x. 17). And, "Upon the land of my people shall come up thorns and briars" (xxxii. 13), where שמיר is combined with קוץ. The word שית never stands alone, but is always joined with שמיר, which the LXX render ἄκανθα καὶ χόρτος; the word in the fifth chapter they render χέρσος ἄκανθαι; that in the seventh, χέρσος and ἄκανθα; so that χέρσος is put for שמיר, and ἄκανθα for שית. The word in the ninth chapter is ἄγρωστις ξηρά, that in the tenth, ὡσεὶ χόρτον τὴν ὕλην. Upon both names the translators are not agreed. Now, this word "smiris" is used by Isaiah alone as the name of a plant. The smiris, as we have seen, is a stone-breaking substance, and the same idea which is rendered in Latin by *saxifraga* is given in the Hebrew word used by Isaiah, so that we may take שמיר ושית to mean saxifraga and thorn[3]. In the North, we have another object, to which are attributed the same properties as to the "Springwort" and schamir, and that is the Hand of Glory. This is the hand of a man who has been hung, and it is prepared in the following manner: wrap the hand in a piece of winding-sheet, drawing it tight, so as to squeeze out the little blood which may remain ; then place it in an earthenware vessel with saltpetre, salt, and long pepper, all carefully and thoroughly powdered. Let it remain a fortnight in this pickle till it is well dried, then expose it to the sun in the dog-days, till it is completely parched, or, if the sun be not powerful enough, dry it in an oven heated with vervain and

---

[3] Cassel, Ueber Schamir, in Denkschrift d. Königl. Akad. der Wissenschaften. Erfurt, 1856, p. 76. The Oriental word "smiris" passed into use among the Greeks as the name of the hardest substance known, used in polishing stones, and is retained in the German "Smirgel," and the English "emery."

fern. Next make a candle with the fat of a hung man, virgin-wax, and Lapland sesame. Observe the use of this herb : the hand of glory is used to hold this candle when it is lighted[4]. Douster Swivel, in the "Antiquary," adds, " You do make a candle, and put into de hand of glory at de proper hour and minute, with de proper ceremonisth ; and he who seeksh for treasuresh shall find none at all!" Southey places it in the hands of the enchanter Mohareb, when he would lull to sleep Yohak, the giant guardian of the caves of Babylon. He—

> " From his wallet drew a human hand,
>   Shrivell'd, and dry, and black ;
>   And fitting, as he spake,
>   A taper in his hold,
>   Pursued : ' A murderer on the stake had died ;
> I drove the vulture from his limbs, and lopt
> The hand that did the murder, and drew up
>   The tendon strings to close its grasp ;
>   And in the sun and wind
>   Parch'd it, nine weeks exposed.
>   The taper . . . But not here the place to impart,
>   Nor hast thou undergone the rites
>   That fit thee to partake the mystery.
>   Look ! it burns clear, but with the air around,
>   Its dead ingredients mingle deathliness[5].' "

Several stories of this terrible hand are related in

[4] Collin de Plancy, Dictionnaire Infernal.   Paris, 1818.
[5] Thalaba the Destroyer, book v.

Henderson's "Folklore of the Northern Counties of England." I will only quote one, which was told me by a labouring man in the West Riding of Yorkshire, and which is the same story as that given by Martin Anthony Delrio in his "Disquisitiones Magicæ," in 1593, and which is printed in the Appendix to that book of M. Henderson.

One dark night, after the house had been closed, there came a tap at the door of a lone inn, in the midst of a barren moor.

The door was opened, and there stood without, shivering and shaking, a poor beggar, his rags soaked with rain, and his hands white with cold. He asked piteously for a lodging, and it was cheerfully granted him; though there was not a spare bed in the house, he might lie along on the mat before the kitchen fire, and welcome.

All in the house went to bed except the servant lassie, who from the kitchen could see into the large room through a small pane of glass let into the door. When every one save the beggar was out of the room, she observed the man draw himself up from the floor, seat himself at the table, extract a brown withered human hand from his pocket, and set it upright in the candlestick; he then anointed the fingers, and, applying a match to them, they began to flame. Filled with horror, the girl rushed up the back stairs, and endeavoured to arouse her master and the men of the house; but all in vain, they slept a charmed sleep; and finding all her efforts ineffectual, she hastened downstairs again. Looking again through the small window, she observed the fingers of the hand flaming, but the thumb gave no light: this was because one of the inmates of the house was not asleep. The beggar began collecting all the valuables of the house into a large sack—no lock withstood the application of the flaming hand. Then, putting it down, the man entered an adjoining apartment. The moment he was gone, the girl rushed in, and seizing the hand, attempted to extinguish the quivering yellow flames, which wavered at the fingers' ends. She blew at them in vain; she poured some drops from a beer-jug over them, but that only made the fingers burn the brighter; she cast some water upon them, but still without extinguishing the light. As a last resource, she caught up a jug of milk, and dashing it over the four lambent flames, they went out immediately.

Uttering a piercing cry, she rushed to the door

of the room the beggar had entered, and locked
it. The whole house was aroused, and the thief
was secured and hung.

We must not forget Tom Ingoldsby's rendering of a similar legend :—

> " Open, lock,
>   To the Dead Man's knock !
>   Fly, bolt, and bar, and band !
>   Nor move, nor swerve,
>   Joint, muscle, or nerve,
> At the spell of the Dead Man's hand !
> Sleep, all who sleep !—Wake, all who wake !
> But be as the dead for the Dead Man's sake !
>
> " Now lock, nor bolt, nor bar avails,
>   Nor stout oak panel thick-studded with nails.
> Heavy and harsh the hinges creak,
> Though they had been oil'd in the course of the week.
>   The door opens wide as wide may be,
>   And there they stand,
>   That murderous band,
>   Lit by the light of the GLORIOUS HAND,
>   By one !—by two !—by three ! "

But, instead of pursuing the fable through
its further ramifications, let us apply the schamir of comparative mythology to the myth itself,
and see whether before it the bolts do not
give way, and the great doors of the cavern of
mysteries expand, and discover to us the origin of the superstitious belief in this sea-prince's

worm, the stone of wisdom, sesame, forget-me-not, or the hand of glory.

What are its effects ?

It bursts locks, and shatters stones, it opens in the mountains the hidden treasures hitherto concealed from men, or it paralyzes, lulling into a magic sleep, or, again, it restores to life.

I believe the varied fables relate to one and the same object—and that, the lightning.

But what is the bird which bears schamir, the worm or stone which shatters rocks ? It is the storm-cloud, which in many a mythology of ancient days was supposed to be a mighty bird. In Greek iconography, Zeus, "the æther in his moist arms embracing the earth," as Euripides describes him, is armed with the thunderbolt, and accompanied by the eagle, a symbol of the cloud.

> "The refulgent heaven above,
> Which all men call, unanimously, Jove [6],"

has for its essential attributes the cloud and its bolt, and when the æther was represented under human form, the cloud was given shape as a bird. It is the same storm-cloud which as "blood-

---

[6] Cicero, De N. Deorum xvi.

thirsting eagle" banquets its "full on the black
viands of the liver" of Prometheus. The same
cloud in its fury is symbolized by the Phorcidæ
with their flashing eye and lightning tooth—

πρὸς Γοργόνεια πεδία Κισθήνης, ἵνα
αἱ Φορκίδες ναίουσι δηναιαὶ κόραι
τρεῖς κυκνόμορφοι, κοινὸν ὄμμ᾽ ἐκτημέναι,
μονόδοντες, ᾶς οὔθ᾽ ἥλιος προσδέρκεται
ἀκτίσιν, οὔθ᾽ ἡ νύκτερος μήνη ποτέ.

(ÆSCH. *Prom.*),

and also by the ravening harpies. In ancient
Indian mythology, the delicate white cirrus cloud
drifting overhead was a fleeting swan, and so it
was as well in the creed of the Scandinavian,
whilst the black clouds were ravens coursing
over the earth, and returning to whisper the news
in the ear of listening Odin. The rushing vapour
is the roc of the Arabian Nights, which broods
over its great luminous egg, the sun, and which
haunts the sparkling valley of diamonds, the
starry sky. The resemblance traced between
bird and cloud is not far fetched: it recurs to the
modern poet as it did to the Psalmist, when he
spoke of the "wings of the wind." If the cloud
was supposed to be a great bird, the lightnings
were regarded as writhing worms or serpents
in its beak. These fiery serpents, ἑλικίαι γραμμο-

εἰδῶς φερόμενοι, are believed in to this day by the Canadian Indians, who call the thunder their hissing. It was these heavenly reptiles which were supposed by the Druids to generate the sun, the famous anguineum so coveted and so ill comprehended. The thunderbolt shattering all it struck, was regarded as the stone dropped by the cloud-bird. A more forced resemblance is that supposed to exist between the lightning and a heavenly flower, blue, or yellow, or red, and yet there is evidence, upon which I cannot enter here, that so it was regarded.

The lightning-flashing cloud was also supposed to be a flaming hand. The Greek placed the forked dart in the hand of Zeus—

> " rubente
> Dextera sacras jaculatus arces ; "

and the ancient Mexican symbolized the sacrificial fire by a blood-red hand impressed on his sanctuary walls. The idea may have been present in the mind of the servant of Elijah when he told his master that he saw from the top of Carmel rising "A little cloud out of the sea, like a man's hand. And it came to pass, that the heaven was black with clouds and wind, and there was a great rain" (1 Kings xviii. 44). In Finnish and Esthonian mythology, the cloud is a little man with a copper hand, who, rising from the water, becomes a giant.

The black cloud with the lambent flames issuing from it was the original of the magical hand of glory.

The effects produced by the lightning are differently expressed. As shattering the rocks, schamir is easily intelligible. It is less so as giving access to the hidden treasures of the mountains. The ancient Aryan had the same name for cloud and mountain. To him the piles of vapour on the horizon were so like Alpine ranges, that he had but one word whereby to designate both. These great mountains of heaven were opened by the lightning. In the sudden flash he beheld the dazzling splendour within, but only for a moment, and then, with a crash, the celestial rocks closed again. Believing these vaporous piles to contain resplendent treasures of which partial glimpse was obtained by mortals in a momentary gleam, tales were speedily formed, relating the adventures of some who had succeeded in entering these treasure-mountains. The plant of life, brought by weasel or serpent, restores life to one who was dead. This myth was forged in Eastern lands, where the earth apparently dies from a protracted drought. Then comes the cloud. The lightning flash reaches the barren, dead, and thirsty land; forth gush the waters of heaven, and the parched vegetation bursts once more into the vigour of life, restored after suspended animation. It is the dead and parched vegetation which is symbolized by Glaucus, and the earth still and without the energy of life which is represented by the lady in the Lai d'Eliduc. This reviving power is attributed in mythology to the rain as well. In Sclavonic myths, it is the water of life which restores the dead earth, a water brought by a bird from the depths of a gloomy cave. A prince has been murdered,—that is, the earth is dead; then comes the eagle bearing a vial of the reviving water— the cloud with the rain; it sprinkles the corpse with the precious drops, and life returns[7].

But the hand of glory has a very different property—it paralyzes. In this it resembles the Gorgon's head or the basilisk. The head of Medusa, with its flying serpent locks, is unquestionably the storm-cloud; and the basilisk which strikes dead with its eye is certainly the

---

[7] Compare with this the Psyche in "The Golden Ass," and the Fair One with the Golden Locks of the Countess d'Aulnay.

same. The terror inspired by the outburst of the thunder-storm is expressed in fable by the paralyzing effect of the eye of the cockatrice, the exhibition of the Gorgon's countenance, and the waving of the glorious hand.

Strained as some of these explanations may seem, they are nevertheless true. We, with our knowledge of the causes producing meteorological phenomena, are hardly able to realize the extravagance of the theories propounded by the ignorant to account for them.

How Finn cosmogonists could have believed the earth and heaven to be made out of a severed egg, the upper concave shell representing heaven, the yolk being earth, and the crystal surrounding fluid the circumambient ocean, is to us incomprehensible: and yet it remains a fact that so they did regard them. How the Scandinavians could have supposed the mountains to be the mouldering bones of a mighty Jötun, and the earth to be his festering flesh, we cannot conceive: yet such a theory was solemnly taught and accepted. How the ancient Indians could regard the rain-clouds as cows with full udders, milked by the winds of heaven, is beyond our comprehension, and yet their Veda contains indisputable testimony to the fact that so they were regarded.

Nonnus Dionysius (v. 163 et seq.) spoke of the moon as a luminous white stone, and Democritus regarded the stars as πέτρους. Lucretius considered the sun as a wheel (v. 433), and Ovid as a shield—

> " Ipse Dei clypeus, terra cum tollitur ima,
>   Mane rubet: terraque rubet, cum conditur ima.
>   Candidus in summo . . . ."—(*Metam.* xv. 192 sq.)

As late as 1600, a German writer would illustrate a thunder-storm destroying a crop of corn by a picture of a dragon devouring the produce of the field with his flaming tongue and iron teeth (Wolfii Memorabil. ii. p. 505) ; and at the present day children are taught that the thunder-crash is the voice of the Almighty.

The restless mind of man, ever seeking a reason to account for the marvels presented to his senses, adopts one theory after another, and the rejected explanations encumber the memory of nations as myths, the significance of which has been forgotten.

The Piper of Hameln

HAMELN town was infested with rats, in the year 1284. In their houses the people had no peace from them ; rats disturbed them by night and worried them by day—

" They fought the dogs, and kill'd the cats,
   And bit the babies in the cradles,
And ate the cheeses out of the vats,
   And lick'd the soup from the cook's own ladles,
Split open the kegs of salted sprats,
Made nests inside men's Sunday hats,
And even spoil'd the women's chats,
   By drowning their speaking
   With shrieking and squeaking
In fifty different sharps and flats."

One day, there came a man into the town, most quaintly attired in parti-coloured suit. Bunting the man was called, after his dress. None knew whence he came, or who he was. He announced himself to be a rat-catcher, and offered for a certain sum of money to rid the place of the vermin. The townsmen agreed to his proposal, and promised him the sum demanded. Thereupon the man drew forth a pipe and piped.

> " And ere three shrill notes the pipe utter'd,
>   You heard as if an army mutter'd ;
> And the muttering grew to a grumbling,
> And the grumbling grew to a mighty rumbling :
> And out of the town the rats came tumbling.
> Great rats, small rats, lean rats, brawny rats,
> Brown rats, black rats, grey rats, tawny rats,
> Grave old plodders, gay young friskers,
>   Fathers, mothers, uncles, cousins,
> Cocking tails and pricking whiskers ;
>   Families by tens and dozens,
> Brothers, sisters, husbands, wives,
> Follow'd the Piper for their lives.
> From street to street he piped advancing,
> Until they came to the river Weser,
> Wherein all plunged and perish'd."

No sooner were the townsfolk released from their torment, than they repented of their bargain, and, on the plea that the rat-destroyer was a sorcerer, they refused to pay the stipulated remuneration. At this the piper waxed wrath, and vowed vengeance. On the 26th June, the feast of SS. John and Paul, the mysterious Piper reappeared in Hameln town—

> " Once more he stept into the street,
>   And to his lips again

Laid his long pipe of smooth, straight cane ;
 And, ere he blew three notes (such sweet,
Soft notes as yet musician's cunning
Never gave to the enraptured air),
There was a rustling, that seem'd like a bustling
Of merry crowds justling, at pitching and hustling,
Small feet were pattering, wooden shoes clattering,
Little hands clapping, and little tongues chattering :
And, like fowls in a farmyard where barley is scattering,
Out came the children running.
All the little boys and girls,
With rosy cheeks and flaxen curls,
And sparkling eyes, and teeth like pearls,
Tripping, skipping, ran merrily after
The wonderful music with shouting and laughter."

The Piper led the way down the street, the children all following, whilst the Hameln people stood aghast, not knowing what step to take, or what would be the result of this weird piping. He led them from the town towards a hill rising above the Weser—

 " When, lo ! as they reach'd the mountain's side,
  A wondrous portal open'd wide,
  As if a cavern were suddenly hollow'd ;
  And the piper advanced, and the children follow'd ;
  And when all were in, to the very last,
  The door in the mountain side shut fast."

No ! not all. Two remained : the one blind, and the other dumb. The dumb child pointed out the spot where the children had vanished, and the blind boy related his sensations when he heard the piper play.   In other accounts, the lad was lame, and he alone was left; and in after years he was sad.   And thus he accounted for his settled melancholy—

> " It's dull in our town since my playmates left;
>   I can't forget that I'm bereft
>   Of all the pleasant sights they see,
>   Which the piper also promised me;
>   For he led us, he said, to a joyous land,
>   Joining the town, and just at hand,
>   Where waters gush'd, and fruit-trees grew,
>   And flowers put forth a fairer hue,
>   And every thing was strange and new;
>   And sparrows were brighter than peacocks here
>   And their dogs outran our fallow deer,
>   And honey bees had lost their stings,
>   And horses were born with eagle's wings;
>   And just as I became assured
>   My lame foot would be speedily cured,
>   The music stopp'd, and I stood still,
>   And found myself outside the hill,
>   Left alone against my will,
>   To go now limping as before,
>   And never hear of that country more."

The number of children that perished was one hundred and thirty.   Fathers and mothers rushed to the east gate, but when they came to the mountain, called Koppenberg, into which the train had disappeared, nothing was observable except a small hollow, where the sorcerer and their little ones had entered.

The street through which the piper went is called the Bungen-Strasse, because no music, no drum (Bunge), may be played in it. If a bridal procession passes through it, the music must cease until it is out of it. It is not long since two moss-grown crosses on the Koppenberg marked the spot where the little ones vanished. On the wall of a house in the town is written, in gold characters—

"Anno 1284 am dage Johannis et Pauli war der 26. Junii dorch einen piper mit allerlei farve bekledet gewesen 130 kinder verledet binnen Hameln gebon to Calvarie, bi den Koppen verloren."

On the Rathhaus was sculptured, in memory of the event—

" Im Jahr 1284 na Christi gebert
Tho Hamel worden uthgevert
hundert und dreiszig kinder dasülvest geborn
durch einen Piper under den Köppen verlorn."

And on the new gate—

" Centum ter denos cum magus ab urbe puellos
Duxerat ante annos CCLXXII condita porta fuit."

For long, so profound was the impression produced by the event, the town dated its public documents from this calamity [1].

[1] Thorpe, Northern Mythology, iii. 119 ; and Grimm, Deutsche Sagen, Berlin, 1866, i. p. 245. Grimm has collected a list of authorities who speak of the event as an historical fact.

Similar stories are told of other places. A man with a violin came once to Brandenburg, and walked through the town fiddling. All the children followed him : he led them to the Marienberg, which opened and admitted him and the little ones, and, closing upon them, left none behind. At one time, the fields about Lorch were devastated with ants. The Bishop of Worms instituted a procession and litanies to obtain the deliverance of his people from the plague. As the procession approached the Lake of Lorch, a hermit came to meet it, and offered to rid the neighbourhood of the ants, if the farmers would erect a chapel on the site, at the cost of a hundred gulden. When they consented, he drew forth a pipe and piped so sweetly that all the insects came about him ; and he led them to the water, into which he plunged with them. Then he asked for the money, but it was refused. Whereupon he piped again, and all the pigs followed him : he led them into the lake, and vanished with them.

Next year a swarm of crickets ate up the herbage ; the people were in despair. Again they went in procession, and were met by a charcoal-burner, who promised to destroy the insects, if the people would expend five hundred gulden on a chapel. Then he piped, and the crickets followed him into

the water. Again the people refused to pay the
stipulated sum, thereupon the charcoal-burner piped
all their sheep into the lake. The third year comes
a plague of rats. A little old man of the mountain
this time offers to free the land of the vermin for a
thousand gulden. He pipes them into the Tannen-
berg ; then the farmers again button up their
pockets, whereupon the little man pipes all their
children away [2].

In the Hartz mountains once passed a strange
musician with a bagpipe. Each time that he
played a tune a maiden died. In this manner he
caused the death of fifty girls, and then he vanished
with their souls [3].

It is singular that a similar story should exist in
Abyssinia. It is related by Harrison, in his " Highlands of Æthiopia," that the Hadjiuji Madjuji are
dæmon pipers, who, riding on a goat, traverse a
hamlet, and, by their music, irresistibly draw the
children after them to destruction.

The soul, in German mythology, is supposed to
bear some analogy to a mouse. In Thuringia, at
Saalfeld, a servant-girl fell asleep whilst her com-

[2] Wolf, Beiträge zur Deutschen Mythologie. Göttingen,
1852, i. 171.
[3] Pröhle, Mährchen, No. 14.

panions were shelling nuts. They observed a little red mouse creep from her mouth and run out of the window. One of the fellows present shook the sleeper, but could not wake her, so he moved her to another place. Presently the mouse ran back to the former place, and dashed about seeking the girl : not finding her, it vanished ; at the same moment, the girl died [4].

Akin to the story of the piper is that made familiar to us by Goethe's poem, the Erlking.

A father is riding late at night with his child wrapped in a mantle. The little fellow hears the erlking chanting in his ear, and promising him the glories of Elf-land, where his daughters dance and sing, awaiting him, if he will follow. The father hushes the child, and bids him not to listen, for it is only the whistling of the wind among the trees. But the song has lured the little soul away, and when the father unfolds his mantle, the child is dead.

It is curious that a trace of this myth should remain among the Wesleyans. From my experience of English dissenters, I am satisfied that their religion is, to a greater extent than any one has sup-

[4] Prætorius, i. 40.

posed, a revival of ancient paganism, which has long lain dormant among the English peasantry. A Wesleyan told me one day that he was sure his little servant-girl was going to die; for the night before, as he had lain awake, he had heard an angel piping to her in the adjoining room; the music was inexpressibly sweet, like the warbling of a flute. " And when t'aingels gang that road," said the Yorkshire man, " they're boun to tak bairns' souls wi' em." I know several cases of Wesleyans declaring that they were going to die, because they had heard voices singing to them, which none but themselves had distinguished, telling them of the—

> " —— happy land
> Far, far away,"

precisely as the piper of Hameln's notes seemed to the lame lad to speak of a land—

> " Where flowers put forth a fairer hue,
> And every thing was strange and new."

And I have heard of a death being accounted for by a band of music playing in the neighbourhood. " When t'music was agaite, her soul was forced to be off."

A hymn by the late Dr. Faber, now very popular, is unquestionably founded on this ancient

superstition, and is probably an unconscious revival
of early dissenting reminiscences.

> "Hark ! hark, my soul ! Angelic songs are swelling
> O'er earth's green fields and ocean's wave-beat shore :
> How sweet the truth those blessed strains are telling
> Of that new life when sin shall be no more !
>
> "Onward we go, for still we hear them singing,
> Come, weary souls, for Jesus bids you come :
> And through the dark, its echoes sweetly ringing,
> The music of the Gospel leads us home.
>> Angels of Jesus, Angels of Light,
>> Singing to welcome the pilgrims of the night."

An idea which I have myself consciously adopted
in a hymn on the severing of Jordan (People's
Hymnal, 3), upon the principle which led the early
Christians to adopt the figure of Orpheus as a symbol of Christ.

> "Sweet angels are calling to me from yon shore,
> Come over, come over, and wander no more."

The music which our English dissenters consider
as that of angels' singing, is attributed by the Germans to the Elves, and their song is called Alpleich
or Elfenreigen. Children are cautioned not to
listen to it, or believe in the promises made in the
weird spirit-song. If they hearken, then Frau
Holle, the ancient goddess Hulda, takes them to
wander with her in the forests.

A young man heard the music, and was filled with

an irresistible longing to be with Dame Holle. Three
days after he died, and it was said of him, " He
preferred the society of Frau Hulda to heaven, and
now till the judgment he must wander with her in
the forest⁵." In like manner, in Scandinavian ballads,
we are told of youths who were allured away by
the sweet strains of the Elf maidens⁶. Their music
is called *ellfr-lek*, in Icelandic *liuflíngslag*, in Norwegian *Huldreslát*.

The reader will have already become conscious
that these northern myths resemble the classic
fable of the Sirens, with their magic lay; of Ulysses
with his ears open, bound to the mast, longing to
rush to their arms, and perish.

The root of the myth is this : the piper is no other
than the wind, and ancients held that in the wind
were the souls of the dead.   All over England the
peasants believe still that the spirits of unbap-
tized children wander in it, and that the wail at
their doors and windows are the cries of the little
souls condemned to journey till the last day.   The
ancient German goddess Hulda was ever accompanied by a crowd of children's souls, and Odin in
his wild hunt rushed over the tree-tops, accompa-

⁵ Zeitschrift für Deutsche Myth. i. 27.
⁶ Svenska fornsanger, 2. 308.   Danske viser, i. 235—240.

nied by the scudding train of brave men's spirits. It is because the soul is thought to travel on the wind, that we open the window to let a dying person breathe his last. Often have I had it repeated to me that the person *in extremis* could not die, that he struggled to die, but was unable till the casement was thrown open, and then at once his spirit escaped.

In one of the Icelandic sagas we have a strange story of a man standing at his house-door, and seeing the souls go by in the air, and among the souls was his own; he told the tale and died.

In Greek mythology, Hermes Psychopompos carries the spirits of the dead to Hades; and in Egyptian fable, Thoth performs the same office. I am satisfied that we have in Hermes two entirely distinct divinities run into one, through the confusion of similar names, that the Pelasgic, Ithyphallic Hermes is an entirely distinct god from the tricksy, thievish youth with winged feet and fluttering mantle. The Pelasgic Hermes (from ἕρμα) is the sun as generator of life, whilst the other Hermes (from ὁρμή) is the impetuous wind, whose representative Saramâ exists as the gale in Indian mythology. Hermes Psychopompos is therefore the wind bearing away the souls of the dead. He has other

atmospheric characteristics: the flying cloak, a symbol of the drifting cloud,—as Odin, the rushing of
storm, is also Hekluberandi, the mantle-bearer ; the
winged Talaria, emblems of the swiftness of his
flight ; and the lyre, wherewith he closes the thousand eyes of Argos, the starry firmament, signifying the music of the blast.

The very names given to the soul, *animus*, ἄνεμος
or *spiritus*, and *athem*, signify wind or breath, and
point to the connexion which was supposed to
exist between them. Our word Ghost, the German
Geist, is from a root "gîsan," to gush and blow, as
does the wind.

In the classic Sirens we cannot fail to detect the
wailing of the rising storm in the cordage, which is
likely to end in shipwrecks. The very name of
Siren is from συρίζω, to pipe or whistle[7], just as their
representatives in Vedic mythology, the Ribhus,
draw their name from *rebh*, to sound, to which the
Greek ῥοιβδέω is akin. The Sirens are themselves
winged beings [8], rushing over the earth, seeking
every where the lost Persephone.

But the piping wind does not merely carry with
it the souls of the dead, and give the mariner

[7] Cognate words, Lat. *susurrus*, Sanskrit *svri*, to sound.
[8] Eurip. Hel. 167.

warning of approaching wreck : it does something besides. Let us lie on a hill-side, and watch the rising gale. All is still and motionless. Presently we hear the whistle in the grass, and then every herb and tree is set in agitation. The trees toss from side to side, and the flowers waver, and rock their bells. All are set dancing, and cannot stop till the piping has ceased. In this we have the rudiment of another myth, that of the musical instrument which, when played, sets every thing a-capering.

Grimm has a story to this effect : a lad obtains a bow which will bring down any thing he aims at, and a fiddle which, when scraped, will make all who hear it dance. He shoots a bird, and it falls into a bush of thorns; a Jew goes into the bush to get the bird, then the lad strikes up a tune on his instrument, and makes the Jew dance in the bush till he has paid him a large sum to obtain rest. In a Walachian story it is the Almighty who gives the lad a bagpipe. The tale runs thus : a boy runs away from his brother with a quern; on the approach of night he hides in a tree. Some robbers come beneath the tree, and spread out their spoils. The lad drops the mill-stone, which puts the robbers to flight, and he thus obtains the gold. Then the story runs on like that of Grimm, only the Jew is replaced by a priest (Schott, xxii).

The same story is found among the modern Greeks, and the hero has a pipe, and his name is Bakala [9].

We have a similar tale in England, published by Wynkyn de Worde, entitled "A merry Geste of the Frere and the Boye," in which the lad receives—

> "———— a bowe
> Byrdes to shete"

and a pipe of marvellous power—

> "All that may the pype here
> Shall not themselfe stere,
> But laugh and lepe about [1]."

In the Icelandic Herauds ok Bosa Saga, which rests on mythologic foundation, a harp occurs which belonged to a certain Sigurd. Bosi slays Sigurd, puts on his skin and clothes, and taking the harp, goes in this disguise to the banquet-hall of king Godmund, where his true-love is about to be wed to another man. He plays the harp, and the knives and plates, the tables and stools, then the guests, and lastly the monarch himself, are set dancing. He keeps them capering till they are too

---

[9] Von Hahn, Griechische Mährchen, No. 34.
[1] Ritson, Pieces of Ancient Poetry.

exhausted to move a limb ; then he casts the bride over his shoulder and makes off[2].

In the mediæval romance of Huon de Bordeaux, Oberon's horn has the same properties ; and in a Spanish tale of the Fandango, at the strains of the tune, the Pope and cardinals are made to dance and jig about.

In that most charming collection of fairy tales, made in Southern Ireland by Mr. Crofton Croker, we meet with the same wonderful tune ; but the fable relating to it has suffered in the telling, and the parts have been inverted.   Maurice Connor, the blind piper, could play an air which could set every thing, alive or dead, capering.   In what way he learned it is not known.   At the very first note of that tune the brogues began shaking upon the feet of all who heard it, old or young ; then the feet began going, going from under them, and at last up and away with them, dancing like mad, whisking here, there, and every where, like a straw in a storm :—there was no halting while the music lasted.   One day Maurice piped this tune on the sea-shore, and at once every inch of it was covered with all manner of fish, jumping and plunging about

[2] Fornmanna Sögur, iii. p. 221.

to the music; and every moment more and more would tumble out of the water, charmed by the wonderful tune. Crabs of monstrous size spun round and round on one claw with the nimbleness of a dancing-master, and twirled and tossed their other claws about like limbs that did not belong to them.

> "John-dories came tripping;
> Dull hake by their skipping
>   To frisk it seem'd given;
> Bright mackrel came springing,
> Like small rainbows winging
>   Their flight up to heaven;
> The whiting and haddock
> Left salt-water paddock
>   This dance to be put in,
> Where skate with flat faces
> Edged out some odd plaices;
>   But soles kept their footing."

Then up came a mermaid, and whispered to Maurice of the charms of the land beneath the sea, and the blind piper danced after her into the salt sea, followed by the fish, and was never seen more.

In Sclavonic tales the magical instrument has a quite opposite effect—it sends to sleep. This signifies the whistling autumn wind, chilling the earth and checking all signs of life and vegetation. But another magical harp—that is, the spring breeze—restores all to vigour. The sorcerer enchants with the tones of his guzla, and all is hushed,—that is, the winter god sends the earth to sleep at the sound of his frozen gale; but, with the notes of the spring zephyr, the sun-god, golden-haired, revives creation, overcoming the charm [3].

It is this marvellous harp which was stolen by Jack when he climbed the bean-stalk to the upper world. In that story the ogre in the land above the skies, who was once the All-father, till Christianity made a monster of him, possessed three treasures: a harp which played of itself enchanting music, bags of gold and diamonds, and a hen which daily laid a golden egg. The harp is the wind, the bags are the clouds dropping the sparkling rain, and the golden egg, laid every morning by the red hen, is the dawn-produced sun. I have not space here to establish these two latter points, but they are repeated in so many cosmogonies, that there can be little doubt as to my interpretation being correct.

Among the Quiches of Guatemala, not a little to our surprise, the magic pipe which causes to dance is to be found. In their sacred book, the Popol-Vuh, the twins Hunahpu and Xbalanque turn their half-brothers into apes. Then they go

[3] Chodzko, Contes des Paysans Slaves, 1864.

to the mother, who asks where the lads are. The twins reply that she shall have them again, if she can behold them without laughing. Then they begin to play on their pipes; at the sound, the transformed brothers, Hunbatz and Hunchouen, are attracted from the forest to the house, they enter it and begin to dance. Their mother laughs at their comical gestures, and they vanish (Popol-Vuh, b. ii. c. 5).

I very much fear that I am leading my readers a sad dance, like one of these strange pipers; I only hope that I shall not, like the Sclavonic dæmon harper, send them to sleep. We must go a little further.

It is curious that the lyre-god Apollo should be called Smintheus, because he delivered Phrygia from a plague of rats. How he performed this feat we do not know; probably it was, after the manner of the Hameln piper, with his lyre, for we find that in Greek fable that instrument has powers attractive to the beasts attributed to it. The rats, as animals loving darkness, may have been regarded as symbols of night, and Apollo driving them from the land may have typified the sun scattering darkness.

Orpheus with his strains allured birds and beasts

around him, and made the trees and herbs to grow. The name Orpheus has been supposed to be identical with the Vedic Ribhus, which, no doubt, in its original form, was Arbhus. This, however, is not certain. Preller supposes Orpheus to come from the same root as ὄρφνη, ἔρεβος, and to signify gloom (Griechische Myth. ii. p. 486) ; but this is most improbable. He was a son of Apollo, and therefore probably a solar god.

It was hardly to be expected that such a charming and innocent myth as that of Orpheus should have been allowed to drop by the early Christians. They made a legitimate and graceful use of it in the catacombs, when they presented it as an allegory of Christ, who, by the sweet strains of His gospel, overcame brutish natures, making the wolf to lie down with the lamb. But a less justifiable adaptation of the figure was that of the mediæval hagiologists, when they took from Orpheus his lyre, and robbed him of his song, and split him into S. Francis and S. Anthony, the former with his preaching attracting the birds, the latter learnedly propounding scriptural types to the fishes.

It is curious that this Orpheus myth should be found scattered among Aryan and Turanian peoples.

In Sanskrit, it is told of Gunâdhya, in connexion with the Sibylline books story. The poet Gunâdhya, an incarnation of Mâljavân, writes with his own blood, in the forest, a mighty book of tales, in seven hundred thousand slokas. He then sends the book by his two pupils, Gunadeva and Nandideva, to king Sâtavâhana, but he rejects it as being composed in the Pisâcha dialect. Gunâdhya then ascends a mountain, and lights a great pile of firewood. He reads aloud his tales, and as he finishes each page, he casts it into the flames. Thus perish one hundred thousand slokas. Whilst the poet reads, stags, deer, bears, buffaloes, and roebucks, in short all the beasts of the forest, assemble and weep tears of delight at the beauty of the tales. In the mean time, the king falls ill, and the doctors order him game. But game is not to be found in the forest, for every living creature of the woods is listening to Gunâdhya. The huntsmen report this to the king, and the monarch hastens to the scene, and offers to buy the wondrous book. But, alas! by this time only one of the seven hundred thousand slokas remains [4].

But this is not the ancient form of the Indian myth. The poet Gunâdhya is the heavenly Mâl-

[4] Katha Sarit Sagara, i., c. 8.

javân incarnate, and the fable properly belongs to some of the heavenly musicians, the Ribhus, Maruts, or Gandharvas.

In the mythology of the Rig Veda, the Ribhus are skilled artists, whose element is the summer's gently stirring breeze. They are akin to the Maruts, the rough winds, with whom they unite in singing a magic song. The Arbhus became in Teutonic mythology the Alben, Elben or Elfen, our Elfs, and in Scandinavian the Alfar. The names are the same : Arbhus became altered into Albhu, by the change of the *r* into *l* ; the *b* in the old German Elbe is replaced in modern German and Norse by an *f*.

The spring and summer breezes were deified by the ancient Aryans. According to the Rig Veda, they slumber in winter for twelve days, and when they waken, the earth is decked with flowers, the trees with foliage, and the floodgates of the streams are unlocked. These Ribhus were the offspring of Sudhanvan, the skilful archer, just as the classic Orpheus was the son of the bow-bearing Apollo. They are probably identical with the Gandharvas, heavenly musicians attending on Indra (Mahâbh. i. 4806). The name Gandharva is derived from *gandh*, to harass, injure, and was applied to them as violent winds rending the clouds and scattering the leaves. They were represented as horses, and, according to some etymologists, are the originals of the Centaurs.

I remember one summer evening ascending a knoll in the district of the Landes in Southern France—once a region of moving sand-hills, now a vast tract of pine-forest. The air was fragrant with the breath of the fir-woods and the luscious exhalations of the flowery acacias. On all sides stretched the pines, basking in the sun, and rolling, like a green sea, to the snowy range of the Pyrenees, which hung in vaporous blue on the horizon—

> " Faintly-flush, phantom-fair—
> A thousand shadowy-pencill'd valleys
> And snowy dells in a golden air."

Perfect stillness reigned : not a sound from bird or beast was audible. Suddenly a strange, at first inexplicable, music vibrated through the air. Tender and distant, as though a thousand harp-strings were set a-quivering by the most delicate fingers, it rose up the scale by fractions of tones, and then descended again. Weird harmonies broke in upon and overflowed the melody, then ebbed away into sobs of music, again to reunite into a continued undulating chant. Not a breath stirred in my immediate neighbourhood, but the music of the forest was unquestionably brought out by a partial breeze, at some little distance. Any thing more solemn and beautiful could hardly be conceived: it was not like earthly instrumental strains, nor like what we deem the music of the spheres—it was the voice of nature expressing its rapture. The Apostle tells us that Creation groans and travails in its pangs—it does so; but it at times exchanges these utterances of pain for an outburst of the joy of its vitality.

This was the wandering harp of Orpheus seeking the lost Eurydice, the song of the Ribhus, the tale-chanting of Gunâdhya, the lay of the sons of Kalew, and the harping of Wainamoinen.

The Esthonian description of the charm of this wood-music is very graphic, and may be set beside Ovid's account of the springing of the trees at the playing of Orpheus.

> " In the dusky pine-tree forest
> Sat the eldest son of Kalew,
>   Singing 'neath a branching fir.
> As from swelling throat he chanted,
> Danced the fir-cones on the branches;
>   Every leaflet was astir.
> All the larches thrill'd, and budding,
>   Burst to tufts of silky green;
> Waved the pine-tops in the sunset,

> Steep'd in lustrous purple sheen.
> Catkins dangled on the hazels,
> On the oak the acorns sprouted,
>   And the black-thorn blossom'd white,
> Sudden wreathed in snowy tresses,
> Fragrant in the evening glory,
>   Scenting all the moonlit night."

Then the second son of Kalew goes to a birch-wood, and sings there. Then the corn begins to kern, the petals of the cherry to drop off, and the luscious fruit to swell and redden, the ripening apple to blush towards the sun, the cranberry and the whortle to speckle the moor with scarlet and purple.

Then the third son intones his lay in a forest of oaks, and the beasts assemble, the birds give voice, the lark sings shrill, the cuckoo calls, the doves coo, and the magpies chatter, the swans utter their trumpet-note, the sparrows twitter, and then as they weary, with sweet flute-like note sad Philomel begins his strain (Kalewpoeg. Rune iii.).

In the Finn mythology, these results follow the playing of Wainamoinen's magic harp. The story of this instrument is singular enough.

Wainamoinen went to a waterfall, and killed a pike which swam below it. Of the bones of this fish he constructed a harp, just as Hermes made his lyre of the tortoise-shell. But he dropped this instrument into the sea, and thus it fell into the power of the sea-gods, which accounts for the music of the ocean on the beach. The hero then made another from the forest wood, and with it descended to Pohjola, the realm of darkness, in quest of the mystic Sampo; just as in the classic myth Orpheus went down to Hades, to bring thence Eurydice. When in the realm of gloom perpetual, the Finn demi-god struck his kantele, and sent all the inhabitants of Pohjola to sleep; as Hermes, when about to steal Io, made the eyes of Argus close at the sound of his lyre. Then he ran off with the Sampo, and had nearly got it to the land of light, when the dwellers in Pohjola awoke, and pursued and fought him for the ravished treasure, which, in the struggle, fell into the sea and was lost; again reminding us of the classic tale of Orpheus.

The effects of the harping of Wainamoinen remind one of those accompanying the playing of the Greek lyrist.

"The ancient Wainamoinen began to sing; he raised his clear and limpid voice, and his light fingers danced over the strings of the kantele, whilst joy answered to joy, and song to song. Every beast of the forest and fowl of the air came about him, to listen to the sweet voice, and to taste the music of his strains. The wolf deserted the swamp, the bear forsook his forest lair ; they ascended the hedge, and the hedge gave way. Then they climbed the pine, and sat on the boughs, hearkening whilst Wainamoinen intoned his joy. The old black-bearded monarch of the forest, and all the host of Tapio, hastened to listen. His wife, the brave lady of Tapiola, put on her socks of blue, and her laces of red, and ascended a hollow trunk to listen to the god. The eagles came down from the cloud, the falcon dropped through the air, the mew flitted from the shore, the swan forsook the limpid waves, the swift lark, the light swallow, the graceful finches perched on the shoulders of the god. The fair vir-gins of the air, the rich and gorgeous sun, the gentle beaming moon, halted, the one on the luminous vault of heaven, the other leaning on the edge of a cloud. There they wove with the golden shuttle and the silver comb. They heard the unknown voice, the sweet song of the hero. And the silver comb fell, the golden shuttle dropped, and the threads of their tissue were broken. Then came the salmon and the trout, the pike and the porpoise, fish great and small, towards the shore, listening to the sweet strains of the charmer" (Kalewala, Rune xxii.).

In one of the heroic ballads of the Minussinchen Tartars, the wind, which is represented as a foal which courses round the world, finds that its master's two children, Aidôlei Mirgän and Alten Kuruptju, which I take to be the morning and evening stars, are dead and buried and watched by seven warriors. The foal changes himself into a maiden, and comes singing to the tomb such bewitching strains that

> " All the creatures of the forest,
> All the wing'd fowl of the air,
> Come and breathless to her listen ;"

and the watchers are charmed into letting her steal away the children, as Hermes stole Io from Argus, and she revives them with the water of life, which is the dew [5].

In Scandinavian mythology, Odin was famous for his Rune chanting ; and the power of bewitching creation with these Runes obtained for him the name of Galdner, from gala, to sing, a root retained in our nightingale, the night-songster ; in gale, a name applied to the wind from its singing powers ;

---

[5] Heldensagen der Minussischen Tataren, v. A. Schiefner. S. Petersburg, 1859, p. 60.

and in the Latin *gallus*, the noisy chanticleer of the farmyard.

A trace of the myth appears in the ancient German heroic Gudrunlied, where the powers are ascribed to Horant, *Norse* Hjarrandi, who is described as singing a song which no one could learn. "These strains he sang, and they were wondrous. To none were they too long, who heard the strains. The time it would take one to ride a thousand miles passed, whilst listening to him, as a moment. The wild beast of the forest and the timid deer hearkened, the little worms crept forth in the green meadows, fishes swam up to listen, each forgetting its nature, so long as he chanted his song." On reading this, we are reminded of that sweet German legend, so gracefully rendered by Longfellow, wherein the parts are changed, and it is no more the birds listening to the song of man, but proud man, with finger on lip and bated breath, listening to the matchless warble of the bird.

"A thousand years in Thy sight are but as yesterday!" mused Brother Felix; "how may that be?" and full of doubt over God's word he went forth to meditate in the forest.

> "And lo! he heard
> The sudden singing of a bird,

A snow-white bird, that from a cloud
Dropp'd down,
And among the branches brown
Sat singing
So sweet, and clear, and loud,
It seem'd a thousand harp-strings ringing.
And the Monk Felix closed his book,
And long, long
With rapturous look
He listen'd to the song,
And hardly breathed or stirr'd."

As he thus listened years rolled by, and on his return to the convent he found all changed—new faces in the refectory and in the choir.

Then the monastery roll was brought forth, wherein were written the names of all who had belonged to that house of prayer, and therein it was found—

" That on a certain day and date,
One thousand years before,
Had gone forth from the convent gate
The Monk Felix, and never more
Had enter'd that sacred door:
He had been counted among the dead.
And they knew at last,
That, such had been the power
Of that celestial and immortal song,
A thousand years had pass'd,
And had not seem'd so long
As a single hour."

Bishop Hatto

O F the many who yearly visit the Rhine, and bring away with them reminiscences of tottering castles and desecrated convents, whether they take interest or not in the legends inseparably attached to these ruins, none, probably, have failed to learn and remember the famous story of God's judgment on the wicked Bishop Hatto, in the quaint Mäusethurm, erected on a little rock in midstream.

At the close of the tenth century lived Hatto, once abbot of Fulda, where he ruled the monks with great prudence for twelve years, and afterwards Bishop of Mayence.

In the year 970, Germany suffered from famine.

" The summer and autumn had been so wet,
    That in winter the corn was growing yet.
    'Twas a piteous sight to see all around
    The corn lie rotting on the ground.

> " Every day the starving poor
> Crowded around Bishop Hatto's door,
> For he had a plentiful last year's store ;
> And all the neighbourhood could tell
> His granaries were furnish'd well."

Wearied by the cries of the famishing people, the Bishop appointed a day, whereon he undertook to quiet them. He bade all who were without bread, and the means to purchase it at its then high rate, repair to his great barn. From all quarters, far and near, the poor hungry folk flocked into Kaub, and were admitted into the barn, till it was as full of people as it could be made to contain.

> " Then, when he saw it could hold no more,
> Bishop Hatto he made fast the door,
> And while for mercy on Christ they call,
> He set fire to the barn, and burnt them all.
>
> " ' I'faith, 'tis an excellent bonfire !' quoth he,
> ' And the country is greatly obliged to me
> For ridding it, in these times forlorn,
> Of rats that only consume the corn.'
>
> " So then to his palace returned he,
> And he sat down to supper merrily,
> And he slept that night like an innocent man;
> But Bishop Hatto never slept again.
>
> " In the morning, as he enter'd the hall
> Where his picture hung against the wall,
> A sweat, like death, all over him came,
> For the rats had eaten it out of the frame."

Then there came a man to him from his farm,

with a countenance pale with fear, to tell him that the rats had devoured all the corn in his granaries. And presently there came another servant, to inform him that a legion of rats was on its way to his palace. The Bishop looked from his window, and saw the road and fields dark with the moving multitude ; neither hedge nor wall impeded their progress, as they made straight for his mansion. Then, full of terror, the prelate fled by his postern, and, taking a boat, was rowed out to his tower in the river,

> "———— and barr'd
> All the gates secure and hard.

> "He laid him down, and closed his eyes ;
> But soon a scream made him arise.
> He started, and saw two eyes of flame
> On his pillow, from whence the screaming came.

> "He listen'd and look'd—it was only the cat ;
> But the Bishop he grew more fearful for that,
> For she sat screaming, mad with fear,
> At the army of rats that were drawing near.

> "For they have swum over the river so deep,
> And they have climb'd the shores so steep,
> And now by thousands up they crawl
> To the holes and windows in the wall.

> "Down on his knees the Bishop fell,
> And faster and faster his beads did tell,
> As louder and louder, drawing near,
> The saw of their teeth without he could hear.

" And in at the windows, and in at the door,
    And through the walls by thousands they pour,
    And down from the ceiling, and up through the floor,
    From the right and the left, from behind and before,
    From within and without, from above and below,
    And all at once to the Bishop they go.

" They have whetted their teeth against the stones,
    And now they pick the Bishop's bones ;
    They gnaw'd the flesh from every limb,
    For they were sent to do judgment on him."

It is satisfactory to know that popular fiction has maligned poor Bishop Hatto, who was not by any means a hard-hearted and wicked prelate. Wolfius [1], who tells the story on the authority of Honorius Augustodunensis (d. 1152), Marianus Scotus (d. 1086), and Grithemius (d. 1516), accompanying it with the curious picture which is reproduced on the opposite page, says, "This is regarded by many as a fable, yet the tower, taking its name from the mice, exists to this day in the river Rhine." But this is no evidence, as there is documentary proof that the tower was erected as a station for collecting tolls on the vessels which passed up and down the river.

The same story is told of other persons and places. Indeed, Wolfius reproduces his picture of

[1] Wolfii Lect. Memorab. Centenarii xvi. Lavingæ, 1600, tom. i. p. 343.

[To face page 450.

BISHOP HATTO.

From Joh. Wolfii Lect. Memorab. Lavingæ (1600).

Hatto in the mouse-tower, to do service as an illustration of the dreadful death of Widerolf, Bishop of
Strasburg (997), who, in the seventeenth year of
his episcopate, on July 17th, in punishment for
having suppressed the convent of Seltzen on the
Rhine, was attacked and devoured by mice or
rats [2]. The same fate is also attributed to Bishop
Adolf of Cologne, who died in 1112 [3].

The story comes to us from Switzerland. A
Freiherr von Güttingen possessed three castles
between Constance and Arbon, in the Canton of
Thurgau, namely, Güttingen, Moosburg, and Ober-
burg. During a famine, he collected the poor of
his territory into a great barn, and there consumed
them, mocking their cries by exclamations of
" Hark! how the rats and mice are squeaking."
Shortly after, he was attacked by an army of mice,
and fled to his castle of Güttingen in the waters of
the Lake of Constance ; but the vermin pursued
him to his retreat, and devoured him. The castle
then sank into the lake, and its ruins are distin-

[2] Id. tom. i. p. 270. See also Königshofen's Chronik.
Königshofen was priest of Strasbourg (b. 1360, d. 1420).
His German Chronicle contains the story of Bishop Widerolf
and the mice.

[3] San-Marte, Germania, viii. 77.

guishable when the water is clear and unruffled[4].
In Austria, a similar legend is related of the mouse
tower at Holzölster, with this difference only, that
the hard-hearted nobleman casts the poor people
into a dungeon and starves them to death, instead
of burning them[5].

Between Inning and Seefeld in Bavaria is the
Wörthsee, called also the Mouse-lake. There was
once a Count of Seefeld, who in time of famine put
all his starving poor in a dungeon, jested at their
cries, which he called the squeaking of mice, and
was devoured by these animals in his tower in the
lake, to which he fled from them, although he
suspended his bed by iron chains from the roof[6].

A similar story is told of the Mäuseschloss in the
Hirschberger lake. A Polish version occurs in old
historical writers.

Martinus Gallus, who wrote in 1110, says that
King Popiel, having been driven from his kingdom,
was so tormented by mice, that he fled to an island
whereon was a wooden tower, in which he took
refuge ; but the host of mice and rats swam over
and ate him up. The story is told more fully by

[4] Zeitschrift f. Deut. Myth. iii. p. 307.
[5] Vernaleken, Alpensagen, p. 328.
[6] Zeitschrift f. Deut. Myth. i. p. 452.

Majolus[7]. When the Poles murmured at the bad government of the king, and sought redress, Popiel summoned the chief murmurers to his palace, where he pretended that he was ill, and then poisoned them. After this the corpses were flung by his orders into the lake Gopolo. Then the king held a banquet of rejoicing at having freed himself from these troublesome complainers. But during the feast, by a strange metamorphosis (*mira quadam metamorphosi*), an enormous number of mice issued from the bodies of his poisoned subjects, and rushing on the palace, attacked the king and his family. Popiel took refuge within a circle of fire, but the mice broke through the flaming ring ; then he fled with his wife and child to a castle in the sea, but was followed by the animals and devoured.

A Scandinavian legend is to this effect[8]. King Knut the Saint was murdered by the Earl Asbjorn, in the church of S. Alban, in Odense, during an insurrection of the Jutes, in 1086. Next year the country suffered severely from famine, and this was attributed to Divine vengeance for the murder of the king. Asbjorn was fallen upon by rats, and eaten up.

[7] Majolus, Dierum Canic. p. 793.
[8] Afzelius, Sagohäfder (2nd ed.), ii. p. 132.

William of Malmesbury tells this story[9]: "I have heard a person of the utmost veracity relate, that one of the adversaries of Henry IV. (of Germany), a weak and factious man, while reclining at a banquet, was on a sudden so completely surrounded by mice as to be unable to escape. So great was the number of these little animals, that there could scarcely be imagined more in a whole province. It was in vain that they were attacked with clubs and fragments of the benches which were at hand ; and though they were for a long time assailed by all, yet they wreaked their deputed curse on no one else ; pursuing him only with their teeth, and with a kind of dreadful squeaking. And although he was carried out to sea about a javelin's cast by the servants, yet he could not by these means escape their violence ; for immediately so great a multitude of mice took to the water, that you would have sworn the sea was strewed with chaff. But when they began to gnaw the planks of the ship, and the water, rushing through the chinks, threatened inevitable shipwreck, the servants turned the vessel to the shore. The animals, then also swimming close to the ship, landed first.

[9] William of Malmesbury, book iii., Bohn's trans., p. 313.

Thus the wretch, set on shore, and soon after entirely gnawed in pieces, satiated the dreadful hunger of the mice.

" I deem this the less wonderful, because it is well known that in Asia, if a leopard bite any person, a party of mice approach directly. . . . . . . But if, by the care of servants driving them off, the destruction can be avoided during nine days, then medical assistance, if called in, may be of service. My informant had seen a person wounded after this manner, who, despairing of safety on shore, proceeded to sea, and lay at anchor ; when, immediately, more than a thousand mice swam out, wonderful to relate, in the rinds of pomegranates, the insides of which they had eaten ; but they were drowned through the loud shouting of the sailors."

Albertus Trium-Fontium tells the same story under the year 1083, quoting probably from William of Malmesbury.

Giraldus Cambrensis (d. 1220), in his "Itinerary," relates a curious story of a youth named Siscillus Esceir-hir, or Long-shanks, who was attacked in his bed by multitudes of toads, and who fled from them to the top of a tree, but was pursued by the reptiles, and his flesh picked from his bones. "And in like manner," he adds, "we read of how by the secret, but never unjust, counsel of God a certain man was persecuted by the larger sort of mice which are commonly called *rati*[1]."

And Thietmar of Merseburg (b. 976, d. 1018) says, that there was once a certain knight who, having appropriated the goods of S. Clement, and refused to make restitution, was one day attacked by an innumerable host of mice, as he lay in bed. At first he defended himself with a club, then with his sword, and, as he found himself unable to cope with the multitude, he ordered his servants to put him in a box, and suspend this by a rope from the ceiling, and as soon as the mice were gone, to liberate him. But the animals pursued him even thus, and when he was taken down, it was found that they had eaten the flesh and skin off his bones. And it became manifest to all how obnoxious to God is the sin of sacrilege[2].

Cæsarius of Heisterbach (Dist. ii. c. 31) tells a tale of a usurer in Cologne, who, moved with compunction for his sins, confessed to a priest, who bade him fill a chest with bread, as alms for

[1] Girald. Cambr. Itin. Cambriæ, lib. xi. c. 2.
[2] Thietmar, Ep. Merseburg. Chronici libri viii., lib. vi; c. 30.

the poor attached to the church of S. Gereon. Next morning the loaves were found transformed into toads and frogs. " Behold," said the priest, "the value of your alms in the sight of God !" To which the terrified usurer replied, " Lord, what shall I do?" And the priest answered, "If you wish to be saved, lie this night naked amidst these reptiles." Wondrous contrition. He, though he recoiled from such a couch, preferred to lie among worms which perish, rather than those which are eternal ; and he cast himself nude upon the creatures. Then the priest went to the box, shut it, and departed ; which, when he opened it on the following day, he found to contain nothing save human bones.

It will be seen from these versions of the Hatto myth, how prevalent among the Northern nations was the idea of men being devoured by vermin. The manner of accounting for their death differs, but all the stories agree in regarding that death as mysterious.

I believe the origin of these stories to be a heathen human sacrifice made in times of famine. That such sacrifice took place among the Scandinavian and Teutonic peoples is certain. Tacitus tells us that the Germans sacrificed men. Snorro

Sturlesson (d. 1241) gives us an instance of the
Swedes offering their king to obtain abundant
crops [3].

"Donald took the heritage after his father Vis-
bur, and ruled over the land. As in his time there
was a great famine and distress, the Swedes made
great offerings of sacrifice at Upsala. The first
autumn they sacrificed oxen, but the succeeding
season was not improved by it. The following
autumn they sacrificed men, but the succeeding
year was rather worse. The third autumn, when
the offer of sacrifices should begin, a great multitude of Swedes came to Upsala ; and now the chiefs
held consultations with each other, and all agreed
that the times of scarcity were on account of their
king Donald, and they resolved to offer him for
good seasons, and to assault and kill him, and
sprinkle the altar of the gods with his blood. And
they did so." So again with Olaf the Tree-feller :
"There came dear times and famine, which they
ascribed to their king, as the Swedes used always
to reckon good or bad crops for or against their
kings. The Swedes took it amiss that Olaf was
sparing in his sacrifices, and believed the dear times

---

[3] Snorro Sturlesson, Heimskringla, Saga i. c. 18, 47.

must proceed from this cause. The Swedes therefore gathered together troops, made an expedition against King Olaf, surrounded his house, and burnt him in it, giving him to Odin as a sacrifice for good crops."

Saxo Grammaticus says that in the reign of King Snio of Denmark there was a famine. The "Chronicon Regum Danicorum" tells a curious story about this Snio being devoured by vermin, sent to destroy him by his former master the giant Lae. Probably Snio was sacrificed, like Donald and Olaf, to obtain good harvests.

The manner in which human sacrifices were made was very different. Sometimes the victims were precipitated off a rock, sometimes hung, at other times they were sunk in a bog. It seems probable to me that the manner in which an offering was made for plenty, was by exposure to rats, just as M. Du Chaillu tells us, an African tribe place their criminals in the way of ants to be devoured by them. The peculiar death of Ragnar Lodbrog, who was sentenced by Ella of Northumberland to be stung to death by serpents in a dungeon, was somewhat similar. Offerings to rats and mice are still prevalent among the peasantry in certain parts of Germany, if we may credit

Grimm and Wolf; and this can only be a relic of heathenism, for the significance of the act is lost.

In Mark it is said that the Elves appear in Yuletide as mice, and cakes are laid out for them. In Bohemia, on Christmas eve, the remainder of the supper is given them with the words, " Mice! eat of these crumbs, and leave the wheat."

If I am correct in supposing that the Hatto myth points to sacrifices of chieftains and princes in times of famine, and that the manner of offering the sacrifice was the exposure of the victim to rats, then it is not to be wondered at, that, when the reason of such a sacrifice was forgotten, the death should be accounted as a judgment of God for some crime committed by the sufferer, as hard-heartedness, murder, or sacrilege. Both Giraldus Cambrensis and William of Malmesbury are, however, sadly troubled to find a cause.

Rats and mice have generally been considered sacred animals. Among the Scandinavian and Teutonic peoples they were regarded as the souls of the dead.

In the article on the Piper of Hameln, I mentioned that Prætorius gives a story of a woman's soul leaving her body in the shape of a red mouse.

According to Bohemian belief, one must not go to sleep thirsty, or the soul will leave the body in search of drink. Three labourers once lost their way in a wood. Parched with thirst, they sought, but in vain, for a spring of water. At last one of them lay down and fell asleep, but the others continuing their search, discovered a fountain. They drank, and then returned to their comrade. He still slept, and they observed a little white mouse run out of his mouth, go to the spring, drink, and return to his mouth. They woke him and said, " You are such an idle fellow, that instead of going yourself after water, you send your soul. We will have nothing more to do with you."

A miller in the Black Forest, after having cut wood, lay down and slept. A servant saw a mouse run out of him. He and his companions went in pursuit. They scared the little creature away, little thinking it was the soul of the miller, and they were never able to rouse him again. Paulus Diaconus relates of King Gunthram that his soul left his body in the shape of a serpent; and Hugh Miller, in his " Schools and Schoolmasters," tells a Scottish story of two companions, one of whom slept whilst the other watched. He who was awake saw a bee come out of the mouth of the sleeper, cross a stream of water on a straw, run into a hole, and then return and disappear into the mouth of his friend. These are similar stories, but the bee and the serpent have taken the place of the mouse. The idea that the soul is like a mouse, lies at the root of several grotesque stories, as that told by Luther, in his "Table-Talk," of a woman giving birth to a rat, and that of a mother harassed by the clamour of her children, wishing they were mice, and finding this inconsiderate wish literally fulfilled.

The same idea has passed into Christian iconography. According to the popular German belief, the souls of the dead spend the first night after they leave the body with S. Gertrude, the second with S. Michael, and the third in their destined habitation. S. Gertrude is regarded as the patroness of fleeting souls, the saint who is the first to shelter the spirits when they begin their wandering. As the patroness of souls, her symbol is a mouse. Various stories have been invented to account for this symbol. Some relate that a maiden span on her festival, and the mice ate through her clew as a punishment. A prettier story is that, when she prayed, she was so absorbed that the mice ran about her, and up her pastoral staff, without attracting her attention. Another explanation is that the mouse is a symbol of the evil spirit, which S. Gertrude overcame [4].

But S. Gertrude occupies the place of the ancient Teutonic goddess Holda or Perchta, who was the receiver of the souls of maidens and children, and who still exists as the White Lady, not unfrequently, in German legends, transforming herself, or those whom she decoys into her home, into white mice.

It is not unlikely that the saying, " Rats desert a falling house," applied originally to the crumbling ruin of the body from which the soul fled.

In the Hatto and Popiel legends it is evident that the rats are the souls of those whom the Bishop and the King murdered.

The rats of Bingen issue from the flames in which the poor people are being consumed. The same is said of the rats which devoured the Freiherr of Güttingen. The rats *mira metamorphosi* come from the corpses of those poisoned by Popiel.

There is a curious Icelandic story, written in the twelfth century, which bears a striking resemblance to those of Hatto, Widerolf, &c., but in which the rats make no appearance.

[4] Die Attribute der Heiligen. Hanover, 1843, p. 114.

In the tenth century Iceland suffered severely from a bad year, so that there was a large amount of destitution throughout the country ; and, unless something were done by the wealthy bonders to relieve it, there was a certainty of many poor householders perishing during the approaching winter. Then Svathi, a heathen chief, stepped forward and undertook to provide for a considerable number of sufferers. Accordingly, the poor starving wretches assembled at his door, and were ordered by him to dig a large pit in his tun, or home meadow. They complied with alacrity, and in the evening they were gathered into a barn, the door was locked upon them, and it was explained to them that on the following morning they were to be buried alive in the pit of their own digging.

"You will at once perceive," said Svathi, "that if a number of you be put out of your misery, the number of mouths wanting food will be reduced, and there will be more victuals for those who remain."

There was truth in what Svathi said ; but the poor wretches did not view the matter in the same light as he, nor appreciate the force of his argument ; and they spent the night howling with despair. Thorwald of Asi, a Christian, who happened to be riding by towards dawn, heard the outcries, and went to the barn to inquire into their signification. When he learned the cause of their distress, he liberated the prisoners, and bade them follow him to Asi. Before long, Svathi became aware that his victims had escaped, and set off in pursuit. However, he was unable to recover them, as Thorwald's men were armed, and the poor people were prepared to resist with the courage of despair. Thus the golden opportunity was lost, and he was obliged to return home, bewailing the failure of his scheme. As he dashed up to his house, blinded with rage, and regardless of what was before him, the horse fell with him into the pit which the poor folk had dug, and he was killed by the fall. He was buried in it next day, along with his horse and hound [5].

In all likelihood this Svathi was sacrificed in time of famine, and the legend may describe correctly the manner in which he was offered to the gods, viz. by burial alive.

In this story, as in Snorro's account of Donald, we have a sacrifice of human beings, taken from a low rank, offered first, and then the chief himself sacrificed.

[5] Younger Olaf's Saga Trygvas., cap. 225.

The god to whom these human oblations were made, seems to have been Odin. In the " Herverar Saga" is an account of a famine in Jutland, to obtain relief from which, the nobles and farmers consulted whom to sacrifice, and they decided that the king's son was the most illustrious person they could present to Odin. But the king, to save his son, fought with another king, and slew him and his son, and with their blood smeared the altar of Odin, and thus appeased the god [6].

Now, Odin was the receiver of the souls of men, as Freya, or the German Holda, took charge of those of women. Odin appears as the wild huntsman, followed by a multitude of souls; or, as the Piper of Hameln, leading them into the mountain where he dwells.

Freya, or Holda, leads an army of mice, and Odin a multitude of rats.

As a rat or soul god, it is not unlikely that sacrifices to him may have been made by the placing of the victim on an island infested by water-rats, there to be devoured. The manner in which sacrifices were made have generally some relation to the nature of the god to whom they were made.

[6] Herverar Saga, cap. xi

Thus, as Odin was a wind-god, men were hung in his honour. Most of the legends we are considering point to islands as the place where the victim suffered, and islands, we know, were regarded with special sanctity by the Northern nations. Rügen and Heligoland in the sea were sacred from a remote antiquity, and probably lakes had as well their sacred islets, to which the victim was rowed out, his back broken, and on which he was left to become the prey of the rats.

We find rats and mice regarded as sacred animals in other Aryan mythologies. Thus the mouse was the beast of the Indian Rudra.

"This portion belongs to thee, O Rudra, with thy sister Ambika," is the wording of a prayer in the Yajur-Veda ; "may it please you. This portion belongs to thee, O Rudra, whose animal is the mouse[7]." In later mythology it became the attribute of Ganeça, who was represented as riding upon a rat ; but Ganeça is simply an hypostasis for Rudra.

Apollo was called Smintheus, as has been stated already. On some of the coins of Argos, in place of the god, is figured his symbol, the mouse[8]. In the temple at Chrisa was a statue of

[7] Yajur-Veda, iii. 57.
[8] Otfr. Müller, Dorier, i. p. 285.

Apollo, with a mouse at his feet [9] ; and tame mice were kept as sacred to the god. In the Smintheion of Hamaxitus, white mice were fed as a solemn rite, and had their holes under the altar ; and near the tripod of Apollo was a representation of one of these animals [1].

Among Semitic nations the mouse was also sacred.

Herodotus gives a curious legend relating to the destruction of the host of Sennacherib before Jerusalem. Isaiah simply says, " Then the angel of the Lord went forth, and smote in the camp of the Assyrians a hundred and fourscore and five thousand: and when they arose early in the morning, behold, they were all dead corpses [2]." How they were slain he does not specify, but as the army was threatened with a "hot blast," and a "destroying wind," it is rendered probable that they were destroyed by a hot wind. But the story of Herodotus is very different. He received it from the Egyptian priests, who claimed the miracle, of which they had but an imperfect knowledge, for one of their gods, and transferred the entire event to their

---

[9] Strabo, xiii. 1.
[1] Ælian, Hist. Animal. xii. 15.
[2] Isa. xxxvii. 36.

own country. "After Amyrtæus reigned the
priest of Vulcan, whose name was Sethon; he held
in no account and despised the military caste of
the Egyptians, as not having need of their services ;
and accordingly, among other indignities, he took
away their lands ; to each of whom, under former
kings, twelve chosen acres had been assigned.
After this, Sennacherib, king of the Arabians and
Assyrians, marched a large army against Egypt ;
whereupon the Egyptian warriors refused to assist
him ; and the priest being reduced to a strait,
entered the temple, and bewailed before the image
the calamities he was in danger of suffering. While
he was lamenting, sleep fell upon him ; and it
appeared to him in a vision that the god stood by
and encouraged him, assuring him that he should
suffer nothing disagreeable in meeting the Arabian
army, for he would himself send assistants to him.
Confiding in this vision, he took with him such
of the Egyptians as were willing to follow him, and
encamped in Pelusium, for there the entrance into
Egypt is ; but none of the military caste followed
him, but tradesmen, mechanics, and sutlers. When
they arrived there, a number of field-mice, pouring
in upon their enemies, devoured their quivers and
their bows, and, moreover, the handles of their

shields ; so that on the next day, when they fled bereft of their arms, many of them fell. And to this day, a stone statue of this king stands in the temple of Vulcan, with a mouse in his hand, and an inscription to the following effect : ' Whoever looks on me, let him revere the gods [3].' "

Among the Babylonians the mouse was sacrificed and eaten as a religious rite, but in connexion with what god does not transpire [4]. And the Philistines, who, according to Hitzig, were a Pelasgic and therefore Aryan race, after having suffered from the retention of the ark, were told by their divines to "make images of your mice that mar the land ; and ye shall give glory unto the God of Israel." Therefore they made five golden mice as an offering to the Lord [5]. This indicates the mouse as having been the symbol among the Philistines of a deity whom they identified with the God of Israel.

[3] Herod. Euterpe, c. 141, Trans. Bohn.
[4] Movers, Phönizier, i. p. 219. Cf. Isa. lxvi. 17.
[5] 1 Sam. vi. 4, 5.

Melusina

From Puoé Churoh (Gironde).

EMMERICK, Count of Poitou, was a nobleman of great wealth, and eminent for his
virtues. He had two children, a son named Bertram, and a daughter Blaniferte. In the great
forest which stretched away in all directions around
the knoll on which stood the town and castle of
Poictiers, lived a Count de la Forêt, related to
Emmerick, but poor and with a large family. Out
of compassion for his kinsman, the Count of Poitou
adopted his youngest son Raymond, a beautiful

and amiable youth, and made him his constant
companion in hall and in the chase. One day the
Count and his retinue hunted a boar in the forest
of Colombiers, and distancing his servants, Emmerick found himself alone in the depths of the wood
with Raymond. The boar had escaped. Night
came on, and the two huntsmen lost their way.
They succeeded in lighting a fire, and were warm-
ing themselves over the blaze, when suddenly the
boar plunged out of the forest upon the Count, and
Raymond, snatching up his sword, struck at the
beast, but the blade glanced off and slew the Count.
A second blow laid the boar at his side. Raymond then with horror perceived that his friend
and master was dead. In despair he mounted his
horse and fled, not knowing whither he went.

Presently the boughs of the trees became less
interlaced, and the trunks fewer; next moment his
horse, crashing through the shrubs, brought him out
on a pleasant glade, white with rime, and illumined
by the new moon; in the midst bubbled up a
limpid fountain, and flowed away over a pebbly
floor with a soothing murmur. Near the fountain-
head sat three maidens in glimmering white dresses,
with long waving golden hair, and faces of inex-
pressible beauty.

Raymond was riveted to the spot with astonishment. He believed that he saw a vision of angels,
and would have prostrated himself at their feet,
had not one of them advanced and stayed him.
The lady inquired the cause of his manifest terror,
and the young man, after a slight hesitation, told
her of his dreadful misfortune. She listened with
attention, and at the conclusion of his story, recommended him to remount his horse, and gallop out
of the forest, and return to Poictiers, as though
unconscious of what had taken place. All the
huntsmen had that day lost themselves in the
wood, and were returning singly, at intervals, to the
castle, so that no suspicion would attach to him.
The body of the count would be found, and from
the proximity of the dead boar, it would be concluded that he had fallen before the tusk of the
animal, to which he had given its death-blow.

Relieved of his anxiety, Raymond was able to
devote his attention exclusively to the beauty of
the lady who addressed him, and found means to
prolong the conversation till daybreak. He had
never beheld charms equal to hers, and the susceptible heart of the youth was completely capti-
vated by the fair unknown. Before he left her, he
obtained from her a promise to be his. She then

told him to ask of his kinsman Bertram, as a gift, so much ground around the fountain where they had met, as could be covered by a stag's hide: upon this ground she undertook to erect a magnificent palace. Her name, she told him, was Melusina; she was a water-fay of great power and wealth. His she consented to be, but subject to one condition, that her Saturdays might be spent in a complete seclusion, upon which he should never venture to intrude.

Raymond then left her, and followed her advice to the letter. Bertram, who succeeded his father, readily granted the land he asked for, but was not a little vexed, when he found that, by cutting the hide into threads, Raymond had succeeded in making it include a considerable area.

Raymond then invited the young count to his wedding, and the marriage festivities took place, with unusual splendour, in the magnificent castle erected by Melusina. On the evening of the marriage, the bride, with tears in her beautiful eyes, implored her husband on no account to attempt an intrusion on her privacy upon Saturdays, for such an intrusion must infallibly separate them for ever. The enamoured Raymond readily swore to strictly observe her wishes in this matter.

Melusina continued to extend the castle, and strengthen its fortifications, till the like was not to be seen in all the country round. On its completion she named it after herself Lusinia, a name which has been corrupted into Lusignan, which it bears to this day.

In course of time, the Lady of Lusignan gave birth to a son, who was baptized Urian. He was a strangely shaped child : his mouth was large, his ears pendulous ; one of his eyes was red, the other green.

A twelvemonth later she gave birth to another son, whom she called Gedes ; he had a face which was scarlet. In thank-offering for his birth she erected and endowed the convent of Malliers ; and, as a place of residence for her child, built the strong castle of Favent.

Melusina then bore a third son, who was christened Gyot. He was a fine, handsome child, but one of his eyes was higher up in his face than the other. For him his mother built La Rochelle.

Her next son Anthony, had long claws on his fingers, and was covered with hair ; the next again had but a single eye. The sixth was Geoffry with the Tooth, so called from a boar's tusk which protruded from his jaw. Other children she had, but all were in some way disfigured and monstrous.

Years passed, and the love of Raymond for his beautiful wife never languished. Every Saturday she left him, and spent the twenty-four hours in the strictest seclusion, without her husband thinking of intruding on her privacy. The children grew up to be great heroes and illustrious warriors. One, Freimund, entered the Church, and became a pious monk, in the abbey of Malliers. The aged Count de la Forêt and the brothers of Raymond shared in his good fortune, and the old man spent his last years in the castle with his son, whilst the brothers were furnished with money and servants suitable to their rank.

One Saturday, the old father inquired at dinner after his daughter-in-law. Raymond replied that she was not visible on Saturdays. Thereupon one of his brothers, drawing him aside, whispered that strange gossiping tales were about relative to this sabbath seclusion, and that it behoved him to inquire into it, and set the minds of people at rest. Full of wrath and anxiety, the count rushed off to the private apartments of the countess, but found them empty. One door alone was locked, and that opened into a bath. He looked through the keyhole, and to his dismay beheld her in the water, her lower extremities changed into the tail of a monstrous fish or serpent.

Silently he withdrew. No word of what he had seen passed his lips; it was not loathing that filled his heart, but anguish at the thought that by his fault he must lose the beautiful wife who had been the charm and glory of his life. Some time passed by, however, and Melusina gave no token of consciousness that she had been observed during the period of her transformation. But one day news reached the castle that Geoffry with the Tooth had attacked the monastery of Malliers, and burned it; and that in the flames had perished Freimund, with the abbot and a hundred monks. On hearing of this disaster, the poor father, in a paroxysm of misery, exclaimed, as Melusina approached to comfort him, "Away, odious serpent, contaminator of my honourable race!"

At these words she fainted; and Raymond, full of sorrow for having spoken thus intemperately, strove to revive her. When she came to herself again, with streaming tears she kissed and embraced him for the last time. "O husband!" she said, "I leave two little ones in their cradle; look tenderly after them, bereaved of their mother. And now farewell for ever! yet know that thou, and those who succeed thee, shall see me hover over this fair castle of Lusignan, whenever a new lord is to come." And with a long wail of agony she swept from the window, leaving the impression of her foot on the stone she last touched.

The children in arms she had left were Dietrich and Raymond. At night, the nurses beheld a glimmering figure appear near the cradle of the babes, most like the vanished countess, but from her waist downwards terminating in a scaly fish-tail enamelled blue and white. At her approach the little ones extended their arms and smiled, and she took them to her breast and suckled them; but as the grey dawn stole in at the casement, she vanished, and the children's cries told the nurses that their mother was gone.

Long was it believed in France that the unfortunate Melusina appeared in the air, wailing over the ramparts of Lusignan before the death of one of its lords; and that, on the extinction of the family, she was seen whenever a king of France was to depart this life. Mézeray informs us that he was assured of the truth of the appearance of Melusina on the old tower of Lusignan, previous to the death of one of her descendants, or of a king of France, by people of reputation, and who were not by any means credulous. She appeared in a mourning dress, and continued for a long time to utter the most heart-rending lamentations.

Brantome, in his eulogium on the Duke of Montpensier, who in 1574 destroyed Lusignan, a Huguenot retreat, says:

"I heard, more than forty years ago, an old veteran say, that when the Emperor Charles V. came to France, they brought him by Lusignan for the sake of the recreation of hunting the deer, which were then in great abundance in the fine old parks of France; that he was never tired of admiring and praising the beauty, the size, and the chef d'œuvre of that house, built, which is more, by such a lady, of whom he made them tell him several fabulous tales, which are there quite common, even to the good old women who washed their linen at the fountains, whom Queen Catherine de Medicis, mother of the king, would also question and listen to. Some told her that they used sometimes to see her come to the fountain, to bathe in it, in the form of a most beautiful woman and in the dress of a widow. Others said that they used to see her, but very rarely, and that on Saturday evening (for in that state she did not let herself be seen), bathing, half her body being that of a very beautiful lady, the other half ending in a snake; others, that she used to appear a-top of the great tower in a very beautiful form, and as a snake. Some said, that when any great disaster was to come on the kingdom, or a change of reign, or a death, or misfortune among her relatives, who were the greatest people of France, and were kings, that three days before she was heard to cry, with a cry most shrill and terrible, three times.

" This is held to be perfectly true. Several persons of that place, who have heard it, are positive of it, and hand it from father to son; and say that, even when the siege came on, many soldiers and men of honour, who were there, affirmed it. But it was when order was given to throw down and destroy her castles, that she uttered her loudest cries and wails. Since then she has not been heard. Some old wives, however, say she has appeared to them, but very rarely [1]."

In 1387, Jean d'Arras, secretary to the Duke of Berry, received orders from his master to collect all information attainable with reference to Melusina, probably for the entertainment of the sister of the

[1] Keightley's Fairy Mythology, 1850, pp. 483, 484.

duke, the Countess de Bar. This he did, making considerable use of a history of the mysterious lady, written " by one of the race of Lusinia, William de Portenach (qu. Partenope), in Italian." This history if it ever existed, has not come down to us; the work of Jean d'Arras is a complete romance. According to him, Helmas, king of Albania (Scotland, or, as the German popular versions have it, Nordland), married a fay named Pressina, whom he found singing beside a fountain. She became his, after having exacted from him an oath never to visit her during her lying-in. She gave birth to three little girls at once, Melusina, Melior, and Plantina. A son of Helmas by a former wife hurried to his father with the joyful news, and the king, oblivious of his promise, rushed to his wife and found her bathing her three children. Pressina, on seeing him, exclaimed against his forgetfulness, and, taking her babes in her arms, vanished. She brought up the daughters until they were fifteen, when she unfolded to them the story of their father's breach of promise, and Melusina, the youngest, determined on revenge. She, in concert with her sisters, caught King Helmas and chained him in the heart of a mountain called Avalon, or, in the German books, Brunbelois, in Northubelon, i.e. Northumberland. At this unfilial act, the mother was so indignant, that she sentenced her daughter Melusina to spend the sabbath in a semi-fish form, till she should marry one who would never inquire into what became of her on that day. Jean d'Arras relates that Serville, who defended Lusignan for the English against the Duke de Berry, swore to that prince upon his faith and honour, "that three days before the surrender of the castle, there entered into his chamber, though the doors were shut, a large serpent, enamelled blue and white, which struck its tail several times against the foot of the bed whereon he was lying with his wife, who was not at all frightened at it, though he was very considerably so ; and that when he seized his sword, the serpent changed all at once into a woman, and said to him : 'How, Serville, you, who have been in so many battles and sieges, are you afraid? Know that I am the mistress of this castle, which I erected, and that soon you will have to surrender it !' When she had ended these words, she resumed her serpent-shape, and glided away so swiftly that he could not perceive her."

Stephan, a Dominican, of the house of Lusignan, developed the work of Jean d'Arras, and made the story so famous, that the families of Luxembourg, Rohan, and Sassenaye altered their pedigrees so as to be able to claim descent from the illustrious Melusina[2]; and the Emperor Henry VII. felt no little pride in being able to number the beautiful and mysterious lady among his ancestors. "It does not escape me," writes the chronicler Conrad Vecerius, in his life of that emperor, "to report what is related in a little work in the vernacular, concerning the acts of a woman, Melyssina, on one day of the week becoming a serpent from her middle downwards, whom they reckon among the ancestors of Henry VII. . . . . But, as authors relate, that in a certain island of the ocean, there are nine Sirens endowed with various arts, such, for instance, as changing themselves into any shape they like, it is no absurd conjecture to suppose that Melyssina came thence[3]."

The story became immensely popular in France, in Germany, and in Spain, and was printed and reprinted. The following are some of the principal early editions of it.

Jean d'Arras, " Le liure de Melusine en frācoys ;" Geneva, 1478. The same, Lyons and Paris, without date ; Lyons, 4to, 1500, and again 1544 ;

---

[2] Bullet, Dissertat. sur la Mythologie Française. Paris, 1771, pp. 1—32.

[3] Urstisius, Scriptores Germaniæ. Frankfort, 1670.

Troyes, 4to, no date. "L'histoire de Melusine fille du roy d'Albanie et de dame Pressine, revue et mise en meilleur langage que par cy devant;" Lyons, 1597. "Le roman de Melusine, princesse de Lusignan, avec l'histoire de Geoffry, surnommé à la Grand Dent," par Nodot; Paris, 1700. An outline of the story in the "Bibliothèque des Romans," 1775, T. II. A Spanish version, "Historia de la linda Melosyna;" Tolosa, 1489. "La hystoria de la linda Melosina;" Sevilla, 1526. A Dutch translation, "Een san sonderlingke schone ende wonderlike historie, die men warachtich kout te syne ende autentick sprekende van eenre vrouwen gheheeten Melusine;" Tantwerpen, 1500. A Bohemian version, probably translated from the German, "Kronyke Kratochwilne, o ctné a slech netné Panně Meluzijně;" Prag, 1760, 1764, 1805. A Danish version, made about 1579, "Melusine;" Copenhagen, 1667, 1702, 1729. One in Swedish, without date. The original of these three last was the "History of Melusina," by Thüring von Ringoltingen, published in 1456; Augsburg, 1474; Strasburg, 1478. "Melosine-Geschicht," illustrated with woodcuts; Heidelberg, 1491. "Die Historia von Melusina;" Strasburg, 1506. "Die Histori oder Geschicht von der edle und schönen Melusina;" Augsburg,

1547 ; Strasburg, 1577, 1624. "Wunderbare Geschichte von der edeln und schönen Melusina, welche
eine Tochter des Königs Helmus und ein Meer-
wunder gewesen ist ;" Nürnberg, without date ; reprinted in Marbach's "Volksbücher." Leipzig, 1838.

In the fable of Melusina, there are several points
deserving of consideration, as—the framework of
the story, the half-serpent or fish-shape of Melusina, and her appearances as warnings of impending misfortune or death. The minor details, as, for
instance, the trick with the hide, which is taken
from the story of Dido, shall not detain us.

The framework of the myth is the story-radical
corresponding with that of Lohengrin. The skeleton
of the romance is this—

1. A man falls in love with a woman of supernatural race.

2. She consents to live with him, subject to one
condition.

3. He breaks the condition and loses her.

4. He seeks her, and—*a.* recovers her ; *β.* never
recovers her.

In the story before us, the last item has dropped
out, but it exists in many other stories which have
sprung from the same root. The beautiful legend
of Undine is but another version of the same

story. A young knight marries a water-sprite, and promises never to be false to her, and never to bring her near a river. He breaks his engagement, and loses her. Then she comes to him on the eve of his second marriage and kisses him to death. Fouqué's inimitable romance is founded on the story as told by Theophrastus Paracelsus in his "Treatise on Elemental Sprites;" but the bare bones of the myth related by the philosopher have been quickened into life and beauty by the heaven-drawn spark of poetry wherewith Fouqué has endowed them.

In the French tale, Melusina seeks union with a mortal solely that she may escape from her enchantment; but in the German more earnest tale, Undine desires to become a bride that she may obtain an immortal soul. The corresponding Danish story is told by Hans Christian Andersen. A little mermaid sees a prince as she floats on the surface of the sea, and saves him in her arms from drowning when the ship is wrecked. But from that hour her heart is filled with yearning love for the youth whose life she has preserved. She seeks earth of her own free will, leaving her native element, although the consequence is pain at every step she takes.

She becomes the constant attendant of the prince, till he marries a princess, when her heart breaks and she becomes a Light-Elf, with prospect of immortality.

Belonging to the same family is the pretty Indian tale of Urvaçî. Urvaçî was an "apsaras," or heavenly maiden ; she loved Puravaras, a martial king, and became his wife, only, however, on condition that she should never behold him without his clothes. For some years they were together, till the heavenly companions of Urvaçî determined to secure her return to her proper sphere. They accordingly beguiled Puravaras into leaving his bed in the darkness of night, and then, with a lightning-flash, they disclosed him in his nudity to the wife, who was thereupon constrained to leave him. A somewhat similar story is told, in the Katha Sarit Sagara (Book iii. c. 18), of Vidû-shaka, who loves and marries a beautiful Bhadrâ, but after a while she vanishes, leaving behind her a ring. The inconsolable husband wanders in search of her, and reaching the heavenly land, drops the ring in a goblet of water, which is taken to her. By this she recognizes him, and they are re-united.

The legend of Melusina, as it comes to us, is by

no means in its original condition. Jean d'Arras, or other romancers, have considerably altered the simple tale, so as to make it assume the proportions of a romance. All that story of the fay Pressina, and her marriage with King Helmas, is but another version of the same story as Melusina.

Helmas finds Pressina near a fountain, and asks her to be his; she consents on condition that he does not visit her during her lying-in; he breaks the condition and loses her. This is the same as Raymond discovering Melusina near a spring, and obtaining her hand subject to the condition that he will not visit her one day of the week. Like Helmas, he breaks his promise and loses his wife. That both Pressina and Melusina are water-sprites, or nymphs, is unquestionable; both haunt a fountain, and the transformation of the lady of Lusignan indicates her aquatic origin. As Grimm has observed[4], this is a Gallic, and therefore a Keltic myth, an opinion confirmed by the Banshee part played by the unfortunate nymph. For the Banshee superstition has no corresponding feature in Scandinavian, Teutonic, or Classic mythology, and belongs entirely to the Kelts. Among others

---

[4] Deutsche Mythologie, i. 405.

there are death portents, but not, that I am aware of, spirits of women attached to families, by their bitter cries at night announcing the approach of the king of terrors.

The Irish Banshee is thus described : "We saw the figure of a tall, thin woman with uncovered head, and long hair that floated round her shoulders, attired in something which seemed either a loose white cloak or a sheet thrown hastily about her, uttering piercing cries.

"The most remarkable instance (of the Banshee) occurs in the MS. memoirs of Lady Fanshawe, so exemplary for her conjugal affection. Her husband, Sir Richard, and she chanced, during their abode in Ireland, to visit a friend, the head of a sept, who resided in an ancient baronial castle surrounded with a moat. At midnight she was awakened by a ghastly and supernatural scream, and looking out of bed, beheld in the moonlight a female face and part of the form hovering at the window. The face was that of a young and rather handsome woman, but pale, and the hair, which was reddish, loose and dishevelled. The dress, which Lady Fanshawe's terror did not prevent her remarking accurately, was that of the ancient Irish. This apparition continued to exhibit. itself for some time, and then vanished, with two shrieks similar to that which had first excited Lady Fanshawe's attention. In the morning, with infinite terror, she communicated to her host what she had witnessed, and found him prepared, not only to credit, but to account for the apparition :—

"'A near relation of my family,' said he, 'expired last night in this castle. We disguised our certain expectations of the event from you, lest it should throw a cloud over the cheerful reception which was your due[5]. Now, before such an event happens in this family and castle, the female spectre whom ye have seen always is visible : she is believed to be the spirit of a woman of inferior rank, whom one of my ancestors degraded himself by marrying, and whom afterwards, to expiate the dishonour done to his family, he caused to be drowned in the castle moat.'"

A very remarkable story of the Banshee is given by Mr. Crofton Croker. The Rev. Charles Bunworth was rector of Buttevant, in the county Cork, about the middle of last century. He was famous for his performance on the national instrument, the

---

[5] Like Admetus in the Alcestis of Euripides. This story of Lady Fanshawe is from a note to "The Lady of the Lake."

Irish harp, and for his hospitable reception and entertainment of the poor harpers who travelled from house to house about the country; and in his granary were deposited fifteen harps, bequeathed to him by the last members of a race which has now ceased to exist.

The circumstances attending the death of Mr. Bunworth were remarkable; but, says Mr. Crofton Croker, there are still living credible witnesses who declare their authenticity, and who can be produced to attest most, if not all, of the following particulars. Shortly before his decease, a shepherd heard the Banshee keening and clapping her hands under a lightning-struck tree near the house. On the eve of his death the night was serene and moonlit, and nothing broke the stillness of the melancholy watch kept by the bedside of the sick man, who lay in the drawing-room, by his two daughters. The little party were suddenly roused by a sound at the window near the bed: a rose-tree grew outside the window, so closely as to touch the glass; this was forced aside with some noise, and a low moaning was heard, accompanied by clapping of hands, as if of some female in deep affliction. It seemed as if the sound proceeded from a person holding her mouth close to the window. The lady who sat by the bedside of Mr. Bunworth went into the adjoining room, where sat some male relatives, and asked, in a tone of alarm, if they had heard the Banshee. Sceptical of supernatural appearances, two of them rose hastily, and went out to discover the cause of these sounds, which they also distinctly heard. They walked all round the house, examining every spot of ground, particularly near the window from whence the voice had proceeded; the bed of earth beneath, in which the rose-tree was planted, had been recently dug, and the print of a footstep—if the tree had been forced aside by mortal hand—would have inevitably remained; but they could perceive no such impression, and an unbroken stillness reigned without. Hoping to dispel the mystery, they continued their search anxiously along the road, from the straightness of which, and the lightness of the night, they were enabled to see some distance around them; but all was silent and deserted, and they returned surprised and disappointed. How much more then were they astonished at learning that, the whole time of their absence, those who remained within the house had heard the moaning and clapping of hands even louder and more distinct than before they had gone out; and no sooner was the door of the room closed on them, than they again heard the same mournful sounds. Every succeeding hour the sick man became worse, and when the first glimpse of the morning appeared, Mr. Bunworth expired.

The Banshee is represented in Wales by the Gwrâch y Rhibyn, who is said to come after dusk, and flap her leathern wings against the window, giving warning of death, in a broken, howling tone, and calling on the one who is to quit mortality by his or her name several times. In Brittany, similar spirits are called Bandrhudes, and are attached to several of the ancient families. In other parts of France, they pass as Dames Blanches, who, however, are not to be confused with the Teutonic white ladies, which are spirits of a different order.

But, putting the Banshee part of the story of Melusina on one side, let us turn to the semi-fish or serpent form of Melusina. Jean d'Arras attributes this to a curse pronounced on her by the fay Pressina, but this is an invention of his own; the true conception of Melusina he did not grasp, and was therefore obliged to forge a legend which should account for her peculiar appearance. Melusina was a mermaid. Her presence beside the fountain, as well as her fishy tail, indicate her nature; she was not, perhaps, a native of the sea, but a stream-dweller, and therefore as closely related to the true mermaid of the briny deep as are the fresh-water fish to those of the salt sea.

The superstitious belief in mermaids is universal, and I frankly confess my inability to account for its origin in every case. In some particular cases the origin of the myth is clear, in others it is not so. Let me take one which can be explained —the Oannes of the Chaldæans, the Philistine Dagon.

Oannes and Dag-on (the fish On) are identical. According to an ancient fable preserved by Berosus, a creature half man and half fish came out of "that part of the Erythræan sea which borders upon Babylonia," where he taught men the arts of life, "to construct cities, to found temples, to compile laws, and, in short, instructed them in all things that tend to soften manners and humanize their lives;" and he adds that a representation of this animal Oannes was preserved in his day. A figure of him sporting in the waves, and apparently blessing a fleet of vessels, was discovered in a marine piece of sculpture, by M. Botta, in the excavations of Khorsabad.

Oannes, from Khorsabad.

At Nimroud, a gigantic image was found by Mr. Layard, representing him with the fish's head as a cap and the body of the fish depending over his shoulders, his legs those of a man, in his left hand holding a richly decorated bag, and his right hand upraised, as if in the act of presenting the mystic Assyrian fir-cone (British Museum, Nos. 29 and 30).

This Oannes is the Mizraimite On, and the Hebrew Aon, with a Greek case-termination, derived from a root signifying "to illumine." Aon was the original name of the god reverenced in the temple of Heliopolis, which in Scripture is called Beth-Aon, the house of On, as well as by its translation Beth-Shemesh, the house of the Sun. Not only does his name indicate his solar origin, but his representation with horned head-dress testifies to his nature. Ammon, Apis, Dionysos are sun-gods; Isis, Io,

Artemis are moon-goddesses, and are all horned. Indeed, in ancient iconography horns invariably connect the gods represented with the two great sources of light. Apparent exceptions, such as the Fauns, are not so in reality, when subjected to close scrutiny. Civilizing gods, who diffuse intelligence and instruct barbarians, are also solar deities, as the Egyptian Osiris, the Nabathæan Tammuz, the Greek Apollo, and the Mexican Quetzalcoatl; beside these Oannes takes his place, as the sun-god, giving knowledge and civilization. According to

A Babylonish seal in the British Museum, from Munter's Babylonier.

the fable related by Berosus, he came on earth each morning, and at evening plunged into the sea; this is a mythical description of the rising and setting of the sun. His semi-piscine form was an expression of the idea that half his time was spent above ground, and half below the waves.

In precisely similar manner the Semitic moon-goddess, who followed the course of the sun, at times manifesting herself to the eyes of men, at others seeking concealment in the western flood was represented as half woman, half fish, with characteristics which make her lunar origin indisputable. Her name was Derceto or Atergatis. On the coins of Ascalon, where she was held in great honour, is figured a goddess above whose head is a half-moon, and at her feet a woman with her lower extremities like a fish. This is Semiramis, who, according to a popular legend, was the child of Derceto. At Joppa she appears as a mermaid. The story was, that she fled from Typhon, and plunged into the sea, concealing herself under the form of a fish. According to Plutarch, the Syrian Tirgata, the Derceto of Palestine, was the goddess of moisture[6]; and Lucan (De dea Syra, c. 14) declares that she was represented as a woman with a fish-tail from her hips downward.

In every mythology, the different attributes of

---

[6] Plutarch, Crass. c. 17. According to Greek mythology, this goddess, under the name of Ceto, "with comely cheeks," is the daughter of Sea and Earth, and wife of Phorcys (Hesiod, Theog. v. 235. 270).

the deity in process of time became distinct gods, yet with sufficient impress of their origin still upon them to make that origin easy to be detected.

As On, the sun-god rising and setting in the sea, was supplied with a corresponding moon-goddess, Atergatis, and Bel or Baal, also a solar deity, had his lunar Baalti, so the fiery Moloch, "the great lord," was supplied with his Mylitta, "the birth-producer." Moloch was the fierce flame-god, and Mylitta the goddess of moisture. Their worship was closely united. The priests of Moloch wore female attire, the priestesses of Mylitta were dressed like men. Human sacrifices characterized the worship of the fire-god, prostitution that of the goddess of water. From her came the names of the hetaræ Melitta, Meleto, Milto, Milesia (Athenæus, lib. xiii.). Among the Carthaginians, this goddess was worshipped, as appears from their giving the name of Magasmelita (the tent of Mylitta) to one of the African provinces. Mylitta was identical with Atergatis; she was regarded as a universal mother, a source of life.

In Greece, the priestesses of Demeter were called Melissæ, the high-priest of Apollo was entitled κύριος τῶν μελλισσῶν. A fable was invented to account for this name, and to connect

them with bees and honey ; but I have little doubt
that it was corrupted from the Semitic designation
of the servants of Mylitta. The Melissæ are sometimes spoken of as nymphs, but are not to be
identified with the Meliadæ, Dryads sprung from
the ash. Yet Melia, daughter of Oceanus, who
plunges into the Haliacmon, strongly resembles
the Syrian goddess. Selene, the moon, was also
known by the name Melissa. Καὶ τὰς Δήμητρος
ἱερείας, ὡς τῆς χθονίας θεᾶς μυστίδας, μελίσσας οἱ
παλαιοὶ ἐκάλουν, αὐτήν τε τὴν Κόρην μελισσώδη,
Σελήνην τε, οὖσαν γενέσεως προστατίδα μέλισσαν
ἐκάλουν [7].

When we remember the double character of
Mylitta, as a generative or all-mother, and as a
moon-goddess, we are able to account for her
name having passed into the Greek titles of
priestesses of their corresponding goddesses Demeter and Selene.

The name Melissa was probably introduced into
Gaul by the Phocian colony at Massilia, the modern
Marseilles, and passed into the popular mythology
of the Gallic Kelts as the title of nymphs, till it was
finally appropriated by the Melusina of romance.

[7] Schol. Theocr. xv. 94. Porphyr. de Antro Nymph.
c. 18.

It may seem difficult at first sight to trace the connexion between the moon, a water-goddess, and a deity presiding over childbirth; yet it is certain that such a connexion does exist. The classic Venus was born of the sea-foam, and was unmistakably one with the moon. She was also the goddess of love, and was resorted to by barren women—as the Venus of Quimperle in Brittany is, to this day, sought by those who have no children.

On the Syrian coast, they told of their goddess plunging into the sea, because they saw the moon descend into the western waters; but the Cretans, who beheld her rise above the eastern horizon of sea, fabled of a foam-born goddess.

In classic iconography the Tritons, and in later art the Sirens, are represented half fish, half human. Originally the Sirens were winged, but after the fable had been accepted, which told of their strife with the Muses, and their precipitation into the sea, they were figured like mermaids; the fish-form was by them borrowed from Derceto. It is curious how widely-spread is the belief in fish-women. The prevalence of tales of mermaids among Celtic populations indicates these water-nymphs as having been originally deities of those peoples ; and I cannot but believe that the circular mirror they are usually represented as holding is a reminiscence of the moon-disk. Bothe, in his "Kronecke der Sassen," in 1492, described a god, Krodo, worshipped in the Hartz, who was represented with his feet on a fish, a wheel to symbolize the moon in one hand, and a pail of water in the other. As among the Northern nations the moon is masculine, its deity was male. Probably the Mexican Coxcox or Teocipactli (i.e. Fish-god) was either a solar or lunar deity. He was entitled Huehueton-acateo-cateo-cipatli, or Fish-god-of-our-flesh, to give him his name in full; he somewhat resembled the Noah of Sacred Writ ; for the Mexican fable related, that in a great time of flood, when the earth was covered with water, he rescued himself in a cypress trunk, and peopled the world with wise and intelligent beings [8]. The Babylonish Oannes was also identified with the flood.

The Peruvians had likewise their semi-fish gods, but the legend connected with them has not descended to our days.

The North-American Indians relate that they were conducted from Northern Asia by a man-fish.

[8] Müller, Geschichte der Amerikanischen Urreligionen. Basel, 1855, p. 515.

"Once upon a time, in the season of opening buds, the people of our nation were much terrified at seeing a strange creature, much resembling a man, riding upon the waves. He had upon his head long green hair, much resembling the coarse weeds which the mighty storms scatter along the margin of the strand. Upon his face, which was shaped like that of a porpoise, he had a beard of the same colour. But if our people were frightened at seeing a man who could live in the water like a fish or a duck, how much more were they frightened when they saw that from his breast down he was actually a fish, or rather two fishes, for each of his legs was a whole and distinct fish. And there he would sit for hours singing to the wondering ears of the Indians the beautiful things he saw in the depths of the ocean, always closing his strange stories with these words :—' Follow me, and see what I will show you.' For a great many suns, they dared not venture upon the water ; but when they grew hungry, they at last put to sea, and following the man-fish, who kept close to the boat, reached the American coast[9]."

It is not impossible that the North-American

[9] Epitomized from Traditions of the North-American Indians, by J. A. Jones. 1830, pp. 47—58.

Indians may have symbolized the sun in the same manner as the Syrians, and that this legend may signify that the early colonists, to reach the New Land, followed the *fish*-course of the sun, which as man goes from East to West, whereas when it dives it swims from West to East, the course taken by the Indians in their canoes. The wanderers in the Canadian forests have also their fish-woman, of whom a tale is related which bears a lively resemblance to that of Undine, and which is not a little like that of Melusina.

One day an Ottawa chief, whilst sitting by the water side, beheld a beautiful woman rise from the flood, her face exquisitely lovely, her eyes blue, her teeth white, and her locks floating over her shoulders. From her waist downwards she was fish, or rather two fishes. She entreated the warrior to permit her to live on earth, as she desired to win a human soul, which could only be acquired by union with a mortal. He consented and took her to his house, where she was to him as a daughter. Some years after an Andirondack youth beheld and loved her. He took her to wife, and she obtained that which she had desired—a human soul.

In the Undine story, a water-maiden, in like

manner and for a like object, is adopted by an old fisherman, and becomes the bride of a youthful German knight. But the Andirondack tribe was ill-pleased at the marriage of their chief with the mysterious damsel, and they tore her from his arms, and drove her back to her original element. Then all the water-spirits vowed revenge at the insult offered to one of their race; they stirred up war between the Ottawas and Andirondacks, which led to the extermination of the latter; one only was rescued, and he was grasped by the fish-wife, and by her borne down to the watery depths below the Falls of S. Anthony. In the German story, the husband is weary with the taunts of those around at having married a water-sprite, and bids her return to her element. Then the spirits of the flood vow his destruction, and send Undine on earth to embrace her faithless lord, and kiss him to death. The name of the fish-woman is in German Meerfrau or Meriminni; in Danish, the Siren is Maremind; and in Icelandic and old Norse, Marmennill; in Irish she is the Merrow; with the Breton peasantry she is Marie-Morgan. In the legendary lore of all these people, there are stories of the loves of a mortal man and a mermaid. According to Mr. Crofton Croker, O'Sullivan

More, Lord of Dunkerron, lost his heart to one of these beautiful water-sprites, and she agreed to be his, but her parents resented the union and killed her.

On the shore of Smerwick harbour, an Irishman, Dick Fitzgerald, caught a Merrow with her *cohuleen driuth*, or enchanted cap, lying on a rock beside her. He grasped the cap, and thereby possessed himself of the nymph, who, however, seemed nothing loth to obtain a mortal husband. They lived together happily for some years, and saw a family of beautiful children grow up at their knees. But one day the Lady of Gollerus, as she was called, discovered her old cap in a corner. She took it up and looked at it, and then thought of her father the king and her mother the queen, and felt a longing to go back to them. She kissed the babies, and then went down to the strand with the full intention of returning to Gollerus after a brief visit to her home. However, no sooner was the *cohuleen driuth* on her head, than all remembrance of her life on earth was forgotten, and she plunged into the sea, never to return. Similar tales are related in Shetland, the Faroes, in Iceland, and Norway.

Vade, the father of the famous smith Velund,

was the son of King Vilkin and a mermaid whom
he met in a wood on the sea-shore in Russia [1].　In
the Saga of Half and his knights is an account of a
merman who was caught and kept a little while on
land.　He sang the following entreaty to be taken
back to his native element—

> " Cold water to the eyes !
> Flesh raw to the teeth !
> A shroud to the dead !
> Flit me back to the sea !
> Henceforward never
> Men in ships sailing !
> Draw me to dry land
> From the depth of the sea [2] !"

In the " Speculum Regale," an Icelandic work of
the twelfth century, is the following description of
a mermaid :—

"A monster is seen also near Greenland, which
people call the Margygr.　This creature appears
like a woman as far down as her waist, with breast
and bosom like a woman, long hands, and soft
hair, the neck and head in all respects like those
of a human being.　The hands seem to people to
be long, and the fingers not to be parted, but
united by a web like that on the feet of water-

---

[1] Vilkina Saga, c. 18.
[2] Halfs Saga ok rekum hans, c. 7.

birds. From the waist downwards, this monster resembles a fish, with scales, tail, and fins. This prodigy is believed to show itself especially before heavy storms. The habit of this creature is to dive frequently and rise again to the surface with fishes in its hands. When sailors see it playing with the fish, or throwing them towards the ship, they fear that they are doomed to lose several of the crew; but when it casts the fish, or, turning from the vessel, flings them away from her, then the sailors take it as a good omen that they will not suffer loss in the impending storm. This monster has a very horrible face, with broad brow and piercing eyes, a wide mouth, and double chin [3]." The Landnama, or Icelandic Doomsday book, speaks of a Marmennill, or merman, having been caught off the island of Grimsey; and the annals of the same country relate the appearance of these beings off the coast in 1305 and in 1329.

Megasthenes reported that the sea which washed Taprobane, the modern Ceylon, was inhabited by a creature having the appearance of a woman; and Ælian improved this account, by stating that there are whales having the form of Satyrs. In 1187, a

[3] Quoted in " Iceland, its Scenes and Sagas," p. 349.

merman was fished up off the coast of Suffolk. It closely resembled a man, but was not gifted with speech. One day, when it had the opportunity to escape, it fled to the sea, plunged in, and was never seen again. Pontoppidan records the appearance of a merman, which was deposed to on oath by the observers.

"About a mile from the coast of Denmark, near Landscrona, three sailors, observing something like a dead body floating in the water, rowed towards it. When they came within seven or eight fathoms, it still appeared as at first, for it had not stirred; but at that instant it sank, and came up almost immediately in the same place. Upon this, out of fear, they lay still, and then let the boat float, that they might the better examine the monster, which, by the help of the current, came nearer and nearer to them. He turned his face and stared at them, which gave them a good opportunity of examining him narrowly. He stood in the same place for seven or eight minutes, and was seen above the water breast-high. At last they grew apprehensive of some danger, and began to retire; upon which the monster blew up his cheeks and made a kind of lowing noise, and then dived from their view. In regard to his form, they declare in their affidavits, which were

regularly taken and recorded, that he appeared like
an old man, strong limbed, with broad shoulders,
but his arms they could not see. His head was
small in proportion to his body, and had short,
curled black hair, which did not reach below his
ears ; his eyes lay deep in his head, and he had a
meagre face, with a black beard ; about the body
downwards, this merman was quite pointed like a
fish [1]."

In the year 1430, after a violent tempest, which
broke down the dykes in Holland and flooded the
low lands, some girls of the town of Edam in West
Friesland, going in a boat to milk their cows,
observed a mermaid in shallow water and embar-
rassed in the mud.

They took it into their boat and brought it into
Edam, dressed it in female attire, and taught it to
spin. It fed with them, but never could be taught
to speak. It was afterwards brought to Haerlem,
where it lived for several years, though still showing a strong inclination for water. Parival, in his
" Délices de Hollande," relates that it was instructed
in its duty to God, and that it made reverences
before a crucifix. Old Hudson, the navigator, in

---

[1] Pontoppidan's Nat. Hist. of Norway, p. 154.

his dry and ponderous narrative, records the following incident, when trying to force a passage to the pole near Nova Zembla, lat. 75°, on the 15th June. " This morning, one of our company looking overboard saw a mermaid ; and calling up some of the company to see her, one more came up, and by that time she was come close to the ship's side, looking earnestly at the men. A little after, a sea came and overturned her. From the navel upward, her back and breasts were like a woman's, as they say that saw her ; her body as big as one of us, her skin very white, and long hair hanging down behind, of colour black. In her going down they saw her tail, which was like the tail of a porpoise, speckled like a mackerel. Their names that saw her were Thomas Hilles and Robert Rayner."

In 1560, near the island of Mandar, on the west of Ceylon, some fishermen entrapped in their net seven mermen and mermaids, of which several Jesuits, and Father Henriques, and Bosquez, physician to the Viceroy of Goa, were witnesses. The physician examined them with a great deal of care, and dissected them. He asserts that the internal and external structure resembled that of human beings. We have another account of a merman seen near the great rock Diamon, on the coast of Martinique. The persons who saw it gave a precise description of it before a notary; they affirmed that they saw it wipe its hands over its face, and even heard it blow its nose. Another creature of the same species was captured in the Baltic in 1531, and sent as a present to Sigismund, King of Poland, with whom it lived three days, and was seen by all the Court. Another was taken near Rocca de Sintra, as related by Damian Goes. The King of Portugal and the Grand-Master of the Order of S. James are said to have had a suit at law, to determine which party the creature belonged to.

Captain Weddell, well known for his geo-graphical discoveries in the extreme south of the globe, relates the following story:—"A boat's crew were employed on Hall's Island, when one of the crew, left to take care of some produce, saw an animal whose voice was even musical. The sailor had lain down, and about ten o'clock he heard a noise resembling human cries; and as daylight in these latitudes never disappears at this season, he rose and looked around, but, on seeing no person, returned to bed. Presently he heard the noise again, rose a second time, but still saw nothing. Conceiving, however, the possibility of a boat being upset, and that some of the crew might be clinging to some detached rocks, he walked along the beach a few steps, and heard the noise more distinctly, but in a musical strain. Upon searching round, he saw an object lying on a rock a dozen yards from the shore, at which he was somewhat frightened. The face and shoulders appeared of human form, and of a reddish colour; over the shoulders hung long green hair; the tail resembled that of the seal, but the extremities of the arms he could not see distinctly. The creature continued to make a musical noise while he gazed about two minutes, and on perceiving him it disappeared in an instant. Immediately when the man saw his officer, he told this wild tale, and to add weight to his testimony (being a Romanist) he made a cross on the sand, which he kissed, as making oath to the truth of his statement. When I saw him, he told the story in so clear and positive a manner, making oath to its truth, that I concluded he must really have seen the animal he described, or that it must have been the effect of a disturbed imagination[5]."

In a splendidly illustrated work with plates

[5] Voyage towards the South Pole, p. 143, quoted by Goss: Romance of Nat. Hist., 2nd Series.

coloured by hand, "Poissons, écrevisses et crabes de diverses couleurs et figures extraordinaires, que l'on trouve autour des Isles Moluques," dedicated to King George of England, and published by Louis Renard at Amsterdam, in 1717, is a curious account of a mermaid. This book was the result of thirty years' labour, in the Indian seas, by Blatazar Coyett, Governor of the Islands of the

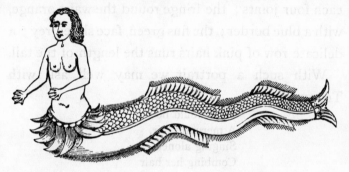

Province of Amboine and President of the Commissioners in Batavia, and by Adrien Van der Stell, Governor Regent of the Province of Amboine. In the 2nd volume, p. 240, is the picture of a mermaid here reproduced, and the subjoined description :—

"See-wyf. A monster resembling a Siren, caught near the island of Borné, or Boeren, in the Department of Amboine. It was 59 inches long, and in proportion as an eel. It lived on land, in a vat full of water, during four days seven hours. From time to time it uttered little cries like those of a mouse. It would not eat, though it was offered small fish, shells, crabs, lobsters, &c. After its death, some excrement was discovered in the vat, like the secretion of a cat." The copy from which I have taken the representation for this work is thus coloured : hair, the hue of kelp ; body, olive tint ; webbed olive between the fingers, which have each four joints ; the fringe round the waist orange, with a blue border ; the fins green, face slate-grey ; a delicate row of pink hairs runs the length of the tail.

With such a portrait we may well ask with Tennyson—

> " Who would be
> A mermaid fair,
> Singing alone,
> Combing her hair
> Under the sea
> In a golden curl,
> With a comb of pearl,
> On a throne ?"

The introduction to the book contains additional information.

The *Avertissement de l'Editeur* says :—" M. Baltazar Coyett is the first to whom the great discovery is due. Whilst governor, he encouraged the fishery of these fishes ; and after having had about two hundred painted of those which were

brought to his home by the Indians of Amboine
and the neighbouring isles, as well as by the Dutch
there settled, he formed of them two collections,
the originals of which were brought by his son to
M. Scott the Elder, who was then chief advocate, or
prime minister, of the Company General of the
East Indies at Amsterdam. He had them copied
exactly. The second volume, *less correct* indeed
in the exactitude of the drawings, but very curious
on account of the novelties wherewith it is filled,
and of the remarks accompanying each fish, was
taken from the collection of M. Van der Stell,
Governor of the Moluccas, by a painter named
Gamael Fallours, who brought them to me from
the Indies, and of which I have selected about
250. Moreover, to check incredulity in certain persons, I have thought fit to subjoin the following
certificates." Among them, the most curious are
those relating to the mermaid.

Letter from Renard, the publisher, to M.
François Valentyn, minister of the Gospel at Dort,
late superintendent of the churches in the colonies,
dated Amsterdam, Dec. 17, 1716.

" Monsieur,
" His Majesty the Czar of Muscovy having

done me the honour of visiting my house, and having had occasion to show the prince the work on the fishes of the Molucca islands, by the Sieur Fallours, in which, among other drawings, is the enclosed plate, representing a monster resembling a Siren, which this painter says that he saw alive for four days at Amboine, as you will be pleased to see in the writing with his own hand, which accompanies this picture, and as he believes that M. Van der Stell, the present Governor of Amboine, may have sent it to you, I remarked that his Majesty the Czar would be much gratified to have this fact substantiated ; wherefore I shall be greatly obliged if you will favour me with a reply.

"I remain, &c."

REPLY.

"Dort, *Dec.* 18, 1716.

"Monsieur,

"It is not impossible that, since my departure from the Indies, Fallours may have seen at Amboine the monster whose picture you had the courtesy to send me, and which I return enclosed ; but up to the present moment I have neither seen nor heard of the original. If I had the creature, I would with all my heart make a present of it to

his Majesty the Czar, whose application in the research of objects of curiosity deserves the praise of
all the world. But, sir, as evidence that there are
monsters in nature resembling this Siren, I may
say that I know for certain, that in the year 1652
or 1653 a lieutenant in the service of the Company
saw two of these beings in the gulf, near the village
of Hennetelo, near the islands of Ceram and Bœro,
in the Department of Amboine. They were swimming side by side, which made him presume that
one was male, the other female. Six weeks after
they reappeared in the same spot, and were seen
by more than fifty persons. These monsters were
of a greenish grey colour, having precisely the
shape of human beings from the head to the waist,
with arms and hands, but their bodies tapered
away. One was larger than the other; their hair
was moderately long. I may add that, on my way
back from the Indies, in which I resided thirty
years, I saw, on the 1st May, 1714, long. 12° 18′,
and on the Meridian, during clear, calm weather, at
the distance of three or four ship-lengths off, a
monster, which was apparently a sort of marine-
man, of a bluish grey (gris de mer). It was raised
well above the surface, and seemed to have a sort
of fisher's cap of moss on its head. All the ship's

company saw it, as well as myself; but although its back was turned towards us, the monster seemed conscious that we were approaching too near, and it dived suddenly under water, and we saw it no more.

"I am, &c.,

"F. VALENTYN."

Letter from M. Parent, Pastor of the church of Amsterdam, written and exhibited before the notary Jacob Lansman.

"AMSTERDAM, *July* 15, 1717.

"Monsieur,

"I have seen with mingled pleasure and surprise the illuminated proofs of the beautiful plates which you have had engraved, representing the fishes of Molucca, which were painted from nature by the Sieur Samuel Fallours, with whom I was acquainted when at Amboine. I own, sir, that I was struck with astonishment at the sight of this work, the engravings of which closely resemble the fishes I have seen during my life, and which, or some of which, I have had the pleasure of eating during the thirteen years I resided at Amboine, from which I returned with the fleet in 1716. . . . Touching your inquiry, whether I ever saw a

Siren in that country, I reply that, whilst making
the circuit of our churches in the Molucca Isles
(which is done twice in the year by the pastors
who understand the language of the country), and
navigating in an *orambay*, or species of galley, between the villages of Holilieuw and Karieuw, distant from one another about two leagues by water,
it happened, whilst I was dozing, that the negro
rowers uttered a shrill cry of astonishment, which
aroused me with a start; and when I inquired the
cause of their outcry, they replied unanimously
that they had seen clearly and distinctly a monster
like a Siren, with a face resembling that of a man,
and long hair like that of a woman floating down
its back; but at their cry it had replunged into
the sea, and all I could see was the agitation of
the water where this Siren had disturbed it by
diving.

"I am, sir, &c.,

"PARENT."

One of the most remarkable accounts of a
mermaid is that in Dr. Robert Hamilton's "History of the Whales and Seals," in the "Naturalist's
Library," he himself vouching for its general truth,
from personal knowledge of some of the parties.
"It was reported that a fishing-boat off the island

of Yell, one of the Shetland group, had captured a mermaid by its getting entangled in the lines." The statement is, that the animal was about three feet long, the upper part of the body resembling the human, with protuberant mammæ, like a woman; the face, the forehead, and neck were short, and resembling those of a monkey; the arms, which were small, were kept folded across the breast; the fingers were distinct, not webbed; a few stiff, long bristles were on the top of the head, extending down to the shoulders, and these it could erect and depress at pleasure, something like a crest. The inferior part of the body was like a fish. The skin was smooth, and of a grey colour. It offered no resistance, nor attempted to bite, but uttered a low, plaintive sound. The crew, six in number, took it within their boat; but superstition getting the better of curiosity, they carefully disentangled it from the lines and from a hook which had accidentally fastened in its body, and returned it to its native element. It instantly dived, descending in a perpendicular direction.

"After writing the above, (we are informed) the narrator had an interview with the skipper of the boat and one of the crew, from whom he learned the following additional particulars. They had the animal for three hours within the boat ; the body was without scales or hair, was of a silver-grey colour above and white below, like the human skin ; no gills were observed, nor fins on the back or belly ; the tail was like that of the dog-fish; the mammæ were about as large as those of a woman ; the mouth and lips were very distinct, and resembled the human. This communication was from Mr. Edmonton, a well-known and intelligent observer, to the distinguished professor of natural history in the Edinburgh University ; and Mr. E. adds a few reflections, which are so pertinent that we shall avail ourselves of them. That a very peculiar animal has been taken, no one can doubt. It was seen and handled by six men on one occasion and for some time, not one of whom dreams of a doubt of its being a mermaid. If it were supposed that their fears magnified its supposed resemblance to the human form, it must at all events be admitted that there was some ground for exciting these fears. But no such fears were likely to be entertained ; for the mermaid is not an object of terror to the fisherman : it is rather a welcome guest, and danger is to be apprehended only from its experiencing bad treatment. The usual resources of scepticism, that the seals and other sea-animals, appearing under certain circumstances, operating on an excited imagination, and so producing ocular illusion, cannot avail here. It is quite impossible that, under the circumstances, six Shetland fishermen could commit such a mistake."

One of these creatures was found in the belly of a shark, on the north-west coast of Iceland, and is thus described by Wernhard Guthmund's son, priest of Ottrardale :—

"The lower part of the animal was entirely eaten away, whilst the upper part, from the epigastric and hypogastric region, was in some places partially eaten, in others completely devoured. The sternum, or breast-bone, was perfect. This animal appeared to be about the size of a boy eight or nine years old, and its head was formed like that of a man. The anterior surface of the occiput was very protuberant, and the nape of the neck had a considerable indentation or sinking. The alæ of the ears were very large, and extended a good way back. It had front teeth, which were long and pointed, as were also the larger teeth. The eyes were lustreless, and resembled those of a codfish. It had on its head long black, coarse hair, very similar to the *fucus filiformis;* this hair hung over the shoulders. Its

forehead was large and round. The skin above
the eyelids was much wrinkled, scanty, and of a
bright olive colour, which was indeed the hue of the
whole body. The chin was cloven, the shoulders
were high, and the neck uncommonly short. The
arms were of their natural size, and each hand had
a thumb and four fingers covered with flesh. Its
breast was formed exactly like that of a man, and
there was also to be seen something like nipples;
the back was also like that of a man. It had very
cartilaginous ribs; and in parts where the skin had
been rubbed off, a black, coarse flesh was perceptible, very similar to that of the seal. This
animal, after having been exposed about a week
on the shore, was again thrown into the sea[6]."

To the manufactured mermaids which come from
Japan, and which are exhibited at shows, it is not
necessary to do more than allude; they testify to
the Japanese conception of a sea-creature resembling the Tritons of ancient Greece, the Syrian On
and Derceto, the Scandinavian Marmennill, and the
Mexican Coxcox.

[6] Quoted in my " Iceland, its Scenes and Sagas."

The Fortunate Isles

IN my article on the "Terrestrial Paradise" I mentioned the principal mediæval fables existing relative to that blessed spot, which was located, according to popular belief, in the remote East of Asia. The Ancients had a floating tradition relative to a vast continent called Atlantis, in the far West, where lay Kronos asleep, guarded by Briareus; a land of rivers, and woods, and soft airs, occupying in their thoughts the position assumed in Christian belief by the earthly paradise. The Fathers of the Church waged war against this object of popular mythology, for Scripture plainly indicated the position of the garden land as "eastward in Eden" (Gen. ii. 8); but, notwithstanding their attempts to drive the western paradise from the minds of men, it held its ground, and was believed in throughout the middle ages, till Christopher Columbus sought and found Atlantis and paradise in the new world, a world in which the theories of the Ancients and of the Mediævals met, for it was truly east of Asia and west of Europe. "The saintly theologians and philosophers were right," are the words of the great admiral in one of his letters, "when they fixed the site of the terrestrial paradise in the extreme Orient, because it is a most temperate clime ; and the lands which I have just discovered are the limits of the Orient ;" an opinion he repeats in his letter of 1498 : "I am convinced that there is the terrestrial paradise," namely that which had been located by SS. Ambrose, Isidore, and the Venerable Bede in the East[1].

The belief in a western land, or group of islands, was prevalent among the Kelts as well as the Greek and Latin geographers, and was with them an article of religion, upon which were founded super-stitious practices, which perpetuated themselves after the introduction of Christianity.

This belief in a western land probably arose from the discovery of objects, unfamiliar and foreign, washed up on the European shores. In the life of Columbus, Martin Vincent, pilot of the King of

[1] Navarrette, Coll. de Documents, i. p 244.

Portugal, picked up off Cape S. Vincent a piece of carved wood ; and a similar fragment was washed ashore on the Island of Madeira, and found by Pedro Correa, brother-in-law of the great navigator. The inhabitants of the Azores said that when the wind blew from the West, there were brought ashore great bamboos and pines of a description wholly unknown to them. On the sands of the Island of Flores were found one day the bodies of two men with large faces, and with features very different from those of Europeans. On another occasion, two canoes were driven on the coast filled with strange men [2]. In 1682, a Greenland canoe appeared off the Isle of Eda in the Orkneys, and in the church of Burra was long preserved an Esquimaux boat which had been washed ashore [3]. On the stormy coast of the Hebrides are often found nuts, which are made by the fishermen into snuff-boxes or worn as amulets. Martin, who wrote of the Western Isles in 1703, calls them " Molluka beans." They are seeds of the *Mimosa scandens*, washed by the gulf-stream across the Atlantic to our shores. Great logs of drift-wood of a strange character are

[2] Herrera, Hist. General, Dec. i. lib. i. cap. 2.

[3] Wallace, An Account of the Islands of Orkney, 1700, p. 60.

also carried to the same coasts, and are used by the islanders in the construction of their hovels.

In 1508, a French vessel met with a boat full of American Indians not far off the English coast, as Bembo tells us in his history of Venice [4]. Other instances have been cited by commentators on the curious fragment of Cornelius Nepos, which gave rise in the middle ages to a discussion of the possibility of forcing a north-west passage to India. Humboldt, in his remarks on this passage, says: " Pomponius Mela, who lived at a period sufficiently near that of Cornelius Nepos, relates, and Pliny repeats it, that Metellus Celer, whilst Proconsul of Gaul, received as a gift from a king of the Boii or Boeti (the name is somewhat uncertain, and Pliny calls him a king of the Suevi) some Indians who, driven by the tempests from the Indian seas, landed on the coasts of Germany. It is of no importance discussing here whether Metellus Celer is the same as the Prætor of Rome in the year of the consulship of Cicero, and afterwards consul conjointly with L. Africanus; or whether the German king was Ariovistus, conquered by Julius Cæsar. What is

[4] Bembo, Hist. Ven. vii. p. 257.

certain is, that from the chain of ideas which lead Mela to cite this fact as indisputable, one may conclude that in his time it was believed in Rome that these swarthy men sent from Germany into Gaul had come across the ocean which bathes the East and North of Asia [5]."

The canoes, bodies, timber, and nuts, washed up on the western coasts of Europe, may have originated the belief in there being a land beyond the setting sun ; and this country, when once supposed to exist, was variously designated as Meropis, the continent of Kronos, Ogygia, Atlantis, the Fortunate Isles, or the Garden of the Hesperides. Strabo says distinctly that the only hindrance in the way of passing west from Iberia to India is the vastness of the Atlantic ocean, but that "in the same temperate zone as we inhabit, and especially about the parallel passing through Thinæ and traversing the Atlantic, there may exist two inhabited countries, and perhaps even more than two [6]."   A more distinct prophecy of America than the vague expressions of Seneca—"Finitam cuique rei magnitudinem natura dederat, dedit et modum : nihil infi-

[5] Humboldt, Essai sur l'Hist. de la Géographie du N. Continent, ii. p. 264, note 2.

[6] Strabo, Geog. lib. i.

nitum est nisi Oceanus.   Fertiles in Oceano jacere
terras, ultraque Oceanum rursus alia littora, alium
nasci orbem, nec usquam naturam rerum desinere,
sed semper inde ubi desiisse videatur, novam exsur-
gere, facile ista finguntur, quia Oceanus navigari
non potest" (Suasoria, I.).   Aristotle accepted the
notion of there being a new continent in the West,
and described it, from the accounts of the Carthaginians, as a land opposite the Pillars of Hercules
(Str. of Gibraltar), fertile, well-watered, and covered
with forests [7].   Diodorus gives the Phœnicians the
credit of having discovered it, and adds that there
are lofty mountains in that country, and that the
temperature is not subject to violent changes [8].   He
however tries to distinguish between it and the Ely-
sium of Homer, the Fortunate Isles of Pindar, and
the Garden of the Hesperides.   The Carthaginians
began to found colonies there, but were forbidden
by law, as it was feared that the old mother settlement would be deserted for the new and more attractive country.   Plutarch locates Homer's Island
of Ogygia five days' sail to the west of Brittia, and
he adds, the great continent, or terra firma, is five
thousand stadia from Ogygia.   It stretches far

[7] Aristot. De Mirab. Aucult. c. 84.
   Diod. Hist., ed. Wessel, tom. i. p. 244.

away towards the north, and the people inhabiting this great land regard the old world as a small island. This is an observation made also by Theopompus, in his geographical myth of Meropis[9].

The ancient theories of Atlantis shall detain us no longer, as they have been carefully and exhaustively treated by Humboldt in the already quoted work on the geography of the New World. We shall therefore pass to the Kelts, and learn the position occupied by America in their mythology.

Brittia, says Procopius, lies 200 stadia from the coast between Britannia and Thule, opposite the mouth of the Rhine, and is inhabited by Angles, Frisians, and Britons[1]. By Britannia he means the present Brittany, and Brittia is England. Tzetze relates that on the ocean coast, opposite Britannia, live fishermen subject to the Franks, but freed from paying tribute, on account of their occupation, which consists in rowing souls across to the opposite coast[2]. Procopius tells the same story, and Sir Walter Scott gives it from him in his " Count Robert of Paris." " I have read," says Agelastes, " in that brilliant mirror which reflects the times of our fathers, the

---

[9] Ælian, Var. Hist. iii. 18.
[1] De Bello Gothico, lib. iv. 20.
[2] Ad Lycophr. v. 1200.

volumes of the learned Procopius, that beyond Gaul, and nearly opposite to it, but separated by an arm of the sea, lies a ghastly region, on which clouds and tempests for ever rest, and which is known to its continental neighbours as the abode to which departed spirits are sent after this life. On one side of the strait dwell a few fishermen, men possessed of a strange character, and enjoying singular privileges in consideration of thus being the living ferry-men who, performing the office of the heathen Charon, carry the spirits of the departed to the island which is their residence after death. At the dead of the night these fishermen are in rotation summoned to perform the duty by which they seem to hold permission to reside on this strange coast. A knock is heard at the door of his cottage, who holds the turn of this singular office, founded by no mortal hand ; a whispering, as of a decaying breeze, summons the ferryman to his duty. He hastens to his bark on the sea-shore, and has no sooner launched it, than he perceives its hull sink sensibly in the water, so as to express the weight of the dead with whom it is filled. No form is seen ; and though voices are heard, yet the accents are undistinguishable, as of one who speaks in his sleep." According to Villemarqué, the place whence the boat put off with its ghostly freight was near Raz, a headland near the Bay of Souls, in the extreme west of Finisterre. The bare, desolate valleys of this cape, opposite the Island of Seint, with its tarn of Kleden, around which dance nightly the skeletons of drowned mariners, the abyss of Plogoff, and the wild moors studded with Druid monuments, make it a scene most suitable for the assembly of the souls previous to their ghastly voyage. Here too, in Yawdet, the ruins of an ancient town near Llannion, has been identified the Ὑάδιτοι of Strabo.

"On the great island of Brittia," continues Procopius, "the men of olden time built a great wall cutting off a great portion of the land. East of this wall, there was a good climate and abundant crops, but west of it, on the contrary, it was such that no man could live there an hour; it was the haunt of myriads of serpents and other reptiles, and if any one crossed the wall, he died at once, poisoned by the noxious exhalations." This belief, which acted as a second wall to the realm of the dead, preserved strict privacy for the spirits. Procopius declares that this tradition was widely spread, and that it was reported to him by many people.

Claudian also heard of the same myth, but confused it with that of the nether world of Odysseus. "At the extreme coast of Gaul is a spot protected from the tides of Ocean, where Odysseus by bloodshed allured forth the silent folk. There are heard wailing cries, and the light fluttering around of the shadows. And the natives there see pale, statue-like figures and dead corpses wandering [3]." According to Philemon in Pliny, the Cimbri called the Northern Ocean Morimarusa, *i.e.* mare mortuum, the sea of the dead.

In the old romance of Lancelot du Lac, the Demoiselle d'Escalot directed that after death her body should be placed richly adorned in a boat, and allowed to float away before the wind; a trace of the ancient belief in the passage over sea to the soul-land.

> " There take the little bed on which I died
>   For Lancelot's love, and deck it like the Queen's
>   For richness, and me also like the Queen
>   In all I have of rich, and lay me on it.
>   And let there be prepared a chariot-bier
>   To take me to the river, and a barge
>   Be ready on the river, clothed in black."
>   TENNYSON'S *Elaine*.

And the grave-digger in Hamlet sings of being at death

[3] In Rufin. i. 123—133.

"... shipp'd intill the land,
As if I had never been such."

Act v. Sc. I.

When King Arthur was about to die, with a mortal wound in the head, he was brought by good Sir Bedivere to the water's side.

"And when they were at the water's side, even fast by the banke, hoved a little barge with many faire ladies in it, and among them all was a queene, and all they had blacke hoods, and they wept and shriked when they saw King Arthur. 'Now put mee into the barge,' said the king; and so hee did softly; and there received him three queenes with great mourning, and so these three queenes set them downe, and in one of their laps King Arthur laide his head. And then that queene said, 'Ah! deer brother, why have ye tarried so long from me? Alas! this wound on your head hath taken over much cold.' And so then they rowed from the land, and Sir Bedivere cried, 'Ah! my lord Arthur, what shall become of mee now ye goe from me, and leave me here alone among mine enemies?' 'Comfort thy selfe,' said King Arthur, 'and do as well as thou maiest, for in mee is no trust for to trust in; for I wil into the vale of Avilion for to heale me of my greivous wound; and if thou never heere more of mee, pray for my soule.' But evermore the queenes and the ladies wept and shriked that it was pity for to heare them. And as soone as Sir Bedivere had lost the sight of the barge, he wept and wailed, and so tooke the forrest [4]."

This fair Avalon—

> " Where falls not hail, or rain, or any snow,
>   Nor ever wind blows loudly ; but—lies
>   Deep-meadow'd, happy, fair with orchard lawns
>   And bowery hollows crown'd with summer sea,"

is the Isle of the Blessed of the Kelts. Tzetze and Procopius attempt to localize it, and suppose that the Land of Souls is Britain ; but in this they are mistaken ; as also are those who think to find Avalon at Glastonbury. Avalon is the Isle of Apples—a name reminding one of the Garden of the Hesperides in the far western seas, with its tree of golden apples in the midst. When we are told that in the remote Ogygia sleeps Kronos gently, watched by Briareus, till the time comes for his awaking, we have a Græcized form of the myth of Arthur in Avalon being cured of his grievous wound. It need hardly be said that the Arthur of romance is actually a demi-god, believed in

---

[4] La Mort d'Arthure, by Sir Thomas Malory, ed. Wright, vol. iii. c. 168.

long before the birth of the historic Arthur. This Ogygia, says Plutarch, lies due west, beneath the setting sun. According to an ancient poem published by M. Villemarqué, it is a place of enchanting beauty. There youths and maidens dance hand in hand on the dewy grass, green trees are laden with apples, and behind the woods the golden sun dips and rises. A murmuring rill flows from a spring in the midst of the island, and thence drink the spirits and obtain life with the draught. Joy, song, and minstrelsy reign in that blessed region[5]. There all is plenty, and the golden age ever lasts ; cows give their milk in such abundance that they fill large ponds at a milking[6]. There, too, is a palace all of glass, floating in air, and receiving within its transparent walls the souls of the blessed : it is to this house of glass that Merddin Emrys and his nine bards voyage[7]. To this alludes Taliesin in his poem, " The Booty of the Deep," where he says, that the valour of Arthur is not retained in the glass enclosure. Into this mansion three classes of men obtain no admission —the tailors, of whom it takes nine to make a

---

[5] Villemarqué, Barz. Breiz, i. 193.

[6] Mém. de l'Acad. Celtique, v. p. 202.

[7] Davies, Mythology of the Druids, p. 522.

man, spending their days sitting, and whose hands, though they labour, are white; the warlocks, and the usurers [8].

In popular opinion, this distant isle was far more beautiful than paradise, and the rumours of its splendour so excited the mind of the mediævals, that the western land became the subject of satyre and jest. It was nicknamed Cocaigne or Schlaraffenland.

An English poem, "apparently written in the latter part of the thirteenth century," says Mr. Wright (S. Patrick's Purgatory), "which was printed very inaccurately by Hickes, from a manuscript which is now in the British Museum," describes Cocaigne as far away out to sea, west of Spain. Slightly modernized it runs thus :—

> " Though Paradise be merry and bright,
>   Cokaygne is of fairer sight ;
>   What is there in Paradise ?
>   Both grass and flower and green ris (boughs).
>   Though there be joy and great dute (pleasure),
>   There is not meat, but fruit.
>   There is not hall, bower, nor bench,
>   But water man's thirst to quench."

In Paradise are only two men, Enoch and Elias; but Cocaigne is full of happy men and women.

[8] Barz. Breiz, ii. 99.

There is no land like it under heaven ; it is there always day and never night ; there quarrelling and strife are unknown ; there no people die ; there falls neither hail, rain, or snow, neither is thunder heard there, nor blustering winds—

> " There is a well fair abbaye
> Of white monks and of grey ;
> There both bowers and halls,
> All of pasties be the walls,
> Of flesh, and fish, and rich meat,
> The like fullest that men may eat.
> Floweren cakes be the shingles all,
> Of church, cloister, bower, and hall.
> The pins be fat pudings,
> Rich meat to princes and kings."

The cloister is built of gems and spices, and all about are birds merrily singing, ready roasted flying into the hungry mouths ; and there are buttered larks and "garlek gret plenté."

A French poem on this land describes it as a true cookery-land, as its nickname implies. All down the streets go roasted geese turning themselves ; there is a river of wine ; the ladies are all fair ; every month one has new clothes. There bubbles up the fountain of perpetual youth, which will restore to bloom and vigour all who bathe in it, be they ever so old and ugly.

However much the burlesque poets of the Middle

Ages might laugh at this mysterious western region of blissful souls, it held its own in the belief of the people. Curiously enough, the same confusion between Britain and Avalon, which was made by Procopius, is still made by the German peasantry, who have their Engel-land which, through a similarity of name, they identify with England, to which they say, the souls of the dead are transported. In this land, according to Teutonic mythology, which in this point resembles the Keltic, is a glass mountain. In like manner the Slaves believe in a paradise for souls wherein is a large apple-orchard, in the midst of which rises a glass rock crowned with a golden palace ; and in olden times they buried bear's claws with the dead, to assist him in climbing the crystal mountain [9].

The mysterious Western Land, in Irish, is called Thierna na oge, or the Country of Youth ; and it is identified with a city of palaces and minsters sunk beneath the Atlantic, or at the bottom of lakes.

" The ancient Greek authors," says M. de Latocnaye in his pleasant tour through Ireland, quoted by Crofton Croker, "and Plato in particular, have

---

[9] Mannhardt, Germanische Mythen, 330 et seq.

recorded a tradition of an ancient world. They pretend that an immense island, or rather a vast continent, has been swallowed up by the sea to the west of Europe. It is more than probable that the inhabitants of Connemara have never heard of Plato or of the Greeks; nevertheless they have also their ancient tradition. 'Our land will re-appear some day,' say the old men to the young folk, as they lead them on a certain day of the year to a mountain-top, and point out over the sea to them; the fishers also on their coasts pretend that they see towns and villages at the bottom of the water. The descriptions which they give of this imaginary country are as emphatic and ex-aggerated as those of the promised land: milk flows in some of the rivulets, others gush with wine; undoubtedly there are also streams of whisky and porter[1]."

The subject of cities beneath the water, which appear above the waves at dawn on Easter-day, or which can be seen by moonlight in the still depths of a lake, is too extensive to be considered here, opening up as it does questions of mythology

[1] Crofton Croker, Fairy Legends of the South of Ireland. 1862, p. 165. See also Kennedy, Popular Fictions of the Irish Celts. London, 1867.

which, to be fully discussed, would demand a separate paper. Each myth of antiquity touches other myths with either hand, and it is difficult to isolate one for consideration without being drawn into the discussion of other articles of belief on which it leans, and to which it is united. As in the sacred symbol of the Church each member predicates that which is to follow, and is a logical consequence of that which goes before, so that the excision of one article would destroy the completeness, and dissolve the unity of the faith—so, with the sacred beliefs of antiquity, one myth is linked to another, and cannot be detached without breaking into and destroying the harmony of the charmed circle.

But to confine ourselves to two points—the phantom western land, and the passage to it.

"Those who have read the history of the Canaries," writes Washington Irving, "may remember the wonders told of this enigmatical island. Occasionally it would be visible from their shores, stretching away in the clear bright west, to all appearance substantial like themselves, and still more beautiful. Expeditions would launch forth from the Canaries to explore this land of promise. For a time its sun-gilt peaks and long shadowy promontories would remain distinctly visible ; but in proportion as the voyagers approached, peak and promontory would gradually fade away, until nothing would remain but blue sky above and deep blue water below.

"Hence this mysterious isle was stigmatized by ancient cosmographers with the name of Aprositus, or the inaccessible [2]." The natives of the Canaries relate of this island, which they name after S. Brandan, the following tale. In the early part of the fifteenth century, there arrived in Lisbon an old bewildered pilot of the seas, who had been driven by the tempests he knew not whither, and raved about an island in the far deep, upon which he had landed, and which he had found peopled with Christians and adorned with noble cities. The inhabitants told him they were descendants of a band of Christians who fled from Spain, when that country was conquered by the Moslems. They were curious about the state of their fatherland, and grieved to hear that the Moslem still held possession of the kingdom of Granada. The old man, on his return to his ship, was caught by a tempest, whirled out once more to sea, and saw

[2] Washington Irving, Chronicles of Wolfert's Roost, and other Papers. Edinburgh, 1855, p. 312.

no more of the unknown island. This strange story caused no little excitement in Portugal and Spain. Those well versed in history remembered to have read that in the time of the conquest of Spain, in the eighth century, seven bishops, at the head of seven bands of exiles, had fled across the great ocean to some distant shores, where they might found seven Christian cities, and enjoy their faith unmolested. The fate of these wanderers had hitherto remained a mystery, and their story had faded from memory; but the report of the old pilot revived the long-forgotten theme, and it was determined, by the pious and enthusiastic, that this island thus accidentally discovered was the identical place of refuge, whither the wandering bishops had been guided with their flock by the hand of Providence. No one, however, entered into the matter with half the zeal of Don Fernando de Alma, a young cavalier of high standing in the Portuguese court, and of the meek, sanguine, and romantic temperament. The Island of the Seven Cities became now the constant subject of his thoughts by day and of his dreams by night; and he determined to fit out an expedition, and set sail in quest of the sainted island. Don Ioacos II. furnished him with a commission, constituting him

Adalantado, or governor, of any country he might discover, with the single proviso, that he should bear all the expenses of the discovery, and pay a tenth of the profits to the crown. With two vessels he put out to sea and steered for the Canaries—in those days the regions of nautical discovery and romance, and the outposts of the known world ; for as yet Columbus had not crossed the ocean. Scarce had they reached those latitudes, than they were separated by a violent tempest. For many days the caravel of Don Fernando was driven about at the mercy of the elements, and the crew were in despair. All at once the storm subsided, the ocean sank into a calm, the clouds which had veiled the face of heaven were suddenly withdrawn, and the tempest-tossed mariners beheld a fair and mountainous island, emerging, as if by enchantment, from the murky gloom. The caravel now lay perfectly becalmed off the mouth of a river, on the banks of which, about a league off, was descried a noble city, with lofty walls and towers, and a protecting castle. After a time, a stately barge with sixteen oars was seen emerging from the river and approaching the vessel. Under a silken canopy in the stern sat a richly-clad cavalier, and over his head was a banner bearing the sacred emblem of the cross. When the barge reached the caravel, the cavalier stepped on board and, in the old Castilian language, welcomed the strangers to the Island of the Seven Cities. Don Fernando could scarce believe that this was not all a dream. He made known his name and the object of his voyage. The Grand Chamberlain—such was the title of the cavalier from the island—assured him that, as soon as his credentials were presented, he would be acknowledged as the Adalantado of the Seven Cities. In the mean time, the day was waning; the barge was ready to convey him to land, and would assuredly bring him back. Don Fernando leaped into it after the Grand Chamberlain, and was rowed ashore. Every thing there bore the stamp of former ages, as if the world had suddenly rolled back for several centuries; and no wonder, for the Island of the Seven Cities had been cut off from the rest of the world for several hundred years. On shore Don Fernando spent an agreeable evening at the court-house, and late at night with reluctance he re-entered the barge, to return to his vessel. The barge sallied out to sea, but no caravel was to be seen. The oarsmen rowed on—their monotonous chant had a lulling effect. A drowsy influence crept over Don Fer-

nando : objects swam before his eyes, and he lost
consciousness. On his recovery, he found himself
in a strange cabin, surrounded by strangers. Where
was he? On board a Portuguese ship, bound for
Lisbon. How had he come there? He had been
taken senseless from a wreck drifting about the
ocean. The vessel arrived in the Tagus, and
anchored before the famous capital. Don Fernando sprang joyfully on shore, and hastened to
his ancestral mansion. A strange porter opened
the door, who knew nothing of him or of his family :
no people of the name had inhabited the house
for many a year. He sought the house of his betrothed, the Donna Serafina. He beheld her on
the balcony ; then he raised his arms towards her
with an exclamation of rapture. She cast upon
him a look of indignation, and hastily retired. He
rang at the door ; as it was opened by the porter,
he rushed past, sought the well-known chamber,
and threw himself at the feet of Serafina. She
started back with affright, and took refuge in the
arms of a youthful cavalier.

"What mean you, Señor?" cried the latter.

"What right have you to ask that question?"
demanded Don Fernando fiecely.

"The right of an affianced suitor!"

"O Serafina ! is this your fidelity?" cried he in a tone of agony.

"Serafina ! What mean you by Serafina, Señor ? This lady's name is Maria."

"What !" cried Don Fernando ; "is not this Serafina Alvarez, the original of yon portrait which smiles on me from the wall ?"

"Holy Virgin !" cried the young lady, casting her eyes upon the portrait, "he is talking of my great-grandmother !"

With this Portuguese legend, which has been charmingly told by Washington Irving, must be compared the adventures of Porsenna, king of Russia, in the sixth volume of Dodsley's "Poetical Collection." Porsenna was carried off by Zephyr to a distant region, where the scenery was enchanting, the flowers ever in bloom, and creation put on her fairest guise. There he found a princess with whom he spent a few agreeable weeks. Being, however, anxious to return to his kingdom, he took leave of her, saying that after three months' absence his return would be necessary.

> "'Three months !' replied the fair, 'three months alone !
> Know that three hundred years are roll'd away
> Since at my feet my lovely Phœnix lay.'

> ' Three hundred years !' re-echoed back the prince :
> ' A whole three hundred years completed since
> I landed here ?' "

On his return to Russia, he was overtaken by all-conquering time, and died. A precisely similar legend exists in Ireland.

In a similar manner Ogier-le-Danois found himself unconscious of the lapse of time in Avalon. He was one day carried by his steed Papillon along a track of light to the mystic Vale of Apples ; there he alighted beside a sparkling fountain, around which waved bushes of fragrant flowering shrubs. By the fountain stood a beautiful maiden, extending to him a golden crown wreathed with blossoms. He put it on his head, and at once forgot the past: his battles, his love of glory, Charlemagne and his preux, died from his memory like a dream. He saw only Morgana, and felt no desire other than to sigh through eternity at her feet. One day the crown slipped from Ogier's head, and fell into the fountain: immediately his memory returned, and the thoughts of his friends and relatives, and military prowess, troubled his peace of mind. He begged Morgana to permit him to return to earth. She consented, and he found that, in the few hours of rapture in Avalon, two hundred years had elapsed. Charle-

magne, Roland, and Oliver were no more. Hugh
Capet sat on the throne of France, the dynasty of
the great Charles having come to an end. Ogier
found no rest in France, and he returned to Avalon,
nevermore to leave the fay Morgana.

In the Portuguese legend, the Island of the
Seven Cities is unquestionably the land of departed
spirits of the ancient Celtiberians; the properties
of the old belief remain: the barge to conduct
the spirit to the shore, the gorgeous scenery, and
the splendid castle, but the significance of the
myth has been lost, and a story of a Spanish
colony having taken refuge in the far western sea
has been invented, to account for the Don meeting
with those of his own race in the phantom isle.

That the belief in this region was very strong
in Ireland, about the eleventh century, is certain
from its adoption into the popular mythology of
the Norsemen, under the name of Greater Ireland
(Ireland hit Mikla). Till the ruin of the Norse
kingdom in the east of Erin, in the great battle
of Clontarf (1114), the Norsemen were brought
much in contact with the Irish, and by this
means adopted Irish names, such as Nial and
Cormac, and Irish superstitions as well. The
name they gave to the Isle of the Blessed, in the

western seas, was either Great Ireland, because there the Erse tongue was spoken,—it being a colony of the souls of the Kelts,—or Hvitramanna-land, because there the inhabitants were robed in white. In the mediæval vision of Owayne the Knight, which is simply a fragment of Keltic mythology in a Christian garb, the paradise is enclosed by a fair wall, " whyte and brygth as glass," a reminiscence of the glass-palace in Avalon, and the inhabitants of that land—

" Fayre vestymentes they hadde on."

Some of these met him on his first starting on his journey, and there were fifteen in long white garments.

The following passages in the Icelandic chronicles refer to this land of mystery and romance.

" Mar of Holum married Thorkatla, and their son was Ari; he was storm-cast on the White-man's land, which some call Great Ireland; this lies in the Western Sea near Vinland the Good (America): it is called six days' sail due west from Ireland. Ari could never leave it, and there he was baptized. Hrafn, who sailed to Limerick, was the first to tell of this; he had spent a long time in Limerick in Ireland."

This passage is from the Landnámabok, a work of the twelfth century. A turbulent Icelander, named Bjorn of Bradwick, vanished from his home. Years after, a native of the same island, Gudlief by name, was trading between Iceland and Dublin, when, somewhere about the year 1000, he was caught by a furious gale from the east, and driven further in the western seas than he had ever visited before. Here he came upon a land well populated, where the people spoke the Irish tongue. The crew were taken before an assembly of the natives, and would probably have been hardly dealt with, had not a tall man ridden up, surrounded by an armed band, to whom all bowed the knee. This man spoke to Gudlief in the Norse tongue, and asked him whence he came. On hearing that he was an Icelander, he made particular inquiries about the residents in the immediate neighbourhood of Brad-wick, and gave Gudlief a ring and a sword, to be taken to friends at home. Then he bade him return at once to Iceland, and warn his kindred not to seek him in his new home. Gudlief put again to sea, and, arriving safely in Iceland, related his adventures, concluding that the man he had seen was Bjorn of Bradwick [3]. Another Icelander

[3] Eyrbyggja Saga, c. 64. Hafniæ, 1787, p. 329.

brought away two children from Vinland, and
they related that near their home was a land,
where people walked about in flowing white robes,
singing processional psalms. Northern antiquarians
attempt to identify this White-man's land with
Florida, where they suppose was settled the Welsh
colony led beyond the sea by Madoc in 1169. I
have little doubt that it is simply an Icelandic reminiscence of the popular Irish superstition relative
to the Soul Island beneath the setting sun.

> " In his crystal ark,
> Whither sail'd Merlin with his band of bards,
> Old Merlin, master of the mystic lore ;
> Belike his crystal ark, instinct with life,
> Obedient to the mighty Master, reach'd
> The Land of the Departed ; there, belike,
> They in the clime of immortality,
> Themselves immortal, drink the gales of bliss
> Which o'er Flathinnis breathe eternal spring,
> Blending whatever odours make the gale
> Of evening sweet, whatever melody
> Charms the wood traveller."
>
> SOUTHEY'S *Madoc*, xi.

This Flath Innis, the Noble Island, is the Gaelic
name for the western paradise. Macpherson, in his
Introduction to the " History of Great Britain," relates a legend which agrees with those prevalent
among other Keltic peoples. In former days there
lived in Skerr a Druid of renown. He sat with his

face to the west on the shore, his eye following the declining sun, and he blamed the careless billows which tumbled between him and the distant Isle of Green. One day, as he sat musing on a rock, a storm arose on the sea; a cloud, under whose squally skirts the foaming waters tossed, rushed suddenly into the bay, and from its dark womb emerged a boat with white sails bent to the wind, and banks of gleaming oars on either side. But it was destitute of mariners, itself seeming to live and move. An unusual terror seized on the aged Druid; he heard a voice call, "Arise, and see the Green Isle of those who have passed away!" Then he entered the vessel. Immediately the wind shifted, the cloud enveloped him, and in the bosom of the vapour he sailed away. Seven days gleamed on him through the mist; on the eighth, the waves rolled violently, the vessel pitched, and darkness thickened around him, when suddenly he heard a cry, "The Isle! the Isle!" The clouds parted before him, the waves abated, the wind died away, and the vessel rushed into dazzling light. Before his eyes lay the Isle of the Departed basking in golden light. Its hills sloped green and tufted with beauteous trees to the shore, the mountain-tops were enveloped in bright and transparent clouds, from which gushed limpid streams, which, wandering down the steep hill-sides with pleasant harp-like murmur, emptied themselves into the twinkling blue bays. The valleys were open and free to the ocean ; trees loaded with leaves, which scarcely waved to the light breeze, were scattered on the green declivities and rising ground ; all was calm and bright ; the pure sun of autumn shone from his blue sky on the fields ; he hastened not to the west for repose, nor was he seen to rise in the east, but hung as a golden lamp, ever illumining the Fortunate Isle.

There, in radiant halls, dwelt the spirits of the departed, ever blooming and beautiful, ever laughing and gay.

It is curious to note how retentive of ancient mythologic doctrines relative to death are the memories of the people. This Keltic fable of the 'Land beyond the Sea," to which the souls are borne after death, has engrafted itself on popular religion in England. The following hymn is from the collection of the Sunday School Union, and is founded on this venerable Druidic tenet :—

" Shall we meet beyond the river,
Where the surges cease to roll,
Where in all the bright For-ever
Sorrow ne'er shall press the soul ?

" Shall we meet in that blest harbour,
    When our stormy voyage is o'er?
Shall we meet and cast the anchor
    By the fair celestial shore?

" Shall we meet with many loved ones,
    Who were torn from our embrace?
Shall we listen to their voices,
    And behold them face to face?"

So is a hymn from the Countess of Huntingdon's
collection :—

" I launch into the deep,
    And leave my native land,
    Where sin lulls all asleep :
For thee I fain would all resign,
And sail for heav'n with thee and thine.

" Come, heav'nly wind, and blow
    A prosp'rous gale of grace,
    To waft from all below
To heav'n, my destined place :
There in full sail my port I'll find,
And leave the world and sin behind."

Or I might quote a poem on " The Last Voyage,"
from the Lyra Messianica, which one would have
supposed to have been founded on the Gaelic
legend told by Macpherson :—

" On ! on ! through the storm and the billow,
    By life's chequer'd troubles opprest,
The rude deck my home and my pillow,
    I sail to the land of the Blest.

The tempests of darkness confound me,
Above me the deep waters roll,
But the arms of sweet Pity surround me,
And bear up my foundering soul.

" With a wild and mysterious commotion
The torrent flows, rapid and strong ;
Towards a mournful and shadowy ocean
My vessel bounds fiercely along.
Ye waters of gloom and of sorrow,
How dread are your tumult and roar !
But, on ! for the brilliant to-morrow
That dawns upon yonder bright shore !

" O Pilot, the great and the glorious,
That sittest in garments so white,
O'er death and o'er hell ' The Victorious,'
The Way and the Truth and the Light,
Speak, speak to the darkness appalling,
And bid the mad turmoil to cease :
For, hark ! the good Angels are calling
My soul to the haven of Peace.

" Now, ended all sighing and sadness,
The waves of destruction all spent,
I sing with the children of gladness
The song of immortal content."

It would be a study of no ordinary interest to
trace modern popular Protestantism back to the
mythologic systems of which it is the resultant.
The early Fathers erred in regarding the ancient
heresies as bastard forms of Christianity ; they
were distinct religions, feebly tinged by contact
with the religion of the Cross.   In like manner, I

am satisfied that we make a mistake in considering the Dissent of England, especially as manifested in greatest intensity in the wilds of Cornwall, Wales, and the eastern moors of Yorkshire, where the Keltic element is strong, as a form of Christianity. It is radically different: its framework and nerve is of ancient British origin, passing itself off as a spiritual Christianity.

In S. Peter's, Rome, is a statue of Jupiter, deprived of his thunderbolt, which is replaced by the emblematic keys. In like manner, much of the religion of the lower orders, which we regard as essentially Christian, is ancient heathenism, refitted with Christian symbols. The story of Jacob's stratagem is reversed: the voice is the elder brother's voice, but the hands and the raiment are those of the younger.

I have instanced the belief in angelic music calling away the soul as one heathen item in popular Protestant mythology—

> " Hark! they whisper! Angels say,
> ' Sister spirit, come away!' "

Another is embodied in the tenet that the souls of the departed become angels. In Judaic and Christian doctrine, the angel creation is distinct from that of human beings, and a Jew or a Catholic would as little dream of confusing the distinct conception of angel and soul, as of believing in metempsychosis.   But not so dissenting religion. According to Druidic dogma, the souls of the dead were guardians of the living ; a belief shared with the ancient Indians, who venerated the spirits of their ancestry, the Pitris, as watching over and protecting them.   Thus, the hymn "I want to be an Angel," so popular in dissenting schools, is founded on the venerable Aryan myth, and therefore of exceeding interest ; but Christian it is not.

Another tenet which militates against Christian doctrine, and has supplanted it in popular belief, is that of the transmigration of the soul to bliss immediately on its departure from the body.

The article *stantis vel cadentis Fidei*, of the Apostles, was the resurrection of the body.   If we read the Acts of the Apostles and their Epistles with care, it is striking how great weight, we find, is laid on this doctrine.   They went every where preaching—1. the rising of Christ ; 2. the consequent restoration of the bodies of Christians. "If the dead rise not, then is not Christ raised ; and if Christ be not raised, your faith is vain.   But now is Christ risen from the dead, and become the first fruits of them that slept.   For as in Adam all

die, even so in Christ shall all be made alive[4]."
This was the key-note to the teaching of the
Apostles ; it runs through the New Testament, and
is reflected in the writings of the Fathers. It
occupies its legitimate position in the Creeds, and
the Church has never failed to insist upon it with
no faltering voice.

But the doctrine of the soul being transported
to heaven, and of its happiness being completed
at death, finds no place in the Bible or the Liturgies
of any branch—Greek, Roman, or Anglican—of
the Church Catholic. Yet this was the tenet of
our Keltic forefathers, and it has maintained itself
in English Protestantism, so as to divest the doctrine
of the resurrection of the body of its grasp on the
popular mind. Among the Kelts, again, reception
into the sacred inner circle of the illuminated was
precisely analogous to the received dissenting
doctrine of conversion. To it are applied, by the
bards, terms such as 'the second birth,' 'the
renewal,' which are to this day employed by
Methodists to designate the mysterious process of
conversion.

But to return to the subject of this article. It is
a singular fact, that only the other day I heard of

[4] 1 Cor. xv. 16, 17, 20, 21.

a man in Cleveland, being buried two years ago
with a candle, a penny, and a bottle of wine in his
coffin : the candle to light him along the road. the
penny to pay the ferry, and the wine to nourish
him, as he went to the New Jerusalem.   I was told
this, and this explanation was given me, by some
rustics who professed to have attended the funeral.
This looks to me as though the shipping into the
other land were not regarded merely as a figure of
speech, but as a reality.

Swan=Maidens

I REMEMBER a long scramble in Iceland, over the ruins of tuff rock in a narrow gorge. My little pony had toiled sturdily up a dusty slope leading apparently to nothing, when, all at once, the ravine terminated in an abrupt scarp, whence was obtained a sudden peep of entrancing beauty. Far away in front gleamed a snowy dome of silver, doubly refined and burnished, resting upon a basement of gentian blue.

> " Some blue peaks in the distance rose,
>   And white against the cold-white sky
>   Shone out their crowning snows."

To the left started sheer precipices of ink-black rock to icy pinnacles, from which fell a continuous powder of white water into a lake, here black as the rocks above it, yonder bluer than the over-arching heavens. Not a sound of animated life broke the stillness, which would have been oppressive, but for the patter of the falling streams. The only living objects visible were two white swans rippling proudly through the clear water.

I have never since felt surprise at superstition attaching itself to these glorious birds, haunting lone tarns, pure as new-fallen snow. The first night I slept under my tent in the same island, I was wakened with a start by a wild triumphant strain as of clarions pealing from the sky. I crept from under canvas to look up, and saw a flight of the Hooper swans on their way to the lakes of the interior, high up, lit by the sun, like flakes of gold-leaf against the green sky of an arctic night.

Its solitary habits, the purity of its feathers, its wondrous song, have given to the wild swan a charm which has endeared it to poets, and ensured its introduction into mythology.

The ancient Indians, looking up at the sky over which coursed the white cirrus clouds, fabled of a heavenly lake in which bathed the swan-like Apsaras, impersonifications of these delicate light cloud-flakes. What these white vapours were, the ancient Aryans could not understand; therefore, because they bore a more or less remote resemblance to swans floating on blue waters, they supposed them to be divine beings partaking of the nature and appearance of these beautiful birds.

The name Apsaras signifies those who go in the water, from *ap*, water, and *saras*, from sr, to go. Those who bear the name skim as swans over the lotus-pond of heaven, or, laying aside their feather-dresses, bathe, as beautiful females, in the limpid flood. These swan-maidens are the houris of the Vedic heaven ; receiving to their arms the souls of the heroes. Sometimes they descend to earth, and become the wives of mortals ; but soon their celestial nature re-asserts itself, and they expand their luminous wings, and soar away into the heavenly deeps of tranquil azure. I have else-where referred to the story of Urvaçi, the Apsaras, and her lover Puravaras. And Somadeva relates the adventures of a certain Niçcayadatta, who caught one of these celestial maidens, and then lost her, but, full of love, pursued her to the golden city above[1]. He tells also of Srîdatta, who beheld one bathing in the Ganges, and, plunging after her, found himself in a wondrous land beneath the water, in the company of the beloved[2].

In the Kalmuk collection of tales called Siddhi-

[1] Katha Sarit Sagara, book vii. c. 37.
[2] Ibid. book ii. c. 10.

Kûr[3], which is a translation from the Sanskrit, is a story of a woman who had three daughters. The girls took it in turn to keep the cattle. An ox was lost, and the eldest, in search of it, entered a cave, where she found an extensive lake of rippling blue water, on which swam a stainless swan. She asked for her ox, and the bird replied that she should have it if she would become his wife. She refused, and returned to her mother. Next day the second sister lost an ox, traced it to the cave, pursued it into the land of mysteries, and saw the blue lake surrounded by flowery banks, on which floated a silver swan. She refused to become his wife, as did her sister. Next day the same incidents were repeated with the third sister, who, however, proved more compliant to the wishes of the swan.

The Samojeds have a wild tale about swan-maidens. Two Samojeds lived in a desolate moor, where they caught foxes, sables, and bears. One went on a journey, the other remained at home. He who travelled, reached an old woman chopping birch-trees. He cut down the trees for her, and drew them to her tent. This gratified the old

---

[3] Siddhi-Kûr, Tale vii.

woman, and she bade him hide, and see what would take place. He concealed himself; and shortly after beheld seven maidens approach. They asked the old woman whether she had cut the wood herself, and then whether she was quite alone. To both questions she replied in the affirmative; then they went away. The old woman then drew the Samojed from his hiding-place, and bade him follow the traces of the damsels, and steal the dress of one of them. He obeyed. Emerging from a wood of gloomy pines, he came upon a beautiful lake, in which swam the seven maidens. Then the man took away the dress which lay nearest to him. The seven swam to the shore and sought their clothes. Those of one were gone. She cried bitterly, and exclaimed, "I will be the wife of him who has stolen my dress, if he will restore it me." He replied, "No, I will not give you back your feather dress, or you will spread your wings, and fly away from me."

"Give me my clothes, I am freezing!"

"Not far from here are seven Samojeds, who range the neighbourhood by day, and at night hang their hearts on the tent-pegs. Procure for me these hearts, and I will give you the clothes."

"In five days I will bring them to you."

Then he gave her the clothes, and returned to his companion.

One day the maiden came to him out of the sky, and asked him to accompany her to the brothers, whose hearts he had set her to procure. They came to the tent, and the man secreted himself, but the damsel became invisible. At night the seven Samojeds returned, ate their supper, and then hitched up their hearts to the tent-pegs. The swan-maiden stole them, and brought them to her lover. He dashed all but one upon the ground, and as they fell, the brothers expired. But the heart of the eldest he did not kill. Then the man without a heart awoke, and entreated to have it returned to him.

"Once upon a time you killed my mother," said the Samojed; "restore her to life, and you shall have your heart."

Then the man without the heart said to his wife, "Go to the place where the dead lie, there you will find a purse, in that purse is her soul; shake the purse over the dead woman's bones, and she will come to life." The woman did as she was ordered, and the mother of the Samojed revived. Then he dashed the heart to the ground, and the last of the seven brothers died.

But the swan-maiden took her own heart and that of her husband, and threw them into the air. The mother of the Samojed saw that they were without hearts, so she went to the lake where swam the six maidens; she stole one dress, and would not restore it till the maiden had promised to recover the hearts which were in the air. This she succeeded in doing, and her dress was restored [4].

Among the Minussinian Tatars these mysterious ladies have lost their grace and beauty. They dwell in the seventeenth region of the earth in raven-black rocks, and are fierce, raging demons of the air. They scourge themselves into action with a sword, lap the blood of the slain, and fly gorged with blood for forty years. In number they are forty, and yet they run together into one; so that at one time there is but a single swan-woman, at another the sky is dark with their numerous wings; a description which makes it easy to identify them with clouds. But there are not only evil swan-women, there are also good ones as well.

Katai Khan lived on the coast of the White Sea, at the foot of gloomy mountains. He had two daughters, Kara Kuruptju (black thimble) and

---

[4] Castren, Ethnologische Vorlesungen über die Altaischen Völker. St. Petersburg, 1857, pp. 172—176.

Kesel Djibäk (red silk) ; the elder evil disposed and in league with the powers of darkness, a friend of the raging swan-woman ; the younger beautiful and good.

> " Kesel Djibäk often riseth,
> In a dress of snowy swan,
> To the realm where reign the Kudai.
> There the Kudai's daughters seven
> Fly on wings of snowy swan ;
> With them sporteth Kesel Djibäk,
> Swimming on the golden lake [5]."

The seven Kudai, or gods of the Tatars, are the planets. Kara Kuruptju is the evening twilight, Kesel Djibäk the morning dawn which ascends to the heavens, and there lingers among the floating feathery clouds. But Kara Kuruptju descends to the gloomy realm of the evil-hearted swan-women, where she marries their son Djidar Mōs (bronzen), the thunder-cloud. These grimly swanlike damsels of the Tatars irresistibly remind us of the Phorcydæ ; κυκνόμορφοι, as Æschylus calls them.

The classic swan myths must be considered in greater detail. They are numerous, for each Greek tribe had its own favourite myths, and additional fables were being constantly imported into

Schiefner, Heldensagen der Minussinischen Tataren. St. Petersburg, 1859, p. 201.

religion from foreign sources.   The swan was with
the Greeks the bird of the Muses, and therefore
also of Apollo.   When the golden-haired deity was
born, swans came from the golden stream of Pacto-
lus, and seven times wheeled about Delos, uttering
songs of joy.

> " Seven times, on snowy pinions, circle round
>   The Delian shores, and skim along the ground :
>   The vocal birds, the favourites of the Nine,
>   In strains melodious hail the birth divine.
>   Oft as they carol on resounding wings,
>   To soothe Latona's pangs, as many strings
>   Apollo fitted to the warbling lyre
>   In aftertimes ; but ere the sacred choir
>   Of circling swans another concert sung,
>   In melting notes, the power immortal sprung
>   To glorious birth [6]."

A picture, this, of the white cloudlets fleeting
around the rising sun.

The Muses were originally nymphs, and are the
representatives of the Indian Apsaras ; and it is on
this account that the swans are their symbols.
Beyond the Eridanus, in the land of the Lygii
(Λίγυες, i.e. the clear-ringing), lived once a songful
(μουσικός) king.   Him Apollo transformed into a
swan [7].   " Cycnus having left his kingdom, accom-

---

[6] Callimachus, Hymn. Delos.   Cf. also Euripides, Iphig.
in Tauris, 1110.

[7] Paus. i. 30, 3 ; Lucian, de Electro, 5.

panied by his sisters, was filling the verdant banks, and the river Eridanus, and the forest, with his complaints; when the human voice becomes shrill, and grey feathers conceal his hair. A long neck, too, extends from his breast, and a membrane joins his reddening toes; plumage clothes his sides, and his mouth becomes a pointless bill. Cycnus becomes a new bird; but he trusts himself neither to heavens nor the air. He frequents the pools and wide meers, and abhorring fires, choses the streams [8]."
This Cycnus was a son of Sthenelus; he is the same as the son of Pelopea by Ares, and the son of Thyria by Poseidon. The son of Ares lived in southern Thessaly, where he slew pilgrims till Apollo cut off his head, and gave the skull to the temple of Ares. According to another version of the story, he was the son of Ares by Pyrene. When Herakles had slain him, the father was so enraged that he fought with the hero of many labours.

Cycnus, a son of Poseidon, was matched against Achilles, who, stripping him of his armour, suddenly beheld him transformed into a swan; or he is the son of Hyrie, who springs from a rock and becomes the bird from which he derives his name,

[8] Ovid, Metam. ii. Fab. 4.

whilst his mother dissolving into tears is transformed into a lake whereon the stately bird can glide.

In the fable of Leda, Zeus, the heaven above, clothed in swan's shape,—that is, enveloped in white mist,—embraces the fair Leda, who is probably the earth-mother [9], and by her becomes the father of the Dioscuri, the morning and evening twilights, and, according to some, of beautiful Helen, that is, Selene, the moon. The husband of Leda was Tyndareos, a name which identifies him with the thunderer, and he is therefore the same as Zeus.

According to the Cyprian legend, Nemesis, flying the pursuit of Zeus, took the form of a swan, and dropped an egg, from which issued Helen. Nemesis is a Norn, who, with Shame, "having abandoned men, depart, *when they have clad their fair skin in white raiment*, to the tribe of the immortals [1]."

Swans were kept and fed as sacred birds on the Eurotas, and were reverenced in Sparta as emblems

---

[9] Λήδα is probably from *lada*, i. e. woman. Leda, however, bears a close resemblance to Leto, the dark-robed (κυανόπεπλος), who takes her name from λανθάνω or λήθω, *lateo*, and signifies darkness, which gives birth to Apollo, the sun, and Artemis, the moon.

[1] Hesiod, W. and D., 200.

of Aphrodite : this is not surprising, as Aphrodite
is identical with Helen, the moon, which swims at
night as a silver swan upon the deep dark sky-sea.
A late fable relates how that Achilles and Helen
were united on a spirit-isle in Northern Pontus,
where they were served by flights of white birds [2].

In the North, however, is the home of the swan,
and there we find the fables about the mystic bird
in great profusion.   There, as a Faroese ballad
says—

> " Fly along, o'er the verdant ground,
>   Glimmering swans to the rippling sound ;"

or, as an Icelandic song has it—

> " Sweetly swans are singing
>   In the summer time.
>   There a swan as silver white,
>   In the summer time,
>   Lay upon my bosom light.
>   Lily maiden,
>   Sweetly swans are singing !"

The venerable Edda of Soemund relates how
that there were once three brothers, sons of a king
of the Finns ; one was called Slagfid, the second
Egil, the third Völund, the original of our Wayland
smith.   They went on snow-shoes and hunted wild

---

[2] Pausan. iii. 19.

beasts. They came to Ulfdal, and there made
themselves a house, where there is a water called
the Wolflake. Early one morning they found, on
the border of the lake, three maidens sitting and
spinning flax. Near them lay their swan plumages :
they were Valkyries. Two of them, Hladgud, the
Swan-white, and Hervör, the All-white, were daughters of King Hlödver ; the third was Olrun, a
daughter of Kiàr of Valland. They took them
home with them to their dwelling : Egil had
Olrun, Slagfid had Swan-white, and Völund All-
white. They lived there seven years, and then
they flew away, seeking conflicts, and did not
return. Egil then went on snow-shoes in search
of Olrun, and Slagfid in search of Swan-white, but
Völund remained in Wolfdale. In the German
story of the mighty smith, as preserved in the
Wilkina Saga, this incident has disappeared ; but
that the myth was Teutonic as well as Scandinavian, appears from the poem on Frederick of
Suabia, a composition of the fourteenth century [3],
wherein is related how the hero wanders in search
of his beloved Angelburga. By chance he arrives
at a fountain, in which are bathing three maidens,

---

[3] Bragur, Leipzig, 1800, vi. p. 204.

with their dresses, consisting of doves' feathers, lying at the side. Wieland, armed with a root which renders him invisible, approaches the bank and steals the clóthes. The maidens, on discovering their loss, utter cries of distress. Wieland appears, and promises to return their bird-skins if one of them will consent to be his wife. They agree to the terms, leaving the choice to Wieland, who selects Angelburga, whom he had long loved without having seen. Brunhild, who was won by Sigurd, and who died for him, is said to "move on her seat as a swan rocking on a wave [4];" and the three sea-maids from whom Hagne stole a dress, which is simply described as "wonderful" in the Nibelungen-Lied, are said to—

"swim as birds before him on the flood [5]."

An old German story tells of a nobleman who was hunting in a forest, when he emerged upon a lake in which bathed an exquisitely beautiful maiden. He stole up to her, and took from her the gold necklace she wore ; then she lost her power to fly, and she became his wife. At one birth she bore seven sons, who had all of them gold chains round their necks, and had the power, which their

[4] Fornaldur-Sögur, i. p. 186.
[5] Nibelungen-Lied, 1476.

mother had possessed, of transforming themselves into swans at pleasure. In the ancient Gudrun-Lied, an angel approaches like a swimming wild-bird.

A Hessian forester once saw a beautiful swan floating on a lonely lake. Charmed with its beauty, he prepared to shoot it, when it exclaimed, " Shoot not, or it will cost you your life !" As he persisted in taking aim, the swan was suddenly transformed into a lovely girl, who swam towards him, and told him that she was bewitched, but could be freed if he would say an "Our Father" every Sunday for her during a twelvemonth, and not allude to what he had seen in conversation with his friends. He promised, but failed to keep silence, and lost her.

A hunter in Southern Germany lost his wife, and was in deep affliction. He went to a hermit and asked his advice ; the aged man advised him to seek a lonely pool, and wait there till he saw three swans alight and despoil themselves of their feathers, then he was to steal one of the dresses, and never return it, but take the maiden whose was the vesture of plumes to be his wife. This the huntsman did, and he lived happily with the beautiful damsel for fifteen years. But one day he forgot to lock the cupboard in which he kept the feather-dress ; the wife discovered it, put it on, spread her wings, and never returned. In some household tales a wicked step-mother throws white skirts over her step-children, and they are at once transformed into swans. A similar story is that of Hasan of Basra in the Arabian Nights.

The old fables of Valkyries were misunderstood, when Christianity had cast these damsels from heaven, and the stories were modified to account for the transformation. The sweet maidens no more swam of their own free will in the crystal waves, but swam thus through the force of an enchantment they were unable to break. Thus, in the Irish legend of Fionmala, the daughter of King Lir, on the death of the mother of Fingula (Fionmala) and her brothers, their father marries the wicked Aoife, who, through spite, transforms the children of Lir into swans, which must float on the waters for centuries, till the first mass-bell tingles. Who does not remember Tom Moore's verses on this legend ?—

" Silent, O Moyle, be the roar of thy water ;
  Break not, ye breezes, your chain of repose,
While, murmuring mournfully, Lir's lovely daughter
  Tells to the night-star the tale of her woes.
When shall the swan, her death-note singing,
  Sleep with wings in darkness furl'd ?
When will heaven, its sweet bells ringing,
  Call my spirit from this stormy world ?

" Sadly, O Moyle, to thy winter-wave weeping,
    Fate bids me languish long ages away ;
Yet still in her darkness doth Erin lie sleeping,
    Still doth the pure light its dawning delay.
When will that day-star, mildly springing,
    Warm our isle with peace and love ?
When will heaven, its sweet bells ringing,
    Call my spirit to the fields above?"

In another version of the story there is no term
fixed for the breaking of the enchantment; but
when the bells of Innis-gloria rang for the mass,
four white birds rose from the loch and flew to
church, where they occupied daily a bench, sitting
side by side and exhibiting the utmost reverence
and devotion. Charmed at the piety of the birds,
S. Brandan prayed for them, when they were transformed into children, were baptized, and then died.

In a Sclavonian legend, a youth was reposing in
a forest. The wind sighed through the trees, filling
him with a tender melancholy which could find no
expression in words. Presently there fluttered
through the branches a snowy swan, which alighted
on his breast. The youth clasped the beautiful
bird to his heart, and resisted all its struggles to
escape. Then the swan changed into a beautiful
girl, who forthwith accompanied him to church,
where they were united.

A weird Icelandic saga tells of a battle fought

on the ice of Lake Vener, between two Swedish kings, assisted by the chief Helgi and King Olaf of Norway, supported by Hromund Greipsson, the betrothed of the king's sister Swan-white. Above the heads of the combatants flew a great swan; this was Kara, the mistress of Helgi, who had transformed herself into a bird. She, by her incantations, blunted the weapons of King Olaf's men, so that they began to give way before the Swedes. But accidentally Helgi, in raising his sword, smote off the leg of the swan which floated on expanded wings above his head. From that moment the tide of battle turned, and the Norwegians were victorious [6].

It is a fair subject for inquiry, whether the popular iconography of the angel-hosts is not indebted to the heathen myth for its most striking features. Our delineations of angels in flowing white robes, with large pinions, are derived from the later Greek and Roman representations of victory; but were not these figures—half bird, half woman—derived from the Apsaras of the Vedas, who were but the fleecy clouds, supposed in the ages of man's simplicity to be celestial swans?

---

[6] Fornaldur Sögur, ii. p. 374.

The Knight of the Swan

"WE rede in the auncient and autentike
cronicles that sometime ther was a noble
king in Lilefort, otherwise named the strong yle, a
muche riche lande, the which kinge had to name
Pieron. And he tooke to wife and spouse Mata-
brunne the doughter of an other king puissaunt
and riche mervailously." By his wife Matabrune,
the king became father of Oriant, "the which after
the dyscease of his father abode with his mother
as heir of the realme, whiche he succeded and
governed peasiabli without to be maried."

One day King Oriant chased a hart in the forest,
and lost his way; exhausted with his ride, he drew
rein near a fountain which bubbled out from under
a mossy rock.

"And there he sat downe under a tree, to the
which he reined his horse the better to solace and

sporte him at his owne pleasure.   And thus as
he was in consolacion there came to him a yonge
damoysel moche grevous and of noble maintene,
named Beatrice, accompanied of a noble knight,
and two squires, with iiii damoyselles, the which
she held in her service and famyliarite."

This Beatrice became the wife of Oriant, much
to the chagrin of his mother, who had hitherto
held rule in the palace, and who at once hated
her daughter-in-law, and determined on her destruction.

The king had not been married many months
before war broke out, and he was called from
home to head his army.   Before leaving, he consigned his wife to the care of his mother, who
promised to guard her with the utmost fidelity.
"Whan the time limited and ordeined of almighti
god approched that the noble and goodly quene
Beatrice should be delivered after the cours of
nature, the false matrone aforsaid went and
delibered in herselfe to execute and put in effecte
her malignus or moste wicked purpose. . . . But
she comen made maners of great welth to the said
noble quene Beatrice.   And sodainly in great
paine and traivable of bodye, she childed vi sonnes
and a faire doughter, at whose birthe eche of them

brought a chaine of silver about their neckes issuing out of their mothers wombe. And whan Matabrune saw the vii litle children borne having echone a chaine of silver at necke, she made them lightli and secretli to be borne a side by her chamberer of her teaching, and than toke vii litle dogges that she had prepared, and all bloudy laide them under the quene in maner as they had issued of her bodye."

Then Matabrune ordered her squire Marks to take the seven children to the river and drown them ; but the man, moved by compassion, left them in the forest on his cloak, where they were found by a hermit who " toke and lapped them tenderly in his mantel and with al their chaines at their neckes he bare them into the litle hous of his hermitage, and there he warmed and sustened them of his poore goodnes as well as he coulde." Of these children, one excelled the others in beauty. The pious old man baptized the little babes, and called the one who surpassed the others by the name Helias. "And whan that they were in the age of theyr pleasaunt and fresshe grene yougth thei reane all about sporting and playinge in the said forest about the trees and floures."

One day it fell out that a yeoman of Queen

Matabrune, whilst chasing in the forest, saw the seven children sitting under a tree eating wild apples, each with a silver chain about his neck. Then he told Matabrune of the marvel he had seen, and she at once concluded that these were her grandchildren; wherefore she bade the yeoman take seven fellows with him and slay the children. But by the grace of God these men's hearts were softened, and, instead of murdering the little ones, they robbed them of their silver chains. But they only found six children, for the hermit had taken Helias with him on a begging excursion. Now, "as soone as their chaines were of, they were al transmued in an instaunt in faire white swannes by the divine grace, and began to flee in the ayre through the forest, making a piteous and lamentable crye."

Helias grew up with his godfather in the forest. The story goes on to relate how that the hermit was told by an angel in vision whose the children were; how a false charge was brought against Beatrice, and she was about to be executed, when Helias appeared in the lists, and by his valour proclaimed her innocence; and how Matabrune's treachery was discovered.

" But for to returne to the subject of the crony-kill of the noble Helias knight of the swanne. It is to be noted that the said Helias knight of the swanne demanded of Kyng Oriant his father that it wolde please him to give him the chaines of silver of his brethern and sister that the goldesmith had brought. The which he delivered him with good herte for to dispose them at his pleasure. Than he made an othe and sware that he wolde never rest tyll he had so longe sought by pondes and stagnes that he had founde his v brethren and his sister, which were transmued into swannes. But our Lorde that consoleth his freendes in exaltinge their good will shewed greatly his vertue. For in the river that ranne about the kinges palays appeared visibly the swannes before all the people. —And incontinent the kynge and the queene descended wyth many lordes, knightes, and gentilmen, and came with great diligence upon the water syde, for to see the above sayde swannes. The king and the queene behelde them piteousli in weeping for sorrow that they had to se theyr poore children so transmued into swannes. And whan they saw the good Helias come nere them they began to make a mervaylous feast and rejoyced them in the water. So he approched upon the brinke: and whan they sawe him nere them, they

came lightli fawning and flickering about him
making him chere, and he playned lovingly their
fethers. After he shewed them the chaynes of
silver, whereby they set them in good ordre before
him. And to five of them he remised the chaynes
about their neckes, and sodeynlye they began to
retourne to theyr propre humayne forme as they
were before." But unfortunately the sixth chain
had been melted to form a silver goblet, and therefore one of the brothers was unable to regain his
human shape.

Helias spent some time with his father ; but a
voice within his breast called him to further adventures.

" After certayne tyme that the victoryous kynge
Helyas had posseded the Realme of Lyleforte in
good peace and tranquilite of justice, it happened
on a day as he was in his palais looking towarde
the river that he apperceived the swanne, one of his
brethren that was not yet tourned into his fourme
humayne, for that his chaine was molten for to
make Matabrune a cup. And the sayd swanne
was in the water before a ship, the which he had
led to the wharfe as abiding king Helias. And
when Helias saw him, he saide in himselfe : Here
is a signification that God sendeth to me for to

shew to me that I ought to go by the guyding of this swanne into some countrey for to have honour and consolacion.

"And when Helyas had mekelye taken his leave of all his parentes and freendes, he made to bere his armures and armes of honoure into the shyppe, with hys target and his bright sheelde, of whiche as it is written the felde was of sylver, and thereon a double crosse of goldè. So descended anon the sayd Helyas with his parentes and freendes, the which came to convey him unto the brinke of the water."

About this time, Otho, Emperor of Germany, held court at Neumagen, there to decide between Clarissa, Duchess of Bouillon, and the Count of Frankfort, who claimed her duchy. It was decided that their right should be established by single combat. The Count of Frankfort was to appear in person in the lists, whilst the duchess was to provide some doughty warrior who would do battle for her.

"Than the good lady as al abasshed loked aboute her if there were ony present that in her need wolde helpe her. But none wolde medle seynge the case to her imposed. Wherefore she committed her to God, praying Him humbly to

succour her, and reprove the injury that wickedly
to her was imposed by the sayd erle."

The council broke up, and lords and ladies were
scattered along the banks of the Meuse.

> " So, as they stray'd, a swan they saw
>   Sail stately up and strong,
> And by a silver chain she drew
>   A little boat along,
> Whose streamer to the gentle breeze,
>   Long floating, flutter'd light,
> Beneath whose crimson canopy
>   There lay reclined a knight.
>
> " With arching crest and swelling breast
>   On sail'd the stately swan,
> And lightly up the parting tide
>   The little boat came on.
> And onward to the shore they drew,
>   And leapt to land the knight,
> And down the stream the little boat
>   Fell soon beyond the sight."
>   SOUTHEY'S *Rudiger*.

Of course this knight, who is Helias, fights the
Count of Frankfort, overcomes him, and wins the
heart of the daughter of the duchess. Thus Helias
became Duke of Bouillon.

But before marrying the lady, he warned her
that if she asked his name, he would have to leave
her.

At the end of nine months, the wife of Helias

gave birth to a daughter, who was named Ydain at the font, and who afterwards became the mother of Godfrey de Bouillon, King of Jerusalem, and of his brothers Baldwin and Eustace.

One night the wife forgot the injunction of her husband, and began to ask him his name and kindred. Then he rebuked her sorrowfully, and leaving his bed, bade her farewell. Instantly the swan reappeared on the river, drawing the little shallop after it, and uttering loud cries to call its brother. So Helias stepped into the boat, and the swan swam with it from the sight of the sorrowing lady.

The romance of Helias[1] continues the story to the times of Godfrey de Bouillon, but I shall leave it at this point, as it ceases to deal with the myth which is the subject of this article. The story is very ancient and popular. It is told of Lohengrin, Loherangrin, Salvius, and Gerhard the Swan, whilst the lady is Beatrice of Cleves, or Else of Brabant. In the twelfth century it seems to have localized itself about the Lower Rhine.

Probably the most ancient mention of the fable

---

[1] Helyas, the Knight of the Swanne. From the edition of Copland, reprinted in Thoms: "Early English Prose Romances," 1858, vol. iii.

is that of William of Tyre (1180), who says : "We pass over, intentionally, the fable of the Swan, although many people regard it as a fact, that from it he (Godfrey de Bouillon) had his origin, because this story seems destitute of truth." Next to him to speak of the story is Helinandus (circ. 1220), quoted by Vincent de Beauvais[2]: "In the diocese of Cologne, a famous and vast palace over-hangs the Rhine, it is called Juvamen. Thither when once many princes were assembled, suddenly there came up a skiff, drawn by a swan attached to it by a silver chain. Then a strange and un-known knight leaped out before all, and the swan returned with the boat. The knight afterwards married, and had children. At length, when dwell-ing in this palace, he saw the swan return again with the boat and chain : he at once re-entered the vessel, and was never seen again ; but his progeny remain to this day."

A genealogy of the house of Flanders, in a MS. of the thirteenth century, states : " Eustachius venit ad Buillon ad domum ducissæ, quæ uxor erat militis, qui vocabatur miles Cigni[3]." Jacob van

---

Specul. Nat. ii. 127.

[3] Reiffenberg, Le Chevalier au Cygne. Bruxelles, 1846 p. viii.

Maerlant (b. 1235), in his "Spieghel Historiael[4]," alludes to it—

> " Logenaers niesdaet an doen,
> Dat si hem willen tien ane,
> Dat tie ridder metter swane
> Siere moeder vader was.
> No wijt no man, als ict vernam
> Ne was noint swane, daer hi af quam
> Als ist dat hem Brabanters beroemen
> Dat si van der Swane siin coemen."

And Nicolaes de Klerc, who wrote in 1318, thus refers to it in his " Brabantine Gests :" " Formerly the Dukes of Brabant have been much belied in that it is said of them that they came with a swan[5]." And Jan Veldenar (1480) says : " Now, once upon a time, this noble Jungfrau of Cleves was on the banks by Nymwegen, and it was clear weather, and she gazed up the Rhine, and saw a strange sight : for there came sailing down a white swan with a gold chain about its neck, and by this it drew a little skiff . . ."—and so on.

There is an Icelandic saga of Helis, the Knight of the Swan, translated from the French by the Monk Robert, in 1226. In the Paris royal library is a romance upon this subject, consisting of about 30,000 lines, begun by a Renax or Renant, and

[4] Maerlant, Fig. 1. 29.
[5] Von Wyn, Avondstonden, p. 270.

finished by a Gandor de Douay.   In the British
Museum is a volume of French romances, contain-
ing, among others, " L'Ystoire du Chevalier au
Signe," told in not less than 3000 lines.

The " Chevelere Assigne," a shorter poem on the
same subject, was reprinted by M. Utterson for the
Roxburghe Club, from a MS. in the Cottonian
library, which has been quoted by Percy and
Warton as an early specimen of alliterative ver-
sification.   It is certainly not later than the reign
of Henry VI.

The next prose romance of Helias is that of
Pierre Desrey, entitled " Les faictz et gestes du
preux Godsffroy de Boulion, aussi plusieurs croni-
ques et histoires;" Paris, without date.   " La
Genealogie avecques les gestes et nobles faitz
darmes du tres preux et renomme prince Godeffroy
de Boulion : et de ses chevalereux freres Baudouin
et Eustace : yssus et descendus de la tres noble et
illustre lignee du vertueux Chevalier au Cyne ;"
Paris, Jean Petit, 1504; also Lyons, 1580.   This
book was partly translated into English, and
printed by Wynkyn de Worde, " The hystory of
Hilyas Knight of the Swann, imprynted by
Wynkyn de Worde," &c., 1512; and in full by
Caxton, under the title, " The last Siege and Con-

queste of Jherusalem, with many histories therein comprised ;" Westmester, fol. 1480.

It is from the first thirty-eight chapters of the French "Faits et Gestes," that Robert Copland translated his Helias, which he dedicated "to the puyssant and illustrious prynce, lorde Edwarde, duke of Buckynghame," because he was lineally descended from the Knight of the Swan. This duke was beheaded, May 17th, 1521.

We need hardly follow the story in other translations.

The romance, as we have it, is a compilation of at least two distinct myths. The one is that of the Swan-children, the other of the Swan-knight. The compiler of the romance has pieced the first legend to the second, in order to explain it. In its original form, the knight who came to Neumagen, or Cleves, in the swan-led boat, and went away again, was unaccounted for : who he was, no man knew ; and Heywood, in his " Hierarchies of the Blessed Angels," 1635, suggests that he was one of the evil spirits called *incubi;* but the romancer solved the mystery by prefixing to the story of his marriage with the duchess a story of transformation, similar to that of Fionmala, referred to in the previous article.

We shall put aside the story of the swan-children, and confine our attention to the genuine myth.

The home of the fable was that border-land where Germans and Kelts met, where the Nibelungen legends were brought in contact with the romances of Arthur and the Sangreal.

Lohengrin belongs to the round table ; the hero who releases Beatrice of Cleves is called Elias Grail.   Pighius relates that in ancient annals it is recorded that Elias came from the blessed land of the earthly paradise, which is called Graele [6].   And the name Helias, Helius, Elis, or Salvius, is but a corruption of the Keltic ala, eala, ealadh, a swan. I believe the story of the Knight of the Swan to be a myth of local Brabantine origin.   That it is not the invention of the romancer is evident from the variations in the tale, some of which we must now consider.

1. Lohengrin.

The Duke of Limburg and Brabant died leaving an only daughter, Else or Elsam.   On his death-bed he committed her to the care of Frederick von Telramund, a brave knight, who had overcome a dragon in Sweden.   After the duke's death, Frede-

---

[6] Hercules Prodicus, Colon. 1609.

rick claimed the hand of Else, on the plea that it had been promised him; but when she refused it, he appealed to the emperor, Henry the Fowler, asking permission to assert his right in the lists against any champion Else might select.

Permission was granted, and the duchess looked in vain for a knight who would fight in her cause against the redoubted Frederick of Telramund.

Then, far away, in the sacred temple of the Grail, at Montsalvatsch, tolled the bell, untouched by human hands, a signal that help was needed. At once Lohengrin, son of Percival, was sent to the rescue, but whither to go he knew not. He stood foot in stirrup, ready to mount, when a swan appeared on the river drawing a ship along. No sooner did Lohengrin behold this, than he exclaimed: "Take back the horse to its stable; I will go with the bird whither it shall lead!"

Trusting in God, he took no provision on board. After he had been five days on the water, the swan caught a fish, ate half, and gave the other half to the knight.

In the mean while the day of ordeal approached, and Else fell into despair. But at the hour when the lists were opened, there appeared the boat drawn by the silver swan; and in the little vessel lay Lohengrin asleep upon his shield. The swan drew the boat to the landing, the knight awoke, sprang ashore, and then the bird swam away with the vessel.

Lohengrin, as soon as he heard the story of the misfortunes of the Duchess Else, undertook to fight for her. The knight of the Grail prevailed, and slew Frederick. Then Else surrendered herself and her duchy to him; but he would only accept her hand on condition that she should not ask his race. For some time they lived together happily. One day, in a tournament, he overthrew the Duke of Cleves and broke his arm, whereat the Duchess of Cleves exclaimed: "This Lohengrin may be a strong man and a Christian, but who knows whence he has sprung!" These words reached the ears of the Duchess of Brabant; she coloured and hung her head.

At night, Lohengrin heard her sobbing. He asked: "My love, what ails thee?"

She replied: "The Duchess of Cleves has wounded me."

Lohengrin asked no more.

Next night she wept again; her husband again asked the reason, and received the same answer.

On the third night she burst forth with: "Husband,

be not angry, but I must know whence you have sprung."

Then Lohengrin told her that his father was Percival, and that God had sent him from the custody of the Grail. And he called his children to him, and said, kissing them: "Here are my horn and my sword, keep them carefully ; and here, my wife, is the ring my mother gave me—never part with it."

Now, at break of day, the swan reappeared on the river, drawing the little shallop. Lohengrin re-entered the boat, and departed never to return.

Such is the story in the ancient German poem of Lohengrin, published by Görres from a MS. in the Vatican ; and in the great Percival of Wolfram von Eschenbach, verses 24,614—24,715.

2. The swan-knight of Conrad von Würzburg resembles Lohengrin and Helias in the outline of the story, but no name is given to the hero. He marries the daughter of the deceased Duke Gottfried of Brabant, and fights against the Duke of Saxony. His children are the ancestors of the great houses of Gelders and Cleves, which bear a swan as their arms.

3. Gerard Swan.

One day Charlemagne stood at his window overlooking the Rhine. Then he was ware of a swan floating on the water, drawing a boat by a silken band fastened round its neck. When the boat came alongside of the quay, the swan ceased to row, and the emperor saw that a knight armed cap-a-pie sat in the skiff, and round his neck hung a ribbon to which was attached a note. Navilon (Nibelung), one of the emperor's men, gave the stranger his hand to help him out of the bark, and conducted him to Charlemagne. The monarch inquired of the stranger his name; for answer he pointed to the letter on his breast. This the king read. It stated that Gerard Swan sought a wife and lands.

Navilon then unarmed the strange knight, and the king gave him a costly mantle. So they went to table. But when Roland observed the man, he asked who he was. Charlemagne replied, " He is a godsend ;" and Roland observed, " He seems to be a man of courage."

Gerard proved to be a worthy knight; he served the monarch well. He soon learned to talk. The king was very fond of him, and gave him his sister Adalis in marriage, and made him Duke of Ardennes[7].

[7] Northern Chapbooks of the Emperor Charlemagne. Nyerup, Morskabsläsning, p. 90.

4. Helias.

In the year 711 lived Beatrice only daughter of Dietrich, Duke of Cleves, at her castle of Nymwegen. One bright day she sat at her window looking down the Rhine, when she saw a swan drawing a boat by a gold chain. In this vessel was Helias. He came ashore, won her heart, became Duke of Cleves, and lived happily with her for many years. One thing alone interfered with her happiness : she knew not whence her husband came, and he had strictly forbidden her to ask. But once she broke his command, and asked him whence he had come to her. Then he gave his children his sword, his horn, and his ring, bidding them never separate or lose these legacies, and entering the boat which returned for him, he vanished for ever [8]. One of the towers of Cleves is called, after this event, the Swan-tower, and is surmounted by a swan.

5. Salvius Brabo.

Gottfried-Carl was King of Tongres, and lived at Megen on the Maas. He had a son named Carl-Ynach, whom he banished for some misdemeanour. Carl-Ynach fled to Rome, where he fell in love with Germana, daughter of the Proconsul Lucius

[8] Grimm, Deutsche Sagen, 1866, ii. p. 267.

Julius, and fled with her from the eternal city. They took ship to Venice, whence they travelled on horseback to Burgundy, and reached Cambray. Thence they proceeded to a place called Senes, and finding a beautiful valley, they dismounted to repose. Here a swan, at which one of the servants aimed an arrow, took refuge in the arms of Germana, who, delighted at the incident, asked Carl-Ynach the name of the bird in his native tongue. He replied " Swana." " Then," said she, " let me be henceforth called by that name, lest, if I keep my former name, I be recognized and parted from thee."

The lady took the swan with her as they proceeded on their journey, and fed it from her hand.

They now reached Florimont, near Brussels, and there Carl-Ynach heard that his father was dead. He was therefore King of Tongres. Shortly after his arrival at Megen, his wife gave birth to a son, whom he named Octavian, and next year to a daughter, whom they called Swan. Shortly after, Ariovistus, King of the Saxones, waged war against Julius Cæsar. Carl-Ynach united his forces with those of Ariovistus, and fell in the battle of Besançon. Swan, his widow, then fled with his children and her husband's body to Megen, fearing her brother Julius Cæsar. There she buried Carl-Ynach, and daily fed her swan upon his grave.

In the Roman army was a hero, Salvius Brabon by name, descended from Frankus, son of Hector of Troy. Cæsar rested at Cleves, and Salvius Brabon amused himself with shooting birds in the neighbourhood. One day he wandered to the banks of the Rhine. On its discoloured waters swam a snow-white swan, playfully pulling at the rope which bound a small skiff to the shore. Salvius leaped into the boat, and cast it loose from its mooring. Then the bird swam before him as a guide, and he rowed after it. On reaching the castle of Megen, the swan rose from the water, and flew to the grave of Carl-Ynach, where its mistress was wont to feed it. Salvius pursued it, bow in hand, and was about to discharge an arrow, when a window of the castle opened, and a lady cried to him in Latin to spare the bird. Salvius consented ; and casting aside his bow and arrow, entered the castle. There he learned the story of the lady. He hastened to Julius Cæsar, and told him that his sister was in the neighbourhood. The conqueror accompanied Salvius to the castle, and embraced Germana with joy. Salvius Brabon then asked the emperor to give him the young damsel

Swan in marriage, and he readily complied with the request, creating him at the same time Duke of Brabant; Octavian took the name of Germanicus, and became King of Cologne, and Tongres exchanged its name for Germania, after the sister of the emperor, its queen [9].

It was in commemoration of the beautiful myth of the Swan-knight, that Frederick II. of Brandenburg instituted the Order of the Swan, in 1440. The badge was a chain from which was suspended an image of the Virgin, and underneath that a swan. The badge of the Cleves order of knighthood was also a silver swan suspended from a gold chain. In 1453, Duke Adolph of Cleves held a tournament at Lille, "au nom du Chevalier au Cygne, serviteur des dames."

On the 13th May, 1548, the Count of Cleves presented the players with a silver swan of considerable value. Charles, Duke of Cleves, attempted, in 1615, to revive the order of the swan. When Cleves fell to Prussia, the Count de Bar endeavoured to persuade Frederick the Great to resuscitate the order, but in vain. With Anne of Cleves, the white swan passed to our tavern signboards.

[9] Jehan le Maire, Illustrations de Gaule. Paris, 1548, iii. pp. 20—23.

The myth is a Belgic religious myth. Just as in the Keltic legends of the Fortunate Isles, we hear of mortals who went by ship to the Avalon of Spirits, and then returned to their fellow-mortals; so in this Belgic fable we have a denizen of the distant paradise coming by boat to this inhabited land, and leaving it again.

In the former legends the happy mortal lives in the embraces of a divine being in perpetual youth; in the latter, a heavenly being unites himself, for a while, to a woman of earth, and becomes the ancestor of an aristocracy.

An Anglo-Saxon story bears some traces of the same legend. A ship once arrived on the coast of Scandia, without rudder or sail; in it lay a boy asleep upon his arms. The natives took and educated him, calling him Scild, the son of Sceaf (the skiff). In course of time he became their king. In Beowulf, it is added that Scild reigned long; and when he saw that he was about to die, he bade his men lay him fully armed in a boat, and thrust him out to sea. Among the Norse such a practice was not unknown. King Haki, when he died, was laid in a ship, the vessel fired, and sent out upon the waves. And the same is told of Baldur. But the shipping of the dead had

no significance in Scandinavian mythology, whilst
it was full of meaning in that of the Kelts.   The
Scandinavian Valhalla was not situated beyond
the Western Sea, but on the summit of a great
mountain ; whereas the Keltic Avalon lay over the
blue waters, beneath the setting sun.   Consequently, I believe the placing of the dead in ships
to have been a practice imported among the
Northern and Germanic nations, and not indi-
genous [1].

The classic fable of Helios sailing in his golden
vessel deserves notice in connexion with the myth
of Helias.   That the sun and moon travel in boats
of silver or gold is an idea common to many
mythologies.   At first sight it seems probable that
Helias is identical with Helios ; but the difficulty
of explaining how this classic deity should have
become localized in Brabant is insurmountable,
and I prefer the derivation of the name Helias,
from the Keltic appellation of the swan.

The necessity of the knight leaving his bride the
moment she inquired his race connects this story
with the Grail myth.   According to the rules of
the order of the Sangreal, every knight was bound
to return to the temple of the order, immediately

[1] Appendix D.

that any one asked his lineage and office. In the popular legend this reason does not appear, because the Grail was a genuine Keltic myth, with its roots in the mysteries of Druidism.

Of the different editions of Lohengrin, Helias, and the other Swan-knight legends, I will give no list, as the principal are referred to in the notes of this article.

The Sangreal

WHEN Sir Lancelot came to the palace of
King Pelles, in the words of Sir Thomas
Malory[1], "either of them made much of other, and
so they went into the castle for to take their repast.
And anon there came in a dove at the window, and
in her bill there seemed a little sencer of gold, and
therewith there was such a savour as though all
the spicery of the world had been there; and forthwith all there was upon the table all manner of
meates and drinkes that they could thinke upon.
So there came a damosell, passing faire and young,
and she beare a vessell of gold betweene her hands,
and thereto the king kneeled devoutly and said
his prayers, and so did all that were there: 'Oh,
Jesu!' said Sir Launcelot, 'what may this meane?'

[1] La Mort d'Arthure, compiled by Sir Thomas Malory;
reprinted from the text of 1634 by Thomas Wright, iii., c. 2,
&c.

This is,' said King Pelles, 'the richest thing that any man hath living; and when this thing goeth about, the round-table shall bee broken. And wit yee well,' said King Pelles, 'that this is the holy Sancgreall which yee have heere seene.'"

The next to see the sacred vessel was the pious Sir Bors. And after that he had seen it, "he was led to bed into a faire large chamber, and many doores were shut about that chamber. And when Sir Bors espied all those doores, he made all the people to avoide, for he might have no body with him; but in no wise Sir Bors would unarme him, but so laid him upon the bed. And right so he saw come in a light that he might wel see a speare great and long which come straight upon him pointlong. And so Sir Bors seemed that the head of the speare brent like a taper; and anon, or Sir Bors wist, the speare head smote him into the shoulder an hand breadth in deepness, and that wound grieved Sir Bors passing sore."

One day, when King Arthur and his court were at Camelot, sitting at supper, "anon they heard cracking and crying of thunder, that hem thought the place should all to-rive; in the midst of the blast entred a sunne-beame more clear by seaven times than ever they saw day, and all they were alighted by the grace of the Holy Ghost. Then began every knight to behold other, and either saw other by their seeming fairer than ever they saw afore, nor for then there was no knight that might speake any word a great while; and so they looked every man on other as they had beene dombe. Then there entred into the hall the holy grale covered with white samite, but there was none that might see it, nor who beare it, and there was all the hall fulfilled with good odours, and every knight had such meate and drinke as he best loved in this world; and when the holy grale had beene borne through the hall, then the holy vessel departed suddenly, and they wist not where it became."

Then the knights stood up in their places one after another, and vowed to go in quest of the Sangreal, and not to return to the round-table till they had obtained a full view of it.

We must leave the knights to start upon their quest, and turn, for the history of the Grail, to the romance of the San Greal, the Perceval of Chrétien de Troyes, written at the close of the twelfth century, and the Titurel and Parcival of Wolfram von Eschenbach, translated into German from romances older than that of Chrétien de Troyes.

When Christ was transfixed by the spear, there flowed from His side blood and water. Joseph of Arimathæa collected the blood in the vessel from which the Saviour had eaten the last supper. The enraged Jews cast Joseph into prison, and left him to die of hunger. But for forty-two years he lay in the dungeon nourished and invigorated by the sacred vessel which was in his possession. Titus released Joseph from prison, and received baptism at his hands. Then Joseph started with the vessel and the blood, or the Sangreal, for Britain. Before he died, he confided the sacred treasure to his nephew. But according to another version of the legend, the Grail was preserved in heaven, till there should appear on earth a race of heroes, worthy to become its guardians. The chief of this line was an Asiatic prince, named Perillus, who came to Gaul, where his descendants allied themselves with the family of a Breton prince. Titurel, who sprang from this heroic lineage, was the one chosen of God to found the worship of the Sangreal among the Gauls. Angels brought the vessel to him, and instructed him in its mysteries. He erected, on the model of the temple at Jerusalem, a magnificent temple to the Grail. He organized a band of guardians of the vessel, and elaborated the ceremonial of its worship.　The Grail, we are told, was only visible to the baptized, and only partially if they were tainted by sin.　To the pure in heart alone was it perfectly visible.

Every Good Friday a white dove descended from heaven, bearing a white oblation which it laid before the Grail.　The holy vessel gave oracles, expressed miraculously in characters which appeared on the surface of the bowl, and then vanished. Spiritual blessings attended on the vision and custody of the sacred vessel ; the guardians, and those who were privileged to behold it, were conscious of a mysterious internal joy, a foretaste of that of heaven. The material blessings are easier to be described. The Grail stood in the place of all food, it supplied its worshippers with the meats they most desired and the drinks most to their taste ; it maintained them in perpetual youth.　The day on which the Grail had been seen, its guardians were incapable of being wounded or suffering any hurt.　If they fought for eight days after the vision, they were susceptible of wounds but not of death.

Every thing in the construction of the temple was full of mystery.　It was erected on Montsalvatsch, of precious stones, gold, and aloe-wood.　In form it was circular ; there were three principal entrances. The knights who watched the Grail were patterns of virtue. All sensual love, even within the limits of marriage, was strictly forbidden. A single thought of passion would obscure the eye and conceal the mystic vessel. The chief of this order of knights was entitled King. As his office was hereditary, he was permitted to marry.

When the faith or the right was in jeopardy, a bell rang in the chapel of the Grail, and a knight was bound to go forth sword in hand to the defence. Wherever he was, should a question be asked him of his condition or office in the temple, he was to refuse to answer, and at once to return to Montsalvatsch.

Titurel reigned four hundred years, and he, to all appearances, seemed of the age of forty. He was succeeded in his office by his son Frimutelle, who transgressed, by loving a damsel, Floramie by name. Consequently he lost the grace of the holy Grail, and fell in a joust, engaged in to give pleasure and do honour to his mistress.

He was succeeded by his son Amfortas, who fell into grievous sin, and was given over by the Grail to be wounded by a lance. Then it was announced that he should not be healed of his wound till one came, pure and young, to Montsalvatsch who would see the mysteries of the sacred vessel, and ask their signification.

This Amfortas is the Pelles or Pellam of the "Mort d'Arthure."

Years passed, and the king lay wounded in his palace. The brotherhood of the Grail was dissolved, and the existence of the temple and its mystic rites was almost forgotten. Sir Thomas Malory gives a different account of the wounding of the king from that in the Romans du San Greal, and makes his healing depend on the arrival of a knight who is a "clean maid," who shall apply to him the sacred blood.

In the fulness of time, Galahad, the Good Knight, came to king Arthur's court, and went forth, with the other knights, to the quest of the holy Grail.

Let us follow Launcelot who was on a ship.

" The winde arose and drove Sir Launcelot more than a moneth throughout the sea, where he slept but little and prayed unto God that he might have a sight of the Sancgreall. So it befell upon a night at midnight hee arived afore a castle on the backe side, which was rich and faire, and there was a posterne that opened toward the sea, and was open without any keeping, save two lions kept the entrie, and the moone shined cleare.

" Anon Sir Launcelot heard a voice that said,
' Launcelot, goe out of this ship, and enter into the
castle where thou shalt see a great part of thy desire.'   Then he ranne to his armes, and armed him,
and so hee went unto the gate, and saw the two
lions ; then hee set hands to his sword and drew it ;
then came there sudainly a dwarfe, that smote him
upon the arme so sone that the sword fell out of his
hand.   Then he heard a voice that said, ' Oh man of
evill faith and poore beliefe, wherefore believest
thou more in thy harneis than in thy Maker ? for
Hee might more availe thee than thine armour, in
whose service thou art set.'—Thne Sir Launcelot
entered in so armed, and hee found no gate nor doore
but it was opened.   And so at the last he found a
chamber whereof the doore was shut, and hee set
his hands thereto for to have opened it, but hee
might not.   Then he enforced him much for to un-
doe the doore.   Then he listened ; and heard a voice
which sung so sweetly, that it seemed none earthly
thing, and him thought that the voice said, ' Joy and
honour be to the Father of heaven.'   Then Sir
Launcelot kneeled downe before the chamber, for
well he wist that there was the Sancgreall in that
chamber.   Then said he, ' Faire sweete Father,
Jesu Christ, if ever I did thing that pleased the

Lord, for thy pittie ne have me not in despite for my foull sins done here before time, and that thou shew me some thing of that which I seek.'

"And with that he saw the chamber doore open, and there came out a great clearenesse, that the house was as bright as though all the torches of the world had beene there. So came hee to the chamber doore, and would have entered, and anon a voice said unto him, 'Flee, Sir Launcelot, and enter not, for thou oughtest not to doe it, and if thou enter thou shalt forethinke it.' And hee withdrew him back, and was right heavie in his mind.

"Then looked hee up in the midst of the chamber, and saw a table of silver, and the holy vessell covered with red samite, and many angels about it, whereof one of them held a candell of waxe burning, and the other held a crosse, and the ornaments of the altar. And before the holy vessell hee saw a good man clothed like a priest, and it seemed that hee was at the sakering of the masse ; and it seemed unto Sir Launcelot that above the priest's hands there were three men, whereof the two put the youngest by likeness betweene the priest's hands, and so hee lift it up on high, and it seemed to shew so to the people. And then Sir Launcelot mervailed not a little, for him thought that the priest was so greatly charged of the figure, that him seemed that heem should have fallen to the ground; and when hee saw none about him that would helpe him, then hee came to the doore a great pace—and entred into the chamber, and came toward the table of silver; and when he came nigh he felt a breath, that him thought was intermedled with fire, which smote him so sore in the visage that him thought it all to-brent his visage, and therewith hee fell to the ground, and had no power to arise."

Sir Galahad, Sir Percival, and Sir Bors met in the forest, and rode together to the castle of King Pelles. There they supped, and after supper they beheld

a great light, and in the light were four angels bearing up an ancient man in bishop's vestments, and they set him down before a table of silver, on which appeared the Sangreal. And this aged prelate was Joseph of Arimathæa, "the first bishop of Christendom." Then other angels appeared bearing candles, and a spear from which fell drops of blood, and these drops were collected by an angel in a box. Then the angels set the candles upon the table, and "the fourth set the holy speare even upright upon the vessel," as represented on an ancient churchyard crucifix, in rude sculpture, at Sancreed, in Cornwall.

Joseph next celebrated the sacred mysteries, and, at the consecration, our Blessed Lord appeared and said, "Galahad, sonne, wotest thou what I hold between My hands?" "Nay," replied the maiden knight, "but if yee tell mee." "This is," He said, "the holy dish wherein I eate the lambe on Sher-Thursday, and now hast thou seene that thou desirest most to see, but yet hast thou not seene it so openly as thou shalt see it in the citie of Sarras, in the spirituall place. Therefore thou must goe hence, and beare with thee this holy vessell, for this night it shall depart from the realme of Logris, that it shall never be seen more heere."

So Galahad, after having anointed the wounded king with the blood which dropped from the spear, and made him whole, departed with his friends Bors and Perceval to the mystic city of Sarras, where he was made king.

The story is somewhat different in the Perceval of Chrétien de Troyes. This romance was commenced by Chrétien at the request of Phillip of Alsace, Count of Flanders; it was continued by

Gauthier de Denet, and finished by Manessier, towards the close of the twelfth century. It is the history of the quest of the San Greal.

Perceval was the son of a poor widow in Wales, brought up by her in a forest, far removed from all warlike images. One day he saw a knight ride past, and from that moment he had no rest, till his mother gave him arms and let him ride to the court of King Arthur. On his way he saw a tent in which lay a beautiful damsel asleep. Perceval took the ring from her finger, ate and drank at the table which was spread in the tent, and then pursued his course. As he entered the court at Cardueil, a felon knight stole the goblet from the king's table. Perceval went in pursuit. One evening he entered a castle where lay a sick king on a couch. The door of the hall opened, and there came in a servant bearing a bleeding lance, others with golden candlesticks, and finally the holy Grail. Perceval asked no questions, and was reproached on his leaving the castle for not making inquiries into the mystery of the Grail. Afterwards he undertook the quest of this marvellous vessel, but had great difficulty in finding again the castle of the wounded king. When his search was crowned with success, he asked the signification of the mystic rite which took place before his eyes, and was told that the king was a Fisher, descended from Joseph of Arimathæa, and uncle of Perceval; that the spear was that which had pierced the Saviour's side, and that the Grail was the vessel in which the sacred blood of Christ had been collected. The king had been wounded in trying to mend a sword which had been broken by a knight named Pertinax, and which could only be welded together by a knight without fear and reproach. The Fisher-king would recover health only when Pertinax died. On hearing this, Perceval sought out and slew Pertinax, healed his uncle, obtained in return the sacred vessel and the bleeding lance, and retired to a hermitage. On his death—

> " Fut au ciel remis sans doutance
> Et le Saint-Graal et la Lance."

It is very certain that Chrétien de Troyes was not the inventor of this mystic tale, for there exists in the "Red Book" a Welsh tale entitled Pheredur, which is indisputably the original of Perceval.

The "Red Book" is a volume of Welsh prose and verse romances and tales, begun in the year 1318, and finished in 1454. It is preserved in the

library of Jesus College, Oxford. Although Pheredur was transcribed after Perceval was composed,
it bears evidence of a higher antiquity.

Pheredur is not a Christian. His habits are
barbarous. The Grail is not a sacred Christian
vessel, but a mysterious relic of a past heathen
rite. The same incidents occur in Perceval as in
Pheredur, but in the former they are modified and
softened, and various points indicative of barbarism
and paganism are omitted.

Pheredur enters a castle, and "Whilst he and
his uncle were discoursing together, they beheld
two young men entering the hall, bearing a lance
of unusual length, from the point of which dis-
tilled three gouts of gore ; and when the company
beheld this, they began to wail and lament. But
the old man continued to talk with Pheredur ; and
as he did not tell Pheredur the reason of what
took place, Pheredur did not venture to ask him.
And when the cries ceased, there entered two
damsels with a basin in which was the head of a
man swimming in blood. Then the company
uttered a piercing wail."

In the Perceval, and in the Mort d'Arthure, the
head is omitted, and to the lance and grail are
attributed a Christian value ; but in the Pheredur

there is no trace whatever of these symbols having any Christian signification.

Pheredur signifies, according to M. de la Ville-marqué [2], "The Companion of the Basin," and is a synonym of Perceval ; Per being a basin, and Këval and Këdur having alike the meaning of companion.

Pheredur is mentioned as well in the Annales Cambriæ, which extend from the year 444 to 1066. Geoffrey of Monmouth also speaks of the reign of Peredure, "who governed the people with gene-rosity and mildness, so that he even excelled his other brothers who had preceded him [3];" and the anonymous author of the " Life of Merlin" speaks of him as the companion and consoler of the bard [4]. Aneurin, the contemporary of Hengst and Horsa, the author of the Gododin, terms him one of the most illustrious princes of the Isle of Britain [5].

Taliesin ben Beirdd, the famous poet of the same age, speaks of the sacred vessel in a manner which connects it with bardic mythology.   "This vessel," he says, "inspires poetic genius, gives wisdom, discovers the knowledge of futurity, the mysteries

[2] Les Romans de la Table-Ronde 1861.

[3] Geoffr. Monm., lib. iii. c. 18.

[4] Vita Merlini, pp. 2. 4.

[5] Villemarqué, Poèmes des Bardes Bretons du sixième siècle, p. 298.

of the world, the whole treasure of human sciences."
And he describes it as adorned like the Grail, with a
beading of pearls and diamonds[6]. One of his poems
contains the history of Bran the Blessed, in which
the mystic vessel occupies a prominent position.

One day, whilst hunting in Ireland, Bran arrived
on the banks of a lake, called the Lake of the
Basin. He saw there a black and hideous giant,
a witch, and a dwarf, rise from the water holding a
vessel in their hands. He persuaded them to
accompany him to Wales, where he lodged them
in his palace, and in return for his hospitality,
received the basin. This vase had the property of
healing all mortal ills, of staunching blood, of re-
suscitating the dead. But those who were restored
to life by it were not enabled to speak, lest they
should divulge the mysteries of the vessel. At a
banquet given by Bran to Martholone, King of Ireland, the Welsh prince presented the bowl to his
guest. He regretted that he had made this present,
when some years later war broke out between the
King of Ireland and himself. Then he found himself unable to cope with his adversary, whose every
slain soldier recovered life by means of the sacred
vessel. But Bran smote off the head of a hostile

[6] Myvvrian, i. pp. 17, 18, 19, 20. 37. 45. 67.

chief, and cast the bloody head into the bowl, when it burst, and its virtues ceased.

This basin was reckoned as one of the thirteen wonders of the Isle of Britain, brought by Merdhyn, or Merlin, in his crystal ark. That it is the same as Ceridwen's cauldron is not improbable. Ceridwen was the Keltic Great Mother, the Demeter, the source of life, and the receptacle of the dead. The story of her cauldron is told in the Pair Ceridwen (vessel of Ceridwen), or Hanes Taliesin (History of Taliesin).

In ancient times there was a man, Tegid Voel by name, who had a wife called Ceridwen, by whom he had a son Morvran ap Tegid, and a daughter Creirwy, both very beautiful; also Aragddu, the most hideous of beings. Ceridwen, knowing that the poor deformed child would have little joy of life, determined to prepare for him the Water of Inspiration. She placed a cauldron on a fire, filled it with the requisite ingredients, and left little Gwion to attend to its seething, and blind Morda to keep up the fire for a year and a day, without suffering the operation to cease for a moment. One day, near the end of the twelve-month, three drops spirted out of the bubbling liquid, and Gwion caught them on his finger. As they scalded him, he put his finger into his mouth, and at once obtained the knowledge of futurity. He saw that Ceridwen would attempt his death, in consequence of his having tasted the precious drops; so he prudently took to flight. Then the cauldron burst and extinguished the fire.

Ceridwen, in her rage, struck Morda on the head, and rushed in pursuit of Gwion the Little. He transformed himself into a hare; then she took the form of a hound. He sprang into a river and took that of a fish; instantly she became an otter. Then he rose from the water as a little bird; but she soared after him as a hawk. Then he dropped as a grain of wheat on a corn-heap; but Ceridwen, instantly taking the shape of a hen, swallowed him. She became pregnant thereby, and in nine months gave birth to a lovely child which she hid in a leather coracle and committed to the waves, on the 29th of April.

In this bardic tale we have certainly a very ancient Keltic myth. What the cauldron signifies it is difficult to ascertain. Some suppose it to represent the ocean, others the working of the vital force of earth, which produces the three seasons which are good, symbolized by the drops. But we know too little of druidic mythology, and those legends which have come to us have descended in a too altered form, for us to place much confidence in such conjectures.

But that this vessel of the liquor of Wisdom held a prominent place in British mythology is certain from the allusions made to it by the bards. Taliesin, in the description of this initiation into the mysteries of the basin, cries out, "I have lost my speech!" because on all who had been admitted to the privileges of full membership secrecy was imposed. This initiation was regarded as a new birth; and those who had once become joined members were regarded as elect, regenerate, separate from the rest of mankind, who lay in darkness and ignorance.

That originally the ceremonies of initiation included human sacrifices is more than probable from the vessel being represented as containing human blood, and a lance forming part of the paraphernalia, from which dropped blood. In the story of Pheredur, the vessel contained a man's head floating in gore. In that of Bran the Blessed, the head is thrown into the basin to destroy its efficacy. Taliesin also refers to Pheredur as "the hero of the bleeding head[7]."

The lance is also referred to by Welsh authors. One of the predictions attributed to Taliesin holds

[7] Myvyrian, i. p. 80.

out to the Britons the hope that "the Kingdom of
Logres (England) shall perish before the bleeding
lance ;" and five centuries later, Chrétien de Troyes
quotes this saying—

> " Il est écrit qu'il est une heure,
> Où tout le royaume de Logres,
> Qui jadis fut la terre ès Ogres,
> Sera détruit par cette lance."

This lance was probably a symbol of war.

The first to adapt the druidic mystery to Christianity was a British hermit, who wrote a Latin
legend on the subject.   Helinandus (d. 1227) says,
"At this time (A.D. 720), in Britain, a marvellous
vision was shown by an angel to a certain hermit :
it was of the basin or paropsis in which the Saviour
supped with His disciples ; concerning which the
history was written by the same hermit, which is
called the Gradal."   And he adds, "In French
they give the name gradal, or graal, to a large,
rather deep vessel, in which rich meats with their
gravy are served to the wealthy[8]."

The date at which lived this anchorite is not
certain, for though Helinandus says he had his
vision in 720, Usher places him later than 1140[9].

After the composition of this legend, the roman-

---

[8] Vincent. Belov. Speculum Hist., lib. xxiii. c. 147.
[9] Usserius, Primordia, p. 16.

cers took possession of the myth and adapted it to Christian chivalrous exigencies. The bardic table of the elect became the round-table of Arthur's knights, and the sacred vessel of mysteries became the Grail. The head of the victim was forgotten, and the sacrificial blood was supposed to be that of Christ.

It is likely that the tradition of the ancient druidic brotherhood lingered on and gained consistency again among the Templars. Just as the Miles Templi fought for the holy sepulchre, so did the soldier of Montsalvatsch for the holy Grail. Both orders were vowed to chastity and obedience, both were subject to a head, who exercised regal authority. The ancient temple of the Grail, like Stonehenge, was circular; so also were the churches dedicated to S. Sepulchre, by the soldier-monks. The charge of heresy was brought against the order of the Templars, and it has been supposed that they were imbued with gnosticism. That this Eastern heresy should have influenced a mediæval Western society, I think very unlikely; no other traces of gnosticism are to be found in the religious history of the Occident, which certainly would have been the case had the heresy been sufficiently powerful to have obtained mastery over an ecclesiastical society.

I think the root of the false doctrine or practices of the Templars must be looked for in the West.

The Templars were charged with having an idol which the Chronicles of S. Denys (which terminate 1461) describe as "an old skin embalmed and polished, in which the Templar places his very vile faith and trust, and in which he confidently believes: and it has in the sockets eyes of carbuncle shining with the brightness of the sky." Abraham Bzov, in his continuation of the "Church History" of Baronius, quotes a charge brought by the Italian bishops against the Templars, to this effect: "They have a certain head, the face pale like that of a man, with black curled hair, and round the neck a gilded ornament, which indeed belonged to no saint, and this they adored, making prayers before it." And one of the questions asked by the Pope of the witnesses was, "whether they had not a skull or some sort of image, to which they rendered divine homage?" So also the Chronicle of Meaux states, that on the first day of the General Council of the Templars, a head with a white beard, which had belonged to a former Grand Master of the Order, was set at midnight before the altar in a chapel, covered with silken robes and precious stuffs. Mass was sung before daylight, and the head was then adored by the Master and the other knights.

It seems to me probable that this head, if there were truth in the charge, was revered because it was part of an ancient druidic rite to produce a head upon a vessel, though for what purposes we do not know. Friar Bacon constructed a head which gave oracles. Possibly some such property was attributed to the Templar, and previously to the druidic head. Livy tells us that a bloody head of an enemy was a national Keltic symbol (xxiii. 24), and that the Boii brought the head into their temples, where they cleansed it and adorned it with gold, and then used it on festivals for a sacred vessel, out of which to make drink-offerings.

To enter with any thing like completeness into the most interesting and intricate subject of druidic mythology and ceremonial would occupy too much space. This paper will necessarily be imperfect; the religion of our British ancestors has yet to be written. Those who have hitherto approached the subject have so done with pre-conceived theories which have caused them to read wrong the sacred myths and rites they were interpreting. Much is to be learned from the Arthurian Romances, much from bardic remains, and much from Breton, Welsh, Gaelic, and Irish folk-lore.

That all thus recovered will be in a corrupted form I am well aware, but a practised eye will be able to restore what is disintegrated, and will know to detect antiquity, though disguised under the newest robe.

A careful study of these sources, conducted by the light of comparative mythology, will, I am satisfied, lead to the discovery that, under the name of Methodism, we have the old druidic religion still alive, energetic, and possibly more vigorous than it was when it exercised a spiritual supremacy over the whole of Britain. With the loss of the British tongue, much of the old terminology has died out, and a series of adaptations to Christianity has taken place, without radically affecting the system[1].

---

[1] Exception has been taken to this remark by some of the reviews; but the writer believes unjustly. Those who have made the fragments of Bardic religious poems, and the scheme of Druidic rites their study, cannot fail with astonishment to note the remarkable coincidence which exists between modern Wesleyanism and the religion of our British forefathers.

Theophilus

A FEW years before the Persian invasion in
538, there lived, in the town of Adana in
Cilicia, a priest named Theophilus, treasurer and
archdeacon. He lived in strict observance of all his
religious duties, was famous for his liberality to the
poor, his sympathy with the afflicted, his eloquence
in the pulpit, his private devotion, and severe asce-
ticism. On the decease of the bishop, by popular
acclamation he was summoned to the episcopal
oversight of the diocese, but his deep humility
urged him to refuse the office, even when it was
pressed upon him by the metropolitan. Seldom
has a *nolo episcopari* been carried out to such an
emphatic refusal as was given by Theophilus. A
stranger was raised to the vacant seat, and the treasurer resumed the course of life he had pursued for
so many years with credit to himself and advan-

tage to others, content in his own mind at having refused the office, which might have aroused his pride, and which certainly would have diminished his opportunities of self-sacrifice. Virtue invariably arouses the spirit of detraction, and Theophilus, by his refusal of the bishopric, was thrust into public notice, and attracted public attention. The consequence was that the evil-minded and envious originated slanders, which, circulating widely, produced a revulsion of feeling towards Theophilus and, from being generally reported, were accepted as substantially true. These stories reaching the ears of the new bishop, he sent for the archdeacon, and without properly investigating the charges, concluding he was guilty, deprived him of his offices.

One would have supposed that the humility which had required the holy man to refuse a mitre, would have rendered him callous to the voice of slander, and have sustained him under deprivation. But the trial was too great for his virtue. He brooded over the accusations raised against him, and the wrongs inflicted upon him, till the whole object of his labour was the clearing of his character. He sought every available means of unmasking the calumnies of his maligners, and exposing the falsity of the charges raised against him. But he found

himself unable to effect his object: one man is
powerless against a multitude, and slander is a
hydra which, when maimed in one head, produces
others in the place of that struck off. Baffled,
despairing, and without a friend to sustain his
cause, the poor clerk sought redress in a manner
which a month ago would have filled him with
horror. He visited a necromancer, who led him at
midnight to a place where four cross-roads met, and
there conjured up Satan, who promised reinstate-
ment in all his offices to the unfortunate Theophilus,
and, what he valued more, a complete clearing of
his character. The priest, to obtain these boons,
signed away his soul with a pen dipped in his own
blood, and abjured for ever Jesus Christ and his
spotless mother.

On the morrow, the bishop discovering his error,
how we know not, sent for Theophilus, and acknowledged publicly that he had been misled by
false reports, the utter valuelessness of which he
was ready frankly to acknowledge ; and he asked
pardon of the priest, for having unjustly deprived
him of his office. The populace enthusiastically
reversed their late opinion of the treasurer, and
greeted him as a saint and confessor. For some
days all went well, and in the excitement of a re-

turn to his former occupations the compact he had made was forgotten. But after a while, as reason and religion resumed their sway, the conscience of Theophilus gave him no rest. He paced his room at nights in an agony of terror, his face lost its colour, his brow was seamed with wrinkles, an unutterable horror gleamed from his deep-set eyes. Hour by hour he prayed, but found no relief. At length he resolved on a solemn fast of forty days. This he accomplished, praying nightly in the church of the Panhagia till the grey of morning stole in at the little windows of the dome and obscured the lamps. On the fortieth night, the Blessed Virgin appeared to him, and sadly rebuked him for his sin. He implored her pardon and all-prevailing intercession, and this she promised him. The following night she re-appeared and assured him that Christ had, at her prayer, forgiven him. With a cry of joy he awoke ; and on his breast lay the deed which had made over his soul to Satan, obtained from the evil one by the mercy of the sacred Mother of God.

The next day was Sunday. He rose, spent some time in acts of thanksgiving, and then went to church where the divine liturgy was being celebrated. After the reading of the gospel, he flung himself at the bishop's feet, and requested permission to make his confession in public. Then he related the circumstances of his fall, and showed the compact signed with his blood to the assembled multitude. Having finished his confession, he prostrated himself before the bishop and asked for absolution. The deed was torn and burned before the people, he was reconciled and received the blessed sacrament, after which he returned to his house in a fever, and died at the expiration of three days. The Church honours him as a penitent, on the 4th February.

The original account of this famous compact with the devil is in the Greek of Eutychianus, disciple of Theophilus, who declares that he relates what he had seen with his own eyes, and heard from the mouth of Theophilus himself. From the Greek of Eutychianus, two early Latin versions are extant, one by Paulus Diaconus, the other by Gentianus Hervetus. The former of these is published in the great work of the Bollandists, who fix the date of the event in 538. The version of Gentianus Hervetus purports to be a translation from Symeon Metaphrastes, who flourished in the tenth century, and who embodied the narrative of Eutychianus in his great collection of the Lives of the Saints.

In the tenth century, Hrosvitha, the illustrious nun of Gandersheim in Saxony, composed a Latin poem on the story of Theophilus. In the eleventh century the legend was versified by Marbodus, Bishop of Rennes. There is a poem on the subject by Gaultier de Coincy. Other rhymed versions have been published by M. Achille Jubinal, and M. Paulin Paris. One of the best of the ancient poems is that of Rutebeuf, a trouvère of the thirteenth century. There are several older miracle plays on mysteries of Theophilus : one in French, published by M. Francisque Michel [1]; another in low German, published by M. Dasent [2]. The latter gentleman has collected a great number of pieces on Theophilus in various European languages, and quotes references to the legend in early French, Anglo-Saxon, Anglo-Norman, and German writers.

Archbishop Ælfric (d. 1006) alludes to the story in his "Homilies;" S. Bernard also, in his "Deprecatio ad gloriosam Virginem Mariam;" Vincent of Beauvais, in his wonderful "Speculum Historiale;" S. Bonaventura, as a passionate devotee to the Virgin, could not omit it from his "Speculum

[1] Le Théâtre Français au moyen âge. Paris, p. 137.
[2] Theophilus, in Icelandic, Low German, &c. London, p. 23.

Beatæ Mariæ ;" Jacques de Voragine inserts it in his
"Golden Legend," and Albertus Magnus includes
it in his "Biblia B. Mariæ Virginis." It is again
mentioned by the great German poet of the twelfth
century, Hartmann von der Aue, and by Konrad
von Würzburg, in the thirteenth century. A Flemish
Theophilus was published by M. Philipp Blom-
maert, from an old MS. of the fourteenth century,
in 1836. To the same century belongs one version
of the Theophilus legend in Icelandic, published
by M. Dasent ; the other is younger by a century.
An old Swedish Theophilus of 1350 exists in the
royal library at Stockholm.

In the cathedral of Notre-Dame, at Paris, are
two sculptured representations of the fable ; one is
on the north porch. In the cathedral of Laon it
is painted on a window in the choir, in eighteen
medallions. It is also to be seen in the church of
S. Peter, at Troyes, and in that of S. Julien at
Mans, in both instances on stained glass.

Further information as to the legend, with the
texts, can be found in—"Theophilus, in Icelandic,
Low German, and other tongues, from MSS. in the
Royal Library, Stockholm, by G. Webbe Dasent,
M.A. Stockholm, 1845 ;" in "E. F. Sommer, De
Theophili cum Diabole fœdere. Halle, 1844 ;" and

in "Miracle de Théophile, mis en vers au com-
mencement du XIIIme siècle, par Gauthier de
Coincy, publié par M. D. Maillet.   Rennes, 1838."

I do not think it improbable that this famous
story may rest on a foundation of truth; indeed
it bears on the face of it tokens of authenticity.
Theophilus is driven from his position by slanders:
this preys on his mind.   By some means he is
reinstated.   The revulsion of feeling upsets his
reason, he undertakes a prodigious fast, goes crazy,
tells a long rambling story about a compact with
the devil, and dies three days after in brain-fever.
His narrative is the only extraordinary item in the
tale.   If we remember that this was told after a
forty-days' fast, and immediately before a mortal
fever, the only thing to be wondered at in the
legend is that any sane persons believed his ravings
to have in them a foundation of truth.

APPENDIX A

The Wandering Jew

IN the Bragda Mágus Saga, an Icelandic version of the Romance of Maugis, but with considerable alterations in the story, is the following very curious passage, which seems to indicate a belief in a life indefinitely prolonged, not attached to the Jew, Cartaphilus. I quote from the edition "Bragda Mágus Saga, med tilheyrandi Fáttum, skrif. af Gunnlaugi Thordarsyni. Kaupmannahöfn, 1858. Cap. 35—40."

"Mágus went before the king (Charlemagne), and greeted him courteously. The king received him well, and asked him his name. He said he was called 'Vidförull.' The king said, 'You are a vigorous man, though you seem very old.'

"Vidförull replied, 'Sire, you say right that I am very old, but I have been much older, and it may fall out that I become younger.'

"'How can that possibly be,' asked the king, 'that you could have been older than you are, and will be younger?'

"Vidförull said, 'That I will make clear to you. Twice have I cast my old skin, and become each time younger than before.'

"When he said this all the guard of the king sprang up, laughing, and said he should not venture to talk such non-sense before the king. Then the king took up the word, and said,

"'Do you mean to say that you have twice cast your skin?'

"'It is quite true, sire !' answered Vidförull.

"The king asked, 'Do you suppose that you will cast it again?'

"'I am sure,' answered Vidförull, 'that in this very month I shall have to slough it off, and that not many days hence.'

"'How old are you wont to be,' asked the king, 'before you cast it?'

"Vidförull replied, 'The time is not always the same. The first time I was aged 330, and then when I had undergone the process I was only about thirty, and I regained all the vigour of youth. . . . . Now, sire, if you wish to know my powers, and see me cast my skin, then show me a seat, and I will remain in your court a few days, till the time comes. . . .

"36. . . . . The second time I cast my skin, I was aged 215; and when I found the time arrive for my change I sought Rome, where then reigned Hermanric.' The king asked how the operation had taken place. Vidförull answered, 'The first time it was rather strange; I was then much more vigorous, though I had lived longer, for then men's ages were longer than they are now, and though I was over 300 years old, I was sturdy and could hunt; and one day as I was at the chase I felt thirst, and I lay down by the water with the intention of drinking; then there flew over me a dragon, which grabbed me up, and carried me off to a lofty crag, where was a cave. Then I . . . . escaped after a struggle, and fled to a beautiful plain, and there, exhausted with age, there came over me a lassitude, and then there peeled off me my first skin, as I was in a fainting fit. A little while after I revived, and I was as hale and hearty as a youth of thirty. . .

37. Now I will tell you how I cast my skin the second time. I had been a little while in Rome, and I learned by a dream that I was to undergo the change. I was then some two ells

taller than before, and I was exceedingly able-bodied and strong, though very old.' (The king then asks him about the heroes of olden time, and Vidförull describes to him their personal appearance, the colour of their hair, eyes, and their stature.) 'And one day I was wrestling in the water with the knights of King Gunnar, and I was reluctant to do it, because I doubted my powers. However, to please the king I went in ; and when I was fresh I held most of the knights under water, but I soon tired, and then came my exhaustion over me, and they then held me under, and I could not rise, so I sank to the bottom, and lay there all day. And I woke up as I was washed ashore ; and it was like as when a man strips off his clothes, for I was younger then again, as though I was thirty.'

"40. It was one festival, in the morning, that the king and his court went to church, and they saw that a great log had come under the hall-wall, and by it stood Vidförull, and he came to the king and greeted him, and he was very cheerful. The king said, 'What is the cause of your merriment?'

"Vidförull replied, 'Sire, you must not be surprised when I tell you that to-day is the time when I shall have to cast my skin, and I should like you and all the court to witness the process.' The guard were right pleased, and laughed for joy. The king smiled and said, 'We must go to church first and hear mass, and after that we shall be ready.' Vidförull said it was well that they should do so. And when all the office was over, the guard scampered out of the church, for all were eager to see what would happen. The king went forth as usual, and back to his hall. And when he got there Vidförull went to him, and fell on his knee, and said, 'Now I wish, sire, that you and all your suite should take your places, and watch me accomplish my desire, for I have long desired to quit this age and become young again.' . . . Then he bared his head, and stroked his arms, and all his body and belly and his legs, then he rolled together the skin he was

in, and lay down before the post, and muttered to himself,
' Away with age, that I may have my desire !'   Then all the
court laughed as loud as they well could, but he lay a little
while motionless.   And, when they were least aware, he
dragged at the post, and worked himself headforemost into
the post, and it closed upon him as his feet entered.   The
king ran to it with all his men, but the beam was solid.
Then they began to discuss what was to be done.

" Earl Uppi said :—' It was a Troll, and he has vanished into
the earth.'   But next they heard a great noise in the beam.
They thought it very strange that the post was at one time
bigger than at another.   And after this had gone on a while,
they saw come out at the end of the beam a man's feet, then
a man as far as to his middle.   They saw the beam shrink
and expand, and it was like a woman in her pangs ; at last
the post contracted, and shot Vidförull completely out, and
he lay a while as though dead ; but when the assistants were
least expecting it, he sprang up, rolled up the skin from off
his head, stepped up to the king, and saluted him.   And they
saw that he was no other than a beardless youth, and fair
faced."

APPENDIX B

Mountain of Venus

(Extract from Vincent of Beauvais: Speculum Historiale, I. xxvi.)

THE youth having returned for his ring to the statue,
"videt digitum statuæ usque ad volam manus recur-
vatum, et quantumvis conatus annulum recuperare, nec
digitum inflectare nec annulum valuit extrahere. Redit ad
sodales, nec illis ea de re quicquam indicavit. Nocte intem-
pesta cum famulo ad statuam revertitur, et extensum ut
initio digitum repperit, sed sine annulo ; jactura dissimulata
domum se confert ad novam nuptam. Cumque thorum
genialem ingressus sponsæ se jungere vellet, sensit impedire
sese et quiddam nebulosum ac densum inter suum conjugis-
que corpus volutari ; sentiebat id tactu, videre tamen nequie-
bat. Hoc obstaculo ab amplexu prohibebatur, audiebat
etiam vocem dicentem : 'mecum concumbe, quia hodie me
desponsasti. Ego sum Venus, cui digito annulum inseruisti,
nec reddam.' Territus ille tanto prodigio nihil referre ausus
est vel potuit; insomnem duxit noctem illam, multum secum
deliberans.

"Sic factum est per multum tempus ut quacunque hora
cum sponsa concumbere vellet, illud idem sentiret et audiret.
Erat sane alias valens et domi aptus et militiæ. Tandem

uxoris querelis commonitus, rem parentibus detulit. Illi habito concilio Palumbo cuidam, presbytero suburbano, rem pandunt. Is autem erat necromanticus et in maleficiis potens. Illectus ergo promissis multis compositam epistolam dedit juveni dicens : 'Vade illa hora noctis ad compitum, ubi quatuor viæ conveniunt, et stans tacite considera. Transient ibi figuræ hominum utriusque sexus, omnisque ætatis et conditionis, equites et pedites, quidam læti et quidam tristes ; quicquid audieris non loquaris. Sequetur illam turbam quidam statura procerior, forma corpulentior, curru sedens ; huic tacitus epistolam trades legendam, statimque fiet quod postulas.' Ille autem juvenis totum implevit prout edoctus erat. Viditque inter cæteros ibi mulierem in habitu meretricio mulam inequitantem, crine soluto per humeros jactato, vitta aurea superius constricto, auream virgam gerentem in manibus, qua mulum regebat ; præ tenuitate vestium pene nuda apparebat, gestus exsequens impudicos. Ultimus dominus turbæ terribiles in juvenem oculos exacuens, ab axe superbo smaragdis et unionibus composito causas viæ ab eo exquirebat. Nihil ille contra, sed protenta manu epistolam ei porrigit ; dæmon notum sigillum non audens contemnere legit scriptum, moxque brachiis in cœlum elevatis ; 'Deus,' inquit, 'omnipotens, quamdiu patieris nequitias Palumbi presbyteri ?' Nec mora, satellites suos a latere mittit qui annulum extorquerent a Venere. Illa multum tergiversata vix tandem reddidit. Ita juvenis voti compos sine obstaculo potitus est diu suspiratis amoribus. Palumbus autem, ubi dæmonis clamorem ad Deum audivit de se, intellexit sibi præsignari finem dierum. Quocirca omnibus in membris ultro truncatis miserabili pœna defunctus est."

APPENDIX C

Pre=Christian Crosses

I HAVE said that the phallic origin attributed to the cross is destitute of evidence. In a work like this, which will be in the hands of general readers, it is impossible to enter into the subject.

I believe I have conscientiously examined the question. If I saw that there was sufficient evidence to substantiate the theory, I would adopt it without hesitation. But I think a better claim may be made for the lightning, and a better still for the ancient instrument of two sticks used for producing fire by friction.

An article on Sun worship in the "English Leader," copied into "Public Opinion" (Sept. 14, 1867), assumes the identity of the cross with the phallus. The article is full of assertions, rather bold and reckless than well supported by evidence.

It asserts on the authority of the Abbé Pluche that the crux ansata was the symbol of the annual inundation of the Nile. The speculations of the learned on the signification of the Egyptian hieroglyphics, previous to the discoveries of Champollion, are, however, devoid of weight. "The crux ansata," it adds, "that is, the cross and circle, was the sign of Venus or sensual love,—the goddess from whose name our word *venery* is derived,—and it is still the astronomical symbol of the planet which bears her name." As we have already seen, the crux ansata was not exclusively the symbol of Astarte ; it was a sign of divinity and was placed near every god to indicate him as being Divine. It appears beside Baal as well as Astarte.

If used more frequently with her than with other deities, it was because it symbolized her power over moisture, she being the Moon. The cross did not belong to her as a goddess of sensuality, but as presiding over the month and its rains ; to Baal it belonged as a year-god guiding the seasons.

The same article refers to the Indian cross as though it were a phallus ; whereas the symbols are entirely and radically distinct, as may be seen by reference to the plates of Müller's " Glauben, Wissen, und Kunst der Hindus."

APPENDIX D

Shipping the Dead

THE following curious passage from Gervase of Tilbury may not prove uninteresting when treating of the transport of the dead by boats.

OTIA IMPERIALIA, Decisio iii. c. 90.

Insigne mirum ac ex divina virtute miraculum audi, Princeps Sacratissime. Caput regni Burgundionum, quod Arelatense dicitur, civitas est Arelas, antiquissimis dotata privilegiis. Hanc ordinatus ab Apostolis Petro et Paulo, Trophimus, qui . . . . deliberavit cœmeterium solemne ad meridianam urbis partem constituere, in quo omnium orthodoxorum corpora sepulturæ traderentur, ut, sicut ab Arelatensi ecclesia tota Gallia fidei sumsit exordium, ita et mortui in Christo undecunque advecti sepulturæ communis haberent beneficium. Facta itaque consecratione solemni per manus sanctissimorum antistitum ad Orientalem portam, ubi nunc est ecclesia ab ipsis in honorem B. Virginis consecrata, illis Christus, pridem in carne familiariter agnitus, apparuit, opus eorum sua benedictione profundens, dato cœmeterio ac illis sepeliendis munere, ut quicunque inibi sepelirentur, nullas in cadaveribus suis paterentur diabolicas illusiones. Ex hujusmodi ergo Dominicæ benedictionis munere, apud omnes majoris auctoritatis Galliarum principes ac clericos inolevit, quod maxima patentum pars illuc sepulturam habent, et quidam in plaustris, alii in curribus, nonnulli in equis, plurimi per dependulum fluentis Rhodani ad cœmeterium Campi Elisii deferebantur. Est ergo omni admiratione dignissimum, quod nullus in thecis positus mortuus ultimos civitatis Arelatensis terminos, quos Rochetam nominant, quantalibet vi ventorum aut tempestate compulsus præterit, sed infra semper subsistens in aqua rotatur, donec applicet, aut ad ripam fluminis ductus cœmeterio sacro inferatur. Mirandis magis miranda succedunt, quæ oculis conspeximus sub innumera utriusque sexus hominum multitudine. Solent, ergo præmisimus, mortui in doliis bituminatis ac in thecis corpora mortuorum a longinquis regionibus fluminis Rhodani dimitti cum pecunia sigillata, quæ cœmeterio tam sacro, nomine eleemosynæ, confertur. Uno aliquo die, nondum decennio delapso, dolium cum mortuo suo descendit inter illud angustum, quod ex alternis ripis castrum Tarasconense et castrum Belliquadri prospectant. Exilientes adolescentes Belliquadri dolium ad terram trahunt, et relicto mortuo pecuniam reconditam rapiunt. Depulsum dolium inter impetuosi amnis fluctus subsistit, et nec vi fluminis præcipitis nec juvenum impulsibus potuit descendere, verum rotans et in se revolvens, eosdem circinabat fluminis fluctus. . . . . Tandem, restituto censu, confestim mortuus sine omni impellentis adjutorio viam aggreditur, et infra modicam horam apud civitatem Arelatensem applicans, sepulturæ honorifice traditur.

APPENDIX E

Fatality of Numbers

THE laws governing numbers are so perplexing to the uncultivated mind, and the results arrived at by calculation are so astonishing, that it cannot be matter of surprise if superstition has attached itself to numbers.

But, even to those who are instructed in numeration, there is much that is mysterious and unaccountable, much that only an advanced mathematician can explain to his own satisfaction. The neophyte sees the numbers obedient to certain laws, but *why* they obey these laws he cannot understand ; and the fact of his not being able so to do, tends to give to numbers an atmosphere of mystery which impresses him with awe.

For instance, the property of the number 9, discovered, I believe, by W. Green, who died in 1794, is inexplicable to any one but a mathematician. The property to which I allude is this, that when 9 is multiplied by 2, by 3, by 4, by 5, by 6, &c., it will be found that the digits composing the product, when added together, give 9. Thus :

$$2 \times 9 = 18, \text{ and } 1 + 8 = 9$$
$$3 \times 9 = 27 \text{ ,, } 2 + 7 = 9$$
$$4 \times 9 = 36 \text{ ,, } 3 + 6 = 9$$

$$5 \times 9 = 45 \text{ and } 4 + 5 = 9$$
$$6 \times 9 = 54 \text{ „ } 5 + 4 = 9$$
$$7 \times 9 = 63 \text{ „ } 6 + 3 = 9$$
$$8 \times 9 = 72 \text{ „ } 7 + 2 = 9$$
$$9 \times 9 = 81 \text{ „ } 8 + 1 = 9$$
$$10 \times 9 = 90 \text{ „ } 9 + 0 = 9$$

It will be noticed that 9×11 makes 99, the sum of the digits of which is 18 and not 9, but the sum of the digits 1×8 equals 9.

$$9 \times 12 = 108, \text{ and } 1 + 0 + 8 = 9$$
$$9 \times 13 = 117 \text{ „ } 1 + 1 + 7 = 9$$
$$9 \times 14 = 126 \text{ „ } 1 + 2 + 6 = 9$$

And so on to any extent.

M. de Maivan discovered another singular property of the same number. If the order of the digits expressing a number be changed, and this number be subtracted from the former, the remainder will be 9 or a multiple of 9, and, being a multiple, the sum of its digits will be 9.

For instance, take the number 21, reverse the digits, and you have 12; subtract 12 from 21, and the remainder is 9. Take 63, reverse the digits, and subtract 36 from 63; you have 27, a multiple of 9, and $2 + 7 = 9$. Once more, the number 13 is the reverse of 31; the difference between these numbers is 18, or twice 9.

Again, the same property found in two numbers thus changed, is discovered in the same numbers raised to any power.

Take 21 and 12 again. The square of 21 is 441, and the square of 12 is 144; subtract 144 from 441, and the remainder is 297, a multiple of 9; besides, the digits expressing these powers added together give 9. The cube of 21 is 9261, and that of 12 is 1728; their difference is 7533, also a multiple of 9.

The number 37 has also somewhat remarkable properties ; when multiplied by 3 or a multiple of 3 up to 27, it gives in the product three digits exactly similar. From the knowledge of this the multiplication of 37 is greatly facilitated, the method to be adopted being to multiply merely the first cipher of the multiplicand, by the first of the multiplier ; it is then unnecessary to proceed with the multiplication, it being sufficient to write twice to the right hand the cipher obtained, so that the same digit will stand in the unit, tens, and hundreds places.

For instance, take the results of the following table :—

37	multiplied by	3	gives	111,	and	3	times	1 =	3
37	„	6	„	222,	„	3	„	2 =	6
37	„	9	„	333,	„	3	„	3 =	9
37	„	12	„	444,	„	3	„	4 =	12
37	„	15	„	555,	„	3	„	5 =	15
37	„	18	„	666,	„	3	„	6 =	18
37	„	21	„	777,	„	3	„	7 =	21
37	„	24	„	888,	„	3	„	8 =	24
37	„	27	„	999,	„	3	„	9 =	27

The singular property of numbers the most different, when added, to produce the same sum, originated the use of magical squares for talismans. Although the reason may be accounted for mathematically, yet numerous authors have written concerning them, as though there were something "uncanny" about them. But the most remarkable and exhaustive treatise on the subject is that by a mathematician of Dijon, which is entitled, " Traité complet des Carrés magiques, pairs et impairs, simple et composés, à Bordures, Compartiments, Croix, Chassis, Équerres, Bandes détachées, &c. ; suivi d'un Traité des Cubes magiques et d'un Essai sur les Cercles magiques ; par M. Violle, Géomètre, Chevalier de S. Louis, avec Atlas de 54 grandes Feuilles, comprenant

400 figures." Paris, 1837. 2 vols. 8vo., the first of 593 pages, the second of 616. Price 36 fr.

I give three examples of magical squares :—

2   7   6

9   5   1

4   3   8

These nine ciphers are disposed in three horizontal lines ; add the three ciphers of each line, and the sum is 15 ; add the three ciphers in each column, the sum is 15 ; add the three ciphers forming diagonals, and the sum is 15.

1	2	3	4		1	7	13	19	25
2	3	2	3		18	24	5	6	12
4	1	4	1		10	11	17	23	4
3	4	1	2		22	3	9	15	16
					14	20	21	2	8

The sum is 10.   The sum is 65.

But the connexion of certain numbers with the dogmas of religion was sufficient, besides their marvellous properties, to make superstition attach itself to them. Because there were thirteen at the table when the Last Supper was celebrated, and one of the number betrayed his Master, and then hung himself, it is looked upon through Christendom as unlucky to sit down thirteen at table, the consequence being that one of the number will die before the year is out. "When I see," said Vouvenargues, "men of genius not daring to sit down thirteen at table, there is no error ancient or modern which astonishes me."

Nine, having been consecrated by Buddhism, is regarded with great veneration by the Moguls and Chinese : the latter bow nine times on entering the presence of their Emperor.

Three is sacred among Brahminical and Christian peoples, because of the Trinity of the Godhead.

Pythagoras taught that each number had its own peculiar character, virtue, and properties.

" The unit, or the monad," he says, " is the principle and the end of all; it is this sublime knot which binds together the chain of causes; it is the symbol of identity, of equality, of existence, of conservation, and of general harmony. Having no parts, the monad represents Divinity; it announces also order, peace, and tranquillity, which are founded on unity of sentiments; consequently ONE is a good principle.

" The number TWO, or the dyad, the origin of contrasts, is the symbol of diversity, or inequality, of division and of separation. Two is accordingly an evil principle, a number of bad augury, characterizing disorder, confusion, and change.

" THREE, or the triad, is the first of unequals; it is the number containing the most sublime mysteries, for every thing is composed of three substances; it represents God, the soul of the world, the spirit of man." This number, which plays so great a part in the traditions of Asia, and in the Platonic philosophy, is the image of the attributes of God.

" FOUR, or the tetrad, as the first mathematical power, is also one of the chief elements; it represents the generating virtue, whence come all combinations; it is the most perfect of numbers; it is the root of all things. It is holy by nature, since it constitutes the Divine essence, by recalling His unity, His power, His goodness, and His wisdom, the four perfections which especially characterize God. Consequently, Pythagoricians swear by the quaternary number, which gives the human soul its eternal nature.

" The number FIVE, or the pentad, has a peculiar force in sacred expiations; it is every thing; it stops the power of poisons, and is redoubted by evil spirits.

" The number SIX, or the hexad, is a fortunate number, and it derives its merit from the first sculptors having divided the face into six portions ; but, according to the Chaldeans, the reason is, because God created the world in six days.

" SEVEN, or the heptad, is a number very powerful for good or for evil. It belongs especially to sacred things.

" The number EIGHT, or the octad, is the first cube, that is to say, squared in all senses, as a die, proceeding from its base two, an even number ; so is man four-square, or perfect.

" The number NINE, or the ennead, being the multiple of three, should be regarded as sacred.

" Finally, TEN, or the decad, is the measure of all, since it contains all the numeric relations and harmonies. As the reunion of the four first numbers, it plays an eminent part, since all the branches of science, all nomenclatures, emanate from, and retire into it."

It is hardly necessary for me here to do more than mention the peculiar character given to different numbers by Christianity. One is the numeral indicating the Unity of the Godhead ; Two points to the hypostatic union ; Three to the Blessed Trinity ; Four to the Evangelists ; Five to the Sacred Wounds ; Six is the number of sin ; Seven that of the gifts of the Spirit ; Eight that of the Beatitudes ; Ten is the number of the Commandments : Eleven speaks of the Apostles after the loss of Judas ; Twelve, of the complete apostolic college.

I shall now point out.certain numbers which have been regarded with superstition, and certain events connected with numbers which are of curious interest.

The number 14 has often been observed as having singularly influenced the life of Henry IV. and other French princes.   Let us take the history of Henry.

On the 14th May, 1029, the first king of France named Henry was consecrated, and on the 14th May, 1610, the last Henry was assassinated.

Fourteen letters enter into the composition of the name of Henri de Bourbon, who was the 14th king bearing the titles of France and Navarre.

The 14th December, 1553, that is, 14 centuries, 14 decades, and 14 years after the birth of Christ, Henry IV. was born ; the ciphers of the date 1553, when added together, giving the number 14.

The 14th May, 1554, Henry II. ordered the enlargement of the Rue de la Ferronnerie. The circumstance of this order not having been carried out, occasioned the murder of Henry IV. in that street, four times 14 years after.

The 14th May, 1552, was the date of the birth of Marguérite de Valois, first wife of Henry IV.

On the 14th May, 1588, the Parisians revolted against Henry III., at the instigation of the Duke of Guise.

On the 14th March, 1590, Henry IV. gained the battle of Ivry.

On the 14th May, 1590, Henry was repulsed from the Fauxbourgs of Paris.

On the 14th November, 1590, the Sixteen took oath to die rather than serve Henry.

On the 14th November, 1592, the Parliament registered the Papal Bull giving power to the legate to nominate a king to the exclusion of Henry.

On the 14th December, 1599, the Duke of Savoy was reconciled to Henry IV.

On the 14th September, 1606, the Dauphin, afterwards Louis XIII., was baptized.

On the 14th May, 1610, the king was stopped in the Rue de la Ferronnerie, by his carriage becoming locked with a cart, on account of the narrowness of the street. Ravaillac took advantage of the occasion for stabbing him.

Henry IV. lived four times 14 years, 14 weeks, and four times 14 days ; that is to say, 56 years and 5 months.

On the 14th May, 1643, died Louis XIII., son of Henry

IV.; not only on the same day of the same month as his father, but the date, 1643, when its ciphers are added together, gives the number 14, just as the ciphers of the date of the birth of his father gave 14.

Louis XIV. mounted the throne in 1643 :

$$1 + 6 + 4 + 3 = 14.$$

He died in the year 1715 : $1 + 7 + 1 + 5 = 14.$

He lived 77 years, and $7 + 7 = 14.$

Louis XV. mounted the throne in the same year ; he died in 1774, which also bears the stamp of 14, the extremes being 14, and the sum of the means $7 + 7$ making 14.

Louis XVI. had reigned 14 years when he convoked the States General, which was to bring about the Revolution.

The number of years between the assassination of Henry IV. and the dethronement of Louis XVI. is divisible by 14.

Louis XVII. died in 1794 ; the extreme digits of the date are 14, and the first two give his number.

The restoration of the Bourbons took place in 1814, also marked by the extremes being 14 ; also by the sum of the ciphers making 14.

The following are other curious calculations made respecting certain French kings.

Add the ciphers composing the year of the birth or of the death of some of the kings of the third race, and the result of each sum is the titular number of each prince. Thus :—

Louis IX. was born in 1215 ; add the four ciphers of this date, and you have IX.

Charles VII. was born in 1402 ; the sum of $1 + 4 + 2$ gives VII.

Louis XII. was born in 1461 ; and $1 + 4 + 6 + 1 = XII.$

Henry IV. died in 1610 ; and $1 + 6 + 1 =$ twice IV.

Louis XIV. was crowned in 1643 ; and these four ciphers give XIV. The same king died in 1715 ; and this date gives also XIV. He was aged 77 years, and again $7 + 7 = 14.$

Louis XVIII. was born in 1755; add the digits, and you have XVIII.

What is remarkable is, that this number 18 is double the number of the king to whom the law first applies, and is triple the number of the kings to whom it has applied.

Here is another curious calculation :—

Robespierre fell in 1794;

Napoleon in 1815, and Charles X. in 1830.

Now the remarkable fact in connexion with these dates is, that the sum of the digits composing them, added to the dates, gives the date of the fall of the successor. Robespierre fell in 1794; $1 + 7 + 9 + 4 = 21$, $1794 + 21 = 1815$, the date of the fall of Napoleon; $1 + 8 + 1 + 5 = 15$, and $1815 + 15 = 1830$, the date of the fall of Charles X.

There is a singular rule which has been supposed to determine the length of the reigning Pope's life, in the earlier half of a century. Add his number to that of his predecessor, to that add ten, and the result gives the year of his death.

Pius VII. succeeded Pius VI.; $6 + 7 = 13$; add 10, and the sum is 23. Pius VII. died in 1823.

Leo XII. succeeded Pius VII.; $12 + 7 + 10 = 29$; and Leo XII. died in 1829.

Pius VIII. succeeded Leo XII.; $8 + 12 + 10 = 30$; and Pius VIII. died in 1830.

However, this calculation does not always apply.

Gregory XVI. ought to have died in 1834, but he did not actually vacate his see till 1846.

It is also well known that an ancient tradition forbids the hope of any of S. Peter's successors, *pervenire ad annos Petri;* i. e. to reign 25 years.

And it is a remarkable fact that all have vacated the throne before that time is complete ; Pius IX. must not reign beyond 1871.

The Popes who have sat longest are

	Years.	Months.	Days.
Pius VI., who reigned	24	6	14
Hadrian I. ,,	23	10	17
Pius VII. ,,	23	5	6
Alexander III. ,,	21	11	23
S. Silvester I. ,,	21	0	4

There is one numerical curiosity of a very remarkable character, which I must not omit.

The ancient Chamber of Deputies, such as it existed in 1830, was composed of 402 members, and was divided into two parties. The one, numbering 221 members, declared itself strongly for the revolution of July; the other party, numbering 181, did not favour a change. The result was the constitutional monarchy, which re-established order after the three memorable days of July. The parties were known by the following nicknames. The larger was commonly called *La queue de Robespierre,* and the smaller, *Les honnêtes gens.* Now the remarkable fact is, that if we give to the letters of the alphabet their numerical values as they stand in their order, as 1 for A, 2 for B, 3 for C, and so on to Z, which is valued at 25, and then write vertically on the left hand the words, *La queue de Robespierre,* with the number equivalent to each letter opposite to it, and on the right hand, in like manner, *Les honnêtes gens,* if each column of numbers be summed up, the result is the number of members who formed each party.

1	2	3	4	5	6	7	8	9	10	11	12	13	14	15	16
A	B	C	D	E	F	G	H	I	J	K	L	M	N	O	P

17	18	19	20	21	22	23	24	25
Q	R	S	T	U	V	X	Y	Z

L—12			L—12
A— 1			E— 5
			S —19
O —17			H— 8
U —21			O—15
E— 5			N—14
U —21			N—14
E— 5			E— 5
D— 4			T—20
E— 5			E— 5
R—18			S —19
O—15			G— 7
B— 2			E— 5
E— 5			N—14
S—19			S—19
P—16			
I— 9			181
E— 5			
R—18			
R—18			
E— 5			
221			

Majority **221**
Minority   181

Total   402

Some coincidences of dates are very remarkable.

On the 25th August, 1569, the Calvinists massacred the Catholic nobles and priests of Béarn and Navarre.

On the same day of the same month, in 1572, the Calvinists were massacred in Paris and elsewhere.

On the 25th October, 1615, Louis XIII. married Anne of Austria, infanta of Spain; whereupon we may remark the following coincidences :—

The name Loys[1] de Bourbon contains **13** letters, so does the name Anne d'Autriche.

Louis was **13** years old when this marriage was decided on. Anne was the same age.

He was the thirteenth king of France bearing the name of Louis, and she was the thirteenth infanta of the name of Anne of Austria.

On the 23rd of April, 1616, died Shakspeare : on the same day of the same month, in the same year, died the great poet Cervantes.

On the 29th May, 1630, King Charles II. was born.

On the 29th May, 1660, he was restored.

On the 29th May, 1672, the fleet was beaten by the Dutch.

On the 29th May, 1679, the rebellion of the Covenanters broke out in Scotland.

The Emperor Charles V. was born on February 24th, 1500 ; on that day he won the battle of Pavia, in 1525, and on the same day was crowned in 1530.

On the 29th January, 1697, M. de Broquemar, president of the Parliament of Paris, died suddenly in that city; next day his brother, an officer, died suddenly at Bergue, where he was governor. The lives of these brothers present remarkable coincidences. One day the officer, being engaged in battle, was wounded in his leg by a sword-blow. On the same day, at the same moment, the president was afflicted with acute pain, which attacked him suddenly in the same leg as that of his brother which had been injured.

John Aubrey mentions the case of a friend of his who was born on the 15th November ; his eldest son was born on the 15th November ; and his second son's first son on the same day of the same month.

At the hour of prime, April 6th, 1327, Petrarch first saw

---

[1] Up to Louis XIII. all the kings of this name spelled Louis as Loys.

his mistress Laura, in the Church of S. Clara in Avignon. In the same city, same month, same hour, 1348, she died.

The deputation charged with offering the crown of Greece to Prince Otho, arrived in Munich on the 13th of October, 1832; and it was on the 13th October, 1862, that King Otho left Athens, to return to it no more.

On the 21st April, 1770, Louis XVI. was married at Vienna, by the sending of the ring.

On the 21st June, in the same year, took place the fatal festivities of his marriage.

On the 21st January, 1781, was the *fête* at the Hôtel de Ville, for the birth of the Dauphin.

On the 21st June, 1791, took place the flight to Varennes.

On the 21st January, 1793, he died on the scaffold.

December 2nd is as remarkable a day in Bonapartist annals as September 3rd in Cromwellian. On that day in 1804, Napoleon I. was crowned. The same day in the next year he won his chief victory of Austerlitz. On December 2nd, 1851, Napoleon III. made himself master of France, on December 2nd, 1852, he was proclaimed Emperor.

There is said to be a tradition of Norman-monkish origin, that the number 3 is stamped on the Royal line of England, so that there shall not be more than three princes in succession without a revolution.

William I., William II., Henry I.; then followed the revolution of Stephen.

Henry II., Richard I., John; invasion of Louis, Dauphin of France, who claimed the throne.

Henry III., Edward I., Edward II., who was dethroned and put to death.

Edward III., Richard II., who was dethroned.

Henry IV., Henry V., Henry VI.; the crown passed to the house of York.

Edward IV., Edward V., Richard III.; the crown claimed and won by Henry Tudor.

Henry VII., Henry VIII., Edward VI.; usurpation of Lady Jane Grey.

Mary I., Elizabeth; the crown passed to the House of Stuart.

James I., Charles I.; Revolution.

Charles II., James II.; invasion of William of Orange.

William of Orange and Mary II., Anne; arrival of the House of Brunswick.

George I., George II., George III., George IV., William IV., Victoria. The law has proved faulty in the last case; but certainly there was a crisis in the reign of George IV.

The number 88 seems to have been fatal to the House of Stuart, and the date September 3, had influence on the fortunes of Oliver Cromwell.

Robert II., the first Stuart king, died in 1388, James II. was killed at the siege of Roxburgh in 1488, Mary Stuart was beheaded in 1588 (new style), James II. dethroned in 1688, Charles Edward died in 1788, and with him the last hopes of the Jacobites. Oliver Cromwell was born September 3, 1599, won the battle of Dunbar September 3, 1650, that of Worcester September 3, 1651, and died September 3, 1658.

As I am on the subject of the English princes, I will add another singular coincidence, though it has nothing to do with the fatality of numbers.

It is that Saturday has been a day of ill omen to the later kings.

William of Orange died Saturday 18th March, 1702.

Anne died Saturday 1st August, 1714.

George I. died Saturday 10th June, 1727.

George II. died Saturday 25th October, 1760.

George III. died Saturday 30th January, 1820.

George IV. died Saturday 26th June, 1830.

THE END.